The "Double Indemnity" Murder

Ruth Snyder, ca. 1920; Judd Gray, ca. 1925

The "Double Indemnity" Murder

Ruth Snyder, Judd Gray, and New York's Crime of the Century

LANDIS MacKELLAR

SYRACUSE UNIVERSITY PRESS

Copyright © 2006 by Syracuse University Press
Syracuse, New York 13244–5160
All Rights Reserved

First Edition 2006
06 07 08 09 10 11 6 5 4 3 2 1

The paper used in this publication meets the minimum requirements of
American National Standard for Information Sciences—Permanence of
Paper for Printed Library Materials, ANSI Z39.48–1984.∞™

All illustrations courtesy of the author.

Library of Congress Cataloging-in-Publication Data
MacKellar, Landis.
The double indemnity murder : Ruth Snyder, Judd Gray,
and New York's crime of the century / Landis MacKellar.—1st ed.
p. cm.
Includes bibliographical references and index.
ISBN 0–8156–0824–1 (pbk. : alk. paper)
1. Snyder, Ruth May, d. 1928. 2. Women murderers—United States—Biography.
3. Murder—Investigation—New York (State)—New York. I. Title.
HV6517.S69M35 2006
364.152'3092—dc22   2006012980

Manufactured in the United States of America

Contents

Illustrations

LANDIS MACKELLAR lives in Vienna and Paris. His interest in the Snyder–Gray murder began when he taught at Queens College in New York City.

•   •   •

In keeping with the narrative style of this book, when secondary sources are cited in the main text and footnotes, only minimal identifying information is given, for example, "According to Kobler, . . ." Full information is contained in the "Sources" section at the end of the book.

PART ONE The Crime

Judd Gray (A) and Ruth Snyder (B) at their arraignment at Jamaica Town Hall Police Court, in Queens, New York, 22 March 1927

1

SUNDAY, 20 MARCH 1927. A crisp morning in Queens Village, the newly developed suburb dividing the borough of Queens from the rolling fields of Long Island. On the corner of 222nd Street and 93rd Road, a compact house, distinguishable from the dozens surrounding it only by its salmon pink color, with shutters and trim in robin's-egg blue.

At seven forty-five, in the house next door, Mrs. Harriet Mulhauser was awakened by a telephone call from her neighbors' daughter, nine-year-old Lorraine Snyder. "Come over to our house quick," the child pleaded. "Mama is very sick!"

Mrs. Mulhauser entered the front door of the Snyder residence and, hearing moans from upstairs, climbed the staircase. She found Mrs. Ruth Snyder sprawled on the top landing. An attractive young blonde, Mrs. Snyder was clad in an abbreviated green nightgown trimmed with lace. Her feet were bound loosely with clothesline, but her hands were untied. Lying next to her was a second length of rope and a loosened gag.

"My God, Ruth, what's happened?" Mrs. Mulhauser asked.

"I got an awful whack on the head," Mrs. Snyder whimpered.

Mrs. Mulhauser telephoned her husband, Louis, and instructed Lorraine to go over and stay at her house. She told Mrs. Snyder to lie still and telephoned the nearest police booth.

When Mulhauser arrived, he went looking for the man of the house, Albert Snyder, in the master bedroom. On the twin bed nearest the door was a heap of sheets and blankets. Mulhauser patted it and felt something hard underneath. Pulling aside the bedding, Mulhauser discovered the pajama-clad body of Albert Snyder, hands tied behind his back with a towel and ankles bound with a red-and-yellow silk necktie. Snyder was

3

lying on his stomach, his face stuffed into the pillow. The pillowcase was smeared with blood. Looped around his neck and digging deeply into the flesh was a length of picture wire, cinched at the back, its loose ends sticking out at odd angles. Next to the body lay a revolver, broken open. Mulhauser pulled a sheet over the corpse and emerged from the bedroom.

"How is Mr. Snyder?" asked Mrs. Mulhauser.

"Dead," he replied.

Mulhauser called another neighbor, George Colyer. The two men carried Mrs. Snyder into Lorraine's room and put her to bed. They said nothing about her husband, nor did she ask. A physician who lived in the neighborhood, Dr. Harry Hansen, was summoned, examined her, and found no evidence that Mrs. Snyder had, as she claimed, received a terrific blow on the head. He told her that the headache she complained of did not appear to be the result of an injury. "Well, then," she replied, "it must be from lying on that cold floor so long."

Patrolmen Robert Tucker and Edmund Schulties responded to Mrs. Mulhauser's call. Sizing up the situation as a case of burglary with violence—only the week before, a suspicious man had been seen prowling around the Snyder residence—they notified the Jamaica Precinct House. Detective Patrolmen Frank Heyner and Harry Kraus arrived at 8:10 A.M. and questioned Mrs. Snyder for five minutes before proceeding to examine the scene. Still, she was told nothing about her husband; still, she did not ask. An ambulance was called, and the accompanying physician, Vincent Juster, ventured that Snyder had been dead for about six hours. He examined Mrs. Snyder and, like Hanson, could find no wound that would explain why she had been unconscious. She was calm and collected.

Murders simply did not happen in middle-class Queens Village, and news of the crime immediately reached the top of the New York City Police Department. By ten o'clock, Deputy Commissioner James Leach was on the scene, and sixty detectives from Queens and Manhattan under the command of Deputy Inspectors James Gallagher and Arthur Carey, respectively, were crawling over every inch of the property.[1] Dr. Howard

---

1. Where the detectives performed such feats of forensic investigation as picking up each other's cigarette butts. Under Police Commissioner George McLaughlin, the

Neail of the New York Medical Examiner's Office, the highest-ranking forensic pathologist in Queens County, examined the body. There was a gash an inch long and a quarter-inch wide on the right side of the head near the forehead. The wound, though ugly, was superficial. Just below it was a slight abrasion and there was another abrasion directly on the back of the skull. There were assorted minor cuts and scrapes—five on the right side of the neck, two on the left side, and a gouge on the left side of the nose.

When Neail turned it over, the body of Albert Snyder was an ugly sight. The face was swollen and blue from strangulation. A cotton rag protruded from his mouth, as though he had vomited on it, and strips of cotton hung like worms from his nostrils. Lying on the pillow was a small cloth pad into which Snyder's mouth and nose had been jammed. Wrapped in a blue, white-dotted bandanna handkerchief with a border of anchors, it reeked of chloroform.

The .38-caliber pistol on the bed was loaded with three rounds, and three loose cartridges were on the floor. A leather holster protruded from under the dead man's pillow. Ever since the prowler scare, Snyder had slept with his gun at hand.[2] Underneath the body, near the shoulders,

---

plainclothes force was organized along pseudomilitary lines. The detectives from Queens were jacks-of-all-trades from the Fourteenth Detective Bureau in Jamaica, which had jurisdiction for Queens Village. The detectives from Manhattan were "murder men," members of the Homicide Squad attached to New York City Police headquarters, where there were also squads specializing, for example, in gambling, prostitution, and white-collar crime. The Manhattan investigators were "detectives' detectives" called in on especially difficult or important investigations falling within their field of expertise. The two teams naturally detested each other. To complicate matters, Queens assistant district attorneys also played an active role in the investigation; because they had a long-standing working relationship with Queens detectives, they also looked on the "murder men" as interlopers. Deputy Inspector Carey was second-in-command of the Central Detective Bureau and head of the Homicide Squad; Deputy Inspector Gallagher was commander of the Fifteenth Detective Bureau in Queens; the head of the Fourteenth was unavailable at the time of the Snyder murder.

2. Snyder had bought the pistol in 1926, when Queens Village was being terrorized by Paul Hilton, "The Radio Burglar," named after his favorite target. Hilton's listening

police found a second length of picture wire, with a gold pencil clipped to it.

Neail also checked Mrs. Snyder for signs of a blow and became the third doctor to conclude that there were none. He could find no explanation, other than fright, for the long period during which she claimed to have been unconscious. He laughed when a detective told him that Mrs. Snyder maintained she had been senseless for five hours: "Five *hours*! Five *minutes* would be more like it!" Her wrists bore none of the expected marks from having struggled free from tight bonds, nor her body any of the expected bruises from having lain on the floor for five hours.

Lorraine, who was being looked after by the Muhlhausers' teenage daughter, told detectives that her father and mother had taken her with them the night before to a bridge party in the nearby neighborhood of Hollis. Normally, she would have stayed home with her grandmother, Mrs. Josephine Brown, who lived with the Snyders, but Mrs. Brown was away on a nursing job. When they returned from the party at about two o'clock in the morning, she was undressed by her mother and put to bed. She immediately fell asleep and knew nothing more until morning, when she was awakened by noises in the hallway. Leaving her bed, she found her mother at the top of the stairs and was told to call Mrs. Mulhauser.

New York City Police Commissioner George McLaughlin arrived on the scene shortly before noon. He asked if Mrs. Snyder had been informed of her husband's death and learned that she had not. "There's something fishy here," a detective told him. "She hasn't even asked about him." McLaughlin went into Lorraine's room, where Mrs. Snyder was still in bed being ministered to by Mrs. Mulhauser.

"Do you know your husband has been injured?" he inquired.

"Has he really?"

"Yes, I'm sorry, but we have just received word that he is dead."

---

days ended when he shot and killed a policeman while evading arrest. He was executed at Sing Sing on 17 February, 1927.

As the commissioner put it later, "A few tears were shed for a minute or two."[3]

According to Mrs. Snyder, she and her husband and daughter had returned from a bridge party at about two o'clock. Her husband dropped her and Lorraine off out front and put the car in the garage. For about five minutes, while she and Lorraine were upstairs and Snyder was seeing to the car, the front door was open. The couple retired and Mr. Snyder, who had drunk a great deal at the party, quickly fell asleep. A few minutes later Mrs. Snyder thought she heard Lorraine in the hallway and, fearing that she might be sick from something she ate at the party, went to her. When she passed her mother's bedroom, a huge man emerged. As he dragged her into the room, Mrs. Snyder had the impression that someone below called up to him. Her assailant was swarthy and had a black mustache; he looked like an Italian. Then came the blow on the head, and she was out cold for the next five hours. When she succeeded in freeing her hands and removing the gag from her mouth, she awakened Lorraine.

The house had been searched—not merely searched but ransacked, systematically turned topsy-turvy. Even the sofa cushions in the living room and the pots and pans in the kitchen were strewn about. The contents of dresser drawers in the master bedroom and Mrs. Brown's bedroom were jumbled on the floor. In the middle of the floor in the master bedroom were Snyder's gold watch, its platinum chain still attached, and his empty wallet. Scraps of an Italian-language newspaper, which seemed to corroborate Mrs. Snyder's description of the man who had struck her, were found on the floor beside the bed. Downstairs in the living room, there was a pint bottle of whiskey on the table with a full glass next to it and a half-smoked Sweet Caporal cigarette in an ashtray. Mrs. Snyder was not a smoker and Albert Snyder smoked cigars.

Detectives—the least romantic and most practical of men, to invert

---

3. Later in the afternoon, Snyder's brothers and sisters hurried to the scene of the tragedy. "Isn't it terrible?" Mrs. Snyder remarked as they huddled at her bedside. "They clipped him twice on the head."

what John Maynard Keynes said about bankers—did not give Mrs. Snyder's story the slightest credence. First, it was clear that she had not received a blow serious enough to knock her unconscious for five hours, nor could she have fainted and remained senseless for so long. Second, since her hands were free, why had she not untied the rope that loosely bound her ankles?

And these were only the most glaring of the inconsistencies in her story. Burglars, who are usually professional and methodical criminals, shun low-payoff risks. Why should the modest Snyder home have been targeted? Nothing of interest—negotiable securities, silver, jewelry, objets d'art—was likely to be found there.[4] The only item definitely missing was the money from Snyder's wallet. But if that was all the robbers were after, they could have jumped him when he put away the car. And why did they not take Snyder's gold watch and platinum chain?

The thoroughness with which the house had been searched was itself suspicious. Time is the essence of the housebreaker's art: the burglar knows what he wants, knows where it is likely to be kept, goes after it, and leaves—no thief, however meticulous, would bother to search beneath sofa cushions and empty out kitchen cabinets.

"There's something funny about that kitchen business," grumbled a detective. "A professional would never bother with the kitchen."

Why were Albert Snyder's clothes, but not Mrs. Snyder's, jumbled? Why was Lorraine's room, and only her room, left undisturbed, as if ensuring that the little girl was not awakened? What kind of burglar carries chloroform and picture wire? Why, knowing that her husband kept a loaded pistol, had Mrs. Snyder not cried out when she was grabbed? And how could the house have been so suffocatingly hot when the police arrived at eight if the coal furnace had been left unattended since the couple returned home at two o'clock in the morning?

Mrs. Snyder's answers were evasive and unsatisfactory. When asked about the whiskey in the living room, she claimed that the only liquor in

---

4. One of the zaniest theories was that Snyder had created a valuable invention in his basement workshop and that the burglars were after the device or plans for it.

the house was a small flask of brandy in the bathroom kept for medicinal purposes. In fact, detectives had found a generously stocked liquor cabinet. She also claimed that jewelry worth two hundred dollars was missing, but in the early afternoon, the supposedly missing items—three rings of modest value and a silver bar pin—were found wrapped in a rag underneath the mattress of Mrs. Snyder's bed.[5] The pillowcase on her side of the bed appeared to have been recently changed and never slept on. Police found a bloodstained pillowcase thrown in the dirty-clothes hamper in the basement. A squirrel coat that Mrs. Snyder claimed was missing was found on the shelf of her closet. Hanging openly in the same closet was a much more valuable leopard-skin coat.

A small calendar pad, kept in the fashion of a diary, contained a number of names. During questioning about these, Mrs. Snyder flushed and stammered when the police came to the entry for one H. Judd Gray, 37 Wayne Avenue, East Orange, New Jersey. The detectives' interest in Mr. Gray increased when a pin bearing the initials "J. G." was found on the floor of the master bedroom and several canceled checks were found made out to H. Judd Gray.

Other canceled checks to the Prudential Life Insurance Company were found, suggesting that Snyder's life had been heavily insured. Asked about her husband's insurance, Mrs. Snyder gave an obviously false response. "It's for one thousand dollars," she said. But that was not nearly enough to account for the checks. "Well," she replied, "it *was* for one thousand dollars; now it's twenty-five thousand dollars."

Lorraine, questioned about life in the Snyder household, made a comment that caused the detectives to exchange glances: "Mommy and Daddy had fights because Mommy stayed out all night long." A neighbor said that Mrs. Snyder often returned late at night by taxi. On one occasion, Albert Snyder had come out and met her on the sidewalk, where the couple had loudly bickered. Asked who kept her away from home at

5. Some reports say the missing jewelry was not discovered until after Mrs. Snyder was taken to the Jamaica police station. Untrue. Police discovered the items in the early afternoon but did not tell Mrs. Snyder until she was at the station.

night, Mrs. Snyder snapped, "None of your business!" When Detective Inspector Carey from Manhattan told her that this did not look like a real burglary, her reply was, "What do you mean? How could you tell?"

"We see lots of burglaries," the patient detective explained. "They are not done this way."

At five o'clock in the afternoon, Mrs. Snyder was informed that she would have to go to the Jamaica Precinct House, located at Jamaica and Flushing Avenues, for further questioning. "I'm too sick," she replied. When detectives insisted, Mrs. Snyder, who had been in bed throughout her questioning, flung off the covers in a rage and leapt out of bed wearing only the nightgown in which she had been found. Tossing her blond hair, she dressed in front of her crimson-faced questioners. She threw on her squirrel coat, jammed a hat down low over her head, and, surrounded by a wedge of detectives, left the little house in Queens Village.

The previous night's partygoers were assembled for questioning. The hosts were salesman Walter Fidgeon and his wife, Serena. The Fidgeon and Snyder couples had met last summer, when the families rented adjoining summer bungalows in Port Jefferson; they were planning to summer again together this year, as well. Guests at the party included George Hough, the brother of Mrs. Fidgeon, and Dr. Arthur W. Stanford. According to the guests, Mrs. Snyder always behaved affectionately toward her husband and the couple had no domestic troubles. On one occasion, though, she went away without him for over a week on a car trip up north.

There had been a great deal of drinking (ginger ale highballs) at the party.[6] The police also learned that Mrs. Snyder had encouraged her husband to drink freely. In contrast, she herself drank practically nothing. Based on her previous drinking behavior, for example, at last year's Halloween party, this was unusual. In the Fidgeon's kitchen at one point, she had complained of not feeling well and said to Mrs. Fidgeon, "Give my share to Al." When a guest offered Mrs. Snyder a drink, she

---

6. According to neighbors, loud parties were held at the Fidgeon residence every Saturday night, for which the couple was ostracized. The previous night's party, they said, had been particularly wild.

again declined and suggested serving it to Mr. Snyder instead. She remarked to Dr. Stanford that she was menstruating and did not feel like drinking. This tallied with the report of Dr. Hansen, the neighborhood doctor who examined Mrs. Snyder. At the party, she and her husband appeared to be on good terms. At one point, she called him "baby lamb," eliciting the good-humored rejoinder, "That's not what you call me at home!"

At one thirty in the morning, a quarrel nasty enough to break up the evening had erupted between Snyder and George Hough.[7] Hough was traced to a hotel in Jamaica, but he was able to prove that he had gone there directly after the party and had not left since.

At eight o'clock Sunday evening, Commissioner McLaughlin returned to the Snyder residence to see how the investigation was progressing. He learned from detectives that there were no signs of forced entry. Mrs. Snyder theorized that the burglars must have pushed the kitchen door key out of the lock from outside and used a skeleton key to open the door. The door key was, indeed, found lying on the kitchen floor, but it was three feet from the door. A detective tried two experiments: first, he placed the key loosely in the lock and slammed the door shut on his way out; then he tried ejecting the key from the lock by poking in a stick from the outside. In both cases, the key fell straight down onto the kitchen floor, coming to rest next to the door. There was only one conclusion: someone had planted the key where it was found.

McLaughlin proceeded to the Jamaica Precinct House. Because Queens District Attorney Richard Newcombe was temporarily unavailable, Mrs. Snyder was being questioned by Assistant District Attorneys

---

7. Snyder had again brought up the story (see chapter 3) about his wife's "card-playing friends" and the disappearance of his wallet a few weeks earlier. "You're a bad sport to blame the loss of your wallet on your wife's friends," Hough said. Albert Snyder responded sharply and the pair had to be restrained from coming to blows. When police asked Mrs. Snyder how much money had been stolen from her husband's wallet, she unhesitatingly replied, "One hundred and ten dollars." "How do you know that?" she was asked, to which she replied, "Because last night when we left the party he pulled out his wallet, counted his money out loud and said, 'Well, at least I got away from *this* party without losing anything!'" [my emphasis].

Thomas Thornton and Peter Daly in the precinct captain's office.[8] McLaughlin joined the group. The commissioner admonished Mrs. Snyder that her robbery story was not believable and asked her to go over again what happened. She told the same tale.

She did admit, however, that for some years she and her husband had not been on good terms. McLaughlin asked Mrs. Snyder if she had ever stayed out all night; she admitted that she had. On those occasions, she generally stayed at the home of her cousin, Ethel Anderson. Mrs. Anderson was the estranged wife of Police Patrolman Edward Pierson of the Twenty-third Precinct in the Bronx. Word was sent to Officer Pierson to present himself in Jamaica.

The questioning continued.

"Mrs. Snyder, we know full well that there was a man whom you know in your house last night," McLaughlin said.

"I can't understand why you say that."

"We also know full well that when you say you were lying upstairs in a faint, you were really downstairs."

"How do you know that?"

"Never mind how we know."

When Pierson arrived, McLaughlin asked Mrs. Snyder to leave the room for a few moments while he questioned the patrolman about persons friendly with his wife and Mrs. Snyder. Pierson mentioned, among others, Judd Gray.

This was getting to be too much. Detective Lieutenant Michael Mc-Dermott wrote the name "H. Judd Gray" on a slip of paper and went down the hall to Mrs. Snyder. She was sitting at a desk drumming her fingers nervously.

"Ruth," McDermott started, "your story's getting more and more balled up. It doesn't fit. Why don't you tell the truth and get it off your chest?"

---

8. As Daly's son recalled over seventy years later, "The telephone rang and Dad went to get it. He came back and said, 'Well, I've got to go to the office. Gallagher says some dame from Queens Village has killed her husband and they've got her cold for murder-one.' "

"What do you think they'd do to me if I told everything?"

"I can't promise you anything, but you might as well come clean."

McDermott held out the slip of paper. "Is that the man who killed your husband?"

"He did it," Mrs. Snyder confirmed.

"Ruth, I'm going to leave you here and go down the hall to the commissioner. When you're ready, I want you to come in and make a clean breast of it."

McDermott went into the precinct captain's office, passed the slip of paper to McLaughlin, and nodded. About two minutes later, Mrs. Snyder entered with a handkerchief to her eyes and announced that she had not been telling the truth. She was sorry for having kept them all there for so many hours (it was now nearly one thirty Monday morning). She could see that she was getting deeper and deeper into trouble. McLaughlin silently held out to her the slip of paper.

"That is the party," she said.

2

GRAY COULD BE FOUND, said Mrs. Snyder, at the Hotel Onondaga in Syracuse. She began to make her statement at one thirty on Monday morning; at one forty-seven, a cable was sent to the Syracuse Police Department. By two thirty, three Syracuse Police Department detectives were at the Onondaga, knocking on the door of Room 743. A slight, owl-faced man with a deeply cleft chin opened it. Dressed only in his underwear, he blinked at the policemen through thick spectacles.

"Mr. Gray?"

"Yes."

"They seem to want you in New York for homicide."

"What's that?"

"Murder."

"Fellows, the most I ever murdered in my life was a little liquor from time to time," Gray joked, pointing to a half-full glass of whiskey on the bedside table.

"You'll have to come with us anyway."

Gray was taken downtown and sat for several hours with other recently arrested prisoners in a holding room, then he was put in a cell by himself. At about eight o'clock Monday evening, he was taken into an interrogation room for questioning by Syracuse Police Chief Martin Cadin.

Gray maintained his composure. He parried questions easily and would sign an affidavit only to the following effect. He was thirty-four years old, married, and lived with his wife Isabel and daughter Jane, age ten, at 37 Wayne Avenue in East Orange, New Jersey. He was employed as the New York State representative for the Benjamin and Johnes Company, a corset and ladies' underwear concern, and had been absent from home for two weeks on his usual upstate route. Ruth Snyder had been a friend of his for some two years; he had never met Mr. Snyder and had no idea who murdered him. He had not seen or heard from Mrs. Snyder since dining with her and Lorraine at Henry's Restaurant on 35th Street in Manhattan at the end of February or beginning of March.

According to Gray, he left Rochester on the afternoon of Friday, 18 March, arriving at Syracuse at eight fifteen in the evening, and checked into the Hotel Onondaga. On the afternoon of Saturday, 19 March, he ate lunch with his friend Haddon Gray (a Syracuse insurance salesman who was no relation) and stopped off twice at the Elks Club for a drink. At six twenty, he posted a letter to Mrs. Snyder and his regular sales report to his employer. He retired at about eight o'clock, instructing the desk to hold telephone calls and leaving a "Do Not Disturb" sign on his door. At eight o'clock Sunday morning, he got up and took a bath. On Sunday evening he ate dinner at Haddon Gray's house, arriving at six o'clock and leaving at ten thirty. Then he stopped by a club for a few drinks with a friend and was just preparing for bed with a nightcap when police took him into custody.

All morning, Gray's story remained intact. The dinner with Haddon Gray was confirmed. Employees at the Onondaga testified that someone certainly occupied Room 743 on Saturday night—in the early evening, the front desk had been asked to hold calls, and the bedclothes and bath towels were in disarray when the maid arrived on Sunday morning.

Detective Lieutenant McDermott and his partner Martin Brown, also of the Fourteenth Detective Bureau in Jamaica, arrived in Syracuse just after lunch and presented their credentials to Police Chief Cadin. He took them into a small room where Gray was sitting. "This is your man," he said. Brown handled the introductions and informed Gray that they would be escorting him on the 5:30 train to New York, where he would be charged with homicide. Gray stuck to his story, insisting he had never left Syracuse.

"Put your hand on the desk, please," asked McDermott, who checked that Gray's hand size conformed roughly to the marks on Albert

Snyder's neck. "You know, we have finger prints all over the house," he lied.

"Not mine, I'll guarantee you that," replied Gray.

"Mrs. Snyder has confessed and implicated you in this crime. How would we know who you were and where to find you if she had not?"

"I have made a statement to Chief Cadin and signed an affidavit and I have nothing further to say."

McDermott left the room and consulted by telephone with Queens District Attorney Richard Newcombe while Brown continued the questioning. When McDermott returned they again queried Gray about his movements and activities in Syracuse. Regarding the crucial time period from late Saturday afternoon to late Sunday afternoon, Gray said that on Saturday evening he wrote letters, worked on samples in his room and went to bed a little after eight o'clock because he did not feel well. On Sunday morning, he woke up at seven thirty and ate breakfast in the restaurant across the street from the hotel.

"Are you known in that restaurant?" they asked.

"No."

"Ever eat there before?"

"No."

"Did you talk to anyone on the way in or out?"

"No."

After breakfast, Gray said, he took a walk until ten o'clock. Where had he walked? Gray did not remember. Then he worked on samples in his room until late afternoon, when he called Haddon Gray's house to confirm a dinner appointment.

When Haddon Gray learned of his friend's predicament, he retained lawyer Nathan Abelson to represent him. At first, Syracuse police refused to admit Abelson, but the lawyer would not leave the police station. Police Chief Cadin finally gave in, called the New York detectives out of the room, and introduced them to Abelson. McDermott said that Gray had not been arrested and that the police officers were not permitted to let anyone interview him, however, they would make an exception if Gray insisted.

He took Abelson's card into Gray.

"There's some big Jew lawyer out there wants to talk to you. Are you interested?"

"No, I don't see what good a lawyer would do me," Gray replied.

McDermott transmitted the message to Abelson, adding that if he wanted to come back in an hour or so, Gray would be given another opportunity to speak to him.[1]

It was clear that no more could be gotten out of Gray in Syracuse, so the detectives left him in Cadin's custody and went to interview Joseph Grogan, manager of the Hotel Onondaga. Grogan confirmed that Gray had checked in on Friday, 18 March, and had been given Room 743. Switchboard records showed that he telephoned the residence of Haddon Gray at 4:41 P.M. on Sunday, 20 March. At the detectives' request, Grogan sent for the chief housekeeper, who in turn summoned chambermaid Mary Barnes. On Sunday morning, said Barnes, she entered Room 743 at about nine o'clock to clean it. On the table, she saw a blue "Do Not Disturb" card and a hotel envelope on which "Bud" was written in pencil. The bed had been slept in and the bath had been used.

When she arrived for work on Monday morning, Barnes continued, she heard that the occupant of Room 743 had been taken away in the middle of the night on a murder charge. When she cleaned the room, therefore, she took the wastebasket and locked it in the closet with her cleaning supplies. She led detectives to the closet, where they emptied the wastebasket into a large envelope.

Back at the unoccupied hotel room placed at their disposal for conducting interviews, McDermott emptied the envelope onto the floor and began to rummage through its contents. The note to "Bud" was found. It read: "Perfect. Call me when you're ready." Additionally, there were two business letters, one envelope addressed to "H. Judd Gray" and bearing a Jamaica postmark from 9:00 A.M. on Saturday, 19 March, a

---

1. This is McDermott's version of events, both in his detective's notebook and in testimony. Gray would later testify that he requested to see a lawyer, but was denied permission.

Long Island Railway train schedule, cigarette butts, match stubs, and a nail.

Last, torn but easily reassembled, was a Pullman ticket stub for the 8:45 A.M. New York to Syracuse train on Sunday, 20 March. So much for Gray's story—they had their man. The only issues still to be resolved were the telephone call to the front desk on Saturday evening and the fact that Gray's room appeared Sunday morning to have been occupied the night before.

Back at Syracuse police headquarters, there were various administrative details to settle. Gray was brought to the station house desk, where McDermott signed him out of the custody of the Syracuse police. He asked for and received permission to leave thirteen dollars with the desk sergeant to be transmitted to the hotel. Haddon Gray approached and asked if he could speak to the prisoner, but the detectives refused to allow the two to exchange more than a few words.

Syracuse detectives slapped Gray jovially on the back by way of an encouraging send-off, and Cadin shook his hand to show there were no hard feelings.

Nattily dressed and smiling, Gray descended the steps of the Syracuse police station handcuffed to Brown and carrying an overcoat over his free arm. The smile disappeared when photographers began to take pictures. "Any New York newspaper that prints my picture in connection with this case will be sued for libel!" he shouted.

Police Chief Cadin gave a news conference after his charge had left: "I've been in police work for over twenty years, and if he is guilty of this crime, he is the calmest individual I've come across in my experience."

It must have been a bizarre train ride. Gray and his escorts sat around a table in a private parlor compartment. Reporters clustered outside and peeked through the doorway whenever anyone went in or came out. Gray regaled his escorts with tales of his adventures in the ladies' underwear trade. They reciprocated by relating the latest bootlegger jokes. Gray addressed McDermott, who led the questioning, as "Mac" and was addressed as "Judd" in return. At one point, Gray remarked, "Someday, we'll all laugh about this."

Gray was questioned until dinner.[2] Detectives showed him one of the Syracuse daily papers, whose headline blared: "MRS. SNYDER CONFESSES!" and read him the high points of her statement. He might as well come across before the "Big Boss" got on, they told him.[3] The "Big Boss" was Queens Assistant District Attorney James Conroy, private secretary to District Attorney Newcombe. Conroy joined the party at Albany along with his colleague Thomas Thornton and Deputy Inspector Gallagher.

"This is the first time I've been in the clutches of the law," Gray remarked affably as hands were shaken all around.

Conroy took over the questioning, which proceeded at a gentle, steady, pace, while Thornton took notes. There were occasional five-minute breaks given over to small talk. Although a stenographer had been brought on board at Albany, she remained in the next car. Conroy did not advise Gray that anything he said could be used against him, but there was no legal requirement for him to do so, because he was not under arrest. After an hour, Conroy and Thornton switched places, with Thornton asking the questions and Conroy taking notes.

Not long after Albany, McDermott said, "Judd, you know, we have the contents of your wastebasket in the hotel."

Gray grew serious and asked, after a moment's silence, "Mac, what was in the wastebasket?"

The detective made no reply. Reporters noticed from their fleeting glimpses through the door that Gray was no longer relaxed and smiling.

"Why the change?" a reporter asked Deputy Inspector Gallagher when the latter emerged to take a break.

"Because he's smiled his last smile," Gallagher replied.

---

2. Which Gray paid for. The detectives were pressed for cash. McDermott had asked the Syracuse Police Department for an eighty-dollar loan, but this was consumed by train fare. He calculated his expenses in the margins of his notebook.

3. Versions differ: "You'd better come across," was Gray's version. McDermott testified that he simply asked Gray why Mrs. Snyder would pick him, of all men in the world, to implicate. Gray replied that he did not know.

At Poughkeepsie, McDermott dropped the other shoe: "Do you know Judd, that we have the ticket that you went back on?"

"Well, gentlemen," Gray said after a pause, "I was in that house that night."

Then he launched into his story.[4]

---

4. The statement given by Gray on the train was noted down by McDermott in his notebook and conforms exactly to the statement Gray gave in New York, and later on the witness stand.

3

THE ROOTS OF ALBERT SNYDER'S MURDER are to be found in the marriage of two utterly incompatible partners, Ruth and Albert Snyder. The Snyders, their daughter, Lorraine, and Mrs. Snyder's mother, Mrs. Josephine Brown, known as "Granny Brown" around the house, moved to Queens Village in 1923. Snyder was born "Albert Schneider" into a large, close German family in 1882. His father Charles ran a bakery store on Grand Street in the Williamsburg section of Brooklyn; the family lived upstairs and his mother, Mary, kept house. When Albert Schneider was in his early twenties, his father retired, sold the bakery, and moved the family into a roomy, three-story, brick-faced house on McDonough Street in Bedford-Stuyvesant.

Schneider was talented with his hands and attended nearby Pratt Institute, where he studied art and graphic design. After graduation, he experienced no difficulty obtaining employment in commercial art studios. His work consisted mainly of layout and dull incidental sketches, but when given the opportunity, he could also paint passable landscapes and seascapes. He never failed to give his profession as "artist."

In his leisure hours, Schneider devoted himself to boats and automobiles and mechanical devices of all kinds. He was an enthusiast of outdoor sports, especially swimming, and he liked roughing it on weekends— hiking, fishing, camping.

When he moved to Bedford-Stuyvesant, Schneider fell in love with Jessie Guischard (gee-SHARD), whose family lived a few blocks from the Schneiders in an apartment house on Decatur Street. Jessie was a cultured and intelligent girl, a graduate of Jamaica Normal School and, after

1906, a schoolteacher at Public School 132 in Manhattan.[1] Jessie's father, Hillaire, was a printer at a publishing company. Despite the French name, both he and his father were New York natives. Jessie's mother, Kate, was an immigrant from Scotland; census takers recorded her native language as "Scotch."

Year after year, Albert and Jessie kept company. And though it is not clear whether they were ever formally engaged, as the newspapers later reported, it was with Albert Schneider at her bedside that Jessie Guischard, age thirty, died of pneumonia on 21 November 1912.[2]

Schneider never really got over Jessie. He treasured his scrapbooks filled with meticulously dated and captioned photographs of her and memorabilia from their expeditions to the Catskills and Adirondacks. Next to his heart, every day until his death, he wore a keepsake pin inscribed "J. G."[3]

Nevertheless, life went on. Within a year of Jessie's death, Schneider found himself working at *Motor Boating Magazine,* a Hearst publication. A year later, in 1914, at the age of thirty-two, he had recovered sufficiently from his grief to pursue Ruth Brown, a secretary who claimed to be nineteen but who was, in fact, twenty-three.[4]

The story of their meeting is straight out of a romance novel. One morning, when a telephone call was misdirected to Schneider at *Motor Boating,* he gave the operator a piece of his mind and slammed down the receiver. Perhaps it was something in her voice, or perhaps he merely sensed he had missed a sexual opportunity. In any case, he called back and

1. "Normal schools" were elite secondary schools designed to produce teachers.

2. According to New York City Death Certificate Number 21,585 for 1912. Jessie Guischard, her mother, and many members of the extended Guischard clan are buried in Cypress Hills Cemetery in East New York. They must have been an unsentimental family: not a single grave is marked.

3. Ironically, this was the "J. G." pin found on the master bedroom floor by police; it had nothing whatever to do with Judd Gray.

4. Her reported age dropped four years between the 1915 New York State Census, taken just before her wedding, and the 1920 U.S. Federal Census. Granny Brown practiced the same deception: she claimed, at the time of the murder, to be fifty. In fact, she was sixty.

apologized; they chatted for a few minutes, and in the end, he invited her to come see about a job with the Hearst organization.

Ruth's father, Harry Brown, came from a fishing village on the coast of Norway and, like practically every other son in the region, had to go abroad to seek his fortune. In America, he met and married Josephine Anderson, who came from a similar village in Sweden, and settled down to earn his living as a carpenter. A son, Andrew, was born in 1889 and, two years later, a daughter, christened Mamie Ruth, who later called herself Ruth May.[5]

During Ruth's earliest years, the family lived in an apartment house at 125th Street and Morningside Avenue in upper Manhattan; then they began a steady migration northward. According to the 1900 U.S. Federal Census, the family lived with two newly arrived Scandinavian boarders (Harry Brown's nephew and brother-in-law) in a rented house on West 138th Street: a neighborhood of rolling meadows in the days when the City College of New York was only a proposal. By 1913, they had moved across the Harlem River to another apartment house on Woodycrest Avenue in the Highbridge neighborhood of the Bronx, a wide-open, green area on the bluffs overlooking the Harlem River.

There is a whiff of upward mobility in this progress from the crowded tenement in Morningside Heights to the more genteel environs of West Harlem, where they could afford to live only by taking in boarders, to the suburban hills of Highbridge, where they owned their apartment and one of their neighbors was a Municipal Court justice.

Yet, if we are to believe Ruth's own recollection, it was a desperately hard life. Harry Brown suffered from epilepsy and was in poor health much of the time. The carpentry and contracting business never seemed to take off, and Josephine Brown was forced to supplement her husband's

---

5. A name change that perhaps revealed something about the restlessness of Mrs. Snyder's childhood. At eleven, she tired of "Mamie" and announced that she wished to be called "May." At twelve, she tired of "May" and decided to go by her middle name, "Ruth." The second switch was never recognized by members of her family, who persisted in calling her "May." She was enumerated as both "Ruth M. Snyder" and "May R. Snyder" in the various federal and state censuses.

meager earnings by working as a sickroom attendant or, as she put it, "practical nurse." In Ruth's version, her childhood was dominated by a sense of deprivation and want—not of necessities, like food, but of the finer things in life, like the fancy dolls and party dresses the neighborhood girls had.

She was a sickly child. At six years of age, she underwent intestinal surgery; at nine, she suffered a severe sunstroke; and at twelve, she underwent a botched appendectomy that caused repeated bouts of misery until finally, at eighteen, she underwent a second operation to correct the first. She tired easily and was unable to keep up with other girls at play and in sports. She was given to fainting, which she blamed on epilepsy inherited from her father.[6]

After eighth grade, Ruth abandoned her education, went to the employment office of the New York Telephone Company, and was hired as a night relief telephone operator.[7] She worked the graveyard shift for fifteen dollars per week, which she turned over to her family without even opening the pay envelope. For two years, she endured this dreary life before leaving to learn typing, stenography and other secretarial skills at a business college.

Then followed what must have been a rather pleasant interlude. She was gainfully employed in a series of daytime office jobs, making enough to help out her family and still keep a bit for herself. In the meantime, her brother, Andrew, had obtained solid middle-class employment as a clerk, first at a steamship company and then at a bank. When he married, he

6. Mrs. Snyder was never formally diagnosed with epilepsy, and cases of inherited epilepsy are extremely rare.

7. According to the *American,* in the summer of her fifteenth year, which would be about the time she left school, Ruth became infatuated with one of her teachers. Her affections were returned, and the pair carried on a romance during the vacation months. When school resumed in the fall, Ruth grew jealous of one of her lover's students and a hair-pulling match ensued on school premises. The upshot of the episode was the dismissal of the teacher. This would explain the sudden decision to leave school: perhaps she was caught fooling around with a teacher, and he was fired and she was expelled, or maybe she quit in disgrace.

and his wife, Margaret, a bookkeeper like himself, moved into a ground floor apartment just down the block on Woodycrest Avenue.

Despite her poor health, Ruth turned out to be a head turner: tall, blonde, and slim with high cheekbones and piercing blue eyes. Boys came into the picture, but nothing serious, just a turn on the dance floor under the watchful eye of a chaperon and a few giggles with the girls the next day. There were teenage socials at her family's church to attend, movies and vaudeville shows to see, and melodramas to read.

It was during these halcyon days that Ruth dialed the wrong number that introduced her to Albert Schneider. By the end of that fateful afternoon, she had been hired as a proofreader and copyist to work in the pool serving *Motor Boating, Cosmopolitan, Hearst's Weekly,* and several other Hearst publications based in the same building.

Albert Schneider meant business. The very first day, he snuck up behind Ruth, played with her hair, and invited her to accompany him to an event called the Kit Kat Ball. She asked a colleague for advice. "Don't go stepping out with *him,* Brownie," she was told, "or you won't come back the same way you went out." When she declined, he invited her to lunch. This she accepted.

He made sexual advances, which Ruth turned down, but they were made and declined in the spirit of good fun; in fact, her respectability seemed to heighten Schneider's interest. When Ruth left a few months later to take a higher-paying job at a lithography company, he came downtown to take her to lunch, dinner, and the theater. Albert Schneider was turning into a serious prospect. He was well read, artistic, and much more established than the other men Ruth had known. Besides, Ruth loved to go out on the town.

At Christmas 1914, Schneider proposed, but Ruth turned him down. Then, at her "twentieth" birthday party in March 1915, he played his trump card. He arrived with a box of chocolates, somewhat disappointing the birthday girl, who had hoped for something more expensive. Inside the box was a second box, a jeweler's box, with a solitaire diamond engagement ring inside.

That did it. On 24 July 1915, she and Albert Schneider were married

in the Brown family's apartment. The family-and-friends-only ceremony was followed by cold salads, sandwiches, cakes, and coffee prepared by Ruth and her mother. Unfortunately the bride was
menstruating and felt miserable; to add insult to injury, Albert Schneider
reacted by losing his temper and returning to his family for the night. It
was an inauspicious beginning.

The newlyweds moved into a rented house on 61st Street in the Bay
Ridge neighborhood of Brooklyn, where Albert Schneider the suitor
quickly turned into Albert Schneider the husband. Gone were the
courtship days of theaters and restaurants; now Schneider wanted to get
back to boating, fishing, and puttering around the house. He threw himself into tinkering and handyman jobs. Between his outdoor pursuits, the
garden, the garage, and the workshop, Ruth hardly even saw her husband
on weekends except when he came in to eat the heavy German food he
preferred. They never went out to restaurants or theaters in the city like
they used to.

Albert Schneider's idea of entertainment was to put on dirty old
clothes and to go out on his boat, berthed on Long Island. This was no
mere pleasure craft for hopping along the shore—it was a thirty-foot
cabin cruiser outfitted for the open sea. Schneider liked to spend the entire weekend on the water with family or friends. The boat was still
named the "Jessie G." when Ruth and Albert were married, but Ruth
prevailed upon him to rechristen it the "Ruth." She also thought the
name "Schneider" looked and sounded too foreign and convinced him
to change it to "Snyder," a step for which her in-laws never forgave her.[8]

8. Of course, thousands of German-Americans found it expedient to change their
names during World War I. It is certain is that the name change occurred after Albert
and Ruth's marriage. Albert was enumerated in the 1915 New York State Census as
"Schneider"; in the 1920 U.S. Federal Census, he is "Snyder." In 1927, Albert's siblings
were as follows: George, 58, retired from the vaudeville stage, residing with his wife in
Belle Harbor, Long Island; Florence, 53, married to one Coakley, a building contractor,
residing in parts unknown; Warren, 50, married and retired from the New York City
Fire Department, living on a farm on Shelter Island with his wife, Marie, and mother-
in-law; Annie, 47, married to real-estate broker Otto Gleichman (or Gluckman) and residing in Woodhaven; Mamie, 40, married to Edward Thake, a foreman at Edison

A fundamental incompatibility emerged between the couple: Snyder, to use his new name, was reluctant to have children, whereas Mrs. Snyder had dreamed of having a family ever since she was a child. A medical condition stood between her and her goal, but after two years of marriage, and without her husband's knowledge, she had a minor operation and was soon pregnant. Snyder was enraged at first, but comforted himself with the thought that perhaps he would have a son to keep him company. When a daughter was born in Bay Ridge Sanitarium on 15 November 1917, he was inconsolable. Worse still, baby Lorraine was difficult and sickly, always crying and causing trouble.

Mrs. Snyder felt she needed some help around the house, so the couple left Bay Ridge and moved next door to Granny Brown's on Woodycrest Avenue. Within a year, though, Snyder decided to borrow against expected rental income to buy a two-family house on Canonbury Road in Jamaica, Queens. The tidy, two and one-half story wooden house had a garden, and there was an empty lot next to it that Snyder aimed to buy. Frictions developed with the tenant family. Why Snyder chose to run rather than fight is unclear, but he sold and moved his household briefly to Hillside Avenue. There is no information available on his domestic circumstances for that time. In 1923, the Snyder family bought its final home in Queens Manor, a new housing development in Queens Village.

Life could be difficult with Albert Snyder. He was compulsive about neatness and order, wanting everything to be a particular way. He lashed out at Lorraine for normal childish behavior like putting her elbows on the table ("Cut out that damned café habit!" he would snap), and he complained incessantly about expenses. However, he provided well for his family. The house cost eleven thousand dollars in 1923; by 1927, he had paid off all but four thousand dollars of the mortgage. He planted rose bushes by the front steps and put up a vine-covered trellis fence that ran along the sidewalk. With his own hands, Snyder built a garage at the side of the house and an elaborate birdhouse for the backyard.

Electric, and residing just around the corner from the Snyders in Queens Village; and Mabel, 41, unmarried, a secretary at Universal Pictures, residing with the Thakes in Queens Village.

At the insistence of his wife, who did not share his taste for the outdoors, Snyder sold the "Ruth" and bought a top-of-the-line, seven-passenger Buick sedan. There was still enough money left over to rent summer bungalows at Long Island resorts, first on Shelter Island and later in Port Jefferson.

Mrs. Snyder, too, did her part to make the best possible home for the family. She polished the white enamel gas stove and put up row upon row of canned fruits and vegetables in the cellar. She sewed chintz curtains for the kitchen and made raspberry-colored silk lampshades for the living room. She hung white lace curtains in the living-room windows and scattered frilly cushions, antimacassars, knickknacks, and family photographs around the room. The small book collection in the living room was dominated by a gigantic, eight-volume edition of the Bible. On the walls were prints and pictures of a pastoral nature—young women lingering knee-deep in lilies—and three oils painted by Albert Snyder himself. Mrs. Snyder furnished the sunroom with white wicker and filled it to overflowing with carefully tended plants.

Albert Snyder earned $115 per week, of which he gave $85 to his wife for running the household. By all reports, she made her housekeeping budget stretch. She almost never went shopping in retail stores and always tried to strike up an acquaintance with salesmen who would sell to friends at wholesale prices. She was well known around Queens Village for her easy familiarity with the tradesmen on Jamaica Avenue, most of whom she knew by first name. They even nicknamed her "Tommy" because she was such a good-natured tomboy.

Years after the murder, a neighborhood boy commented, "Most of the folks thought she was pretty fast. But us kids liked her. She was a great cutup."[9]

If a neighbor is to be believed, it was no accident that she knew every man in town. "She wasn't interested in women. She'd hardly ever speak to a woman on the street, but every man in the neighborhood was on speaking terms with her. She made it a point to nod to every strange man she saw and soon would establish a casual friendship with him."

9. As quoted in Kobler.

Sister-in-law and Queens Village neighbor Mamie Thake was harsher:"She was man-crazy, and she married above her station. We knew none of her friends. She and they were on a different social plane from us. They weren't our kind of people. We only tolerated her for Albert's sake."

Albert Snyder's father died in 1917, the year Lorraine was born, and his mother died in 1919, followed by Mrs. Snyder's father in 1920. When the Snyder couple moved to Queens Village, Granny Brown came to live with them, occupying the spare bedroom. The arrangement gave Mrs. Snyder help around the house and provided her the companionship she was not getting from her husband. Nor did Albert Snyder mind having the old lady in the house. She kept his wife out of his hair, and she was often away from home nights because of her nursing work.

"Maybe you should give her a present for helping out," Mrs. Snyder asked her husband when Granny had been with them for a few months.

"Why should I?" he replied. "She never gave me one."

At the best of times, there was an uneasy truce at the Snyder residence. Sometimes there would be an outright battle and the couple would refuse to speak to each other for days on end. And Albert Snyder's temper, always ugly, was becoming vicious. When a neighborhood boy sent a baseball through the kitchen window, Snyder pursued the terrified offender down the street, into the boy's own living room, where he pummeled him within an inch of his life. Once in a fit of rage after Lorraine refused to eat her oatmeal, Snyder ran upstairs threatening to kill himself with his pistol. The little girl, crying uncontrollably, ran up after him and threw her arms around him, which brought him back to his senses. On the rare occasions when the couple ate out, Snyder complained all through dinner that they could have eaten the same meal at home for a quarter of the expense. One evening, he and a waiter exchanged words and, with a sweep of his muscular forearm, Snyder sent plates, glasses, food, drinks, and silver crashing to the restaurant floor.

To make matters worse, the Snyder household was haunted by Jessie Guischard. Sitting pensively in her long skirt and frilly blouse, she looked down at them from the bedroom wall in the formal photograph that had followed them wherever they had moved. Every time there was an argument, Albert Snyder would drag in Saint Jessie.

When the marriage first began to deteriorate, Snyder would try to in-terest his wife in sex and she would refuse. Then there was a stage where he would force himself on her. Eventually, things got to the point where he stopped bothering her altogether. One day, Mrs. Snyder's photograph disappeared from his desk at *Motor Boating Magazine*. He never men-tioned her name in the office again.

Finally, as if his rotten moods and hair-trigger temper were not enough, Albert Snyder was becoming a heavy drinker.[10] He made his own beer and wine in the cellar and consumed bootleg whiskey steadily in the evenings; all of his friends were drinkers, too. In fact, Mrs. Snyder liked it when he got drunk at parties, because at least then she could let loose, too. She had to watch out, though, because just a few drinks could send her off the deep end. At one party, she wound up sitting in Albert Snyder's lap singing, "I'll tell the whole wide world I've got the best hus-band in the whole wide world." Another time, after a skinny-dipping party on Shelter Island, she passed out naked, dripping wet, on Granny Brown's bed. And once, after a bridge party in Queens, when she had to take the wheel from her drunken husband, she was pulled over by a traf-fic cop. It looked bad for a few minutes—she was tipsy herself, she had been speeding, she had no driver's license, and Albert Snyder was dead to the world. But her gift for gab paid off, and the cop let her go with a warning. Snyder was still so drunk when they got home that she had to lift him out of the car.

Sometime during that evening, he had lost his wallet, which con-tained seventy-five dollars. The next day, hung over, he complained loudly in front of Mrs. Snyder's brother, Andrew, and his sister-in-law

---

10. A reporter who toured the house wrote that Snyder's basement workshop was strewn with empty whiskey, wine, and beer bottles. "He drank much more than anyone seems to have known," said Granny Brown. "And when he was drunk he was ugly and domineering." Snyder was accustomed to consuming eight to ten ounces of ethyl alco-hol nightly, a total roughly equivalent to six to eight generous bar shots of whiskey. That Snyder was able, on the night of his death, to drive home and go to bed under his own steam despite a blood alcohol concentration of 0.3 percent (indicating acute intoxica-tion) says a great deal about his alcoholic capacity.

Margaret that one of Ruth's "card-playing friends" had stolen his wallet. "Nice crowd she runs around with!" he snarled, gesturing. He was like a broken Victrola from that day on—crank him up and all he wanted to do was talk about was his missing wallet.

In the 1920s, no woman was forced by law to live with a husband she had ceased to love. As evidenced by the marital comings and goings of the rich, divorce was an acceptable expedient. But Mrs. Snyder wanted not only a divorce but also alimony and, most of all, custody of Lorraine, who, by then, was an adorable nine-year-old. Under New York law, the only way she could have all this was to prove cruelty or adultery.

Albert Snyder was not reluctant to deliver the occasional slap, but in the 1920s, cruelty meant depraved cruelty. As for adultery, it was a definite possibility. Her husband seemed to dress better and come home later on Wednesdays, and she once found a pair of theater matinée ticket stubs in his pocket, which enraged her in light of his refusal to take her out. She suspected he might be running around with girls from the office, but she was never able to catch him at it.

Her husband could of course be framed for adultery. Mrs. Snyder knew all the angles in this area; she and her best friend Ethel Pierson, who was also her cousin, were constantly hatching schemes to get Ethel out of her marriage.[11] Mrs. Snyder could arrange for a female friend to place her husband in a compromising situation, which she and an independent witness would conveniently "discover." For one reason or another, though, Mrs. Snyder never followed through on any of her ideas. Maybe it was just too much to handle by that time. After ten years of dealing with her husband, Ruth Snyder was going a bit crazy. She suffered fainting spells, palpitations of the heart, hot flashes, headaches, and abdominal pains. Her menstrual periods were a misery. When a doctor diagnosed her with anemia, she took up Christian Science for a few weeks, but to no avail.

Once, things got so bad she went across the street and sobbed to her

---

11. Ethel Pierson was the daughter of Granny Brown's brother, John Anderson, a store inspector in the Bronx.

neighbor Mrs. Mulhauser, "I am going to go into the city and get drunk and end it all on account of that husband of mine!"

Sometime in June 1925, Mrs. Snyder and her hairdresser friend Kitty Kaufman were having lunch at Henry's, a Swedish restaurant at 34th Street and 5th Avenue. Dining with them was Harry Folsom, a stocking and hosiery man who used to sell to Mrs. Snyder and her friends. In walked an old friend of Folsom's. "Why, there's Judd Gray! Hey, Judd! Come on over and join the fun!"[12]

12. Mrs. Snyder, trying to present herself as a victim, reports in her autobiographical pamphlet, "Ruth Snyder's Own True Story," that Folsom telephoned Gray and suggested that he come to Henry's for lunch because there was going to be a cute blonde from Queens Village there.

4

HENRY JUDD GRAY was born in 1892 into a family very different from Mrs. Snyder's. His father, Charles, came from Connecticut stock dating back to the landing of the *Mary and John* in 1630, a fact repeatedly drilled into the young Judd. Charles Gray was a jeweler who eventually rose to be co-owner of the Gray-Howes Company, a jewelry-manufacturing firm in downtown Newark. His mother, Margaret, née Carr, was the daughter of a commercial traveler who had accumulated a small fortune in the ladies' intimate-apparel trade, working for the Empire Corset Company.

Gray was born in Cortland, New York, but his family moved to northern New Jersey when he was a youngster. They lived first in Jersey City, then moved to East Orange, and settled eventually on Reynolds Terrace in the affluent village of South Orange. Gray grew up in roomy suburban homes where the hardwood floors were covered with Oriental rugs; the bookshelves bore all the correct Victorian titles—Dickens, Dumas, Stevenson, Thackeray—and there was always an Irish girl to cook and do the heavy work.

Like Mrs. Snyder, Gray was a sickly child. Among his earliest childhood memories were falling behind the other boys in school and not being able to go out to parties that his hardy sister, Margaret, older by three years, could attend. When he was eleven or twelve, he suffered a bout of pneumonia that nearly killed him and made him an invalid for months. A few years later, when a handful of sand was tossed in his face during some playful tussling, Gray came close to losing an eye and was left with permanently impaired sight.

In addition to illness, three main themes run through Gray's childhood as he later described it. First, he was stupifyingly religious. Second, he adored his mother and older sister. Third, he yearned to be one of the fellows. At ten, he became a self-appointed factotum for a group of older neighborhood boys—"splendid youths from cultured and representative families," he later recalled—so he could be in their company. At Barringer High School in Newark, a top-notch college preparatory school, he concentrated on sports and fraternity activities because these brought him closer to "the type of lads I wanted to meet." Gray eventually became president of his fraternity, chairman of the Dance Committee, manager of the basketball team and, despite his small size and poor eyesight, quarterback of the football team.

At sixteen, Gray met the woman who would become his bride: Isabel Kallenbach, daughter of lithographer Ferdinand Kallenbach, who lived on Van Siclen Avenue in East New York. Even Gray's falling in love was motivated by a desire to be one of the gang. His sister was engaged to be married to Harold Logan, a salesman and office manager for a Newark stamping and stove firm so he, too, needed a sweetheart.

Not long after he and Isabel began dating, family financial circumstances—Charles Gray's rise from mere jeweler (as he gave his occupation in the 1900 U.S. Federal Census) to manufacturer of jewelry was a rocky one—forced Gray to leave high school and abandon his ambition to become a medical doctor. His father proposed to take him on as a salesman at Gray-Howes, but Mrs. Howes put her foot down. If the boy was to come in, then he would have to learn the ropes like everybody else, which meant starting as a factory apprentice. Thanks to her stubbornness, there followed a *David Copperfield*-like interlude during which Gray, wearing a workman's apron, stood all day at a jewelry press making blanks for earrings.

Despite the gloss he later attempted to apply to the time, for a boy with Gray's aspirations, it was a miserable experience—noisy, grimy, filled with the foul-mouthed banter of the factory hands. When he was finally able to shed the apron and become a commercial traveler for the firm, it was a blessed relief. Accompanied by his proud parents, dressed in his best suit of clothes, carrying jewelry worth fifteen thousand dollars in his black sample bags, and with thoughts of Isabel in his head, Gray set off from Grand Central Terminal for the life of a traveling salesman.

Although Gray did not like to be away from his mother and Isabel, the drummer's restless life was not without its charm. The value of their wares placed jewelry salesmen at the pinnacle of the sales profession, and Gray's companions of the road were older, well-established, responsible men of the very sort he admired. In 1914, however, Gray made a momentous decision. When his maternal grandfather collapsed and died at the Gray family Christmas dinner, the Empire Corset Company, in which the old man had accumulated a substantial interest, offered Gray a piece of his grandfather's old territory. After conferring with his father, Gray accepted.

The differences between the jewelry and ladies' undergarment businesses could not have been greater. Where the jewelry business was understated, the corset business was ostentatious. In the jewelry trade, buyers were mostly men; in the corset trade, needless to say, they were almost exclusively women. The responsibility of carrying jewelry samples worth thousands of dollars had imposed a strict code of behavior—no drinking and little socializing. But wining and dining were as much a part of Gray's new trade as they had been discouraged in his old one.

Gray and Isabel Kallenbach announced their engagement and were married in Trinity Church, Brooklyn, in November 1915. He was twenty-three and she was twenty-four. At first, the couple lived in East New York with Mrs. Kallenbach, but Gray did not feel at home in his mother-in-law's house.[1] To make matters worse, when Isabel announced

---

1. In June 1915, a few months before the wedding, Mr. Ferdinand and Mrs. Rebecca Kallenbach were enumerated in the New York State Census as living together at 35 Van Siclen Avenue. Gray, in his memoir, *Doomed Ship,* specifies that Mrs. Kallenbach was alone at 35 Van Siclen when he and Isabel moved in after the wedding. If so, Ferdinand had departed the scene in the previous four months. In the 1920 U.S. Federal Census, Mrs. Kallenbach was enumerated as married—not widowed—living alone and head of her own household at 55 Hendrix Street, just a few steps from 35 Van Siclen Avenue. Boarding with her in this establishment were an aged widow, the latter's widowed daughter, and three unmarried granddaughters. No Ferdinand Kallenbach was enumerated in 1920 anywhere in the states of New York, New Jersey, or Pennsylvania (where he

that she was pregnant only a few months after their marriage, Mrs. Kallenbach disapproved.[2] By the time Jane was born in August 1916, the couple had been apartment hunting for several months. They found nothing to their taste in Brooklyn, so they rented half of a two-family house on Berwyn Street in Orange, New Jersey, just a few blocks from Gray's family.

In 1917, the faltering Gray-Howes Company was sold to an investor, John Rindell, who renamed it the "Gray-Rindell Company." Charles Gray remained president and Mrs. Howes disappeared from the scene.

When the Great War came along, Gray wanted to enlist, but because Isabel and his mother objected, he contented himself with volunteer work for the Red Cross and helping out in bond drives. Upon his death in 1920, Charles Gray's interest in Gray-Rindell passed to Mrs. Gray, who sold it to a large Newark jewelry manufacturer, Lon Reynolds, who in turn took over as president. In recognition of her position as the widow of the founder, Mrs. Gray became secretary of the new company and Gray's brother-in-law, Harold Logan, quit the stove business to take over the day-to-day running of the firm. The job could have been Gray's for the asking, but he liked the corset trade and was doing well in it.

In 1921, Gray changed firms, leaving Empire State Corset for a more responsible position with the Benjamin and Johnes Company, purveyors of the Bien Jolie line of female underwear. This was a big step up. In addition to being a major manufacturer, Benjamin and Johnes had outlets in the most fashionable shopping districts of Paris, London, and New York. Gray and Isabel were able to buy an $18,000 house on Wayne Avenue in East Orange. Only two blocks from Washington Elementary School and just across Harrison Avenue from Orange Park, it could not have been better situated for a family with a young child. There was room to spare, so Mrs. Kallenbach sold the house in East New York and

---

was born). What happened? A universally reported story has it that Kallenbach was so upset when his daughter married Gray that he abandoned his family, warning that no good would come of a son-in-law with a cleft chin!

2. Gray describes Mrs. Kallenbach as "disgruntled" in *Doomed Ship*; he also describes Isabel as irritated and unenthusiastic about the pregnancy.

moved in with them. Gray joined the Elks and sang in their choir, which gave concerts at churches, schools, hospitals, and prisons; he also taught Sunday school at the local Methodist church. Gray's mother sold the house in South Orange and bought one closer to her son on Lawrence Avenue in "The Mountain," an exclusive West Orange neighborhood. His sister, Margaret, and her husband, Harold, dutifully moved with her.

In East Orange as they had in Queens, the attractions of matrimony soon began to fade. Because of Gray's constant travels, he and Isabel hardly even saw each other before the wedding. Then Jane was born and the family moved to New Jersey. Isabel objected to her husband's absences from home and disliked the fast crowd he mixed with in his trade. Gray tried a few times to include her in the nightclubbing and theatergoing with which he entertained his customers, but she was upset that he paid more attention to his flashy buyers than he did to her. When he came home from entertaining in New York, she complained that he had liquor on his breath. Finally, Gray gave up and stayed in the city when taking clients out. During his road trips, Gray wrote and telephoned often, but when he came home he felt like a visitor, as if he was cluttering up the place. Invariably, Isabel would have already arranged a program at the country club—bridge with one group of family friends, tennis with another—but she would have done so to suit herself, Mrs. Kallenbach, and his mother, not him.

Barely thirty years old and doomed to a life of bourgeois respectability, Judd Gray was about to embark on the love affair of a lifetime.

5

HENRY JUDD GRAY joined the little party at Henry's, where quite a few highballs were consumed and lunch stretched into the mid-afternoon. He and Mrs. Snyder hit it off so well that they lingered over their glasses after Folsom and Mrs. Kaufman had left.

At four o'clock, Gray's business responsibilities forced the occasion to come to an end. According to Mrs. Snyder, Gray insisted that she come to his Benjamin and Johnes office and accept a free corset; the next day, he telephoned her at home and asked her to write to him while he was on the road.[1] According to Gray, there was no stopping off at his office, and he was completely surprised when a letter from Mrs. Snyder arrived for him at his hotel in Easton, Pennsylvania. He thought it might be from Isabel, with whom he had quarreled before leaving, but it turned out to be from Mrs. Snyder, who gave her mother's measurements and asked if Gray could arrange to have a corset sent to her. A blank check was enclosed. Gray sent off an order slip to his company, charged the corset to samples, and tore up the check. The two accounts are equally plausible.

Gray returned to New York in late July. Again, stories diverge. According to Gray, Harry Folsom invited Gray to a nightclub dinner, and Gray, on arrival, was surprised to find Mrs. Snyder among the guests. According to Mrs. Snyder, Gray telephoned Queens Village on 4 August,

---

1. Gray was fastidious when it came to corsets. In conversation, his preferred term was "garment"; to the enumerator for the 1920 U.S. Federal Census, Gray evasively gave his line as "Dry Goods." Mrs. Snyder shared his delicacy, always taking care to refer to the garments as "corselettes."

just after a particularly nasty fight between the Snyders, and invited her to dinner at Henry's with Folsom and another woman.[2]

Wherever the dinner took place and however it came about, cocktails flowed freely. Folsom and his date had to leave early, but Mrs. Snyder and Gray stayed and talked. When they left for Penn Station, Gray prevailed upon Mrs. Snyder to stop off at his office. The office was empty. She complained of sunburned shoulders; he suggested applying camphor ice he happened to have in his bag. She slipped down her dress, he tenderly ministered to her, and one thing led to another.[3]

It was love at first sight for the two frustrated suburbanites, and a striking pair they made. Gray wore bookish, round-framed, tortoise-shell glasses and was the epitome of sartorial elegance: white silk shirt, silk tie, suit with vest, elk's tooth watch fob, gloves, hat, silk scarf, overcoat. Mrs. Snyder's clothes, by contrast, were flashy, cheap, and wholesale; she completed the effect by chewing gum incessantly. Gray, who what with his wife, mother, sister, and mother-in-law was practically suffocated by fe-

2. In July 1925, claims Mrs. Snyder in "Own True Story," there was a row on Shelter Island when a friend loudly accused Albert Snyder of making a pass at his wife and slugged him. Humiliated by the public scandal, Mrs. Snyder returned to Queens Village, and her subdued husband followed shortly afterward. It was at precisely that moment of domestic crisis that Gray, whom she had met at luncheon a few weeks previously, telephoned out of the blue and invited her to the dinner date that resulted in the loss of her virtue. As she left the house, Mrs. Snyder recounts, her husband demanded where she was going and, when she refused to tell him, slapped her. "Go where you please and with whom you please and be damned!" he shouted. "I've been playing around for years and I have no intention of stopping, so you might as well do the same!" The only problems with this plausible tale are that it is totally self-serving on Mrs. Snyder's part and that there is absolutely no evidence to corroborate it. Gray referred to the Shelter Island incident in his testimony but dated it after the beginning of his affair with Mrs. Snyder. He does not mention it in *Doomed Ship*.

3. Mrs. Snyder claimed on the witness stand that the pair did not have sexual intercourse until September, and then only in the decency of a bed at the Hotel Imperial. Under cross-examination, she could not even remember whether it took place at night or in the day. In "Own True Story," she abandons this straitlaced version and goes along with Gray's tale of heavy breathing on the office floor.

male respectability, had discovered in Mrs. Snyder the most exciting, un-inhibited woman he had ever met. Mrs. Snyder, alternately ignored and mistreated by Albert Snyder, had found in Gray a companion who lis-tened to her dreams, bought her flowers, and initiated lovemaking with tender caresses instead of crude groping.

His nicknames for her were the wildly Oedipal "Momsie," "Mommy" (or "Momie," as Ruth would sign herself in letters to him), and several close variants. Gray's nickname, used by Mrs. Snyder and his close friends, was a decidedly neutral "Bud."

The journalist Ben Hecht referred to the Snyder-Gray love affair as "peculiarly uninteresting," but for the two protagonists, it was all-consuming. They became inseparable. Whenever he could, Gray stayed in New York on business and Mrs. Snyder would make some excuse about visiting friends to be with him. At first they stayed at the Imperial, and then later at the Waldorf-Astoria. If Granny Brown could not take care of Lorraine, Mrs. Snyder would bring her along and let her amuse herself in the lobby while the pair went upstairs.[4] On Thursday nights, Albert Snyder's bowling night, she and Gray had a steady telephone date. Soon Mrs. Snyder was inviting him to Queens Village for lunch while her husband was at work.

They corresponded ardently. Gray left his route list with her, and Mrs. Snyder sent letters, sometimes two and three a day, in advance to the var-ious hotels where he was expected. She instructed the postman, George Marks, to deliver into her hands only all letters addressed to "Mrs. Jane Gray" at the Snyder address. "They're from one of my boyfriends," she bantered easily. The telephone bill, too—"Al hit the ceiling once when he saw the long-distance charges," she chirped.

No one seemed to mind the arrangement. Granny Brown met Gray a few times during the day in Queens Village and told him that it was all

---

4. Kobler states that Lorraine amused herself by riding the elevators and parading up and down Peacock Alley, the famous mirrored hallway that connected the original Wal-dorf and Astoria hotel buildings. In their unpublished play "Dead! A Love Story," William Styron and John Phillips specify that Lorraine read *Black Beauty* in the lobby. All the hotel employees seem to have known her.

right if he took her daughter out so long as he got her home again at night.[5] "Now, we've just got to do something about this, Ruth," she would say from time to time. "It don't look right!" But, most of the time, she kept quiet. After all, Ruth wasn't a baby any more, and she sure wasn't getting what a girl needed from that old crab Snyder.[6] And though Albert Snyder shouted at his wife about her overnight absences, he had long ago withdrawn to the workshop, the garden, and the garage. Lorraine thought Uncle Judd was an awful nice man—much nicer than mean old Daddy. She got to go with him and Mommy to restaurants and the theater and he gave her fancy silk underwear at Christmas. As. for Mrs. Isabel Gray, between the church, the club, and the house, she did not have a clue what her husband was up to.[7]

In September 1925, relations between Ruth and Albert Snyder became especially tense. Mrs. Snyder felt she could grit her teeth and carry on if she had to, but there was one thing that she insisted on: getting Lorraine out of the house and into a good convent school. She had even worked a little selling stock in a dental supply firm door to door to save

5. That Granny Brown encouraged and facilitated her daughter's liaison with Gray—apart from passive-aggressive nagging—is clear. One self-related incident defines the character of Granny Brown. Gray once put to her the straightforward, albeit perhaps typically male, suggestion that, in view of the intolerable conditions in the Queens Village household, the two women should take Lorraine and move out to an apartment, whereupon Mrs. Snyder could initiate divorce proceedings. Granny Brown replied, "Why, how could I move at my age and with all my things?"

6. Mrs. Snyder testified that "the old crab" (like "the governor") was Gray's nickname for Albert Snyder, not hers. In *Doomed Ship,* Gray writes that both Mrs. Snyder and Granny Brown called Albert Snyder "the old crab." He says of his first visit to Queens Village:"I left the charming suburban home with the impression that the whole household was entirely devoid of affection for the master of it—just affection for each other."

7. "A shrewd wife at home might have saved Gray," observed H. L. Mencken. "She might have anesthetized him with gin, fixed him with a fishy eye, and got the truth out of him, and having got it, she might have laughed him back to sense, as wise wives have been doing since the end of the Stone Age. But at home there was only an unimaginative drudge, as sensitively virtuous as Mr. Gray himself. So he went roaring down the road to ruin."

up tuition. Then came a showdown. Ranting and raving, Albert Snyder refused even to consider sending Lorraine away from home and forbade any further discussion of the subject.

Shortly after the argument, Mrs. Snyder became interested in insurance. How much did Gray carry? Oh, about twenty or thirty thousand dollars' worth, he replied; it was a good investment for a family man. What a pity Al carried so little, Mrs. Snyder mused, only a measly $1,000 policy with the Prudential. And he had suffered two accidents over the summer while working on the car in the garage. One time, the jack slipped and the car almost crushed him; the second time, he needed to crank-start it and the crank flew off, hitting him on the head, and knocking him unconscious. Not to mention all that swimming and fishing and whatnot.

In the first week of November, Leroy Ashfield, sales agent for the Queens branch office of the Prudential Life Insurance Company, rang the Snyder doorbell in the course of making his regular monthly collection rounds. Mrs. Snyder made him comfortable in the living room and declared that it was high time for her husband Al to take out some substantial insurance. Could Ashfield drop by one evening later in the week to talk him into it? Surely, together, they could convince him. She had already managed to interest her husband in another $1,000 policy, but they could afford more because Mrs. Snyder was receiving her father's legacy in installments from her mother.[8] This would be a good way to save.

Maybe, if Al wouldn't take out a big policy on the spot, they could encourage him to sign a blank form and think things over. That way, if Mrs. Snyder was able to convince him afterward, why, she and Ashfield could just fill in the required details and not have to bother Mr. Snyder for another signature!

The insurance salesman came out on the appointed evening, and things went exactly as Mrs. Snyder had suggested. Her husband willingly

8. One Christmas, Granny Brown gave her daughter five hundred dollars—a not inconsiderable sum—from the estate. This family inheritance seems a bit at odds with Mrs. Snyder's memories of unremitting poverty.

took out one thousand dollars in life insurance, then signed a blank policy application form and said that he would consider purchasing further
insurance at a later date. After all, he was well over forty; life insurance
was expensive at his age.

Albert Snyder must have been a quick decision maker because the
next day Mrs. Snyder called on Ashfield in his office. Al had made up his
mind—he wanted a policy for either twenty-five thousand or fifty thousand dollars, with Mrs. Snyder as beneficiary and double indemnity in
case of death by misadventure. He wanted to pay for it on the "Modified
Life Plan"—"Buy now, pay later" would be a more accurate description—in which premiums would be at half-rate for the first five years and
then correspondingly greater after that. At no point during this meeting
was the $1,000 policy for which Albert Snyder had applied through reg-
ular methods even mentioned.

Ashfield understandably decided to write a policy for the larger of the
two sums mentioned by Mrs. Snyder and filled in the application form
that Albert Snyder had signed.[9] Then there was a hitch. Double-
indemnity life insurance automatically included a disability income
clause based on the size of the policy. Word came down from upstairs
that, given Snyder's current income, the Prudential would not write a
policy that provided for income in excess of five hundred dollars per
month, and the proposed policy was for five hundred and twenty.

Ashfield, an ambitious young salesman, had a solution to the problem. He typed up a Prudential amendment form requesting that the application for a single $50,000 policy be changed to an application for one
$45,000 policy with double indemnity and one $5,000 policy without it.
Then he traced Albert Snyder's signature onto the amendment form.
The three new policies were issued 16 November 1925, contingent on
the results of Albert Snyder's medical examination. Ashfield hand-
delivered them to Mrs. Snyder, who asked him to follow the same practice with all receipts for premium payments. She again took aside the
much-instructed postman and told him that, like letters to Mrs. Jane

9. It was "a rather large policy for the neighborhood," Ashfield testified drily in *Prudential Life Insurance Company v. Snyder et al.*

Gray and telephone bills, all mail from the Prudential Life Insurance Company was to be placed in her hands only.[10]

None the wiser, Albert Snyder went down to the Prudential's medical office and passed his physical examination with flying colors. An annoyance at best while alive, he was now worth ten times his annual income dead—and twenty times in case of death by misadventure.

10. The postman George Marks testified that Mrs. Snyder was within her rights to make such requests. He stated that he mde 585 stops on his route, twice a day. When asked at how many other stops he was given similar instructions, he answered none, just the Snyder residence.

6

IF THERE IS NO HONOR among thieves, there is even less among murderers. Ruth Snyder and Judd Gray sang as loud as they could as soon as they could.

At the Jamaica Precinct House, Mrs. Snyder began by describing her miserable home life, her affair with Gray, and the fact that he was the only one who would listen to her troubles.

"Things became unbearable and I was looking for a way out, and in talking with Mr. Gray a method was proposed, whereby we were talking about getting rid of him [Albert Snyder]."

She said matters reached a crisis at the end of February when her husband threatened to "blow her brains out." She wrote this to Gray, who asked whether she thought Snyder was serious. She replied that he was certainly capable of it in one of his fits of temper. To this, Gray said that they should get Snyder before he got her.

They met for lunch on Saturday, 5 March, and Gray gave her a window sash weight—an iron bar some eighteen inches in length and a bit smaller than a rolling pin in diameter, weighing five pounds—and told her to take it home. If anything was to be done, he said, the sash weight was the weapon to use. Police would find the sash weight, Mrs. Snyder said, in a tool box in the basement of the Snyder home. Detective Patrolman Frank Heyner was dispatched to look for it. When he returned, Mrs. Snyder identified the weapon and signed an evidence tag that was attached.[1]

1. Many accounts state that the sash weight was found before Mrs. Snyder was taken to the precinct house, and that its discovery contributed to the unraveling of the crime.

45

According to Mrs. Snyder, Gray came to the Snyder residence on the night of Monday, 7 March, planning to hit Snyder on the head with the sash weight when he was asleep and then to chloroform him. The deed went undone, however, because both parties "got cold feet and cried like babies."

"Go on home," Mrs. Snyder told Gray, "you're not going to do it."

On Saturday, 12 March, there was another quarrel in the Snyder home, and Albert Snyder issued an ultimatum: either get out of the house or he would kill her. Once again, Mrs. Snyder wrote to Gray, and there was a repetition of their previous correspondence: Gray asked whether she thought Albert Snyder would really do it; she replied that he was capable of anything. In response, Gray said that they were going to "deliver the goods" on the night of Saturday, 19 March. Mrs. Snyder received this letter on the previous Wednesday or Thursday. She informed Gray that she and her husband would be at a party and that her mother would be away. Gray was instructed to wait in Granny Brown's room. On Saturday morning, Mrs. Snyder received a letter from Gray stating that he would be at the house at about eleven thirty that night.

Mrs. Snyder left the cellar and kitchen doors unlocked when she and her husband and daughter left for the Fidgeon party, where she was careful not to drink too much. After the party, Snyder dropped her and Lorraine at the front door, and Mrs. Snyder took Lorraine upstairs, undressed her, and put her to bed. Gray was in her mother's room, the door of which was open a crack, and Mrs. Snyder told him, "I'll see you in a little while." She undressed and got into bed; about ten minutes later, her husband did the same. After half an hour, when she was sure that her husband was asleep, she got out of bed and went to Gray.[2]

This is untrue. Heyner found the weight early Monday morning, buried beneath some wiring and faucets and parts of an old electric chandelier in a toolbox in Albert Snyder's basement workshop. He had rummaged through the box earlier but thought nothing of the sash weight. Concerned about being spotted by reporters carrying the bludgeon, Heyner slipped the sash weight up his overcoat sleeve, put his hand in his pocket, and walked out of the house stiff-armed.

2. Albert Snyder was deaf in his right ear. It has become part of the folklore of the

As planned, Mrs. Snyder had that afternoon brought the sash weight from the cellar and left it for Gray in her mother's room. She had also left a quart of liquor, most of which he had drunk by the time she got home.[3] Following their plan, Gray had brought with him one and a half ounces of chloroform in a brown eight-ounce medicine bottle, some cotton rags, and a blue bandanna handkerchief.

Gray soaked one of the rags with chloroform and wrapped it in the bandanna. There was a brief, whispered conversation in which Mrs. Snyder told Gray that it was either her or her husband. They kissed; then Gray walked down the hallway (only a matter of three feet) into the master bedroom. Mrs. Snyder followed and stood outside the doorway. All lights in the house were off, but the streetlight in front of the house cast a beam of light into the bedroom.

Mrs. Snyder saw Gray raise the sash weight and strike. She heard a thud, and her husband groaned twice. Gray tied the injured man's hands behind his back, placed the chloroform-soaked pad over his mouth, jammed his face into the pillow, and covered his head with blankets. Then he tied Snyder's feet. Leaving the bedroom, Gray commented, "I guess that's it," peeled off a pair of rubber gloves he had worn, and went into the bathroom. He discovered bloodstains on his shirt, so Mrs. Snyder went into the bedroom and found a blue silk shirt for him. Gray changed in Granny Brown's bedroom. The slayers then took the stained shirt and sash weight down to the cellar; they burned the shirt in the furnace and put the murder weapon into a toolbox, sprinkling it with ashes

---

case that Mrs. Snyder made sure that he was sleeping on his good left ear when she went to Gray. Apart from stipulating that he was sleeping on his left side, Mrs. Snyder does not mention this in her statement, nor does Gray, nor did the prosecution raise the issue at the trial. They did ask Mrs. Snyder whether her husband was deaf in one ear. She replied yes, but did not know which one, an answer which can hardly have pleased the all-male jury. It may have been through habit or accident that Albert Snyder went to sleep for the last time with his good ear to the pillow.

3. Mrs. Snyder makes no mention in her statement of a small bottle as well as the quart bottle—a crucial difference, repeated in testimony, between her version of events and Gray's (see appendix A).

to make it appear as though it had been there for a long time. When they were finished, they went up to the living room and paused to rest.

According to Mrs. Snyder, while they were sitting in the living room, Gray decided to make sure of the job by strangling Snyder with picture wire. He had brought two lengths of wire with him, one of which had been lost in the confusion.[4] Gray and Mrs. Snyder returned to the master bedroom, where Gray tightened the remaining length of wire around Snyder's neck.

The couple then set about turning the house upside down to fake a burglary. They emptied out the drawers in all the bedrooms except Lorraine's. Mrs. Snyder removed the wallet from her husband's pocket and gave Gray the contents. Proceeding downstairs, they continued to throw things about. To support the burglary story, they scattered bits of an Italian newspaper on the bedroom floor, and they removed Snyder's pistol from its holster and placed on the floor next to the bed.[5]

The pair then returned to the living room, where they remained for some two hours, until it was close to dawn and time for Gray to leave. Mrs. Snyder lay down on her mother's bed and Gray tied her with clothesline. She stayed in that position for about two hours, after which she grew tired of waiting to be discovered. She wriggled out of bed, maneuvered to the head of the stairs near the door of Lorraine's bedroom, and woke up her daughter.

It was all very simple, said Mrs. Snyder in closing: "I was in love with Mr. Gray and Mr. Gray loved me, and if my husband hadn't said that he would take my life we would not have thought of taking his life."

Having made a clean breast of the past, Mrs. Snyder turned her

---

4. This was the piece of wire later found underneath Snyder's body, with Gray's gold pencil clipped to it. Despite widespread reports to the contrary, the pencil was not found attached as a tightener to the wire around Albert Snyder's neck.

5. Mrs. Snyder does not specify how the Italian-language newspaper was procured. Gray claimed in his statement that he picked it up on impulse in the train. In his testimony, he said that he wrapped the chloroform bottle in it. Neail's autopsy report (used as a source in chapter 1) states that the pistol was found on the bed, not on the floor.

thoughts to the future. "What is the least I can get for this?" she asked Detective Lieutenant McDermott.

"Well, I suppose the least they could give you would be a suspended sentence," replied the dumbfounded McDermott.

"And the next lowest?"

"One year."

When she had finished her preliminary statement shortly after two o'clock Monday morning, McLaughlin asked if she could give them a photograph that would help identify Gray. She said there was one in a suitcase that she and Gray had left in the storage room at the Waldorf, so the proceedings were interrupted while detectives took her into the city. There was no claim ticket for the bag, so Mrs. Snyder had to point it out. Bellhop Raymond Bruen, a conscientious sort, asked Mrs. Snyder to identify some of the contents of the bag before allowing it to be opened. She mentioned two bathrobes and a framed photograph of herself and Gray. When a detective could not open the bag with the key provided by Mrs. Snyder, she did the honors. In the suitcase, as she had promised them, they found a photograph of herself and Gray.

Everyone was hungry, so she and her escorts went to Rigg's Restaurant on 33rd Street, where Mrs. Snyder had ham and eggs. Then she was taken to the offices of District Attorney Newcombe at the Queens County Courthouse in Long Island City, where her story was filled out in a question-and-answer session lasting until eight thirty Monday morning.

Having answered questions on and off for twenty-four hours, Mrs. Snyder slept in the office of Assistant District Attorney Daly from nine o'clock to one o'clock in the afternoon while her statement was being transcribed. When she was shown the full statement, Mrs. Snyder, either on her own initiative or at Daly's suggestion, asked for it to be reduced to a more manageable summary. She also objected that "kill" sounded "so brutal." As she requested, "get rid of" was substituted. She then went back to sleep for most of the afternoon and the early evening. At eight o'clock on Monday evening, she read over the condensed statement, initialed each of its eight pages, and signed.

For the most part, she was in good spirits. There were a few crying fits, and once she seemed close to fainting, but when someone splashed a little cold water on her face, she protested sharply that her new permanent would be ruined. She asked if a hairdresser could be called in and, when told that this was impossible, borrowed a curling iron from a matron and did her own hair. She joked with matrons that she would never get married again and, in a more serious vein, asked, "What do you think they will do about the insurance?"

"Do you believe in God?" a detective asked her.

"Not really."

"You should put your trust in God and perhaps he will help you."

Mrs. Snyder's mind, however, was on earthly concerns: she ate heartily from a tray of sandwiches, followed up with cake and coffee, and, as the evening grew late, stretched out on the couch in Daly's office and slept.

7

BEFORE LEAVING SYRACUSE, Gray was able to ask Haddon Gray to arrange for a lawyer and a representative of Benjamin and Johnes to meet the train at Grand Central Terminal. Perhaps not coincidentally, the police decided to get off at 125th Street on the excuse that they wanted to avoid reporters. Gray was hustled off the train and down the stairs into a waiting police sedan. Some enterprising pressmen had anticipated the dodge, and the little group was forced to fight its way through a mob. The police car had to evade pursuit before it headed to District Attorney Newcombe's office, arriving at one thirty Tuesday morning. Newcombe and Police Commissioner McLaughlin met the party and a stenographer was called in.

Throughout his statement, Gray seemed more concerned with his interrogators' opinion of him than with the situation he was in. He had a very fine little wife and wonderful daughter, a good many friends, too. Whether he would when this was all over remained to be seen.

"This thing," as Gray called it, all began with Mrs. Snyder. In October or November 1925, she revealed that she was having troubles at home; in November or December, she mentioned that she was planning to increase her husband's life insurance to fifty thousand dollars.[1]

Despite Gray's attempts to dissuade her—"I told her she was terrible"—Mrs. Snyder made repeated attempts on her husband's life. In December 1926 and January 1927, according to Gray, she gave Snyder

1. There is a mistake in the transcription of Gray's confession. The statement reads "1926," but Gray is obviously referring to 1925. Gray testified that Mrs. Snyder showed him Albert Snyder's $5,000 policy over lunch at Henry's during the summer of 1926.

sleeping powders on two occasions and bichloride of mercury tablets once when he had a persistent case of the hiccoughs, and then again on a subsequent occasion. On one occasion, she turned on the gas while her husband was taking a nap.

"She started then to hound me on this plan. I said absolutely no. Then I didn't see her as often as I did. I was reaching the point where I was beginning to get afraid."

Mrs. Snyder persisted, threatening to inform his wife of their relationship if he did not help her in her designs.

According to Gray, the plan that resulted in Albert Snyder's death dated back to the end of February or the beginning of March. In the weeks since then, Gray said, he had been "in a literal hell." Buckling under constant pressure from Mrs. Snyder, he purchased a sash weight to be used as a club, a bottle of chloroform, and a blue bandanna handkerchief. The picture wire he took from his office. Gray gave the sash weight to Mrs. Snyder on Saturday, 5 March, during lunch at Henry's Restaurant; he kept the chloroform.

On Monday, 7 March, Gray received a telephone call from Mrs. Snyder and, at her bidding, went to Queens Village that evening, but ended up walking around the neighborhood for two and a half hours and "absolutely gave up any idea of it." [2] Gray went on the road that night, but Mrs. Snyder barraged him with letters. When he telephoned her on Thursday, 17 March, she told him that she and her husband would be going to a party on Saturday night and that she would leave the doors of the house open so that he could get in. She wrote him that he would find the sash weight, a pair of pliers, and a small bottle of whiskey under the pillow on her mother's bed.

Gray described fabricating his complicated, indeed overcomplicated alibi—one detective remarked that no innocent man could possibly have so tight a story. On the morning of the murder, he called on customers in

---

2. Gray's statement does not confirm Mrs. Snyder's story of a midnight conference during which the slayers lost their nerve, nor did his interrogators raise the subject. Gray testified at his trial that it simply did not occur to him to mention it in his statement.

Syracuse. At lunch, he asked Haddon Gray to help him out. He was going on a date with a girlfriend in Albany, he told his old friend, and he was worried that his wife or employer might find out that he was fooling around. Could Haddon Gray go to the Onondaga around six o'clock, let himself into Room 743 with the extra key that Gray would give him, post some letters that Gray would leave on the bed, telephone the desk to request that calls be held, and hang a "Do Not Disturb" sign on the door when he left? Could he then return first thing in the morning and mess up the bed so it would appear to have been slept in? Haddon Gray was willing to help out his chum.

This explained one mystery that had been unresolved since Mrs. Snyder's confession. On Sunday afternoon, a letter from Gray, addressed to "Mrs. J. Gray" and postmarked Syracuse, 19 March, at 8:30 P.M., had been delivered to the Snyder residence. Since the last train for New York left Syracuse at 5:30, there was no way that Gray could have sent this letter and murdered Snyder the same night.

Gray arrived at Grand Central Terminal shortly after 10:00 P.M. and reached the Snyder residence at midnight. He entered through the kitchen door and waited in Granny Brown's bedroom as arranged. The sash weight, pliers, and a small bottle of whiskey were, as Mrs. Snyder had promised, hidden under the pillow. Gray had brought a briefcase containing the bottle of chloroform, wrapped in an Italian newspaper, two pieces of picture wire, the blue bandanna handkerchief, some cotton rags, and a piece of gauze.[3] The gold pencil clipped to the piece of wire found under Snyder's body might be his: he owned one just like it and didn't know where it was.

As he sat in Granny Brown's room, Gray continued, he really did not think that he would go through with it. It was the whiskey that was to blame, he thought.

"She had given me, I guess, a small bottle, together with a larger bottle, which I think was probably my undoing, . . .because even when I

---

3. Gray had also brought a pair of rubber gloves, although he left this out of his statement. The gauze was used to gag Mrs. Snyder.

was sitting there I firmly in my own mind absolutely said it would not go through.[4] But it did, unfortunately."

He started to leave, but just as he did, the Snyders returned. "Absolutely stumped," he bounded upstairs and ducked back into Granny Brown's bedroom. Mrs. Snyder came upstairs and took Lorraine into the little girl's bedroom. Passing back down the hallway, she asked from the doorway if he was there. Assured that he was, she went into the master bedroom and undressed.

After her husband was asleep, she returned. "You are going to do it, aren't you?" she asked.

"I think I can," he replied.

Figuring that he could steal away, Gray suggested that she should go back to bed and that he would come in later. No such luck; she stayed put.

Mrs. Snyder went first into the bedroom, Gray said. He followed with the sash weight. Taking aim at the head of the sleeping man, Gray struck. Albert Snyder, merely stunned, lunged up and grabbed his assailant by the necktie, causing Gray to drop the weapon. Mrs. Snyder then picked it up and "started to belabor him." At this point, said Gray, "I scarcely knew what happened for a short time." Mrs. Snyder had the bottle of chloroform and handkerchief. Gray didn't know whether she gagged him or not."[5] She gave Gray a necktie to bind Snyder's hands, but he was shaking and could not do it. Mrs. Snyder took over and tied her husband's hands with a towel; somehow Gray managed to tie Snyder's feet with the necktie. As to the picture wire, Gray said he had lost it. If a length of it had been tied around Snyder's neck, it must have been Mrs. Snyder who did it.

Gray then went into the bathroom, where he noticed blood on his shirt and vest. Things were hazy; he didn't know precisely where he was and couldn't seem to collect his thoughts. Mrs. Snyder brought him a new blue shirt belonging to her husband, and he put it on. He did not

4. The " 'larger bottle' " is the quart referred to by Mrs. Snyder in her statement.

5. It is hard to determine just how the injured man was chloroformed in the midst of this chaos. In his trial testimony, Gray claimed not to remember a thing about it.

know what she did with his own shirt until she called him down to the cellar and told him that she had burned it and her own bloodstained robe in the furnace. He thought that she had also burned her nightgown.

Mrs. Snyder showed him the toolbox where she had hidden the sash weight. Gray had wrapped the weight in paper, hoping that the blow would hurt less that way, but the paper was gone; it must have been Mrs. Snyder who took it off. Gray put some more coal on the furnace, came upstairs, and started to throw things around to make it look like there had been a robbery.

Then, the statement continued, he and Mrs. Snyder sat down in the living room, and he had three or four drinks. They decided to blame the assault on a burglar. Gray suggested that, in view of the upheaval, she make it two burglars instead of one. "That is as far as plans went," said Gray. He sat there "more or less in a daze" until he noticed it was starting to turn light.

Mrs. Snyder brought some rope from downstairs, and Gray tied her hands and feet and gagged her loosely with a piece of gauze. Just before being tied up, Mrs. Snyder gave Gray some money from her husband's wallet and threw the wallet on the master bedroom floor. She gave him her husband's revolver; he broke it open and placed it on the floor. He had not seen the revolver until after Snyder was dead. Just before he left, she gave him various poisons and sleeping powders to dispose of. He carried these deadly odds and ends away with him in his briefcase.[6]

Gray walked over to Springfield Boulevard and waited for a bus.[7] There was a man standing at the bus stop; a policeman from the nearby police booth was shooting at milk bottles for target practice.[8] "I wouldn't want that fellow shooting at me!" Gray remarked to his fellow passenger

6. Together with his rubber gloves (Gray's statement mentions taking them away, but not bringing them) and, according to his trial testimony, the empty chloroform bottle. Gray thought that he wore buckskin gloves during the slaying. There is no mention anywhere of what became of the pliers.

7. This description of Gray's movements is somewhat filled out from his testimony.

8. Rules on the discharge of service revolvers were evidently looser than they are today!

after the cop hit one. When the bus came, it was crowded. There was a minor dispute over the fare: either he put in too much or too little, he couldn't remember. Getting out at Jamaica Station, he learned that there was no train until after eight o'clock, so he took a taxi to 59th Street and Broadway.[9] From there, he took the subway to Grand Central Terminal, where he ate breakfast in Mandel's and caught the 8:45 train for Syracuse. As the train passed over the Hudson, Gray heaved the briefcase into the water.

Arriving in Syracuse at four fifteen in the afternoon, Gray's statement continued, he returned to the Hotel Onondaga and found things just as planned. He telephoned Haddon Gray and said that he was in trouble. Could Haddon come over in his car? No, he couldn't, Haddon Gray said, his car was being painted, but he could get a lift with a friend, independent insurance salesman Harry Platt.

When the two arrived, Gray told a story he had concocted.[10] Mrs. Albert Snyder, his "Momsie," had telegraphed him to meet her at her home in Queens Village rather than in Albany, as previously planned. While he was there, two burglars burst into the house. Afraid for his life, he hid behind the clothes in the bedroom closet while the burglars beat Momsie, and her husband. When he cautiously emerged several hours later, there was no sign of Momsie and her husband was lying on the floor. Gray lifted him, dead or unconscious, onto the bed, staining his shirt and vest with blood in the process. There was still no sign of Momsie, so Gray left the house and made his way back to Syracuse. What was he to do now?

---

9. A taxi ride from Jamaica Station to midtown Manhattan was as expensive in 1927 as it is today. Any hack would be bound to remember being hailed at six thirty on a Sunday morning by a fare who splurged so freely. Gray seems to have done everything possible to make sure that his movements after leaving the Snyder residence were observed and remembered. Yet, in his pathetic way, Gray did attempt to cover his tracks, for example, taking the taxi to 59th Street and then the subway to Grand Central Terminal instead of going directly to the station.

10. Why tell his friend anything at all? Because Gray had once shown him a photograph of Mrs. Snyder, told him that he was having an affair with her, and asked what he thought of her looks. Haddon Gray was bound to make a connection when the murder hit the papers, so Gray had to make up some story.

Haddon Gray and Platt suggested that he get rid of the bloody vest, together with the suit to which it belonged, and the gloves and hat he had worn. Gray agreed, and Platt, promising to dispose of them, took the articles away in a small black leather suitcase.

His Syracuse friends were completely innocent, insisted Gray; they knew nothing about the true story.

Later, Gray went over to Haddon Gray's for supper, where he and his friend consumed a large amount of liquor. After dinner, he played marbles with Gray's children and reviewed their Sunday school worksheets. Before leaving, he made a date with them to return the next night for another game of marbles. On the way back to the hotel, Gray stopped by a club for a few more drinks. When detectives knocked at his door, he was just about to have a nightcap and go to bed.

It had indeed been, as District Attorney Newcombe put it, a "remarkable piece of police work." In less than forty-eight hours of intense, coordinated investigation, police from Queens, Manhattan, and Syracuse had apprehended the culprits and obtained confessions from both. Each tended to lay more of the blame on the other, but the only real difference was that Gray said that the woman had struck her husband, whereas Mrs. Snyder claimed she had not. No matter: each statement, if accepted into evidence, was sufficient to send the party who made it to the electric chair.

GRAY SIGNED HIS STATEMENT at four o'clock Tuesday morning, whereupon he was allowed to make a phone call. Not surprisingly, he called his mother. Then he was formally placed under arrest and driven from the district attorney's office to the Jamaica Precinct House to be fingerprinted and photographed. After this, Detectives McDermott and Brown took him across the street for a meal. Mrs. Snyder, who had been sleeping on Assistant District Attorney Daly's couch only a few doors away, was woken up a few minutes after Gray left. She was also formally placed under arrest and taken to Jamaica for booking. The pair was kept for a few hours in separate holding cells at Richmond Hill Precinct House, where there was a matron for Mrs. Snyder, then driven in separate cars to New York City Police Headquarters in Manhattan to appear in the morning lineup.

A custom dating back to the days of the Bow Street runners in London, the lineup consisted of displaying the previous twenty-four hours' intake of prisoners before detectives to see if any were recognized in connection with other crimes. Mrs. Snyder, first to arrive at eight thirty, was taken by elevator to the fourth floor. As she was led down the corridor toward the auditorium where the detectives waited, her knees buckled, and she had to be supported by her escorts. Chief Police Surgeon Daniel Donovan examined her and ordered that she be returned to Queens without undergoing the ordeal. When she left the building, there was a crowd waiting, and she displayed some spirit, pulling up her collar, tugging her hat down over her head, and holding her hands over her face. She was placed in a police sedan, which was immobilized for about five minutes by the crush of vehicles and spectators. Trapped in the public's view, she leaned forward in the backseat to hide herself.

The car in which she left was the one that had brought Gray, who was shackled to a burglar accused of breaking into a dozen Richmond Hill homes. The crowd mobbed Gray and his companion as they emerged from the car, and Gray half-ran to the door, dragging the hapless thief behind him. Though impeccably dressed in a clean white shirt and blue suit, topped off by a gray overcoat, he appeared tired and in need of a shave.

As he was led down the hallway, Gray passed Chief Surgeon Donovan's office, where Mrs. Snyder was being revived with smelling salts. "A fine mess *she* has gotten me into!" he remarked when he caught sight of her through the open door.

Gray was the first of the twenty or so prisoners displayed, bathed by a searchlight, on a small stage. "This is Henry Judd Gray, accused of the Queens Village murder," intoned the officer in charge as over one hundred detectives sized up the prisoner. "Have you ever been convicted of a crime?" asked the officer. "Why, no!" replied Gray, surprised by the question.

When he was led away, his escorts tried to evade photographers and curiosity seekers by taking him through a different door than the one they had used on the way in. As a result of the maneuver, the small party was pursued down the hall by a crowd two hundred strong. Displaying fear at this point, Gray was unceremoniously hustled out the nearest doorway—as luck would have it, the "Commissioner's Arch," normally reserved for the entrances and exits of the Police Commissioner himself.

Gray was handcuffed to two accused housebreakers and placed in a police sedan. He received an unexpected tour of New York City as the police, seeking to elicit confessions from his companions, drove the burglars past some of the sixty-five houses they were accused of robbing.

Back in Queens, Gray was taken to Jamaica Town Hall, where Mrs. Snyder had preceded him, for preliminary arraignment in Police Court. The sidewalk was jammed with onlookers, and traffic had to be diverted away from Jamaica Avenue, as hundreds milled around in the street. Men and boys climbed the scaffolding of a construction site across the street in the hope of glimpsing the famous pair through the windows. Those lucky enough to have gotten into the dim, stuffy courtroom stood on benches and craned their necks. Mrs. Snyder and Gray, following directly behind her, were led in surrounded by attorneys and detectives. They appeared to touch once. According to one story, Gray reached out and took Mrs. Snyder's hand for a moment but, receiving no response, let it drop. Another story reports that the pair instinctively held hands for a moment and exchanged grim smiles.

Attorney Edgar Hazelton, whom Granny Brown had retained for her daughter along with his partner, Dana Wallace, entered a not-guilty plea for Mrs. Snyder—a mere formality given that a guilty plea would not be accepted on a first-degree murder charge. After doing so, he commented, "The defendant Snyder has been held since Sunday morning in custody with no sleep, no opportunity to rest and little food. She is held on an alleged confession which she now repudiates on the ground that it was made under duress and force."

Theodore Groh, who with his senior partner, James Hallinan, had been retained on Gray's behalf by Haddon Gray, likewise entered a not-guilty plea and made a similar statement. The State availed itself of the forty-eight-hour delay to which it was entitled if it did not wish to proceed further with the arraignment. Attorneys for both sides requested that their clients be subjected to no further questioning without the presence of counsel—a case of closing the barn door after the horse has bolted if ever there was one. The prosecution agreed without argument.

"They've talked themselves into a bad fix," commented Groh after the hearing. "This is what comes of persons talking before they engage counsel."

The prisoners were taken through the magistrate's office and out Town Hall's back door. They were placed in a Black Maria, Mrs. Snyder in front and Gray in back, and taken to Queens County Jail, where they would be imprisoned throughout their trial. The jail was housed in two buildings directly behind the Queens County Courthouse in Long Island City and was connected to it by an enclosed elevated walkway, known fancifully as the courthouse's "Bridge of Sighs," and a subterranean passage. Both prisoners had fourth-floor cells with a view—Gray in the southeast corner of the south building facing out over a rear courtyard, and Mrs. Snyder in the northwest corner of the north building facing out over Pearson Street. It seemed symbolic: the two prisoners were as far apart as they possibly could be while being held in the same jail.

By this time, it was apparent to newspapermen that the Snyder-Gray case was not only an important news story but, in fact, the story of the year. The New York press was at its zenith during the years surrounding the Snyder-Gray case. The *New York Times,* then as now the newspaper of record, made an effort to restrict the column space devoted to the Snyder-Gray murder. Its competitors for the highbrow market—the *American* (Hearst), the *Herald Tribune* (the two had merged in 1924), the *Evening Journal* (Hearst), the *Telegram* (Scripps-Howard), the *World,* the *Sun,* and the *Post* (not yet a tabloid)—were less dainty, but nonetheless made some attempt to respect the limits of taste. But the tabloids—Hearst's *Daily Mirror,* Patterson's *Daily News* and, on the lunatic fringe, MacFadden's *Evening Graphic*[1]—depended on stories like the Snyder-Gray case for their existence and knew no restraint.

Gray's family had begun to experience what it meant to deal with the press even before he was brought back to New York Monday night. Jour-

---

1. Known familiarly as the "PornoGraphic," the *New York Evening Graphic* was founded and published by Bernarr MacFadden (born Bernard McFadden; he changed his name on a whim—one of many). MacFadden was a health-food and physical-culture guru whose interests ran to bathing beauties and free love. While the *Graphic* is remembered mostly as the ancestor of today's "Elvis Is Alive" tabloids, it nonetheless published straight news and had an active social conscience: for example, as well as promoting fitness and healthy living, it opposed capital punishment. The paper's alumni included Walter Winchell, whose first job in journalism was with the *Graphic;* television variety-show host Ed Sullivan, who progressed from sports to gossip to covering Broadway; and film director John Huston, who was quickly fired for mishandling a murder story. Among the *Graphic's* innovations were its "composographs"—photo manipulations in which the faces of celebrities were superimposed on photographs of persons in provocative situations (Valentino being welcomed into heaven by Caruso, for example). The *Graphic* lasted eight years, from 1924 to 1932, before folding under the weight of an advertising boycott and cumulative libel judgments.

nalists notified Mrs. Isabel Gray and her mother, Mrs. Kallenbach, of Gray's arrest first thing Monday morning, whereupon a doctor was summoned to treat both women for shock and prostration. One reporter knocked on the door in the afternoon and tried to pass himself off as a police detective. Another showed up at the principal's office at Washington Elementary School and demanded an interview with Gray's daughter, Jane. The worried principal sent the girl home. After school, twenty-five of Jane's loyal schoolmates trooped to the house to show their support and were disappointed when a police guard refused to let them any farther than the front sidewalk.

As soon as they heard the news, Gray's mother, sister, and brother-in-law had hurried to Wayne Avenue from their home a few minutes away. It was obviously a case of mistaken identity. After all, Gray was a common name and salesmen were forever handing out business cards. All Monday night, lights burned at 37 Wayne Avenue as a council of war was held. When Gray telephoned his mother at four o'clock, plans for his defense were already under way. If he had made a confession, he must have been insane when he made it.

By six o'clock, the clutch of reporters staking out the house had grown to a small army, and the police guard was barely able to keep them at bay. Finally, at seven thirty, Mrs. Isabel Gray appeared on the front porch and made a brief statement: she would believe all this only when she heard it from Judd's own lips. She did not intend to go into New York to visit her husband, at least not until the excitement died down. As reporters spoke to her, the postman arrived, bearing one of the letters that her husband had asked Haddon Gray to mail from Syracuse on Saturday. It was, Mrs. Isabel Gray sadly explained, Judd's regular "weekend letter."

Late in the morning, Gray's wife, accompanied by his sister, Margaret, and brother-in-law, Harold Logan, made a lame attempt to sneak out the back door and into a vehicle parked down the street. No one was fooled by the ruse, and a caravan of reporters pursued the trio to the lower Broadway offices of Samuel Miller, an attorney whom the Gray family had retained on the advice of family friend William Millard, himself a well-known New York attorney. When they emerged an hour and a half later, accompanied by Miller, Gray's wife was less assured: "Of course, I'm married to him . . . I can't stand this." By this time, the crowd had grown to several hundred.

At Queens County Courthouse, District Attorney Newcombe questioned Mrs. Gray for twenty minutes, after which she was permitted to see her husband in a room on the Bridge of Sighs. It was hardly a private meeting. The *Daily News,* under the headline "WIFE AIDS KILLER," moralized "it was the first cleanly touch in the whole sordid tragedy." The *Daily Mirror* led off its story with "Henry Judd Gray sent for his wife yesterday. They always do." The flashbulbs of forty cameras exploded as Gray was led down the hall in handcuffs. On meeting, Gray and his wife embraced, kissed, and wept. Detectives withdrew to a far corner, and the couple sat down to converse. Incessantly twisting the buttons on his coat, Gray let his wife do most of the talking. The meeting lasted forty minutes.

Handcuffed again, Gray was led back into the swarm of photographers. One of them lunged from a crouching position and exploded a charge of flash powder practically in Gray's face. The prisoner's knees gave way, and he would have fallen had he not been supported by his guard.

In the early evening, accompanied by her escorts, Mrs. Gray returned to New Jersey, forlornly holding the traveling case her husband had brought down from Syracuse. Gray's mother had not been idle while the others were in Manhattan: indeed, no sooner had they gone into the house than Harold Logan emerged to read a written statement, purportedly from Mrs. Isabel Gray:

> I will stand by my husband, no matter what happens. . . . I have engaged counsel for him and will see the case through. I will spare no expense to save him. He must have been insane when he did it, and I believe he is insane now. When I talked to him this afternoon, he was irrational. He said, "I am very sorry I did it. The woman held a hammer over my head, and I had to do it. She had a strange influence over me."

Granny Brown had been busy as well. On Tuesday afternoon, to rapt reporters assembled in the Snyder living room, she proclaimed that Ruth was incapable of violence: she kept a canary and could not bring herself to have her aged cat put to death. The same with some Easter chicks she gave to Lorraine when, in due course, they became roosters and their crowing annoyed the neighbors. Al and Ruth had never loved each other after they married. Ruth liked to dance and laugh; her husband had been sulky and unfriendly. Ruth never drank until after Prohibition and, even now, only took a glass or two to be a good sport. Snyder used to fly into fits of rage; sometimes when he had lost his temper Ruth would turn white and tremble like a leaf. There was nothing between Gray and Ruth: they were just good friends.

On Tuesday night, funeral rites and a viewing were held in Albert Snyder's home. There was a simple service for family and friends before a crush of casual acquaintances arrived. All of the staff members of *Motor Boating Magazine* attended (although not, as the *Long Island Daily Press* idiotically claimed, all the greats of world motorboat racing). So did representatives of the Queens Village Democratic Club, the Shelter Island Boat Club, and the Spare Bowling Club. Snyder had not been a churchgoer, but he had been a friend of Reverend Everett Lyons of the landmark Queens Village Dutch Reformed Church, where Lorraine went to Sunday school. The minister's remarks were simple and brief—the most memorable being, "I'd rather be this faithful man at rest in his coffin here than be one of those persons who are responsible for his death." He closed with "Good-bye, Al." [2]

Then Granny Brown and Snyder's brothers, George and Warren, took up stations at the door as everyone who had the slightest excuse to mourn Albert Snyder showed up to pay respects. Unknowns were refused entrance and those who could prove their credentials were admitted in batches of fifteen or twenty. People who were turned away lingered unashamedly on the sidewalk, circling the house in a crowd of two hundred.

---

2. By the following Sunday, Lyons had hit his stride and, his congregation swollen to at least twice its normal size, preached on the text, "Though the wicked go hand in hand, they will be punished."

As guests entered, they were directed left into the living room. The staircase leading to the second floor was barred by a rope bearing a Queens County crime investigation seal.[3] Albert Snyder lay in an open black oak casket directly below the room in which he had been murdered. Having seen what they came to see, visitors retraced their steps to the foyer, passed through the dining room into the kitchen, and went out the back door.

On Wednesday morning at ten o'clock, as mounted policemen held the curious throng at bay, the battered body of Albert Snyder was laid to rest in the Schneider family plot at Mount Olivet Cemetery in Maspeth. Mrs. Snyder was denied permission to attend the burial. As consolation, she was allowed to wear mourning in her cell. Roughly fifteen mourners left the Snyder home in five motorcars; Lorraine cowered and hid her face as the undertaker led her down the front steps. Somber crowds lined the streets between Queens Village and Maspeth.

The burial was tense. Granny Brown's press conference the day before had infuriated the Schneider family. At the graveside, the Schneider and Brown families did not exchange a word. The undertaker handed each mourner a piece of the floral arrangement that had been on the coffin, and they dropped the flowers in the grave as they filed past. Granny Brown accepted her small wreath but defiantly refused to consign it to Albert Snyder's grave. Still clutching it, she took Lorraine by the hand and walked to a waiting car.

A few hours after her husband was buried, Mrs. Snyder gave her first press interview in a small room on the second floor of the courthouse. It was originally scheduled for eight thirty in the morning, but Hazelton, her attorney, begged for a few hours' delay on the grounds that his client had slept badly. The reporters agreed and waited patiently until two of them, taking a stroll to relieve the boredom, discovered to their indignation that Mrs. Snyder was being photographed down the hallway for a

---

3. Soon removed. The door and windows of the master bedroom were, however, nailed and taped shut until the end of the trial, in case the jury wished to view the room as it had been found.

Daily News exclusive.[4] The press mutinied and demanded that the interview take place immediately.

There were two more wrinkles. First, Hazelton demanded that all questions be written down and that he and his client have an hour together to discuss answers. Second, he insisted that only three reporters, all female, be present at the interview; the others would have to get their copy secondhand. The reporters had little choice. True to Hazelton's word, an hour later, the elected trio was admitted to the tiny room in which Mrs. Snyder sat. Hazelton sat by her side, holding the written questions, which he himself posed and some of which he peremptorily answered. All questions about the actual crime had been barred.

Given all the screening and preparation, Mrs. Snyder was poised. Her only show of emotion was the frequent prefacing of answers with "God, no!" Gray had been her first real lover, Mrs. Snyder said, and she reached this stage "only after Albert Snyder eliminated love from the house." Gray had never given her any money. As for gifts, last Christmas, he had given her the plain blue bag she was presently carrying. "Mrs. Snyder plays no favorites, even in jail," commented the *Mirror,* noting that she carried her lover's bag while wearing her husband's wedding band. How about the fancy underwear that was his stock in trade, did Gray ever give her any of that? Yes, she replied, but those weren't gifts; they were necessities. She was "terribly, awfully sorry" about what happened. When asked how she felt about Gray now, she answered "I love him still, in spite of all he has done."

Naturally, Lorraine was a major theme. Lorraine knew nothing of the situation. When she came to visit tomorrow, Mrs. Snyder would tell her that Mama was sick and would have to stay in the hospital for a long time. When Lorraine left, Mrs. Snyder would kiss and hug her and tell her

---

4. While the equipment was being set up, Mrs. Snyder remarked that she expected to be free soon. An expression of sympathy from the photographer was dismissed with a shrug and "Oh, well . . ." When he suggested that she put her handkerchief to her eyes in a show of grief, Mrs. Snyder grinned broadly, cautioning the cameraman not to take any photographs while she was laughing.

pretty things. She would say "Lorraine, be a good little girl and your Mama will be home soon."

"God, no!" she had nothing to do with this murder. "I don't know what I was saying when the police got that statement from me. I was so tired that I would say yes to anything they asked me. I deny absolutely any part in the crime." Strangely, in view of loving Gray still, "Any consideration, affection or love I had ever had for Gray has turned to hate for two reasons; first, for his cruel and barbarous murder of my poor husband and, second, because he tried to entangle me in it." At this point, she turned to Hazelton and asked, "Should I say that I am innocent?" The attorney smiled and nodded.

Thus cued, Mrs. Snyder gazed straight ahead and rattled off an obviously memorized statement: "The police have told a number of things about me and tried to fasten things on me that are untrue. These stories at this time make me out in a very bad light before the public. I ask every mother, every daughter, and every wife to withhold judgment until she has heard it all and I am sure that they will find some sympathy, some consideration, some understanding for me in this terrible sorrow which is mine."

Legal developments came at a brisk pace on Wednesday. Haddon Gray and Harry Platt, brought down from Syracuse on the overnight train, spent an uncomfortable four hours being questioned by Newcombe. Haddon Gray continued to assert the impossibility of his friend's involvement in the Snyder murder. "Judd couldn't have done such a thing. He played clean football and didn't have a dirty streak in him." He denied all knowledge of having assisted in disposing of the contents of a black bag as described in Gray's statement. But, taken at eleven o'clock to Gray himself, Haddon Gray heard his friend's confession from his own lips.

"Did you do this thing, Judd?" he asked.

"Yes, Had, I did. Frightfully sorry to have gotten you into this mess, old man."

Haddon Gray then began to cooperate with investigators, as did Harry Platt. Platt admitted that he gave Gray's garments, with instructions to burn them, to Michael Mahoney, the janitor of the Onondaga County Savings Bank Building, where Platt's office was located. Alerted by telephone, Syracuse detectives rushed to the building, but the superintendent had already carried out his instructions. The grip had been given to one Anthony Boehm, who had in turn passed it to his wife, Anna, a cleaning lady, who incinerated is in the boiler room of the Onondaga Printing Company.

Haddon Gray's attorney in Syracuse telegraphed his New York associate, Joseph Shalleck, who showed up at the courthouse in Long Island City Courthouse demanding to see his client.[5] Newcombe refused and ordered Shalleck to leave the premises. For four hours, Shalleck defiantly sat outside the District Attorney's office. At noon, there was a scene between the attorney and Newcombe's secretary, James Conroy, which ended with Shalleck storming off down the hallway to obtain a writ of habeas corpus from New York Supreme Court Justice Stephen Callaghan.[6] The latter granted a writ giving the State until two o'clock that afternoon to show cause why Haddon Gray and Platt should not be discharged. Learning of Shalleck's move, Newcombe immediately hustled Haddon Gray through the crowd of photographers into the Grand Jury room where indictments were being considered. He was safely inside and testifying, beyond benefit of counsel, by the time that Shalleck returned with his precious writ.

Having given testimony, Haddon Gray was freed with a warning not to discuss the case. "He didn't know a thing about the murder plans," Newcomb told reporters. "He has told a full story and he is completely exonerated from blame."

Back in Syracuse, Haddon Gray was still loyal to his friend: "I can't understand Judd. I don't pity him now that he has told me that he did it. But I don't understand. He's not particularly weak. He did not drink to

5. The suave, droopy-eyed, pipe-smoking Shalleck was a major figure. As president of the Monongahela Democratic Club in Manhattan, he was personal adviser and lawyer to Tammany Hall kingpin Jimmy Hines.

6. Contrary to all linguistic logic, in New York State, the Supreme Court is the state trial court, not the highest state appeals court.

excess as I'd call it. I don't think he's insane or will use such a defense. The woman must have had him hypnotized. She was certainly the instigator of it." Her method of hypnotizing Gray, the press reported, was to stroke his cheek with her fingertips while gazing intently into his eyes. The *Evening Journal* did a lurid "composograph" of Mrs. Snyder putting the whammy on Gray; jagged rays projected from her eyes into his.

At four o'clock in the afternoon, almost exactly as Mrs. Snyder was being led from her press conference back to her cell, the Grand Jury returned a joint indictment for first-degree murder, alleging that the prisoners had feloniously, willfully, and with malice aforethought killed and murdered Albert Snyder against the peace and dignity of the people of New York.

Mrs. Snyder and Gray were brought before Justice Callaghan at ten o'clock Thursday morning to finish the arraignment begun two days earlier. Attorneys separated the prisoners as they stood before the bench. The pair did not so much as exchange a glance. Mrs. Snyder leaned forward on the chest-high railing that ran around the court clerk's desk in front of the bench and shifted uneasily from foot to foot. She appeared alert and composed. Granny Brown and Mrs. Snyder's brother, Andrew, were in the courtroom to lend moral support. No one appeared from the Gray family. Not-guilty pleas were entered for both defendants. Mrs. Snyder's attorneys moved for a separate trial and were joined in this by Hallinan for Gray. Justice Callaghan replied that the decision on separate trials would have to be made before the judge who heard the case. The State proposed a trial date of 4 April; all trials that could interfere had been postponed or transferred to other courts. When attorneys from both defense teams stated that they had other trials on that date, Callaghan set the trial date for 11 April and ordered the prisoners held without bail.

As Gray was led from the courtroom, a reporter shouted at him, "Mrs. Snyder is placing all the blame on you. What are you going to do about it?"

"I'm going to stand on my two feet and fight it to the finish!" Gray snapped back.

The pair was taken downstairs to the courthouse basement and led into the tunnel that connected to the basement of the jail. Photographers had laid an ambush in the tunnel. The moment Mrs. Snyder came into view, there was a roar as twenty flashbulbs exploded simultaneously. Mrs. Snyder buckled, but, supported by matrons, was hurried through the throng.

For the first time since her arrest, Mrs. Snyder was permitted a visit with Granny Brown. Visiting conditions in the Queens County Jail were excellent: the two were allowed to converse privately in the prisoners' communal dining room; later, they often took lunch together there. A visit with Lorraine had been scheduled, but was postponed until Friday.

Mrs. Snyder gave another interview to reporters, expounding on the same themes that had been brought up on Wednesday. She used a number of the same lines, but changes of nuance indicated that the accusations against Gray were becoming more serious.

He had murdered her poor husband in a cruel, barbarous manner despite all her efforts to prevent him, she said. Then he had tried to put the blame on her. He had taken the initiative in it all, had gotten her into this pickle, and now he wanted her alone to suffer the consequences.

She loved nature too much to hurt a living thing. She had two canaries at home. She had seen her dear aged mother, so old and feeble, just today. Must she tell people that she is innocent? Surely, the public did not believe the awful things the police had said. When she got out, which should be soon, she would devote her life to her dear little girl, for whom she lived.

With that, Mrs. Snyder ended the interview, explaining that she could not talk any more because it was too weakening.

Weak or not, and despite a shaky start, Mrs. Snyder quickly adapted to her new situation. She had been in a state of hysteria on Tuesday night: her screams caused the forty other female prisoners to complain. On Wednesday night, according to jail matrons, she slept a bit but babbled, moaning at one point, "They buried him and I wasn't there." On Thursday night, she slept normally and, the next day, began to take an interest in the case. She asked a matron whether there would be women on the jury and was disappointed to hear that New York law did not permit women to serve on murder juries at the time. "A woman could see my case better than a man," she observed.

9

ON FRIDAY, 25 MARCH, it was divulged that a four-ounce medicine bottle of whiskey that Gray had taken from his grip on the train, but was prevented from drinking, was poisoned with bichloride of mercury. New York City Toxicologist Dr. Alexander Gettler[1] said that never in his professional experience had he seen so concentrated a toxic dose—the equivalent of perhaps twenty tablets in half a pint of whiskey. The normal test for mercury was to heat a copper wire, dip it in a solution containing the suspected substance, and examine it under a microscope for a silver-colored deposit. In this case, a penny dropped into the whiskey instantly turned silver. A single ounce at this concentration would be fatal. A sober man would have noticed the bitter taste, but a drunken man might have tossed off the drink without realizing that it had been doctored.

Speculation, encouraged by confusion over exactly where the whiskey had been found, ran riot. Initial reports placed it in the Snyder residence; the next editions placed it in Gray's hotel room. The third wave of reports correctly established that the bottle was in the bag Gray had brought down from Syracuse.

The prevailing theory was that Mrs. Snyder had given Gray the deadly concoction when he left Queens Village in the hope of getting rid of him after he had served his purpose. Competing explanations were that the lovers had been prepared to poison Snyder but decided on other

---

1. One of the most eminent twentieth-century forensic toxicologists, Gettler was born in 1883 and became chief chemist of Bellevue Hospital in 1915. His scientific activities ranged widely, but he is mostly remembered as a developer of methods for the detection and measurement of toxic substances in body fluids.

methods—the autopsy had found no trace of poison in Snyder's body—or that they had intended to move on to murdering Isabel Gray. Someone even suggested that Albert Snyder had poisoned the whiskey himself in an attempt to kill his wife and her lover before they killed him!

The poisoned whiskey focused attention on Gray's claim that Mrs. Snyder had attempted to murder her husband on numerous occasions. According to Snyder's relatives, one afternoon in July 1926, Mrs. Snyder went out to the store while Al took a nap in the living room. When she returned an hour later, her husband was staggering around the garden, almost overcome by gas fumes. Mrs. Snyder professed horror and said that she must have kicked off the gas tube by accident when she went out. The next time they were in the house, Snyder's sisters tried to kick the tube off and found that it was nearly impossible. When an almost identical incident occurred in January or February 1927, Albert Snyder joked at a Schneider family gathering that his wife had twice barely escaped widowhood by way of gas.

Evidence of the crushing banality of the relationship between Gray and Mrs. Snyder was, meanwhile, emerging in letters turned in by an innkeeper in Easton, Pennsylvania. They had been mailed by Mrs. Snyder to wait until called for. The first was postmarked Queens Village, 24 February, at 8:40 A.M.:

My Own lover boy,

Gee, but I'm happy. Oh, ain't I happy. Tomorrow's my lucky day.

I'm so very happy, dear, I can't sit still enough to write what I'm thinking of.

You'll excuse it this time, too, won't you, hon? Went down to the movies in Q[ueen]s and saw *Johnny get your hair cut.* Jackie [Coogan] is certainly a sweet kid and a marvelous actor. Wouldn't be a bad idea if I had me a haircut—it's beginning to luka like da wop. Wassa guda writin'—huh? All I keep thinking of is U.A. [?] and you, you darn lovable little cuss. I could eatcha all up. Could I get lit & put out this blaze what's so much bother to me? Ah yes—hon, let's get good and "plastered"; ain't that a nice word? Beginning to think I'm already that way on nothing.

Hurry home, darling, I'll be waiting for you.

All my love,

Your Momie

The second letter mailed to Easton was postmarked the same day Jamaica, Queens at 2:40 P.M.:

My very own sweetheart,

About this time tomorrow, I'll be leaving. Ethel [Anderson] called me up and wanta to see me—what about I don't know. I'm going to see if we can meet downtown somewhere, so I won't have that long trip up [from Manhattan to the Bronx] and back alone.

Are you figuring on coming in about 6 o'clock? Could I meet you at the train? Where does she land?

Maybe you'll call me tonight. Who knows, huh? And say when, where and how you'll arrive. I'm having a young lady here this afternoon. She's quite interested in Sid. So here's hoping she might be able to down or cram math in her head. Come home with twenty percent. Now I ask you, ain't that grand?

Goodbye sweetie, old darling—

Love and kisses,

Your Momie

P.S. Not as always.

It was hinted that "Come home with twenty percent" was a coded message concerning the murder plot. The truth was more mundane. Ethel Anderson, having separated from her husband Edward "Sid" Pierson, wanted to divorce him because she was involved with another man.[2]

2. The identity of Ethel Anderson's male companion was never established. Her neighbors stated that Mrs. Anderson, a male escort, and another couple, perhaps Mrs. Snyder and Gray, were once so affectionate in the lobby of Mrs. Anderson's apartment building that residents called the police. Patrolman Pierson, questioned, had no comment other than to say that he felt certain bridge-playing acquaintances of his estranged wife and Mrs. Snyder were responsible for the destruction of both homes. "I had the ill fortune," he moped, "to wed an extravagant wife." His involvement in the Snyder-Gray case put so much pressure on Pierson that he resigned from the police force.

The woman in question was to be used to compromise Sid, and Ethel Anderson promised to pay twenty percent of her divorce settlement for services rendered.

A tragicomic snag blocked Mrs. Snyder's hoped-for visit with Lorraine. The problem was jailhouse rules. Mrs. Snyder's press conferences had taken place after newspapers obtained a New York Supreme Court order calling on Queens County Jail Warden Henry Fox to make his prisoner available, which he did in the adjoining courthouse. To minimize publicity, the district attorney's office obtained a subsequent order preventing Fox from allowing his prisoner out of the jail proper, from which reporters were barred. Also barred from the jail, unfortunately, were children under sixteen.

On Sunday afternoon, Gray and Mrs. Snyder met from a distance in the jail chapel, where they attended the Protestant service. Both participated actively; Mrs. Snyder was visibly annoyed when the two large black women on either side of her swayed, shouted, and enthusiastically clapped their hands during the hymns. Many prisoners were more interested in glimpsing their celebrated new neighbors than in the service. Gray and Mrs. Snyder, on the men's and women's sides of the chapel, ignored each other. Protestant chaplain Reverend Hill Johnson, who was moonlighting from his regular post at Ascension Episcopalian Church, was placed under orders not to reveal to the press even the hymns and texts that had been chosen.

Warren Schneider retained counsel to protect the interests of Lorraine, who stood to become a very wealthy young lady soon. First, there was the ninety-seven thousand dollars of life insurance: ninety thousand under the double-indemnity policy; five thousand under the straight policy; one thousand under the policy that Albert Snyder signed knowingly; and one thousand under the preexisting Prudential policy. Then there was the equity in the Queens Village house, the Buick sedan, and a handful of liquid financial assets. In effect, he sought to become her legal guardian.

The Schneider family's move to take Lorraine prompted Granny Brown to move her press campaign into high gear. From this moment on, she and Lorraine were available to any reporter who made the trip to

Queens Village. Photographs from the family album were sold to the highest bidder. Guided tours of the house were given, with attention drawn to the many examples of Mrs. Snyder's excellent housework. "How many wives today put up fruit?" Granny Brown asked as she showed reporters the jar-filled shelves in the basement. As for Albert Snyder, "He was a puttering, old-womanish man," she sniffed. He hated animals; he wouldn't let Lorraine have a kitten, and he made Mrs. Snyder get rid of her bulldog, Babe.[3]

The star of the show was little Lorraine. Mama had bought her the pretty shoes she was wearing, she said. They had cost seven dollars. When Daddy found out, he said, "Aw, why'd you go and pay so much!" Mama and Daddy used to always argue about money. Daddy once gave her a piggy bank, but all he gave her to put in it was one nickel. Daddy used to give her an awful slapping even for little things, like not cleaning her plate.

"No, I didn't love my daddy—not like I love my mama. He never read to me or helped me say my prayers. Mama used to read to me. I like fairy tales best, Cinderella and [Goldilocks and] the Three Bears."

One evening, Granny Brown escorted reporters into Lorraine's room for a bedside interview. Mama gave her the pretty, pink ruffled pillow on the radiator. Mama gave her the big doll that used to be hers when she was young. Mama made the dress worn by the big doll; it had been Lorraine's when she was little. Mama put the calendar with the picture of Jesus and the little lambs on the wall. Mama was teaching her hymns. They had been learning "Rock of Ages" just before Mama had to go away to the hospital.

---

3. But there were, among the photographs on the auction block, plenty of shots of Albert Snyder together with Babe, the two appearing to make a happy pair. And among the lovingly catalogued photographs from Snyder's bachelor days was one of a dog and kitten labeled "My First Family." On the other hand, Gray relates in *Doomed Ship* that Albert Snyder once summarily ordered that all animals in the household be taken away by a local animal protection league. As for Mrs. Snyder, there is no question: she loved animals and had an uncanny rapport with them. In Queens County Jail, she managed to domesticate a mouse with breadcrumbs, succeeding to the extent of training the creature to wear a small collar attached to a piece of string.

"Every night after I say 'Now I lay me down to sleep' I say, 'Please God, bring Mama home.' I hope he does it real soon."

Well coached by Granny Brown, and with the old lady at her side to fill in details where required, Lorraine recounted a series of domestic vignettes starring Albert Snyder. An example:

> Once, he grabbed a piece of bread from me and scraped off some of the butter. He was always saying I had too much to eat. I cried and said I wanted lots of butter. Then he got angry and hit me. I ran behind a chair because I was afraid of him. My mother was angry, too, because she stood right up to my father and said things. He rushed out of the room and returned a few minutes later with a revolver in his hand. My father yelled "I'll kill the both of you!" Only he used some swearwords. He pressed the revolver against my mother.

She also had things to say about Judd Gray,

> Before all this happened I liked Judd Gray better than I liked my Daddy and I don't care who knows it. He was much nicer to me. He took me along when I went out with Mama. He always gave me ten cents and candy. He gave me some pink underwear, too, bloomers and a vest. Now I *hate* Judd Gray! When I see his picture in the papers I stick my tongue out at it! I hate Jane Gray, too. I thought I might write to her, but now I know that her father killed my father.

The Lorraine card was played again when Mrs. Snyder's poetic talents were first inflicted upon the public. Commenting that it was only one of many works written by their prisoner, jail authorities made public a poem entitled either "To My Mother" (according to the *Daily Mirror*) or "Retribution" (according to the *American*), which began, "Just a thought on cheerful things, things I used to know, / Joys that mother loving brings, watching Lorraine grow." It was hinted that further works would be released soon; Mrs. Snyder was also reported to be immersed in the works of Schopenauer, Nietzsche, and Kant.

Reports of how Gray spent his time were more prosaic and undoubtedly more accurate: he smoked incessantly and played checkers with his guards. Sometimes his mind was not on the game and his partners needed to remind him that it was his turn to make a move.

Members of the New York State Prison Commission, a largely philanthropic organization staffed by leading citizens, stopped by to inquire whether the famous prisoners had any complaints. Mrs. Snyder had none; Gray, however, spiritedly protested against "indecent exposure" to photographers and the press. Jail officials accordingly drafted plans to erect plywood partitions and detail extra policemen to protect him and Mrs. Snyder from reporters when they were led between the courtroom and their cells.

Preparations for the trial accelerated as March turned into April. District Attorney Newcombe exuded confidence. He toured the Snyder residence to familiarize himself with it; one day, he met Lorraine, who described him as "a very nice man."[4]

Detective Lieutenant McDermott and Assistant District Attorney Conroy took the sleeper to Syracuse on Wednesday, 30 March, to wrap up odds and ends. They visited the boiler room of the Onondaga Savings Bank Building, where the stoker emptied six waiting barrels of ashes for them. Nothing remained of the incinerated grip except a few twisted chunks of metal. The night watchman was able to confirm that on the night of Sunday, 20 March, he had taken Haddon Gray, Judd Gray, and Harry Platt to the sixth floor of the building.

All persons directly connected with the Syracuse end of the case had been ordered to present themselves at police headquarters at noon. Mrs. Anna Boehm failed to show up, and Syracuse detectives scoured the town for her. While they searched, Harry Platt, Haddon Gray, Michael Mahoney, and Anthony Boehm all went over their stories again and expressed relief that they had told the truth and gratitude for the courtesy with which they had been treated. Haddon Gray hoped the trial would go ahead on 11 April, as scheduled. He said he was a nervous wreck and was already making plans to go to Bermuda for a vacation. Mrs. Anna

---

4. Something on which all agreed. Mrs. Snyder said she was glad that it was Newcombe who would be prosecuting her because he was "a likeable man."

Boehm, when she was finally found, expressed her intention to obtain a medical certificate stating that she could not attend the trial because she was pregnant. It would do no good, McDermott and Conroy explained to her, she would be subpoenaed and would have to attend, whether she liked it or not.

Attorneys Hazelton and Wallace said that their preparations for Mrs. Snyder's defense were complete. Granny Brown used her life's savings to pay them. An attempt had been made in Queens Village to start a defense fund for Mrs. Snyder, but its organizers dissolved the fund after it failed to reach ten dollars. "It's bad enough for Queens Village and its people," said one woman, "to have the disgrace of this happening here without being asked to pay for it!"

Gray's defense team was, by contrast, in chaos. Hallinan and Groh had fallen out with the Gray family almost immediately. They felt that they were retained to defend Gray in court while Miller was to defend the interests of the family. Miller disagreed. When Miller announced that he would seek a change of venue for Gray's case, Hallinan and Groh were astonished—they had no such plan. Hallinan and Groh exited the scene on the pretext that they had other, more pressing work.

On Wednesday, 6 April, it was reported that the Gray family had retained Edward "Death House" Reilly, who had successfully used a "mama's boy" diminished-capacity defense to win acquittal of a client on a first-degree murder (though not on a reduced) charge in the beating death of his mother-in-law. Reilly proudly announced from Albany that he was taking matters in hand, an assertion flatly refuted by Miller: "I am the only attorney retained by the family and I'll run the whole thing myself. I have heard nothing from Reilly." Reilly withdrew from the case as quickly as he had entered it.[5]

Max Steuer was approached on Gray's behalf, but rejected the case

---

5. In addition to suffering from alcoholism, Reilly was slowly going mad from the syphilis that would eventually kill him in 1940. "Death House," known also as "The Bull of Brooklyn," liked to boast that he had defended fifteen hundred murder cases and lost only six. He is best known today for his inept defense of Richard Bruno Hauptmann in the Lindbergh kidnapping trial.

when his fee could not be met.[6] Then, on Thursday, 7 April, William Millard, the distinguished attorney who had referred the Gray family to Samuel Miller, announced that he would be acting together with his "old friend" Miller for Gray's defense. In welcoming Millard aboard and commenting on the frequent changes of personnel, Miller remarked that the Gray family had suffered from "too much friendly advice."

Adding to the confusion was a widening internal split. Gray's mother and sister wanted to pour money and effort into their wayward boy's defense. Mrs. Isabel Gray, betrayed and with a daughter to look after, saw things differently. Unlike the other two women, she was nowhere to be seen supporting her husband. She never returned to the Queens County Jail, despite her mother-in-law's pleas to give at least the appearance of loyalty. When Miller arranged for her to be interviewed by some newspaper "sob sisters," she failed to appear. Far from the expected story, a piece along the lines of "Gray to Face Fate Alone" appeared, leaving the elder Mrs. Gray to deny that Isabel had completely abandoned her husband. Miller tried to settle the affair by releasing what he called an "eminently sensible" letter from Isabel to her husband, but it dealt mostly with practicalities such as where the checkbook was kept.

The best way for reporters to settle matters was, of course, to interview Mrs. Isabel Gray, but there was a problem. She had gone with her mother, Mrs. Kallenbach, and her daughter, Jane, to live with her older sister, Mrs. Ethel Brundage, in Norwalk, Connecticut. Frank Brundage, a banker, was a leading figure in the upper-crust suburban town and happened to be police commissioner, a voluntary position. He threatened to have police lock up the first newspaperman to come to his house. The entire police force of the township turned out to protect the residence, and Brundage himself, conveniently deputized, attempted to arrest seven

6. Like Joseph Shalleck, Max Steuer was a Tammany Hall maven. Steuer successfully defended the owners of the Triangle Shirtwaist Factory against charges of manslaughter in the famous 1911 fire that killed 147 female employees. And when *New York Evening Graphic* publisher Bernarr MacFadden and circulation manager Otis Scattergood were charged under a New York statute forbidding publications comprised entirely of crime, sensation, and lewdness, he got them off.

reporters for obstructing the sidewalk. Disgusted, the reporters decided to take up their cause with the mayor of Norwalk. On the way, the driver of their car was pulled over and arrested for speeding and driving an overloaded vehicle. Passengers and driver alike were taken to the police station, where a magistrate charged them with being a public nuisance. The chief of police warned them to be on the 4:50 train or they would spend the night in jail. They did not have long to consider their options—the train left in five minutes. They were on it.

Mrs. Margaret Gray's faith in her boy remained unshakable. One of her letters read:

My darling boy,

Your dear letter came this morning and the telegram last night. So thoughtful, just as you always have been. I thought of you all day, dearie. We just went out on some errands and Margaret cooked me a lovely dinner, as usual, and there was a lovely dessert sent in by an old friend you know down the street.

I can only write a few lines as I want Harold [Logan] to take this out. I want to tell you, dear, about the shoes. The guard told me I could not bring you shoes on account of drugs—they said they would have to loosen the heels, etc. and they would be no good—but you can send out and buy a pair, so that is what I want you to do. Have them get you a pair of rubber sneaks of some kind, dearie. If you have not money enough, get it of Mr. Miller and I will return it to him. You cannot be comfortable with your feet hurting. I am so sorry.

I will be over in a day or two and bring fresh underwear and stockings. I had quite a talk with the guard last time and he told me were not allowed to bring much on account of drug addicts. I had never even thought of that phase of it.

Yes, dearie, Harold has been just wonderful, doing everything in his power—Harold has done nothing for days but go from place to place—but he is really a saint and a real man.

The sun is shining this A.M. and that makes things look a bit brighter. Then your good letter helped to cheer me.

I think it is bad company that is the undoing of many—and then, as

I told you many times, dearie, that this whiskey going around was not fit to drink. Also I always thought that steady tippling weakened the brain. A person's ideals cannot be too high and their homes must be founded on rock and not sand, and all families need to be under the arm of the church with the seal of the church upon them and theirs. I know my precious boy can see that now, can't you?

Dearest, do not trouble much about what you know of the Episcopal retreat.[7] Just your teachings will be alright. We are all for the same destination, only in different routes. The seal of the Presbyterian church is still in you—from baptism. Just have faith and great repentance for your great sin—and a love of the Master is all you need. We all send just heaps of love and kisses—to my precious boy.

Your ever devoted,

Mother

A passage from another letter reads, "My darling boy—I must talk to you a little before I go to bed. You seem oh! so very, very far away. I never dreamed my precious boy could go so far away that I could not touch him, or that he would ever be in trouble that his mother could not be near to hold his hand and comfort him . . . Your mother's arms are close about you and her loving kisses are on your lips."

Well dressed and looking younger than her sixty years, Mrs. Gray gave a formal interview in South Orange on the afternoon of Palm Sunday, 10 April. The journalists were driven up to her house in a butcher's meat wagon. Like Hazelton in Mrs. Snyder's first interview, Samuel Miller sat next to Mrs. Gray and filtered questions. The family's white Pomeranian, Nicky, was also present. Mrs. Gray complained that there was too much smoke and directed Margaret to open a window. As reporters crowded into the room, she offered her own seat to one and would not sit until more chairs had been obtained and her audience was comfortable.

Judd must have been insane when he did it, she began. He was normal, obedient, and considerate. He was so kind. He had been brought up

---

7. Gray switched from the Methodist to the Episcopalian church to please Isabel; if he was baptized a Presbyterian, as the letter states, he was on his third denomination.

properly and did not have a violent temper. He had been very close to his father. He drank liquor only socially, and never to excess. For that matter, no one in the Gray family was much of a drinker. If there had been anything wrong with his marriage, Judd would have told her about it.

A reporter asked whether Gray was particularly susceptible to the influence of others. Well, he must have been in this case, Mrs. Gray replied. Was he repentant? She certainly hoped so.

"Mother love can't be shaken. I'm thinking about the boy I knew for thirty-five years. He must be brought back to himself. He's in a daze now. He's a different person. It wasn't my son who committed this terrible, terrible crime."

She dragged out the old story of the *Mary and John* again. A practical reporter—one of the who-what-where-when-how school—interrupted by asking precisely where in Connecticut the landing had taken place. Her monologue interrupted, Mrs. Gray suddenly turned indignant. "I see no reason why our whole family history should be dragged into this," she said. "Why, no member of our family was ever accused of a crime before!" The interview had clearly come to an end.

That Sunday, Gray and Mrs. Snyder awoke at six, took baths, had prunes, bread, and coffee for breakfast, and mopped their cells. Mrs. Snyder gave her face a massage, polished her fingernails on the prison blanket, and plucked her eyebrows with her fingers, making an uneven job of it in the tiny, distorting cell mirror. Lunch consisted of boiled beef, potatoes, bread, and coffee. The Protestant church service was held just when Mrs. Gray was meeting the press on Wayne Avenue. Gray, described as "morbid and depressed," was wracked with sobs during the singing of one hymn.[8] Mrs. Snyder glared at Gray with open contempt when his sobs became audible on the women's side of the chapel.

Back in her cell, she read detective magazines and asked the matrons two questions: "Will Judd Gray be in court tomorrow?" (her attorneys were to argue their motion for a separate trial), and "Will I have to face

---

8. When security restrictions were lifted, jail officials revealed that the hymn in question was "Lead Kindly Light," which begins: "Lead kindly light amid th' encircling gloom; / The night is dark and I am far from home."

those damned photographers again?" Mrs. Snyder's appetite remained strong and she sent out for a meal of roast chicken and spaghetti from Minotti's Restaurant nearby, complaining afterward that there was not enough sauce.

"It is rumored in Long Island City," wrote Damon Runyon in the *American,* "that Minotti's spaghetti is worth going to jail for."

Tony, the deliveryman from Minotti's, complained that neither Mrs. Snyder nor Gray gave tips. Pete, who brought in normal jail fare from the courthouse restaurant, had this to say: "That Gray, he knows he's in bad. Lost his appetite and many pounds. He orders food, but only drinks his coffee. I never see him smile once. She's not so worried. Good appetite. Gray, he's a hell of a fellow, but she's no damn good."

PART TWO   The Trial

Courtroom sketches of the defendants, April 1927

10

BECAUSE THE QUEENS COUNTY COURT judge who would normally have had jurisdiction was recovering from an appendectomy, the case was transferred to New York State Supreme Court, to be tried before Justice Townsend Scudder. A native of Long Island, Scudder was descended from the captain of the *Mayflower* and had been educated by private tutors in Europe before graduating from Columbia University Law School in 1888. The first Democrat in an old-line Republican family, he was known to be Governor Alfred Smith's choice to succeed him when he stepped down in the autumn to run for President.[1]

At the time of the Snyder-Gray trial, Scudder was a widower, his first wife having died in 1924. His passions were Freemasonry—he was a masonic grand master and had been received at almost all the royal courts of Europe—and dogs. He claimed to have exhibited, in 1874, at the second dog show ever held in the United States, and he owned 125 dogs, mostly cocker spaniels.

Justice Scudder detested criminal trials and was an outspoken opponent of capital punishment. When criminal cases, especially capital ones, appeared on his docket, he was usually able to find another judge with whom to trade. When the Snyder-Gray case came up, he searched in vain for a way out, but there was none.

Even as early as 1927, it was accepted practice that the Queens district attorney would concentrate on administration and leave most courtroom advocacy to his assistants. Such was the notoriety of the Snyder-Gray

---

1. As events unfolded, Franklin Roosevelt came forward to run for governor in 1928 and Scudder deferred to him.

case, however, that Richard Newcombe felt compelled to appear in court. Newcombe was a graduate of Andover and had received his law degree from New York Law School in 1900. Despite his avuncular appearance, he was only forty-six at the time of the Snyder-Gray trial.

The two assistant district attorneys on whom Newcombe relied for the bulk of the work were Peter Daly and Charles Froessel, both in their mid-thirties. Daly worked his way through Fordham University Law School as a clerk in Perry's Drugstore,[2] graduating in 1914. At the time of the Snyder-Gray case, Daly was flush from his success in prosecuting "Radio Burglar" Paul Hilton for murder. Charles Froessel had worked as an office boy to support himself through high school and New York Law School, from which he graduated in 1913. Before becoming assistant prosecutor, he had served as counsel to the Queens County sheriff.

On Mrs. Snyder's team, Edgar Hazelton ("ED-gaaa" behind his back), a native of Queens and a product of Saint Lawrence University Law School in Brooklyn (now defunct), had been the youngest-ever judge to sit on the New York City Municipal Court. He possessed an excellent legal mind, but was not a particularly strong trial advocate and was distracted by Queens County Republican politics. His partner, Dana Wallace,[3] was the reverse, a mediocre lawyer but a brilliant courtroom advocate. Wallace, a Maine native, had attended Dartmouth, Yale, and Brooklyn Law School, from which he graduated in 1900. Having studied drama at Yale, his forte was courtroom theatrics, and he had never lost a

2. Located in the lobby of the Pulitzer Building on Park Row, Perry's Drugstore was a favorite hangout for journalists. "Doc" Perry dispensed shots of whiskey on the house; these were invariably followed by an orange juice chaser poured into the just-drained shot glasses to destroy the evidence.

3. Wallace was the son of "Blackbear" Wallace, owner and skipper of the *Marie Celeste,* subject of one of the great maritime mysteries of all time. In 1872, shortly after Captain Wallace gave up command of the vessel, she set sail from New York to Genoa with a cargo of raw ethyl alcohol. She was found five weeks later, drifting in the mid-Atlantic with sails set and no one aboard. Theories abound, but the mystery has never been solved.

murder case.[4] A Republican-turned-Democrat-turned-Republican, Wallace had held the office of Queens district attorney from 1921 to 1923, when Newcombe trounced him at the polls despite Wallace's excellent record of convictions. At the time of the Snyder-Gray trial, Wallace was a confirmed alcoholic.

Hazelton and Wallace despised each other. Wallace's towering ego—he offered at one point to defend Mrs. Snyder and Gray simultaneously and swore that he could get both of them off if allowed to run each defense his own way—grated on Hazelton. Wallace, for his part, regarded Hazelton as a politically ambitious martinet and a publicity hound. The two disagreed on the best strategy for defending Mrs. Snyder. Hazelton, the good schoolboy, wanted to sort out her story and offer a defense based on the law; Wallace, the showman, regarded this as a waste of time and preferred to sow doubt and confusion with irrelevant theories and facts. Accordingly, he threw his energy into efforts to uncover evidence that could be used to insinuate that Gray and his Syracuse insurance-business friends had plotted to ensnare Mrs. Snyder in a murder-for-profit scheme.

On Gray's side, Samuel Miller was an unknown quantity because of his youth. A brilliant graduate of Georgetown University Law School, he had gained experience in corporate and tax law as a staff member of the U.S. Treasury and was a certified public accountant as well as an attorney. But he had passed the bar examination only two years previously and had never argued a criminal case.

Although nominally the junior member of the Gray team, William Millard was far senior to Miller in experience. In fact, Millard had referred the case to Miller (who had been involved in some real estate dealings with him) in order to give the young attorney's career a boost. Millard had graduated from Columbia University and New York Law

---

4. Once, to demonstrate how a defendant's husband had (allegedly) beaten her, Wallace threw himself so violently on the courtroom floor that he fractured his shoulder. The jury barely bothered to retire before acquitting the woman. When she came up to thank him, Wallace, in pain, snarled, "Aw, get outta here! You're guilty as hell!"

School and, while assistant corporation counsel for the City of New York from 1898 to 1917, had been charged with the monumental task of rewriting the entire sanitary code. After spending several years in private practice, Millard had served as an assistant U.S. attorney from 1921 to 1925, before returning to private practice. At the time of the Snyder-Gray trial, Millard was active in Republican politics in the Bronx; however, as a close friend of Theodore Roosevelt, he had been among the founders of the Progressive Party.

Gray's defense team, still in disarray, requested a delay. Scudder gave them until Monday, 18 April, on the tenuous excuse that it would be better if a trial of such sensational dimensions did not overlap with Holy Week.

Scudder was faced with the critical decision of whether to try the defendants jointly. Only a year before, the matter would have been out of his hands. In 1829, New York State had, by statute, overridden the common-law tenet that in cases of joint indictment, separate trials could be granted only at the discretion of the trial judge. Thus, for almost a century, any jointly indicted defendant in New York State had the right to demand a separate trial. In 1926, however, in response to an upswell in the public's perennial desire to get tough on crime, the New York State Assembly passed, and Governor Smith signed, a comprehensive criminal law reform package known collectively as the "Baumes Law," named after committee chairman Caleb Baumes. Among measures such as mandatory life sentences for repeat offenders (fourth conviction) and tougher handgun laws, there was a provision restoring the rule of common law in the area of joint trials.[5]

Outside of crime thrillers, a state's willingness to incur the expense of bringing defendants to trial usually implies a fair degree of certainty that they committed a crime at least close to the one with which they are charged. Whether or not this can be proven in court is another matter, but if the evidence is weak, the case is unlikely to come to trial in the first place. Given this state of affairs, it is easy to see why joint trials put the

---

5. It had formerly been standard procedure for gangs of petty hoodlums to wear down complainants by demanding separate trials.

prosecution at an advantage. Even when the presiding judge scrupulously instructs the jury as to the evidence to be considered against each defendant, it is almost inevitable that the case presented against one will incriminate the other as well. In a joint Snyder-Gray trial, this would be especially true of the defendants' confessions, assuming they were admitted into evidence.

The path of least resistance for the defense was for each defendant to take the witness stand and blame the other. This would be much easier in a separate trial, where the other party would not be in court to fight back. In a joint trial, however, Mrs. Snyder and Gray would be caught between the Scylla of cross-examination by the State and the Charybdis of cross-examination by the codefendant's counsel. Tactically, then, each defendant would be better off if tried separately.

Strategically, it was a different matter. Gray stood to profit from a coattails effect: no Queens County jury had ever convicted a woman of capital murder, and if Mrs. Snyder deserved the benefit of doubt, then so, assuredly, did he. Moreover, the contrast between the two defendants was completely in favor of the man: Gray looked good in a joint appearance; Mrs. Snyder looked bad.

A large part of this was her own fault. She affected mourning attire that would have done credit to a suburban Lady Macbeth: a straight-cut black crepe dress, tight-fitting and short, a head-hugging black velvet turban, black silk stockings, and black kid gloves. The unfortunate effect of the turban was to emphasize her square jaw, giving her a grim, determined look that won her nicknames such as "Granite Woman," "Ice Queen," "Ruthless Ruth," and "The Viking Vampire." Applying makeup to soften the effect was out of the question for a woman on trial for her life in 1927. For jewelry, Mrs. Snyder wore a long black jet bead necklace, looped through at the neck and hanging almost to her waist. She fingered it constantly, sometimes pulling it so tight that the beads dug into her neck. Her platinum wedding band stood out conspicuously.

Ever the irrepressible "Tommy," Mrs. Snyder persisted in inappropriate public behavior, bantering with photographers and reporters, yawning conspicuously, joking with matrons, and allowing herself to be photographed reading various tabloid newspapers for publicity shots.

She refused to be photographed kissing Granny Brown, complaining, "My face won't show that way!" When a photographer asked her to cross her legs, she giggled, "Are you sure it will look ladylike?" She struck poses even when no cameramen were around as if hoping to attract one, and some of these—like placing her elbow on the table, resting her chin upon her hand and staring fixedly into space—became tableaux familiar to those involved in the case.

As bad as were Mrs. Snyder's appearance and demeanor, her attitude was worse; she proved from the outset to be a difficult, stubborn, unrealistic client. She insisted on releasing silly handwritten statements to the press through jail matrons. All discussions of her situation had to be predicated on how unjust it was. She barely acknowledged the possibility of a long term of imprisonment, let alone that she stood in the shadow of the electric chair. To more than one listener, she commented that she expected to be free soon. She refused to discuss anything short of a full acquittal, blowing up, for example, at the suggestion that she undergo a sanity examination on the chance that it might support a diminished-responsibility defense.

Legally speaking, a full acquittal could be obtained only by proving that everything resulting in Albert Snyder's death was done either without her knowledge or under compulsion, which in law means fear of immediate grievous physical harm. Thus all would depend on her description of events in the Snyder residence on the fatal night.

Mrs. Snyder had already told two different stories. The first was when police interviewed her in Queens Village. The second was in her signed statement. Now she told a third story, in which she claimed to have fought with Gray to prevent him from committing the murder.

In this new version, Mrs. Snyder had left the doors open for Gray not so he could murder Albert Snyder, but so she could persuade him to abandon his murderous intentions and tell him that she wanted to break off their love affair. During this conversation, held in the living room, she went upstairs to the bathroom. While she was there, Gray came upstairs, entered the master bedroom, and clubbed Albert Snyder. Mrs. Snyder, hearing the blow, rushed into the room, grappled with Gray, struggling frantically to save her husband, and then fainted. While she was unconscious, Gray completed his work. When she returned to her senses, Gray said, "You're in this as deep as me and you'd better play along." She was terrified, and this fear of Gray, combined with police duress, led her to lie to the police when they arrived and to keep lying at the station house.

What was Gray's motive? The insurance money, claimed Mrs. Snyder, which he intended to extort from her after the claim had been settled.

Thin as this convoluted story reads on paper, it would sound thinner yet in court when contrasted with the simple and coherent version of events in Mrs. Snyder's signed statement. Wallace, if not Hazelton, was of the opinion that Mrs. Snyder's grip on reality was weak and dreaded putting her on the witness stand.

Worse still, Mrs. Snyder and Gray did not meet as equals in the court of public opinion. With scarcely a voice of moderation or reason to be heard, the public had ganged up on Mrs. Snyder, with her peroxide-blonde hair, her freewheeling personality, and her Jazz Age style. She was vilified coast to coast, in conversations across back fences and luncheon tables, in sermons and after-dinner speeches, and, most important, in the headlines and columns of the tabloid press.

Although there was not a glimmer of evidence to support the claim, it was said that Mrs. Snyder had carried on affairs with dozens of sales-men.[6] It was also said that she had blackmailed her other lovers to finance the high life she led with Gray. She was labeled an "erotomaniac," a woman of insatiable sexual desires. Her "abnormal tastes" ran to "unnatural love," the latter perhaps a reference to fellatio, then sufficiently exotic to be a felony offense in New York State.[7] The practices that had

6. Thus the calendar pad with Gray's name on it that had been found in the Snyder residence became a "love diary" detailing Mrs. Snyder's encounters with Gray and twenty-eight other men. The *Daily Mirror* headline screamed: "28 SHEIKS IN SNYDER PROBE!" In fact, the "love diary" was no more than a red leather-bound book, found on Mrs. Snyder's dresser, that listed the names and addresses of the salesman acquaintances from whom Mrs. Snyder bought wholesale.

7. In 1935, a New York jury acquitted Vera Stretz of fatally shooting her lover, Dr. Fritz Gebhart, on the strength of her defense that he ordered her to commit fellatio on him. That Gebhart was an enthusiastic supporter of National Socialism made her lawyer's task easier.

corrupted him were so filthy, the press reported, Gray was going to request that women be barred from the courtroom during his testimony.

Women, sadly, were Mrs. Snyder's most relentless persecutors. Gray's sister, Margaret, summed up the feelings of most of her sex in a written statement distributed to reporters:

> I have never realized how much tragedy is concealed in the houses all around us. This is created by evil women. Most of their depredations upon happy domestic life don't become public. Few come to such a dreadful pass as the catastrophe in our own family. Dozens of letters come to me from women who are suffering from the "other woman's" lack of conscience.

Mrs. Serena Fidgeon, the Snyders' hostess on the night of the murder, in whose home bootleg liquor flowed and suburbanites caroused every Saturday night, had this comment for the *Telegram*: "Mr. Snyder was a very fine, home-loving man, much too good for that type of woman. I absolutely despise her. If anyone had to be killed, it should have been Mrs. Snyder."

Mrs. Snyder also suffered from a decision on the part of newspaper editors to avoid the mistakes they had made when covering the Hall-Mills trial the year before.[8] On that occasion, emphasis on the human el-

---

8. In September 1922, the bodies of Reverend Edward Hall, pastor of the Episcopal Church of Saint John the Evangelist in New Brunswick, New Jersey, and choir singer Mrs. Eleanor Mills, wife of the church sexton, were discovered on an abandoned lover's lane. They had been shot to death. Scattered love notes and the disposition of the bodies, arranged to lie side by side, suggested a revenge motive, as did the fact that the choir singer's tongue and larynx had been removed. Suspicion fell on the minister's widow, Mrs. Frances Stevens Hall, who came form a wealthy society background, her two brothers, William ("Willie") and Henry, and their cousin Henry Carpender. Despite an eyewitness, hog farmer Mrs. Jane Gibson ("the Pig Woman"), the grand jury failed to return an indictment. Not until 1926, following revelations that Reverend Hall and Mrs. Mills had planned to elope, were indictments brought against Mrs. Hall, her brothers, and Carpender, whom the Pig Woman identified as the actual shooter. Henry Carpender's case having been separated, Mrs. Hall and her brothers were tried first. The Pig Woman, who was suffering from cancer and testified from a stretcher, did not make a be-

ement had resulted in messy coverage that succeeded neither in reporting the case as news nor in making of it a high human drama. There was no secret about the new approach. The headline in *Editor and Publisher* for 23 April ran: "PRESS TRYING TO DEBUNK GRAY-SNYDER TRIAL," followed by "Sob-sister Stuff Notably Lacking in Majority of Stories." Not only was sob-sister stuff lacking, so were the sob sisters themselves. The most prominent of the few women assigned to cover the Snyder-Gray trial was Sophie Treadwell of the *Herald Tribune,* who had trekked through the mountains of Mexico at the height of the civil war to obtain an exclusive interview with Pancho Villa and had reported from the front lines during the Great War. Sentimentality, needless to say, was not the predominant tone in Treadwell's reportage.

Having cast Mrs. Snyder as a suburban Messalina, the press portrayed Gray as the sinner redeemed, the stray sheep returned to the fold, the prodigal son come home—and he shamelessly played to the role.[9] Gray's religious convictions, always strong, became all-consuming.

Gray simplified matters by sticking to the story he had told in his statement. Moreover, in contrast to Mrs. Snyder, he was a model client from a lawyer's point of view—he retained counsel, told them his story, listened to their advice, and issued his instructions, whereupon he left

---

lievable witness. Henry Stevens established a credible alibi and "Willie," a mental defective, delighted spectators by tying the prosecuting attorney up in knots. Mrs. Stevens and her brothers were acquitted and the charges against Carpender were dropped. They eventually settled a libel suit against the *Daily News* out of court. The crime has never been solved, and there are many theories.

9. Even the supporting players had to fit stock roles. Gray's mother had, said the *Daily Mirror,* "the support of years of breeding which have left their cultural imprint upon her" and a "well—modulated voice, with an instinctive choice of the right word and phrase." According to the *Evening Journal,* she looked like "a smart young businesswoman." All of this was contrasted with the drab, careworn, apron-draped Granny Brown, whom John Kobler, in his introduction to *The Trial of Ruth Snyder and Judd Gray,* dismissed as "a born drudge." Isabel Gray was described cruelly by the *Daily News* as "a shabby little wife," her coat "of inferior quality," her hat "not smart," and her plain black shoes "a far cry from the nifty alligator pumps that Mrs. Snyder wore in court." Albert Snyder was "sturdy," "home-loving," and "the old-fashioned type."

them alone. He was serious, modest, and attentive in public appearances and did not give reporters so much as the time of day. Nor did he have any need to. The harder Mrs. Snyder tried to clear herself, the more the press gravitated to Gray's side.

The task before Mrs. Snyder's attorneys was difficult enough, but it was almost impossible with the contrite little underwear salesman beside her at the defense table. Nothing, by contrast, could suit Gray's lawyers better than to have the universally detested "Blonde Borgia" heap blame and abuse on their client, the very picture of remorse.

On Monday, 11 April, counsel appeared before Justice Scudder to argue the issue of separate trials. When Wallace rose to present his motion in favor of a separate trial for Mrs. Snyder, Miller complained that he had not been served with a copy.

"There were so many attorneys of record," Wallace replied, "I didn't know who to send it to."

Wallace based his argument on two points. First, a joint trial might deprive Mrs. Snyder of her right to trial by a jury of her peers: jurors acceptable to Mrs. Snyder and the prosecution might be challenged by Gray. Second, Wallace argued, were the technical difficulties that such a trial would involve. In a joint trial, Justice Scudder would find himself constantly cautioning the jury as to what evidence was to be considered against which defendant and it would be impossible for any jury to follow such legal acrobatics.

District Attorney Newcombe, arguing against Wallace's motion, responded that, as the State alleged that the accused had committed the crime together, they should be tried together. In a separate trial, Mrs. Snyder could blame Gray, and he would not have the chance to reply, Newcombe said.

Miller, speaking for Gray, also opposed the motion and promised to submit a supporting affidavit by the afternoon. The acts of the defendants were "so inseparably interwoven and interlocked," he said, that there was danger of a grave miscarriage of justice if the two were not tried together.

The merits of the motion aside, it was two against one, Gray and the People against Mrs. Snyder. In a ruling released the next day, Justice Scudder rejected Wallace's motion without legal comment.

Gray, unlike Mrs. Snyder, had no objection, albeit little interest, when his counsel suggested that he be examined by a panel of "alienists," the psychiatric experts who had dramatically entered American jurisprudence a few years before when they provided Clarence Darrow with the arguments that saved Leopold and Loeb from the gallows.[10] If even one of the examiners declared Gray insane, his attorneys would stand a chance of getting him off with an amended plea of "guilty, but insane." Such a victory would, coincidentally, be manna from heaven for Mrs. Snyder, as a legally insane Gray could not testify, nor could his statement be used as evidence. "SANITY TEST TO SAVE GRAY!" screamed the *Evening Journal*'s headline. Granny Brown was sarcastic: "Crazy, eh? Him? That's a good one!"

A panel of four was selected: for the defense, Doctors Thomas Cusack, an expert on the degenerative effects of bootleg whiskey, and Siegfried Block; for the prosecution, Doctors Sylvester Leahy, a personal friend of Newcombe, and Stephen Jewett. Sanity examinations followed a predictable pattern. Experts retained by the defense invariably declared the accused insane and experts retained by the State invariably found them sane. The public was even more contemptuous of forensic psychiatry than it is today. Dr. Cusack, head of the team, was determined that this case would be different. This time, whichever way the examination went, the panel would present a unanimous finding.

On 14 and 15 April, Gray was taken from his cell to a room in the

---

10. Nathan "Babe" Leopold and Richard "Dickie" Loeb were the precocious teenaged scions of wealthy Chicago families. Besotted with affection for each other and operating under the delusion that they were Nietzschean supermen, in 1924, they kidnapped and brutally murdered a younger boy from their neighborhood, Bobbie Franks. The motive was not money but their ambition to commit "the perfect crime." The murder was almost immediately discovered and the culprits were arrested, whereupon each confessed. In one of the most brilliant criminal defenses in American history, lawyer Clarence Darrow advised them to plead guilty and throw themselves on the mercy of the sentencing judge. The prosecution vigorously argued that psychiatric testimony should not be permitted at the sentencing hearing since the defendants were not pleading insanity, but Judge John Caverly ruled that it could be admitted in mitigation. Darrow's oratory won the day: Leopold and Loeb escaped with life sentences.

courthouse and subjected to a battery of what passed for sanity tests at the time. Typical of these were walking a chalk line, whirling around quickly, and answering a series of rapid-fire questions. Samples of his blood and spinal fluid were taken, the latter a painful waste of time, for analysis. An X-ray machine was brought in from Saint John's Hospital and a useless X-ray of the brain was made. Gray was cooperative but tense.

The result of the examination, to Cusack's frustration, was the usual split. He and Dr. Block leaned toward insanity, Doctors Leahy and Jewett toward sanity. All Friday night and into Saturday, the team wrangled, finally settling on a compromise solution. Block and Cusack, the latter of whom deliberated for two hours on his knees in a darkened chapel, admitted that Gray knew the meaning and quality of his act. Thus, on the one hand, he was sane within the meaning of the law. On the other hand, because Gray was weakened by raging Oedipal forces and corrupted by liquor and the new sexual practices to which Mrs. Snyder had introduced him, he suffered from diminished capacity.

The proposed compromise was that the panel would declare Gray "not insane" and competent to stand trial on the capital charge. At the same time, they would privately convey to Gray's counsel and to District Attorney Newcombe their reservations and willingness to testify, if called to do so, in support of a plea of guilty to the charge of second-degree murder.

This they did, but, in the commotion surrounding the trial, their offer seemed to vanish into thin air, leaving only the panel's official conclusion that Gray was fit to stand trial. Puzzled and frustrated by the lack of interest in their opinion, the psychiatrists went back to their consulting rooms.

Both defendants took advantage of the Easter holiday weekend to release statements. Gray's, his first extended communication of any kind to the press, was issued through his family and revealed him to be in a philosophical mood: "I want to warn all men against bad liquor and evil women. If I had not taken to drink I would never have met the woman who has placed me in the position I am now in. Bad liquor and evil women make a combination too strong for any man."

Mrs. Snyder was more expansive, delivering to reporters a six-hundred-word statement written in flowing Palmer-method longhand and entitled "To the Public." After a set-piece affirmation of her innocence, she attacked Gray:

> I know Judd Gray as well as any woman knows a man. I know him better now than I ever did before. I know that he is a coward, a low, cringing, sneaking jackal, the murderer of my husband, who is now trying to hide behind my skirts to try to drag me down into the stinking pit that he himself willingly wallowed in; to brand me as a woman who killed her husband.
>
> I am a mother! I love my child and I loved my child's father. God! Can you mothers and wives read this and appreciate the terrible, stifling ordeal I am going through at this time? Easter Sunday. Holy Week!
>
> I wish I was home with Albert and Lorraine. Oh, what a tragic difference a few months make.
>
> I feel sorry for Mrs. Gray. She is a wife and her lot must be hard to know that her husband could be sent to the depths that he has, that he is a coward so low and rotten that he seeks to drag himself to safety over the body of a woman he has wronged.
>
> I defy Gray to disprove his relations with scores of women. His conscience must be of iron if he has any conscience at all. The women in his life! And he reads the Bible! What a fantastic lie!

On Saturday, Mrs. Snyder was serenaded under her jail window by a ukelele orchestra from the Metropolitan Printing Company in Long Island City. "I wish I had a dance floor and a good partner," she commented to a matron. She employed a burnt matchstick to give herself a manicure. On Sunday, Hazelton and Wallace had the privilege of going over the case with her in the courtroom so she could become accustomed to the surroundings. When Assistant District Attorney Daly dropped in to show his wife and children the setting for the drama, Mrs. Snyder gave him a friendly wave.

11

THE SETTING FOR THE TRIAL was appropriately spectacular. As *New York Times* architecture critic Christopher Gray wrote decades later, "It is easy to call the Queens County Courthouse grand, but much harder to call it good."

The original courthouse, a two-story French Second Empire-style edifice with an imposing attic story crowned by a mansard roof, was completed in 1874. A fire gutted the building in 1904, and the county court was forced to adjourn sine die to Flushing Town Hall. In 1906, architect Peter Coco submitted his design for the new courthouse to the Municipal Art Commission. The surviving original walls were to be retained, but the mansard roof was to be replaced with two extra stories and the attic story to be capped with a magnificent pergola or domed pavilion. All surviving external detail was to be stripped and replaced by a rococo pastiche, which the Arts Commission rejected. Queens Borough President Joseph Bermel, who had fixed it with New York Mayor George McLellan for the courthouse plans to go through without being reviewed for architectural merit, was outraged at the Art Commission's action. Coco toned down his design somewhat, and the new structure, described as "Neo-English Renaissance," for lack of a better term, was completed in the spring of 1909.[1]

The trial would be held in the main courtroom on the third floor, of-

---

1. The following year, Coco was convicted in his own courthouse of financial irregularities during the course of construction; he went to prison in 1912. Bermel was no longer in the picture; the first snow had not fallen on the courthouse roof before financial scandal forced him to resign from office.

ficial home of Part One of the New York State Supreme Court, Criminal Term. This was, and still is, one of the most breathtaking courtrooms in the country. Trial scenes from the 1922 movie *Manslaughter,* directed by Cecil B. DeMille, had been filmed there. Its most striking feature, rising from the center of its forty-foot ceiling and corresponding to Coco's pergola, was a magnificent stained-glass skylight, one of the largest in the world, depicting the scales of justice balanced on a flaming torch. The skylight's predominant greens and oranges, combined with the courtroom's cream yellow marble wall facings, gave rise to rich, almost lurid, lighting effects.

The room could accommodate 250 spectators in comfort, 500 under the sardine-can conditions that were expected. In the end, more than 2,000 jammed themselves into the chamber. The bad acoustics gave rise to so many complaints that, with the approval of the court, a Long Island broadcasting company placed two loudspeakers in the rear corners of the courtroom. The judge's bench, the witness chair on a raised dais to the judge's left, and the defense and prosecution tables were equipped with microphones wired into the sound system. This was the first use of audio equipment in New York legal history.

The court clerk sat, as customary, in something looking like a bank teller's cage just in front of the bench. Apart from this, the configuration of the courtroom was unusual. Not one, but two jury boxes flanked the bench. The jury was seated in the box to the judge's left next to the witness chair. The other jury box was reserved for courtroom artists, "trained seals"—literati, evangelists, philosophers, and other notables retained as feature writers by newspapers—and invited guests, most eminent members of the bar.[2] The prosecution occupied a table facing the main jury box and thus perpendicular to the bench; the defendants and their counsel occupied a table at a right angle to this, facing the bench. A few chairs were set up in front of the spare jury box so that the defendants' families could be spared the indignity of sitting with the public.

---

2. At one point, a visiting British judge even availed himself of the courtesy prevailing between judges to sit next to Justice Scudder, where he took copious notes for no apparent reason—force of habit, perhaps.

Conditions were so cramped that someone discovered that no chairs had been reserved for the defendants, an omission immediately corrected.

The defense table had been moved close to the bench, leaving enough space in the front of the courtroom to array sixteen long narrow tables in four banks of four rows apiece. These were to accommodate the accredited reporters—more than one hundred of them. On the back of each folding chair was the number of its assigned occupant.

A truckload of communications equipment was driven up and unloaded over the weekend. Western Union and the Postal Telegraph Company installed four telephones, ten telegraph lines and a wireservice teletype machine in a conference room down the hall from the courtroom. In the courthouse basement, another twenty-four direct telegraph lines went out to newspapers in eighteen cities. At the peak of the trial, one hundred thousand words per day were wired. This is a puny count when compared to the 1 million words per day transmitted during the Hall-Mills trial, but a comparison would be unfair—the Hall-Mills trial was held in the wilds of New Jersey, so all but the largest newspapers relied on wire-service copy rather than sending their own reporters. Some old hands among the press reminisced about the Guldensuppe-Nack murder trial held in the original Queens County Courthouse in 1898.[3] To submit copy for that trial, resourceful reporters had employed carrier pigeons; the birds made the trip to Park Row in eight minutes.

On Monday morning, spectators began lining up outside the courthouse at six o'clock. Their hopes were in vain: on the opening day of the

3. In 1897, barber Martin Torczewski (alias Martin Thorn) and Giuseppe "Bath House Willie" Guldensuppe, a masseur, boarded with Mrs. Augusta Nack, a midwife, in Manhattan. Mrs. Nack was sexually involved with both men. She and Thorn determined to murder Guldensuppe, which they accomplished by luring him to Woodside, Queens, where Mrs. Nack had rented a cottage. Thorn shot him and, after dismembering the body in a bathtub, disposed of it in several parcels scattered across the city. When body parts began to turn up, the crime unraveled. Mrs. Nack testified against Thorn, receiving a light sentence in return, and Thorn was executed at Sing Sing. The case is perhaps best known for an anecdote in which police, hoping to shock a confession out of Mrs. Nack, confronted her with a pair of severed legs and asked her if they were Guldensuppe's. "I wouldn't know," she demurred. "I never saw Willie's legs."

trial, every square inch would be used to accommodate the jury panel, consisting of two hundred prospective jurors. As the panel was whittled down, the public would be accommodated gradually, but the opening-day ban was absolute. Policemen surrounded the courthouse to keep hopeful spectators at bay. The crowd watched enviously as those with passes were admitted and cheered when they caught a glimpse of lawyers. Inside the courtroom, reporters jostled each other for elbow room, and uniformed newspaper messenger boys scurried around delivering copy to the telegraph and teletype operators.

At ten o'clock, the court clerk shouted, "All rise, please!" and called the court to order. The defendants were brought in from a door to the right of the bench.[4] Gray came first, looking dazed and befuddled, a beaten man. Mrs. Snyder, escorted by Mrs. Irene Wolfe, the imposing matron who was to accompany her throughout the trial, walked with a lively step. A piece of white tape split the defense table in half and two placards identified territory: "S" to the left away from the jury, "G" to the right and next to it. Gray, as if to ensure that he would not have to look at Mrs. Snyder, moved his mahogany armchair to the end of the table, crossed his left leg over his right, folded his hands in his lap, and gazed straight ahead at the jury box like a zombie. Mrs. Snyder settled into a chair at the far end of the table and stared daggers at his back.

Oceans of ink were spilled in homage to Mrs. Snyder's beauty. In fact, claiming to be thirty-two but actually thirty-six, Mrs. Snyder looked that and more when she entered the courtroom. Strain had hardened her face and given her eyes a haunted, empty cast; ten years of light housework and heavy dinners had made her rather dumpy. Sophie Treadwell described Mrs. Snyder as "fattish," something Damon Runyon was forced to admit: "Ruth is no sylph, really. She hoists up to one-fifty, but has it nicely distributed." As though trying to talk himself into it, he continued, "She is not bad looking. I have seen much worse. She is thirty-three and looks just about that, though you cannot tell much about blondes. She has a

---

4. The prisoners were led across the "Bridge of Sighs" from the jail to the second floor of the courthouse, where they were carried up in a back elevator to holding pens just off the courtroom.

good figure, slim and trim, with narrow shoulders. She is of medium height and I thought she carried her clothes off rather smartly."

Mrs. Snyder, unconvinced by the ballyhoo, referred to herself as "homely" and wondered why, if she was so alluring, no man ever fell for her before Gray.

In a procedure repeated ad nauseam in coming days, the first set of twelve potential jurors was ushered into the jury box and the indictment against the defendants was read. All members of the panel, in accordance with New York State law at the time, were male. The State began the questioning.

Did any of the prospective jurors have conscientious objections to the death penalty for first-degree murder? Five raised their hands and were immediately excused.

District Attorney Newcombe then zeroed in on prospective juror number 5, a railroad inspector. Would the fact that one defendant was a woman cause him to hesitate in reaching a verdict? he asked. Not at all, was the reply.

Were any of the prospective jurors acquainted with anyone involved in the case? Number 8 had a slight acquaintance with Newcombe, but stated that this would not affect his opinion. Hazelton moved that all panel members who knew counsel be excused by consent and no one disagreed. Number 8 departed the jury box.

Newcombe pronounced himself satisfied with the remaining prospective jurors and Hazelton rose for Mrs. Snyder. According to the rules, her attorneys had to question the panel before Gray's because she was the first defendant listed in the indictment. Under this arrangement, Gray's team would have to use their precious peremptory challenges only if Mrs. Snyder's counsel failed to challenge first. Hazelton pointed this out forcefully to Scudder, but the judge saw no reason to alter the accepted procedure. He had, in fact, already been generous. He could have assigned the State thirty peremptory challenges and the defendants fifteen apiece. Instead, Scudder gave each defendant thirty and the State sixty, reasoning that it was better to err on the side of caution in a capital case.

Hazelton began his questioning with prospective juror number 5.

Had he read that this was a "burning" jury? Halelton asked. No, the juror answered. Had he heard that the defendant Snyder was pregnant? No. Had he read that a short period before her husband's death, Mrs. Snyder had increased his life insurance? Number 5 acknowledged that he had, but said it would not affect his opinion. Did he understand that a defendant must not be convicted on the uncorroborated evidence of an accomplice? Yes. If the defendant Snyder chose not to take the stand in her own defense, would he hold this against her? No. Did he understand what duress meant, and that a confession obtained under duress cannot be held against a defendant? Yes.

Hazelton sat down, and Millard rose to examine for Gray. Had any of the prospective jurors already formed an opinion regarding the guilt or innocence of the defendant Gray? he asked. Numbers 2, 3, and 11 said they had. Would that prevent them from giving a fair verdict? Yes, affirmed the trio. Millard moved that they be excused for cause, and with Scudder's assent, the three left the jury box. Number 1 was peremptorily challenged by Hazelton, leaving only numbers 5 and 6 in the box.

Hazelton took up the questioning again. Was prospective juror number 5 an open-minded man? Yes, number 5 replied. If he had formed any earlier impressions of the case, could he put them entirely aside? Number 5, confused by the question, was excused for cause.

Had number 6 formed any opinion at all on the case? Hazelton asked the remaining prospective juror. Yes, but only one, and he would be able to put it aside. Well, would it require evidence to cause him to change this opinion? Yes, it would require evidence. Excused for cause.

It had taken just over one and a quarter hours to work through the first batch of twelve prospective jurors.

The monotony of the proceedings quickly began to take a toll on Mrs. Snyder. At noon, the lunch whistle at a nearby factory sounded and she asked, "When do we eat?"

Gray also found the procedure boring. During the lunch break, in one of his rare public statements, he commented, "It is a tedious matter, sitting here hour after hour in the courtroom in one position. I wish I did not have to appear in court today because I did not sleep well last night."

The reference to poor sleep sent reporters scurrying for more information. A prisoner in the cell tier just below Gray's had attempted to commit suicide by hanging, but the homemade rope broke and he tumbled down onto the floor of his cell, breaking his leg. His screams of pain brought the guards, who administered emergency medical attention and removed the injured man to a cell adjacent to Gray's, where his moans kept Gray awake.

On Tuesday morning, Justice Scudder opened the proceedings with a pep talk to the prospective jurors.

"It has ever been the pride and boast of old Queens County that there was no necessity for calling a special or 'blue ribbon' jury list. From the rank and file of our citizens it has always been possible to select a fair and impartial jury. Now, let us see to it that this boast continues justified." [5]

He then returned to the point Hazelton had made the day before, that Gray was benefiting unfairly from the Snyder team's peremptory challenges. Counsel for Mrs. Snyder had already used five of their allotted thirty challenges; Gray's team had used only one. Scudder had undergone a change of heart. Gray was now to lead until the two teams were equal and, from that point on, the two defense teams would alternate in leading off the questioning of successive panels. Hazelton beamed, and even Miller and Millard had to admit the fairness of the arrangement.

The pace was slow. The first time Gray's team peremptorily challenged a juror acceptable to Mrs. Snyder, Hazelton turned theatrically to the bench. "Through this joint trial," he intoned, "where the issues are not joined, the defendant, Mrs. Snyder, is being deprived of her right to a trial by a jury of her peers." Hazelton took the opportunity to even the score with Gray's attorneys the next time a juror acceptable to the latter was found. During the morning session, of the seventy-four prospective jurors examined, only one was selected.

The one who satisfied all three batteries of lawyers was William

---

5. The casting of trial participants in stock roles was particularly shameless in the case of Justice Scudder, whom the press portrayed as a kindly but stern grandfather figure. For all the New York press knew, he chewed tobacco and beat his dogs. The accent in which the judge spoke was described by the *Daily News* as "Oxonian," and by the *Daily Mirror* as "Harvard." Scudder never saw the inside of either university.

Young of Elmhurst, publicity manager and press agent for the Empire Hotel on Upper Broadway. A fat man in his early thirties, he was installed, smiling and obviously pleased with himself, in a comfortable chair in the back of the courtroom. As the only juror selected for a full day, he drew the attention of at least fifty photographers when he was escorted to or from the courthouse by the two sturdy deputy sheriffs who ate lunch and dinner with him.

Young was the only catch on Tuesday. On Wednesday, the first panel included Charles Meissner, a gardener who was married and the father of three children. Worries about his business and personal affairs might prevent him from devoting his full attention to the case, he complained. This was his busiest time of the year. Admonished by Scudder regarding his civic duties, Meissner allowed that he could overcome his personal concerns. The prosecution was satisfied. After each had grilled Meissner, attorneys for the defendants glanced warily at each other to see if either side would challenge. Gray whispered a word in Samuel Miller's ear, Miller nodded, and the trial had its second juror. Meissner walked to the back of the courtroom and joined Young, who was sitting with his chair tilted back against the wall.

Starched collars wilted and tempers rose as the mercury hit an unseasonable 86°. Scudder threatened to work through the evening until the jury was completed. But the pace did not pick up; panel after panel was dismissed without yielding a juror. Scudder became sharper in his questioning of prospective jurors. When one claimed he was "tenderhearted," Scudder responded, "Do you realize that, if all citizens were like you, there could be no juries and no courts?"

A: "Yes."

Q: "You lack the stamina to keep the State going?"

A: "Yes."

Q: "This tenderheartedness is something inherent in you which makes it impossible for you to be an impartial juror?"

A: "Yes."

Q: "You are hopeful that there will be some more hard-hearted men than yourself?"

A: "Yes."

The offending party, released from his misery, scuttled out of the courtroom.

Then Scudder had an inspiration: he announced to prospective jurors that anyone excused on the grounds of opposition to capital punishment would be called again for jury duty in a noncapital case in May. He also became more pointed in examining those who had formed opinions from the press.

Q: "Do you mean to say that your mentality is such that sworn evidence cannot remove the impression created by reading one-sided stories in the press?"

A: "Yes."

Q: "Does this not indicate a deficit in intelligence?"

A: "Yes."

Excused for cause.

Q: "Is there any reason why you cannot serve?"

A: "I cannot eat restaurant food on account of dyspepsia."

Excused for cause.

Granny Brown was not in court, but Gray's mother and sister attended from the beginning. Mrs. Gray was one of the most animated of those present, greeting acquaintances from the press rows with a smile and wave. Gray never once looked back over his shoulder at her. Mrs. Snyder, on the other hand, turned and examined the features of her former lover's relations with curiosity. They returned her gaze with visible contempt. Sitting in the back of the courtroom were Warren Schneider and two of Albert Snyder's sisters. All of the dead man's siblings attended at one time or another.

Just before the close of proceedings on Wednesday, the lawyers selected the third and fourth jurors: Harry Arnold, an unemployed plumber from Far Rockaway, and Alfred Kraemer, a clerk from College Point, Long Island. Scudder was becoming even more stubborn about granting challenges for cause and the two defense teams were beginning to conserve their peremptory challenges: the Snyder forces retained seventeen of its original thirty and Gray's attorneys had twenty. The State had twenty-three challenges left.

On Thursday, it finally began to look as though a jury could be picked within the week. The day got off to an auspicious start when the first panel yielded Herman Ballweg, who had been a Borough Hall saloonkeeper until Prohibition sent him into the construction business. The subsequent panels were unfruitful until late afternoon, when two additional jurors were selected within an hour of each other: John Schneider (no relation to Albert Snyder), a florist from Astoria, and John Connolly, a driver for Macy's department store from Long Island City.

On Friday, Scudder took over preliminary questioning himself and weeded out obviously unsuitable candidates twice as fast as the attorneys for the State and defense. Out of every panel of twelve, five to seven were immediately excused for opposition to capital punishment and warned that they would soon be recalled for a noncapital case. The first success of the day was Louis Ruckdaschel, an employment manager from College Point; then, at one o'clock, Everett van Vranken, an executive secretary from Woodhaven, was selected. In the late afternoon, two additional jurors were found acceptable: George Ziegler, a printer from Flushing, and John Vanderheide, a clerk from Maspeth, Long Island.

Appearing in court for the first time, Granny Brown sat two feet away from Mrs. Gray, but the two women did not even exchange looks of recognition. Just after the midday recess, during which Mrs. Snyder read aloud to reporters from supporting letters she had received, the sound of an Italian street band playing "Nearer My God to Thee" as they marched in a funeral was heard in the courtroom. Mrs. Snyder dropped her head. Gray sat stoically until the band had passed.

A cheer went up at six o'clock when the twelfth juror, Frederick Grob of Richmond Hill, a piano maker, was selected, but the public display was immediately suppressed by Scudder, who announced that he was exercising his prerogative to excuse Harry Arnold. Although he added that this decision in no way reflected upon Mr. Arnold, there were immediate mutterings about attempted jury fixing. Scudder then explained: Arnold had been a neighbor of Albert Schneider's brother George in Far Rockaway.

In reality, the mutterings were not far from the truth. The story (as told in Detective Lieutenant McDermott's notebook) offers a glimpse into Dana Wallace's approach to legal practice.

At nine o'clock Friday morning, Court Clerk Joe Hardy pulled Mc-
Dermott aside during the morning lineup. "That's a fine bum Harry
Arnold you got on the Snyder–Gray jury," Hardy said. "He goes running
around with some married blonde in a Buick touring car; he never
works, his brother, Christie, don't work either, and their mother has to
go out and do housework to give them money." Hardy did not know the
blonde woman's name, but his wife might.

This was enough to arouse McDermott's suspicions, and he put off
other business to do some background work on Harry Arnold. He and
his partner Martin Brown tracked down Mrs. Hardy at the house of a
friend, but she could add no information. They then went to the home
of one Patrolman Shylock, whose beat included Arnold's neighborhood.
Yes, Arnold hung out with some married blonde. Even more intriguing,
Shylock recounted a street-corner conversation he had overheard a few
nights before. Tommy "Dusty" McKenna, one of Wallace's courthouse
errand runners, was boasting, "We almost had him on the jury," referring
to an unnamed resident of Rockaway.

McDermott and Brown drove past Arnold's house but were unable to
stop because they were observed by a number of men milling around a
United Cigar Store just opposite. They proceeded to the Fifty-second
Precinct Station House, where they asked about Arnold. "Harry Arnold
on a jury? Get him off," replied a detective. "He hangs out with Dusty
McKenna at the track and shooting dice." Arnold, it developed, had been
arrested a number of times under other names at dice games.

McDermott and Brown telephoned Deputy Inspector Gallagher and
relayed their findings; Gallagher, in turn, arranged for a note to be passed
up to Scudder on the bench. At four fifteen, Scudder declared a brief recess and met in his chambers with Gallagher, McDermott, and Brown,
who set their findings before him. He dismissed the policemen and called
in counsel. Although no evidence suggested that Wallace had acted im-
properly, there was no way the gambling partner of his flunky McKenna
was going to sit in judgment on Mrs. Snyder. Court reconvened and,
after the twelfth juror had been selected, Scudder excused Arnold and
instructed counsel to continue examining prospective jurors.

Shortly after seven o'clock, the final juror was selected: Phillip Mc-

Cabe, an electrical instructor in an Elmhurst trade school. The chosen twelve trooped into the jury box and were sworn by the court clerk. Three hundred and ninety panel members had been examined to find twelve good men and true. The resulting jury was as representative of the men of Queens County as could be expected. Its members ranged from twenty-nine to sixty-three; most were in their mid-thirties. Ten were married, two were widowers, and eleven had children, although Newcombe had managed to weed out prospective jurors with daughters close in age to Lorraine Snyder and Jane Gray. They were split evenly between white—and blue-collar occupations; none occupied a position of distinction (Kraemer was judged to be the best heeled) and they were, almost without exception, fat. All were clean-shaven save Ballweg. There were seven Germans, three Irishmen, and two Dutchmen.

The jurors were to be sequestered in the Kew Gardens Inn during the trial, but before adjourning court, Scudder allowed them to spend the weekend at home provided they did not discuss the case. With a sigh of relief that jury selection had been completed within the week, all legal parties went home.

12

Day 1, Monday, 25 April

THE SNYDER-GRAY TRIAL was the event of the New York spring social season. The courtroom was packed with celebrities who had managed to obtain the coveted entrance pass that exempted them from waiting in line. David Wark Griffith, the Hollywood filmmaker, descended from his limousine outside the courthouse and declared that he was considering a film about the case. David Belasco, the dean of American theater, who affected clerical garb in his role as the self-appointed "Bishop of Broadway," scribbled notes and declared that, far from being the stoic she appeared, Ruth Snyder was a woman exploding with passion. "I thought it a matter of public duty to attend," he declared. "I think it will prove to be one of the most dramatic trials in history." Also representing Broadway were innumerable lesser lights; sitting together, they became known to trial regulars as "The Actor's Equity Section."

Maurine Watkins, whose hit musical *Chicago* had a plot with distinct similarities to the Snyder-Gray case, came as feature writer for the *Telegram* and was accompanied by Francine Larrimore, the female lead.[1]

---

1. The *Telegram's* intellectual pretensions also led it to retain Will Durant, whose recently published *The Story of Philosophy* was said, fantastically, to be one of Mrs. Snyder's favorite books. It was stated in the *New Yorker,* 8 October 1927, p. 96, that Durant was "the worst reporter that the Snyder-Gray trial ever had (and that's no faint praise)." Damon Runyon wondered how a philosopher could be concerned about blondes and still be a philosopher. According to Emil Gauvreau's "Thou Shalt Not Kill," the *Graphic* responded to the *Telegram's* pompous enlistment of Durant by publishing the impressions

Also retained as feature writers were playwrights Samuel Shipman and Willard Mack, novelist William Woodward and short-story writer Fanny Hurst. Olga Petrova and Natasha Rambova, ex-wives of the recently deceased Rudolph Valentino and both screen stars in their own right, wrote up their impressions of the case. The four-times married and divorced playwright Peggy Hopkins Joyce was hired by the *Daily News* to do a feature series, which opened with the definitive declaration "Judd Gray hasn't got 'It.' "[2] There were plenty of vaudevillians like Nora Bayes, who made friends with Mrs. Margaret Gray, and the magician Thurston, who was asked by reporters to conjure up a few more press seats. Mae West, just released from ten days in the workhouse for staging her farce *Sex* on Broadway, covered the case for the *National Police Gazette*.[3]

Among the clergy in attendance was the city's most powerful hellfire and damnation preacher, Reverend John Roach Stratton, pastor of Calvary Baptist Church near Carnegie Hall, who wrote for the *Evening Journal*.[4] The great Billy Sunday himself, who gave New York its nickname when he thundered, "If America is the Garden of Eden, then New York

---

of its own philosopher—the "Great Schnozola" himself, vaudevillian Jimmy Durante. Durante was an intimate of *Graphic* writer (later television impresario) Ed Sullivan and others on the staff, so the story has a ring of truth.

2. Joyce obviously rubbed Damon Runyon the wrong way because he went out of his way to insult her in print at every opportunity. She was "Joyce, the famous grass-widow"; her dress was "distressing green"; her vehicle was "a little-old last year's Rolls-Royce." He wrote, "You can bet Peggy never had any trouble getting rid of her husbands, but at least she didn't kill 'em."

3. Like the *Graphic,* the *National Police Gazette* exists only in incomplete form, and the years 1927–1928 appear to be lost.

4. Stratton, one of the most important religious opinion leaders in the nation, had been an adviser to the prosecution in the Scopes Monkey Trial and was an implacable political enemy of New York governor Alfred Smith. His involvement in the Snyder-Gray case raised controversy in religious circles, which Stratton dismissed in a passage with a contemporary tone: "I have consented to [review the Snyder case] because I feel the time is ripe when all patriotic citizens should do all in their power to unveil the hidden dangers growing out of political, educational, and religious modernism and resulting in the appalling wave of vice and crime which is now menacing the very foundations of our republic."

is a big, rotten apple," put in an appearance. Evangelist Aimée Semple McPherson, covering the trial for the *Evening Graphic,* inveighed against "Sex Love" and exhorted young men to set their sights on "a girl like Mother . . . not a red-hot cutie."

Nobility was represented by the Marquess and Marchioness of Queensberry, who attended, they claimed, to learn about American justice. On the first day, coached by Tin Pan Alley songwriter Irving Berlin, the royal pair threw themselves into the difficult task of eating an overstuffed New York delicatessen sandwich from an illicit lunch box perched on the knees. Like all others who smuggled in food, they were immediately befriended by the courthouse cat, who showed up every day around lunch hour. According to the marquess, punters at the Racquet Club were giving five-to-one odds against Mrs. Snyder's being convicted on the capital charge.

Off-duty cops had privileged access and were among the more boisterous spectators, especially after lunch, when many were drunk. Women in the crowd were evenly divided between Queens housewives and their better-dressed Manhattan counterparts. Despite the warmth of the season, many ladies insisted on wearing their fur coats; a number brought opera glasses.

Outside, those unable to gain access to the courthouse lined the sidewalks hoping for a glimpse of celebrities as they made their entrances and exits. Patients and staff at Saint John's Hospital, glued to the windows, had grandstand seats for the show. Dozens of baby carriages made the sidewalk congestion even worse and automobile traffic was snarled as the crush of humanity spilled out into the street. Long Island City merchants complained that business was ruined by the crowd; merchants elsewhere in Queens blamed a rash of daylight robberies on the fact that police had been assigned to courthouse duty.

A man showed up with a cartload of wood and began constructing a food stand on the sidewalk in front of the courthouse; interrupted by police, he proudly flourished a permit giving him exclusive rights to the Snyder-Gray hotdog and soda pop concession, for which he had paid one hundred dollars. It took the police an hour to convince the crestfallen entrepreneur that he had been duped and would have to move elsewhere.

Every wire service and major American newspaper was represented, as was the *Times* of London. A correspondent from the weekly newspaper in Mrs. Snyder's father's hometown in Norway attended to keep relatives and acquaintances in the old country informed. Mrs. Snyder's paternal grandparents were solid, comfortably middle-class people, the correspondent said. It was inconceivable, descended from such stock, that Mrs. Snyder could have done this thing.

When court opened just after eleven o'clock, Mrs. Snyder entered erect and defiant, her gaze held high over the crowd. Gray seemed to wobble and stumble as he was led in. Those who had been notified that they were potential witnesses were directed to remove themselves to the men's and ladies' lounges next door, and Scudder indicated to the State to begin.

District Attorney Newcombe's opening address—as befitting a prosecutor holding all the trumps—was moderate and to the point. Newcombe sketched the situations of Mrs. Snyder and Gray before the murder, stating that Albert Snyder, "a bit of the old-fashioned type," was an encumbrance to the pair. In fall 1925, Albert Snyder did express interest in taking out a $1,000 life insurance policy, but the State would prove that he was unaware that two policies totaling $50,000, one for $45,000 and another for $5,000, had been taken out on his life. Both policies named Mrs. Snyder as beneficiary; the larger one was a double-indemnity policy paying twice the face value in case of death by misadventure.

The State would prove that the slaying was the result of "constant and repeated planning" on the part of the defendants. The murder was first scheduled for Monday, 7 March, and accordingly on Friday, 4 March, in Kingston, Gray bought a sash weight and a bottle of chloroform. On Saturday, 5 March, he ate lunch with Mrs. Snyder and Lorraine at Henry's Restaurant and gave the sash weight to Mrs. Snyder, who took it back to "that lovely little home"—Newcombe used the phrase repeatedly—in Queens Village. On the night of Monday, 7 March, Gray went to Queens Village as planned, but something went wrong.

"Whether it was an act of Providence or what that left the poor devil, Albert Snyder, to live a couple of more weeks I don't know, but the crime was not consummated that night."

The murder was rescheduled for Saturday night, 19 March. Mrs. Snyder told Gray that her mother would be away all night on a nursing job and that the Snyders would be out late at a party. Newcombe described Gray's preparation of an alibi in Syracuse, his journey from Syracuse to Grand Central Station and from there to Queens Village, his entering by the kitchen door that Mrs. Snyder had left open, and his waiting in Granny Brown's room with the bottle of whiskey that Mrs. Snyder had provided.

Newcombe then switched to Mrs. Snyder. At the Fidgeon party, she complained that she was not herself and asked that her drinks be given to Albert Snyder. Newcombe described the Snyders returning from the party, Mrs. Snyder putting Lorraine to bed, undressing and going to bed herself, waiting for her husband to fall asleep, and sneaking out to Gray. Avoiding details, Newcombe painted the murder itself with the broadest of strokes: they stole into the room, stunned Snyder with the sash weight, tied his hands and feet, chloroformed him, and throttled him with picture wire.

The crime had been committed at three o'clock, but Gray and Mrs. Snyder were occupied until six o'clock in "planning and conceiving and scheming and God knows what else—I don't want to know."

Commenting on the discovery and investigation of the crime, Newcombe remarked, "The appearance of robbery was so far-fetched and far-drawn that it did not look like a robbery." Mrs. Snyder persisted in her story for some time, but then told the truth in a confession that the State would introduce into evidence. Gray, apprehended in Syracuse based on information provided by Mrs. Snyder, likewise claimed innocence for some time, but eventually confessed. Based on the confessions and other evidence, the State would ask for verdicts of guilty of first-degree murder.

Newcombe had taken only thirty minutes to introduce the State's case. Attorneys for both defendants exercised their right to defer opening addresses until after the State had presented its evidence.

The first witness, Warren Schneider, was called and testified to identifying his younger brother's body at the morgue. Called next were Dr.
Howard Neail of the Medical Examiner's Office and Dr. Alexander Gettler, the New York City toxicologist. Neail read his autopsy report into
the record. He had found that the immediate cause of death was strangulation with the picture wire. However, under Newcombe's prompting,
he testified that stunning Snyder with the sash weight, administering
chloroform, and burying his face in the pillow while he was bound hand
and foot would have been sufficient to eventually cause his death.

Wallace cross-examined for Mrs. Snyder. Were the blows to Albert
Snyder's head sufficient to cause death? No, replied Neail. How about
the strangulation? Yes.

This held out a glimmer of hope for Mrs. Snyder if it could be proven
that she sought to prevent Gray from further actions after the blows were
struck.

Miller cross-examined for Gray.

Did not the abrasions on Snyder's neck indicate that there was a struggle? he asked Neail. Not necessarily, was the doctor's answer.

Gray's claim that a struggle had taken place was central to his version
of events, and this was not a good beginning for his defense. Miller, visibly flustered by the answer, tried several times to rephrase the question.
At each turn, he was blocked by Hazelton, who objected that Neail was
qualified to testify to the condition of the corpus delicti and the cause of
death, not to judge whether there had been a struggle. A simple rephras-
ing would have allowed Miller to elicit that the forensic evidence was
consistent with a struggle, but the inexperienced attorney was out of his
depth. Gray was paying a price for having hired a family practitioner to
undertake a criminal defense.

Gettler testified that he had established the presence of 44.8 mil-
ligrams of chloroform per kilogram of brain tissue and a 0.3 percent
blood alcohol concentration (BAC), the latter consistent with acute intoxication. No other poisons were present in the blood, brain, or stomach. Laboratory tests indicated the presence of blood on the sash weight,
but in quantities insufficient to establish whether it was human.

Joseph Farrell, office manager of the Waldorf, was called, and the crowd murmured in expectation of the titillation to follow. "Why, there's the man from the Waldorf!" Mrs. Snyder remarked to Wallace, as though she had just spotted an acquaintance at a cocktail party. Farrell testified that he was acquainted with Gray and knew him to frequently register with Mrs. Snyder, whom he knew as Mrs. Gray. They usually stayed in Room 872. Farrell was asked to examine several pages of the Waldorf register on which, either in Gray's handwriting or in Mrs. Snyder's handwriting, the couple was registered as "Mr. and Mrs. H. J. Gray." After the noon recess, Farrell returned to the stand and identified over fifty registration slips.

Waldorf bellboy Raymond Bruen testified that detectives brought Mrs. Snyder to the hotel in the early morning hours of Monday, 21 March, and that she identified a red leather suitcase in the checkroom. Police Lieutenant James Smith took the stand and identified the "honeymoon bag" as it was placed into evidence over the objection of Gray's attorneys, who argued that it was not binding upon their client because no conspiracy had been established. Justice Scudder pointed out to the jury that the bag was to be considered only as evidence against the defendant Snyder. As spectators sat on the edge of their seats and strained their ears, Lieutenant Smith enumerated the bag's contents. The bag was taken to the jury box, and the jurors poked through it for a few moments.

Leroy Ashfield of the Jamaica Branch of the Prudential Life Insurance Company took the stand. Not surprisingly, Ashfield was no longer employed by the Prudential or any other insurance company. Ashfield testified that he agreed to the proposal made by Mrs. Snyder when he called on her during the first week of November 1925. Regarding the dubious proceedings that ensued on the night of 14 November, Ashfield insisted that he had not intended to deceive Albert Snyder. He had no reason to believe, when Mrs. Snyder called at his office the next day, that Mr. Snyder was unaware of the insurance to be taken out.

Ashfield testified that Mrs. Snyder personally paid all premiums either in cash or by check made out by her on the account she jointly held with Albert Snyder. She fell into arrears. The one-month grace period for overdue payment would have expired on 14 March 1927. Shortly before the 13th, Ashfield received a letter from Mrs. Snyder containing a signed blank check made out to the Prudential. In the letter, which he had discarded, Ashfield was asked to calculate the premiums due and to fill in the required amount. This he did, in the amount of two hundred sixty-one dollars. The canceled check was produced in court, identified by the witness, and placed in evidence.

Day 2, Tuesday, 26 April

Newcombe, who skipped back and forth so as to confound as much as possible in jurors' minds the cases against the two accused, began the morning with the manner in which Gray's confession had been obtained. Detective Lieutenant Charles Dorschel established that Gray signed a statement in District Attorney Newcombe's office at three o'clock on the morning of Tuesday, 22 March. He identified a map drawn by Gray to indicate the location of the hardware store in Kingston where he purchased the sash weight. Millard objected to admission of the sketch into evidence until after he had questioned the witness to ascertain if duress had been used to obtain it. Newcombe obligingly turned the witness over to Millard.

Was Gray represented by counsel when he drew the map, or had he asked to be represented? Millard asked. Dorschel didn't know. Had Gray been tired or sleepy? Dorschel had no way of knowing.

Millard asked Scudder if he might call further witnesses to inquire into the circumstances under which the sketch was obtained. The real question, of course, was whether Gray's statement was admissible, but whichever way Scudder ruled on the map would also be the way he would rule on the confession. With Scudder's agreement, Detective Lieutenant Michael McDermott was called and related meeting Gray in Syracuse and informing him that he was to be taken to New York in connection with the death of Albert Snyder in Queens Village.

Q: "Did Gray seem to realize the seriousness of his position?"

A: "No, until the train reached Poughkeepsie, he behaved as though the whole thing was a joke."

Q: "Do you think that Gray was motivated by fear when he finally admitted having been in the Snyder residence?"

A: "No."

Q: "Had Gray been warned that whatever he said might be used against him?"

A: "Not in my hearing."

Q: "Did you prevent Gray from seeing an attorney in Syracuse?"

A: "No, Gray said that he saw no need for a lawyer."

Q: "Did anyone say to Gray something to the effect 'You better come through now or you'll get yours when you get to New York'?"

A: "No."

Q: "How about 'We have plenty of ways of getting it out of you?' "

A: "No."

Q: "How about 'One way would be to beat you up, but we're not going to have to do that'?"

A: "I told him in the presence of Lieutenant Brown that we did not wish to mistreat him, that Lieutenant Brown and I thought that we were educated enough to get him to tell us what he knew about this case."

Q: "Do you know what the 'third degree' is?"

A: "Well, I know what people in the outside life—outside the Police Department—feel that it is."

Q: "You don't know of any such thing, of course, existing?"

A: "No, sir."

Q: "Did Gray appear exhausted when he dictated his statement to the police stenographer in the district attorney's office?"

A: "No, he was still fresh, going strong."

Millard was now ready to make his formal objection to admission of the sketch as evidence. The drawing was not made voluntarily, he argued, but as the result of methods employed by the police and members of the district attorney's office from the time Gray was taken into custody in Syracuse to the time the train reached Poughkeepsie.

It was no use. Justice Scudder ruled that it would be up to the jury to decide whether evidence introduced had been obtained voluntarily and that this and other pieces of evidence were admitted only on the understanding that the jury would determine their value. He cautioned the jury that the sketch, if they held that it was given voluntarily, was evidence only in the case of the defendant Gray.

The Kingston sketch opened the floodgate for testimony highlighting the active role taken by Gray in preparing for the slaying. Mrs. Margaret Hamilton, a buyer for a corset shop in Kingston, was called and affirmed that the sketch correctly identified the location of the Winne Hardware Store, located half a block from her own place of business. She had seen the defendant Gray in the vicinity on Friday, 4 March. Arthur Bailey, a store clerk, testified that he sold a sash weight to Gray on that day. John Stanford, a stock clerk, testified to bringing the sash weight from the stockroom. Gray would deny none of this, and his lawyers did not cross-examine any of these witnesses.

Martin Mulenthal, a portly waiter with a thick German accent, took the witness stand and related how Gray and Mrs. Snyder came together at least once a month to Henry's Restaurant. He remembered that they came, accompanied by a little girl, to luncheon on Saturday, 5 March. They ate the Saturday special, chicken fricassee.

Reginald Rose, a station clerk for the New York Central Railroad Company, testified that on the evening of Saturday, 19 March, Gray arrived at Grand Central Station with a group of passengers from Buffalo and approached him requesting a ticket to Syracuse on the 8:45 train the next morning. He remembered the sale because he had been able to sell Gray a Pullman car ticket only as far as Albany; the Albany-Syracuse leg was a regular fare. He identified the ticket stub that had been found in Gray's wastebasket at the Hotel Onondaga, and it was placed into evidence.

Members of the Fidgeon party had been conspicuous since the beginning of the trial, sitting together outside the courtroom, joking and laughing as they enjoyed their moment of fame. Walter Fidgeon was a jolly little man with a small mustache and a puffy red face that bore witness to many evenings of the sort that preceded Albert Snyder's death. Called to the stand, he testified that Mrs. Snyder refused liquor on the night of Saturday, 19 March, and suggested that the drink offered to her be given to her husband. Dr. Arthur Stanford corroborated the story, adding that Mrs. Snyder had complained of menstrual discomfort.

Newcombe called the State's star witness on the confessions, former Police Commissioner McLaughlin. McLaughlin had resigned from the force shortly after the Snyder murder to become vice president of the Postal Telegraph Company.[5] Even taking into account the excesses of reporters, who described him as "sartorially perfect," "concise," "matter-of-fact," "dignified," and "sure of himself," McLaughlin was a formidable witness. Mrs. Snyder showed signs of nervousness during his testimony, leaning forward intently to listen and twisting her jet beads around her neck.

McLaughlin described being called to the Snyder home, interviewing Mrs. Snyder as she rested in Lorraine's bed, and seeing her later that evening at the station house. He summarized the main points of the statement that Mrs. Snyder had made to him.[6]

Q: "What was Mrs. Snyder's condition when she made her statement?"

A: "Well, she had a handkerchief to her eyes, but she was perfectly normal and composed."

Switching to Gray, Newcombe established the circumstances under which his statement had been taken and the thrust of its contents.

Q: "And what was Gray's condition when he made his statement?"

A: "Why, I thought he had a remarkable memory and told a very coherent story in a good, straightforward manner."

McLaughlin was excused without cross-examination: lawyers for the defense had no desire to tangle with the former police commissioner. In departing, McLaughlin came across Warren Schneider huddled in an armchair in the district attorney's office on the second floor of the courthouse. Schneider, overcome with grief, had rushed from the courtroom on hearing McLaughlin read Mrs. Snyder's description of the slaying

---

5. McLaughlin's resignation after only fifteen months in office had much to do with gambling raids that he had authorized on Democratic political clubs, thus embarrassing Tammany Hall and the police officers who had been paid for protection. The raids once netted six hundred-thousand dollars in a single Friday-night swoop.

6. In effect, Mrs. Snyder confessed twice—once in her oral confession to McLaughlin, which was quite rushed, and again in the written statement that she reviewed and signed later. McLaughlin's testimony was devastating evidence that the written statement was a free and fair representation of what Mrs. Snyder wanted to say. Gray confessed three times, twice orally—on the train from Syracuse and to Newcombe and McLaughlin in New York City—and a third and final time in his signed statement.

from his notes. "I saw Mr. Gray raising what I took to be the sash weight I had given him. I heard a thud. I think I heard my husband groan twice." McLaughlin comforted the bereaved brother for a few moments before going about the business of the Postal Telegraph Company.

Assistant District Attorney Peter Daly was sworn in and described the taking of Mrs. Snyder's statement, including the naps she took from mid-Monday morning to early afternoon and from midafternoon to early evening. Wallace tried to insinuate that text had been inserted into the statement by pointing out that Mrs. Snyder's initials did not appear on two crucial pages. His fishing expedition was in vain, however, as the explanation was simple: in a mix-up, pages from the carbon copy had been inserted into the original document.

At this point, Mrs. Snyder's attorneys played one of their few legal cards. A confession is inadmissible until the basis of the charge has been established. The basis of the charge against Mrs. Snyder was, argued Hazelton, the existence of a conspiracy to murder Albert Snyder. But the State had brought forward no evidence, apart from the confessions themselves, to indicate that such a conspiracy had existed. They had only brought evidence of assignations at the Waldorf and Henry's Restaurant.

This was splitting legal hairs, and Justice Scudder would have none of it. He ruled that the basis of the indictment was the murder of Albert Snyder, not conspiracy.

As it was late morning, Scudder adjourned court after instructing that both defense teams should be provided with copies of Mrs. Snyder's confession. In the afternoon session and repeatedly in the days to come, Mrs. Snyder's legal team elaborated on their objection, but Scudder never wavered from his ruling. Millard then objected to the admission of Mrs. Snyder's confession on the ground that it was not binding upon Gray. This elicited only the inevitable caution to the jury about what was to be taken against whom, and the statement was admitted into evidence. Speaking slowly and without a trace of emotion, Newcombe read Mrs. Snyder's confession into the trial record.

13

Day 3, Wednesday, 27 April

FOR THE FIRST TIME since the start of the trial, police were hard-pressed to keep order. The doors were opened at nine o'clock, and the courtroom was jammed within ten minutes. All conceivable tricks to gain access were brought into play. One enormous woman rushed to the door waving a piece of paper and shouting: "Subpoena! Subpoena!" The subpoena turned out to be a coal bill—and an unpaid one at that. Another woman and her two daughters proudly announced that they were the family of Deputy Inspector Gallagher, a notoriously desirable bachelor about town.

At ten o'clock, the prisoners made their usual entrance—Mrs. Snyder, icy and composed; Gray, wilted and confused.

It was now time for Gray's confession. Assistant District Attorney Conroy identified the statement and testified to being present when it was signed. Samuel Miller, whose colleague Millard had failed to bar the Kingston sketch from evidence, rose and asked the court for permission to pose questions related to the taking of Gray's statement. Permission was granted, but the line of questioning was as fruitless as Millard's grilling of Detective Lieutenant McDermott: Conroy simply denied all insinuations of impropriety. Detective Lieutenant Martin Brown was called and filled in a few more details about the train ride. Attorneys for Gray then objected to admitting the confession on the grounds that it had been made under duress. As expected, Justice Scudder overruled, and District Attorney Newcombe rose and read Gray's statement into the record. Gray slumped in his seat, his fingers fluttering aimlessly over his face.

During the hour devoted to the reading of Gray's confession, Mrs. Snyder acted out a pantomime. She nodded emphatically at the portion recounting Albert Snyder's threats against her life, rolled her eyes in mock amazement when Gray accused her of having made attempts on her husband's life, and shook her head and repeatedly mouthed the words "No! No! No!" when Gray described her actions during the murderous assault on Albert Snyder.

Newcombe, continuing his tactic of shifting from defendant to defendant, turned to the circumstances under which the crime was discovered. He called Mrs. Mulhauser, first on the scene, who testified to Mrs. Snyder's position, attire, and condition on the morning of the murder and who related Mrs. Snyder's claim that she had been struck on the head. Mrs. Mulhauser had run her fingers all through Mrs. Snyder's hair but found no evidence of a wound. She also testified that the ropes that bound Mrs. Snyder's ankles had been extremely loose.

During cross-examination, Wallace produced the first of several red herrings, that between the aborted 7 March murder attempt and the successful one on 19 March, Gray had made a secret trip to Queens Village intending to murder Snyder on his own. Prodded by Wallace, Mrs. Mulhauser testified that on Saturday, 12 March, neighborhood children saw a man with glasses looking through the windows of the Snyder residence and trying the doors.[1] When Louis Mulhauser was called to identify the first policemen on the scene, Wallace used his cross-examination to corroborate the story of a lurking stranger.

Vincent Juster, the ambulance surgeon, and Harry Hansen, the neighborhood general practitioner who was the first doctor to examine Mrs. Snyder, were called and both testified that they had found no evidence of physical injury to Mrs. Snyder. Juster's record for Mrs. Snyder contained the words "shock and concussion," qualified by a question

---

1. This was the prowler scare which had caused Albert Snyder to sleep with his loaded revolver close at hand.

mark in the margin. Despite grilling from Wallace, Juster maintained that he had written the question mark at the time he made the note, not after a subsequent visit to the district attorney's office. Further descriptions of the scene of the crime and the condition of Mrs. Snyder were given by Patrolmen Tucker and Schulties, the first lawmen on the scene, and by Detective Patrolman Frank Heyner, who had arrived minutes later.

It fell to Heyner to identify a parade of exhibits, all marked with iden-tification tags that Gray had signed during the taking of his statement. Admitted into evidence were the pistol found next to Snyder's body, the towel and necktie with which Snyder's hands and feet were bound, the gold pencil that was found attached to a piece of picture wire under Snyder's body, the blue handkerchief that had been used to wrap the chloroform-soaked cotton rag, and the rag itself. The last exhibit was Snyder's bloodstained pillowcase, pulled with a flourish from the fruit jar into which it had been stuffed.

Spectators were subdued as these gruesome objects were introduced and their identification tags were read by the witness: " 'This is the towel that was referred to in my statement,' signed H. Judd Gray"; " 'This is the necktie that was referred to in my statement,' signed H. Judd Gray"; " 'This is the pencil referred to in my statement,' signed H. Judd Gray"; and so on. Gray sat with eyes averted, but Mrs. Snyder was not fazed: she shifted in her chair and craned her neck to see the exhibits better.

Under hostile and occasionally argumentative cross-examination by Wallace, Heyner described returning to the Snyder residence to find the sash weight in the basement. He spent an uncomfortable few minutes de-fending himself for having taken no steps to preserve fingerprints. He claimed that, in his professional opinion, the sash weight was highly un-likely to retain fingerprints. He also defended his handling of Albert Snyder's wallet, his pistol, and the gold pencil found on the bed.

Wallace relied on his cross-examination of Heyner to establish that Mrs. Snyder had been subjected to duress. He led the detective through a minute account of Mrs. Snyder's treatment from just after eight o'clock Sunday morning, when Heyner arrived on the scene of the crime, to noon Tuesday, when she was arraigned at Jamaica Police Court. Nothing in Heyner's answers conflicted with Assistant District Attorney Daly's previous testimony that Mrs. Snyder had taken two substantial naps on Monday. About all Wallace was able to accomplish was to remind jurors of Mrs. Snyder's condition by eliciting that, at one point, she had asked Heyner to bring her a sanitary napkin from her purse.[2] Millard took over cross-examination and had even less success in his attempt to show that Gray was held under unacceptable conditions.

Heyner stepped down, and the prosecution shifted its focus to the arrangements under which Mrs. Snyder had stored the insurance policies on her husband's life. The superintendent of the safe-deposit department of the Queens Bellaire Bank testified that Mrs. Snyder held two boxes in his bank—one under the name of "Ruth M. Snyder" and one under the name of "Ruth M. Brown." The latter was rented in July 1926. A bank cashier testified to the opening of the boxes by representatives of the district attorney's office. The box registered to "Ruth Brown" was found to contain, in addition to Granny Brown's will, nothing but life insurance policies—the original Prudential $1,000 policy on Albert Snyder's life, the three policies taken out during Leroy Ashfield's visit, and a $1,000 New York Life policy on Mrs. Snyder's life—as well as related premium payment receipts and cancelled checks. All other Snyder family documents—house deed, mortgage agreement, wills, fire, burglary. and automobile insurance policies, stocks and bonds—were in the box registered to "Ruth Snyder."

Day 4, Thursday, 28 April

The State's final witness of consequence was Haddon Gray: gullible, loyal, betrayed, and about as close to an accessory after the fact as it is possible to be and still keep out of jail. At the time of his testimony, a rumor swept the press benches that his wife intended to sue him for divorce because of his involvement in the case. "Go ahead and ask her about it," he

---

2. As no matron was available, Detective Lieutenant McDermott insisted on accompanying Mrs. Snyder into the bathroom and sat on the edge of the tub with eyes averted while she performed the necessary operation. This earned him a scolding from his wife, to whom he replied that he didn't trust Mrs. Snyder any farther than he could throw her.

replied cooly when a reporter confronted him with the news. "I'm inclined to think it's bunk."

Haddon Gray had nothing to fear from the law. Justice Scudder was downright solicitous in reminding him that he was not required to answer questions that he thought might incriminate him, and the prosecution treated him with kid gloves. During his friend's testimony, Judd Gray sat looking at the floor.

After establishing that the two Grays had been boyhood friends, Newcombe moved to the morning of Saturday, 19 March. The witness confirmed the Syracuse story as set forth in Gray's confession: the excuse of an assignation with "Momsie" in Albany, the request to mail letters, to hang out the "Do Not Disturb" sign, to call the desk, and to rumple the bed. Gray's Syracuse friend testified that, after performing these tasks, he left the note that had been found in Room 743. He received a telephone call from Gray late Sunday afternoon, drove to the Hotel Onondaga in Harry Platt's car, and heard Gray's story about being in Queens Village when an assault on "Momsie" and her husband took place.

Miller cross-examined, asking questions designed to emphasize that his client had not been able to communicate with a lawyer when he was a prisoner in Syracuse. Wallace, for Mrs. Snyder, was rougher on the witness. He brought out the extent to which Haddon Gray had deceived the police. When he went to the police station on Monday morning, having learned of his friend's arrest from a newspaper report, he revealed nothing of what he knew. By early afternoon, he knew that Gray was under investigation in connection with the notorious Snyder murder, but still he kept silent. When, on Tuesday morning at three o'clock, detectives knocked at the door of his home, announced that his friend had confessed, and asked for a black bag, Gray falsely claimed that he knew nothing about such a bag. Haddon Gray continued lying, Wallace established, until after he had heard of his friend's involvement from his own lips.

Despite failing to uncover even a shred of evidence, Wallace tried to sow suspicion that the two Grays, along with Harry Platt, had conspired to murder Snyder for the insurance money that would be paid out on his death. The cross-examination reached a nadir when Wallace elicited that several of Haddon Gray's friends in Syracuse were lawyers.

Q: "You know several lawyers, do you not?"

A: "I know a number of lawyers."

Q: "Very intimate with some of them?"

A: "Some."

The Court: "We will not consider this any reflection."

The prosecution rested in *State of New York v. Snyder and Gray*. Following luncheon recess, defense attorneys for both defendants made the inevitable pleas for dismissal of the indictment, which were met by the equally inevitable denials. Court adjourned until the next day, when it would begin hearing *Snyder v. Gray* and *Gray v. Snyder*.

14

Day 5, Friday, 29 April

COURTROOM CONDITIONS on Friday morning were the worst in New York legal history. Despite the presence of thirty uniformed police controlling access to the building, the courtroom was mobbed. Anticipating chaos when Mrs. Snyder took the stand, Justice Scudder issued the first of countless admonitions, all ignored, against public displays.[1]

Hazelton rose to make a combative opening statement in defense of Mrs. Snyder. He started off with the character issue. The defense would prove that Mrs. Snyder was not the "demimonde" that she had been portrayed to be. She was a moderate drinker, not much of a dancer, and no social butterfly. She had been a faithful wife to Albert Snyder in the early years even though Snyder had rejected her after only three months of marriage. Snyder doted on a dead sweetheart and repeatedly told Mrs. Snyder that he would have been happier had his former love lived. Yet it was not until Mrs. Snyder met Gray that her domestic world, unhappy though it was, unraveled. "Judd Gray found in that disorganized home, found in that home of no love, a willing victim for his nefarious purpose and design.

"[Gray], we will prove to you, was a perfect lover," promised Hazelton. Realizing the stark contrast between the sheikh he described and the broken specimen huddled in his armchair before the jury, he added, "He was not the man you see now." Mrs. Snyder would not deny that she had

---

1. Mrs. Snyder's attorneys argued in their appeal that the behavior of the public was so atrocious that Justice Scudder ought to have declared a mistrial.

registered with Gray at hotels, but she was being tried for murder, not adultery. Far from denying improper relations, Mrs. Snyder would even testify to a long upstate trip she took with Gray in the fall of 1926.

The defense would prove that it was Gray, not Mrs. Snyder, who broached the idea of insurance in latter part of 1925, when he commented to Mrs. Snyder that he himself carried insurance worth thirty thousand dollars and that Albert Snyder should take out more. Besides, Hazelton said, what was more natural, in view of Snyder's accidents in the garage, than deciding to take out more insurance? The defense would prove that Albert Snyder was in no way deceived about the insurance— "no subterfuge, no concealment about it." It was discussed in his presence, he signed a blank form, promised to think it over, and, after consulting with his wife, decided to take out a fifty-thousand-dollar policy. The checks used to pay the premiums were drawn on a joint bank account and Albert Snyder knew all about them. The defense would prove that, when the premiums became too heavy, Mrs. Snyder went on two occasions to the office of the Prudential Life Insurance Company to inquire about canceling the policies. She was told that she would lose her money unless she continued payments on the policies for three years, at which point she could get her money out.

Gray sponged money off of Mrs. Snyder all the time. "Sixty some-odd dollars to pay an installment on his automobile. He never returned it. Fifty dollars for another purpose. Never returned it. Twenty-five or thirty for another purpose. Never returned it. And then a year ago last February, when he heard that her mother gave her five hundred dollars as a Christmas present, he got two hundred and fifty of it away from her . . . and she never got that back either," Hazelton said.

Yes, in the summer of 1926, "a little accident" had occurred when the gas was inadvertently turned on while Albert Snyder lay sleeping in the living room.[2] It was after this that Gray began evincing an interest

---

2. Hazelton had to address the purported murder attempts because they were in Gray's statement, and he was sure to testify to them. Hazelton employed "little" three times in four sentences: "We will prove it to you how a *little* accident did happen with the windows open in the summertime. There is a *little* jet coming up out of the floor. The

in the demise of "the governor"—his term for Albert Snyder, not Mrs. Snyder's. She did not take Gray seriously until after she returned from lunch at Henry's Restaurant with Gray and Lorraine on Saturday, 5 March. When she opened the bundle Gray had given her, she was horrified to find not only the empty whiskey bottle she had asked for in order to make a lamp, but also a sash weight and a note that read, "I am coming out Monday night to get the governor; put this sash weight under the pillow in Mother's room." Also enclosed were some powders that she was directed to give to Albert Snyder before he went to bed. She threw them down the sink instead.

When Gray came to the house, Mrs. Snyder prevented him from going any farther than the kitchen pantry. Gray then said that he would come back on Thursday, Albert Snyder's bowling night, and kill him in the garage, but she talked him out of it. That evening, Mrs. Snyder returned the sash weight to Gray, who took it with him when he left.

Then, on Saturday, 12 March, a week before the murder, the neighborhood children observed Gray—the mysterious prowler about whom Mr. and Mrs. Mulhauser had testified—lurking around the Snyder residence.

A few days later, Gray sent Mrs. Snyder a letter in a large, thick envelope: "I am going to go through with this matter. You and the governor are going to a party Saturday night and I will be out Saturday night to deliver the goods. Have a weight under the pillow." Why "a weight," and not "the sash weight"? asked Hazelton. Because Mrs. Snyder had forced him to take the sash weight with him on Monday night.[3] The envelope

---

husband was lying on the couch snoozing. Someone hit that jet, the windows were wide open, and a *little* gas escaped." Emphasis added. According to George Schneider's version of how his brother told the story, Albert Snyder came within an inch of being asphyxiated. When Mrs. Snyder returned to the house, he was staggering around the garden like a drunken man trying to clear his head. Although Mrs. Snyder later testified to it, Hazelton did not refer to the winter gas incident in his opening.

3. Hazelton did not raise the obvious question as to why Gray asked for "a weight" when he could have, as in fact Mrs. Snyder claimed he did, simply brought the sash weight out with him.

also included more powders, which Mrs. Snyder was advised to give the governor before going out. Again, she threw them away.

The Snyders did go to the Fidgeon party on Saturday night. And Mrs. Snyder did suggest that her drinks be given to her husband, but then why not? She was not an excessive drinker, nor, for that matter, was Albert Snyder.[4] Mrs. Snyder would admit that she left the doors of the house open for Gray, but it was not so he could murder her husband. It was so she could have it out with him— end the affair once and for all.

Mrs. Snyder waited until her husband was asleep and then stole into her mother's bedroom to see Gray. Gray had been drinking: he always drank when he came to the house; that was why she had left him a bottle of whiskey under her mother's pillow. Gray kissed her and she felt rubber gloves on his hands when he caressed her face. "My God, Judd," she gasped, "you're not going to do that, are you?" "I know you don't want me to do it," said Gray. "That's why you didn't put a weight under the pillow as I asked. But I am going to go through with it." He brandished Albert Snyder's revolver as he spoke, paralyzing Mrs. Snyder with fear.

Groans of disbelief swept the courtroom, Scudder rapped for order, and Hazelton wheeled around to confront the public. "Her story, we will maintain, is just as reasonable and possible of being believed as his," he shouted, pointing his index finger in the air.

Turning again to the jury, he continued. Mrs. Snyder managed to coax Gray downstairs to the living room, still hoping that she could persuade him to leave. Gray pointed the revolver at her and threatened to kill her and then himself. Panic-stricken though she was, Mrs. Snyder persisted in trying to dissuade the drunken fiend. Finally, it seemed to work; he calmed down and gave her the pistol, which she put on the piano.

At that moment, a hygienic crisis arose. The stress of knowing that Gray was coming out to Queens Village had caused the early onset of Mrs. Snyder's menstrual period; now her nervousness was making her

---

4. "Albert was not an excessive drinker, but he would have a good time, perhaps, at a party, and take eight or ten highballs, even as you and I." The bottom line is that Snyder's blood alcohol concentration was 0.3 percent that night.

bleed more heavily.[5] Mrs. Snyder went upstairs to the bathroom to change her sanitary napkin. While doing so, she heard Gray come upstairs. She thought he was coming to get his hat and coat out of her mother's bedroom before leaving. Then she heard a heavy thud.

Hazelton banged the defense table with his open hand to simulate the sound and tore loose his collar.[6]

> She rushes out. She is in the hall looking down from the bathroom, towards the room, the death room, in which Snyder is, and there she sees Judd Gray . . . striking him with this weight [Hazelton waves sash weight]. Albert Snyder, we will prove to you, never moved after Judd Gray gave him that first thud on the head, and the doctor's [Neail's] evidence bears it out. Albert Snyder, we will prove to you, never arose, as is said in the confession of Judd Gray, and grabbed him by the collar and fought with him. He lay there unconscious. The hand that grabbed him by that collar and pulled the collar . . . from the neck, was what? It was the hand of Ruth Snyder taking Judd Gray from off her husband, whom he was belaboring with the sash weight. . . . He pushed her, and she fell. She is a woman who faints very easily, and she fell. She fell . . . and she swooned [ripple of mock swoons sweeps across courtroom], in spite of what anyone may think, and her story is just as reasonable and probable as his.

Hazelton paused for breath and pointed at the floor to indicate Mrs. Snyder's position. When she recovered, he went on, she was horrified to find her husband dead and bloodstains on her nightgown where Gray

5. Mrs. Snyder's female troubles were the butt of cruel jokes and endless witty repartee on the part of reporters. Hazelton's infelicitous wording in addressing the all-male jury hardly helped: "That [knowing that Gray was coming out] resulted in a condition upon the part of Mrs. Snyder which you can well realize, and, being a human being, she reacted the same as you or I would under those same or similar circumstances."

6. The loose-collar trick was an old courtroom standby. Some say it originated with evangelist Billy Sunday. Sophie Treadwell was dismissive: "Copy was short that day and reporters made much of the collar-ripping scene." Wallace was in the habit of bringing along dime store spectacles that he would "accidentally" smash while thumping the table.

had pushed her. "You're in this as deep as me," he told her, and described how they were going to fake a robbery. Gray washed up and got a new shirt from Albert Snyder's closet. He then went down to the cellar and burned his own bloody shirt. Gray had already drugged Snyder with chloroform while Mrs. Snyder was unconscious. When he came back from the cellar, Gray was inspired to strangle Snyder by tightening picture wire around the unconscious man's neck with a gold pencil.[7]

Then Gray announced that he was going to take Snyder's money and her jewelry to support the burglary story. He would be in touch in a few months when Snyder's insurance money was paid. It was only at this point that Mrs. Snyder realized what was really going on—it was the insurance! Gray wanted to extort the insurance money from her! Her defensive instincts aroused by the realization that Gray was after her property, Mrs. Snyder rushed into the master bedroom and hid her jewelry under the mattress.

Mrs. Snyder would concede that the aftermath of the crime—the burglary scheme, her falsehoods, and the like—was as had been established by the prosecution. But Hazelton painted a grim picture of Mrs. Snyder in police custody—no sleep, no food, grilled by one detective after another, denied permission to see her mother or consult a lawyer.

Why did they keep hounding her? Because she had not told them the one thing they wanted to hear—that she had been Gray's willing coconspirator. The police had an opportunity when they got their hands on Gray's confession.

"Judd Gray confessed on the train. Some detectives got off at 125th Street. . . . We will prove to you that word got down here to the po-

---

7. "So after the fellow was dead," Hazelton continued, "he goes up to murder him for the second time and takes the picture wire that he brought with him from Syracuse and ties it around his neck and, *I believe,* fastens it with that little pencil. *I believe* that is why the pencil was found, his pencil was found in the bed. *I maintain* that is the logical conclusion." Emphasis added. Never has an advocate sounded less convinced—and with good reason, because the question of the pencil has never been explained. See appendix A for further commentary.

lice . . . as to what Judd Gray had said. Then started the work of dovetailing the two, boiling down what she had said so that it would fit in with Mr. Gray's confession."

His loose collar flapping, Hazelton closed with a rosy picture of Mrs. Snyder sewing clothes, filling the cellar shelves with jars of fruit preserves, and teaching little Lorraine to say her prayers. "Woman is just as God intended her to be were it not for some man; and we will prove to you that Mrs. Ruth Snyder is just as God intended her to be were it not for her incompatible husband and the deceiver Gray, who, taking advantage of the conditions that were there, stole himself into the house."

Hazelton sat down, exhausted, and Scudder instructed counsel for Gray to proceed. Miller, who was rather fat and pomaded his hair, made an imposing presence in the well of the courtroom. Because this was his first big case, his wife and a number of legal acquaintances had come to hear him. Miller launched into a harangue about the court, the responsibilities of counsel, and the like, rambling on until Scudder intervened and told him to get to the point. Thus prodded, Miller promised that the defense would prove that Gray's statement was not voluntary.[8] Counsel for the defendant Gray would present "the most tragic story that has ever gripped human heart, a story of the human triangle, of illicit love, of unnatural relations and of dishonor."[9] Then Miller went off on another tangent about the truth in its pristine glory prevailing so long as American institutions endure, prompting Scudder to again interrupt and to tell him to stick to the matter at hand.

8. Trying to keep Gray's statement out was well and good, but since it had been admitted and Gray would deny virtually nothing in it, what was the use of claiming duress? There is a chance, as Wallace angrily claimed in his closing address to the jury, that Gray meant to fight when the trial opened but decided to make a clean breast of it after he heard Mrs. Snyder's testimony against him.

9. According to Damon Runyon, counsel for Mrs. Snyder and Gray agreed to stay away from the question of "unnatural relations." The agreement held up, apart from casual references, until Millard's closing argument up for Gray, drawing an angry retort from Wallace during his summation on behalf of Mrs. Snyder. It did not, however, prevent Gray, on direct examination, from complaining about being worn out by excessive sexual intercourse during the couple's upstate road trip.

Again reminding jurors that they would hear the most tragic story ever narrated in a court of justice, Miller gave a preview Gray's "love slave" defense:

> The defendant was driven into this tragedy by a force not his own, dominated by a will not his own; and powerless to struggle against that controlling superpower which was gripping him and driving him and directing his energies and faculties, and he struggled to loosen himself from this dominion and from the catastrophe it was leading into, but without avail . . . He was dominated by a cold, heartless, calculating mastermind and master will. He was a helpless mendicant of a designing, deadly, consciousless, abnormal woman, a human serpent, a human fiend in the guise of a woman. He was in the web, he was hemmed in the abyss; he was dominated, he was commanded, he was driven by this malicious character. He became inveigled and was drawn into this hopeless chasm, when reason was gone, when mind was gone, when manhood was gone and when his mind was absolutely weakened by lust and by passion and by abnormal relations.

What Gray's opening lacked in substance, it made up for in brevity: Hazelton had held forth to the jury for one hour and sixteen minutes; Miller, for only eleven minutes.

15

MRS. SNYDER'S DEFENSE opened with two witnesses called to prove that she had tried to cancel her husband's insurance policies. Unfortunately, the manager of the Prudential's Jamaica branch did not recall any conversation with Mrs. Snyder about her husband's policies. His predecessor, who had since moved to the Richmond Hill branch, remembered that Mrs. Snyder once called at the office. Asked what the visit concerned, he replied that he couldn't recall.

Granny Brown was the next witness. Yes, she had seen Gray at her daughter's house a number of times. The first time, they had discussed a corset for her, and the stock market. The second time, they had discussed a corset for her daughter, and the stock market. The third time, she had protested to her daughter that it didn't look right to have Gray coming to the house. She never saw him again.

When she learned that her daughter had been taken away by the police, she went with Lorraine to District Attorney Newcombe's office, arriving at about ten o'clock Monday morning. Newcombe refused to allow her to see her daughter, whom she could hear crying hysterically in the next room. Mrs. Brown planted herself in a chair and said, "You can kill me if you want to, but I won't move without seeing my daughter." District Attorney Newcombe threatened to put Lorraine in the Children's Society if Mrs. Brown did not leave immediately, but a gentleman coaxed her into returning home by promising that Ruth would be along presently.

District Attorney Newcombe cross-examined and asked where Mrs. Brown had been at the time her son-in-law was murdered. She had been cooking and cleaning for Mr. William Code of Kew Gardens, who was convalescing from surgery.

Q: "Do you remember Mr. Code telling you on Saturday that he as going to stay in town all Saturday night?"

A: "Yes, but—"

Q: "Do you remember telephoning the Snyder house that day?"

A: "I called up my daughter every day as a rule."

Q: "And you told her that Mr. Code was going away, didn't you?"

A: "No, I didn't."

Q: "You knew Mr. Code was going away, didn't you?"

A: "Not until he came home in the afternoon."

Q: "Mr. Code told you that he wasn't going to be home Saturday night, didn't he?"

A: "Yes, sir."

Q: "And you talked with your daughter on Saturday?"

A: "Yes, I talked with her early."

Q: "You knew that you weren't going to be needed in the Code home on Saturday night?"

A: "I was needed, I was needed."

Justice Scudder interrupted to explain to Granny Brown that she must confine herself to yes and no answers on cross-examination.

The Court: "Wait a minute, Madam. Just pay attention to the question, and then try to answer the question only. The question which was just put to you is whether you knew that you were not going to be needed on Saturday night."

The Witness: "Oh."

The Court: "So, you see, the answer to that would be yes or no."

The Witness: "I see."

Newcombe resumed.

Q: "Mr. Code told you you would not be needed Saturday night, didn't he?"

A: "He did not, no."

Q: "He told you he was not going to be home Saturday night, didn't he, Mrs. Brown?"

A:"Yes, but he wanted—can I speak?"

Exasperated, Scudder intervened again:"No, no, you cannot speak."

Newcombe then turned to Granny Brown's version of what happened when she came to his office.

Q:"Do you not recall that, far from threatening to send Lorraine away to the Children's Society, I rejected the suggestion when it was put forth by someone else and insisted that Lorraine go home with you?"

A:"Not as I understood you."

Q:"Did I not provide a car to drive you and Lorraine home?"

A:"I do not know whose car took us home."

Q:"Well, it was not your own car, was it?"

A:"No, it was not."

As the afternoon session, which would find Mrs. Snyder on the stand, drew near, there was a virtual riot in the courthouse. A counterfeiter had managed to sell several hundred bogus court passes. When those with legitimate passes learned that the courtroom was already filled for the afternoon session, there was a brawl. Hats were knocked off, clothes ripped, and punches exchanged. A woman was narrowly saved from being propelled over the marble railing surrounding the third floor gallery. The public areas on three entire floors of the courthouse—stairways, galleries, hallways—were mobbed, and the crowd was broken up only by the liberal application of policemen's nightsticks.

"Ruth May Snyder," called Hazelton, and the widow, still in black and wearing the ever-present jet beads, approached the witness stand. Justice Scudder explained to her that she was under no obligation to testify and that, if she did take the stand, she would be forced to undergo hostile cross-examination. "I will take it," Mrs. Snyder replied.

Hazelton began with where she had been born, what schools she had attended, and where she had lived. He established that she was a good housewife and mother and that she and her husband did not get along. How soon after marriage had they begun quarreling? Almost right away, after two or three months. Every time they fought, Albert Snyder would bring up Jessie Guischard, and how much happier he would have been if she had lived. The fights intensified after Lorraine's birth because Albert Snyder had wanted a boy.

Mrs. Snyder then described meeting Gray through Harry Folsom in Henry's Restaurant in July of 1925. They had commenced their sexual relations around September at the Hotel Imperial.

Under direct examination, Mrs. Snyder's modulated voice, which may have been an advantage as a telephone operator, made her answers sound pat and rehearsed. Her voice was "strange and metallic," wrote the *American*. According to their feature author, Rita Weiman: "The woman's voice fell, brittle as glass. No depth, no tremor—a crisp, dominating, ruthless voice that seems utterly to lack tenderness. One feels that attempt at emotion would splinter it. Her lips snapped together on her answers, a thin, sharp line."

Mrs. Snyder also had an annoying habit of prefacing her answers with a breathless little "Why," as if all this was the most normal thing in the world and she was surprised to be asked about it.

Q: "Where else did you go with him?"

A: "Why . . . we went to the Frivolity Club, and the Monte Carlo and we frequently had dinner at the Waldorf."

Q: "How often did you see him?"

A: "Why . . . once or twice or three times a week if he was in town."

Equally maddening was her recurrent use of "just" to qualify the extent of her remembrance or knowledge: "I don't . . . *just* remember," "I don't . . . *just* know," with a helpless pause after the "don't" and the percussive "just" delivered with an earnest little bob of the head.

She had never drunk to excess in her life, nor did she smoke. When asked how many highballs she drank in an evening, Mrs. Snyder claimed to take a little one and try to make it last all night long. Asked if Gray had ever borrowed money from her, she said yes, stating that in February 1926 he had borrowed two hundred dollars to repay a debt to an ex-girlfriend named "Alice," known more familiarly as "Snooks," and adding that he had never paid her back. When Hazelton wanted to know where had she gotten the money, she said it had been part of her mother's Christmas present of five hundred dollars; Gray had found out about the present. Another time, she said, he had borrowed ninety dollars to make a car payment and on still another occasion, thirty-five dollars when he was short of pocket money.

One of Mrs. Snyder's tasks was to explain her husband's stupendous life insurance policy. As usual, she blamed Gray.

Q: "Did Gray ever talk to you about insurance?"

A: "Yes, he asked me if my husband was insured, and I told him my husband did not carry very much and he said I ought to get him insured."

Q: "Did you speak to your husband about insurance after that?"

A: "I had been after my husband for years to take out insurance, particularly after the two accidents in the garage. I encouraged insurance and he said, 'Well, we will see' and I finally got him to consent to having Mr. Ashfield come up and talk insurance to him."

She described the two accidents and then Hazelton brought her back to the insurance.

Q: "What was the talk that you and your husband had about the insurance when Mr. Ashfield called?"

A: "I don't . . . *just* recall the words."

Q: "Well, did your husband sign the two applications?

A: "He did."

Q: "Did you and your husband talk over the insurance after Mr. Ashfield left?"

A: "Yes, and my husband consented to taking out some. He did not specify any particular amount. He said he thought he could carry whatever I thought I could spare out of the money he gave me."

Q: "Were the two policies then taken out and delivered to you?"

A: "Yes."

Q: "When you got your policies home, did you show them to your husband?"

A: "Yes."

Q: "Did you and your husband keep a bank account, a joint account?"

A: "Yes, we had everything together."

Q: "Now what was the amount of the premiums, if you know?"

A: "About twenty dollars a week."

Q: "Did you and your late husband ever have a talk about the premiums?"

A: "Yes, my husband figured, too, that it probably might have been a little bit too heavy for us to carry."

Q:"What did you do?"

A:"I went down to the Jamaica branch and I spoke to some gentleman down there. He said the insurance could not be reduced, and he suggested inasmuch as this kind of policy would be payable in three years, that I should stick it out if I possibly could do it, and I told my husband what he had said. He said, 'Well, as long as you have kept it in that long, go right ahead with it.' "

Had Mrs. Snyder heard in court about an incident in which her husband was almost asphyxiated by gas? She launched into a breathless recitation:

> Well, on one occasion it happened in the summer [1926], and that was when somebody had touched the cock that is right in back of the couch or right by the side of the couch, and that was accidental, and the second attempt was the time when he was sick with the hiccoughs, and sometime in February, I believe, or January [1927], he was lying on the couch, and he lit the heater himself and while he was lying on the couch my mother and the baby went out, and I did not want to stay alone in the house, so I went out, and he had this heater going, and the radio going, and while he was asleep I stooped over to turn off the radio, and, doing so, I stepped on the gas pipe, and I had my hat and coat on ready to go out, and I knew nothing at all about it until he—when I came home he was on the street and I asked him what the trouble was, and he said that he was almost asphyxiated, that the tube had left the cock on the floor, and I wrote Mr. Gray about this.

The slip of the tongue that turned "second occasion" into "second attempt" sounded awful; it gave clear indication of a prepared response. Wallace, sitting at the defense table, was observed to wince.

Q:"And what did Gray write back to you?"

A:" 'It's too damn bad the hose wasn't long enough to put in his nose.' "[1]

---

1. Precisely what Gray would accuse Mrs. Snyder of remarking to him. On the subject of heating, Mrs. Snyder joked in the Sing Sing Death House, "I always asked my husband to get an electric heater but he was too cheap. Now it looks as though I'm finally going to get one."

Q:"When was it that Gray first spoke to you about getting rid of your husband?"

A:"My last stop at the Waldorf. . . . Sometime in February."

Q:"And what did he say to you then?"

A:"Well, I don't *just* recall the words." . . .

Q:"Did he say something about doing away with himself?"

A: "He said that if I didn't consent to letting him do what he had thought of doing that he would get rid of both himself and myself."

Hazelton turned to the lunch on Saturday, 5 March, when the sash weight changed hands. On that date, Mrs. Snyder testified, she brought Lorraine to town to see an eye doctor. Gray had suggested that the three have lunch at Henry's. Gray left the restaurant early and gestured toward the chair before leaving, saying, "There's a package there—take it home." When she got home, Mrs. Snyder discovered it held three items she had asked Gray to procure for her: a whiskey bottle out of which she intended to make a lamp—you could buy a light fixture that fit into the top of the bottle and fill the bottle with colored water—a corset, and a rolling-pin-like device known as a "flesh reducer." The parcel contained, in addition, the sash weight and a letter.

"In that letter," Mrs. Snyder testified, "it said, 'I am coming over Monday night.' I do not just recall whether it said, 'to do the job' or 'finish the governor.' I cannot just recall, because those sayings had been said in so many letters."

Q:"Were there any powders in that letter?"

A:"Yes, there were."

Q:"Did he say anything about the powders?"

A:"He said I should give my husband one of those powders when he went to sleep or at suppertime."

Q:"What did you do with those powders?"

A:"I threw them down the sink."

Q:"What did you do with the sash weight?"

A:"I put it down in the cellar."

Q:"Did Judd Gray come out the following Monday night?"

A:"He did."

Q:"What time did he arrive at your home?"

A: "About eleven twenty."

Q: "Did you let him in the house?"

A: "I let him as far as the pantry."

Q: "Was your husband up at that time or had he retired and was he asleep in bed?"

A: "He was asleep in bed."

Q: "Did Judd Gray tell you why he came that night?"

A: "He said he had come to finish the governor."

Q: "And what did you say to him?"

A: "I said, 'Judd, you can't do such a thing.' "

Q: "How long did he remain there and talk with you, would you say?"

A: "Possibly five or six minutes."

Q: "Did he say when he was going to return?"

A: "Yes, when I gave him back the sash weight, he said, 'Well, if I can't do it tonight, I am coming back Thursday night and get him in the garage.' "

Mrs. Snyder was taking a giant step back from her statement, and contradicting Gray's, when she claimed that she had returned the sash weight to Gray. Both defendants said in their statements that Mrs. Snyder was in possession of the sash weight on Saturday, 19 March, and that she hid it in her mother's room for Gray's use. Now, she claimed to have practically thrust it into Gray's hands as she pushed him out the pantry door on Monday evening.

Mrs. Snyder claimed that she received a midweek communication from one of Gray's friends alerting her that she would shortly receive a large letter. She telephoned the Post Office and found that it had arrived; because it was past home delivery hours, she walked down and picked it up. In it, she found two more packages of powders and a note: "Give one and one-half or possibly two to the governor before you go to the party on Saturday night." The note went on to say that Gray would be over on Saturday night to finish the job, and directed her to leave the doors open for him.

Hazelton elicited that Mrs. Snyder had planned a large birthday party for the week after her husband's murder; she named some of the sixteen guests who had been invited.

"Had you bought any supplies for the party?" Hazelton asked. Mrs. Snyder, evidently a meticulous hostess, answered without hesitation: "Six bottles of Scotch whisky, two bottles of rye and two other bottles of Scotch, a bottle of gin, a bottle of vermouth and a bottle of grenadine."[2]

Mrs. Snyder related going with her husband and Lorraine to the Fidgeon party, drinking very little there, and returning home at two o'clock in the morning. While her husband was undressing, she spoke to Gray for a moment in her mother's room. She told him to remain quiet and that she would return in a few minutes. She and her husband went to bed and twenty or thirty minutes later, when she judged that Albert Snyder was asleep, she slipped down the hall to Gray.

Q: "Did any talk take place between you and Gray?"

A: "Considerable talk."

Q: "And what did he say to you and what did you say to him?"

A: "When I walked over to him he kissed me, and I immediately felt the rubber gloves that he had on his hands and I said, 'Judd, what are you going to do?' "

Q: "What did he say to you?"

A: "He said, 'If you don't let me go through with it tonight, I am going to get the pair of us.' And he then had my husband's revolver, that he had gotten from under my husband's pillow, and he had it in my mother's room, and he said, 'It's either him or it's us.' I grabbed him by the hand and I took him downstairs to the living room."

Q: "When he went down with you did he have his hat and overcoat on?"

A: "No, he had that laying on my mother's bed."

Q: "Did you give Gray any weight that night?"

A: "No, he took the weight away with him Monday night that he was out to the house."

---

2. Eleven bottles of liquor and one of vermouth for a party of under twenty persons. If, as Hazelton said, Mrs. Snyder and her husband were not great drinkers, some of their friends certainly were. The quart of Tom Dawson whiskey that Gray drank was part of this inventory.

Q: "Did you put any weight under the pillow that night?"

A: "I put a bottle of liquor under the pillow, no weight."

Q: "Did you put any pliers under the pillow?"

A: "No."

Q: "After he got downstairs did you and he have any talk?"

A: "I was trying to plead with him to try and get him to change his mind and get the idea out of his mind. We stayed down there quite a while, and in my excitement I had said things to him that probably enraged him. I went upstairs to go to the bathroom."

Q: "Well, now, why did you go to the bathroom?"

A: "Through my excitement, I was flowing."

Q: "Your excitement brought about a certain condition?"

A: "I was in that condition, but it brought it on greater."

Q: "Did you go to the bathroom?"

A: "I came upstairs to go to the bathroom and before I had gotten upstairs I said, 'I will bring your hat and coat down to you,' and while—I was in the bathroom taking care of myself when I heard this terrific thud. I immediately opened up the door and ran down the hall to see Mr. Gray leaning over my husband."

Q: "When you saw your husband was he lying down or was he up around Gray?"

A: "My husband was lying down. Mr. Gray was kneeling on his back."

Q: "What did you do?"

A: "I ran in and I grabbed Mr. Gray by the neck, pulled him off, and in wrestling with me, he pushed me to the floor, and I fainted, and I remembered nothing until I came to again and saw my husband all piled up with blankets. I pulled the blankets off—"

An interlude of tears followed, and Matron Wolfe hastened to the witness's side to comfort her.

After composing herself, Mrs. Snyder went on. While she was attempting to untie her husband, Gray returned to the bedroom and pulled her away from the dying Albert Snyder. Gray led her back into her mother's room, where he laid out his plan: "I have gone through with it and you have to stand just as much of the blame as I have. We can frame up a burglary; we will both get out of it. They will never know that I did it anyway." Mrs. Snyder had sat there confused, listening while Gray instructed her on the story that she should tell the police.

Hazelton pressed her for details of her state of mind.

Q: "Were you afraid at that time?"

A: "I was heartily afraid. I saw what a terrible mess he had made out of things, and I couldn't see any way out other than to do as he asked me to do."

Q: "What did he tell you to do?"

A: "He said, 'Mommy, you stay up here, you are in no fit condition to do anything. I am going downstairs and mess up all the things, and I am coming up here to mess up all the things, to carry out the idea that it was a robbery. You stay up here until I come back.' "

Q: "What happened to your jewelry that night?"

A: "He said to me, . . . 'Give me your jewelry.' And when he said that to me it came to my mind that he was probably out to get more than my jewelry. So I ran into my room and took my jewelry from out of the box I had previously kept it in and threw it under the mattress." [3]

Q: "Did he say when you would hear from him again or see him?"

A: "He said, 'You won't see me for a couple of months, and when you do,' he said, 'by that time the insurance will have been in your hands or they will have saved it or given it to you—' I don't just know the exact words he used, but he said it would take at least a couple of months for the insurance to be settled."

Q: "Was that the first time that he had mentioned insurance to you from the time that he told you he was insured for thirty thousand dollars and your husband ought to be insured?"

A: "Yes."

Hazelton returned to Mrs. Gray's statement that Gray had tied her up and left her on her mother's bed.

Q: "Did you let him do that?"

A: "I did. I had to."

---

3. In the *Daily Mirror* exclusive "My Last Story," Mrs. Snyder claims to have been overcome with sentimental feelings about her jewelry.

Q:"Why did you let him do that?"

A:"Because I was afraid if I did not go in with what he asked me to do that he would finish me that night."

Q:"Did the police question you?"

A:"They did."

Q:"Had you been up all day Saturday?"

A:"Yes."

Q:"Had you been up all Saturday night?"

A:"Yes."

Q:"What time did the police start questioning you?"

A: "As soon as they got there, a little after eight o'clock Sunday morning."

Q:"What time were you taken to the station house?"

A:"About seven o'clock Sunday evening."

Q:"Had the police been questioning you all day?"

A:"All day long."

Q:"Did they question you at the station house?"

A:"Yes."

Q:"How long did you remain at the station house?"

A:"Until two o'clock Monday morning."

Q:"How many different detectives questioned you while you were at the station house, would you say?"

A:"Several of them."

Q:"Were they questioning you all the time?"

A:"Continually."

Q:"Did you have anything to eat that day?"

A:"No. "

Q:"Had you had any sleep at all?"

A:"Not a bit."

Q: "Before you signed your last paper did the detective tell you whether or not Judd Gray had told his story?"

A:"Yes."

Q: "Did they tell you anything that Judd Gray had said, if you remember?"

A:"I don't . . . *just* remember."

Q: "Did you feel weak or strong?"

A: "I was very, very weak, because I hadn't had any sleep, and I hadn't but very, very little food, and I was in a physical condition that would make me feel miserable even without all this trouble that I had."

Then Hazelton enumerated a series of points in the confession that Mrs. Snyder now denied, implying that detectives had altered the statement after they talked to Gray.

Q: "Did you say that you saw Gray tie your husband's hands behind his back?"

A: "I did not."

Q: "Did you write Gray that it was better for you to get your husband before he got you?"

A: "No, I did not."

On the crucial matter of the sash weight,

Q: "Did you say in your confession, 'Judd Gray told me to take home a window weight in case we were going to do anything; that was the way we were going to do it'?"

A: "I did not."

Q: "Did you say, 'I had brought the window weight up from the cellar that afternoon'?"

A: "When I said that I meant I brought it up from the cellar Monday morning, from the Saturday he gave it to me; I unwrapped it and put it in the cellar, and I brought it up Monday and rewrapped it to give it to Mr. Gray Monday night when he came to the house."

Contrary to her confession, she had seen neither the chloroform, nor the blue handkerchief, nor the cotton rags before Snyder was murdered. Also contrary to her confession, she had not brought Gray one of her husband's shirts, he had found it himself. She and Gray had not burned their bloodstained garments in the furnace together; Gray had burned the clothes himself. She had not given Gray money from Albert Snyder's wallet; he helped himself.

It was only five o'clock, but Hazelton pleaded that the witness had been answering questions nonstop for three hours and needed a break. Agreeing, Justice Scudder adjourned court until Monday morning.

16

GRAY SPENT THE WEEKEND doing some hard thinking. On Friday evening, he complained, "I never said a thing against her in my life." On Saturday, he had the luxury of a barber shave under the eyes of a guard. "I'm going to tell the truth," he said. "I don't care who gets hurt now."

Mrs. Snyder spent hours twisting her moistened hair around her fingers in an attempt to make curls. She was satisfied with her performance on the stand with one exception: having broken down and wept. "I feel bad that I had to interrupt the court by my emotional outburst. But when the tale of my husband's murder had to be told, my inner self caused me to break."

Hazelton was dismayed by the laughter and groans with which spectators derided Mrs. Snyder's story. Over the weekend, he considered the idea of asking that women, the prime offenders, be barred from the courtroom.

Day 6, Monday, 2 May

In response to the turbulent conditions on Friday, the contingent of policemen on court duty was more than tripled to one hundred. Passes were checked at every point of entry: at the doorway to the building, at the elevator, for those who took the stairs at each landing, and finally at the door to the courtroom itself. Outside the building, one determined young woman managed to reach a second-floor window by climbing a wall and then perching on a railing. She was able to clamber halfway into the courtroom before police dragged her down.

Mrs. Snyder resumed her testimony, and Hazelton finished off his direct examination with a few minor questions. He then turned to Gray's attorney Millard: "Now the witness is yours for examination in accordance with the Court's rule. I take exception to Mr. Millard's cross-examining this witness because it places her in the position of being cross-examined twice." Justice Scudder noted the exception and motioned to Millard to begin.[1]

Q: "Ruth Snyder, why did you place a quart bottle of whiskey for Judd Gray under the pillow in your mother's room on the night of the murder?"

A: "He asked me to."

Q: "When?"

A: "In a letter he wrote to me."

Q: "When did you receive that letter?"

A: "I do not just recall, but it was during the week previous to the murder."

Q: "What did you do with the sash weight after you discovered it upon opening the package you took home from Henry's Restaurant?"

A: "I took it and put it down in the cellar, after I unwrapped it."

Q: "Why did you put it in the cellar?"

A: "Because I had every intention of giving it back to him after I read his note that he was coming out Monday night."

Q: "Did you know what that sash weight was for?"

A: "After reading the note, yes."

Q: "Then why did you place it in the cellar?"

A: "Because I didn't want to have it anywheres around."

Q: "Why did you not throw it away?"

A: "Because I felt it should go back to him, inasmuch as he gave it to me."

Q: "Well, did you believe that that sash weight was to be used in killing your husband?"

A: "I didn't believe anything, because I knew that if I gave it back to him he would have to take it away again."

1. All three legal teams adopted a "good cop, bad cop" strategy in examining major witnesses—the good cops, Hazelton for Mrs. Snyder, Newcombe for the People and Miller for Gray, conducted direct examination and stayed above the fray; the bad cops, Wallace, Froessel, and Millard, went for blood in cross-examination.

Q:"You knew you were giving it into his possession when you gave it back to him?"

A:"Yes, and I also told him that I didn't want him to go through with it, of getting away—of doing away with my husband."

Mrs. Snyder sat composedly in the elevated wooden armchair that served as the witness stand, her elbows on the arm rests, her hands clasped in her lap and her turbaned head cocked slightly to one side. She was cold, glib, and self-assured under hostile questioning, repeatedly replying to leading questions with the calm demurral, "I wouldn't say that." Mrs. Snyder's attitude on cross-examination seemed to be "It's so if I say it's so."

Q:"Did you warn your husband?"

A:"No."

Q:"Did you believe that Judd Gray wanted to kill your husband?"

A:"I thought I could talk Judd Gray out of it."

Q:"But you never mentioned the subject to Albert Snyder?"

A:"I could not mention it to my husband."

Q:"Why?"

A:"Because I was ashamed of the disgrace that might come out of it . . ."

Q:"Isn't it a fact, Mrs. Snyder, that you knew when you went with Albert Snyder to that party just what was going to take place that night?"

A:"No, I did not know what was going to take place because, as I said before, I had every intention of telling Judd Gray that I didn't want to see him anymore."

Q:"Isn't it a fact, Mrs. Snyder, that you wanted to be seen that night with Albert Snyder on seemingly, or apparently, good terms?"

A:"No, I was no different that night to my husband than any other night . . ."

Q:"Do you know of any reason on earth why Judd Gray would want to kill Albert Snyder?"

A:"Yes, for the insurance money."

Q:"Was there any insurance money with Judd Gray as beneficiary?"

A:"No, I was the beneficiary, but he would have eventually gotten it out of me."

Q:"How?"

A: "Through the same scheme that he got money out of me before."

Q: "It could only be done through you, Mrs. Snyder, couldn't it?"

A: "That's true."

Millard asked in which safe-deposit box the insurance policies were kept, the box she held jointly with her husband or the one she held personally under her maiden name of "Ruth Brown"? In her own box, answered Mrs. Snyder.

Q: "Why?"

A: "Because that was the first one I had taken out and everything of importance went in that except the deeds and things for the house, and they went in the second one."

Q: "Were the forms for both the $1,000 and $50,000 policies signed in blank, or just the latter?"

Mrs. Snyder pretended not to understand the question.

A: "The small one was signed the same night as he signed the other one. They were both signed together."

Q: "In blank?"

A: "They were both signed together."

Q: "In blank, then."

A: "I don't recall if they were in blank or how, but they were both signed at the same time."

Q: "Wasn't the smaller policy, Mrs. Snyder, made out when he signed it?"

A: "I really couldn't say. Mr. Ashfield attended to all that with him, and he took the forms back with him."

The only way Mrs. Snyder could undo the damage of her confession was by repudiating it, expecially regarding the murder weapon.

Q: "Why did you say in your statement to the police that you had brought the sash weight up from the cellar to have it ready for Gray?

A: "I may have said that, but I didn't know what I was saying at the time I made that confession."

Q: "You know that you said it?"

A: "I don't remember if I said it or not."

Q: "Why did you change your testimony here on Friday, and state that you gave the sash weight back to Gray?"

A: "I didn't change it, I did just as I did."

Millard turned to the alleged previous attempts on Albert Snyder's life.

Q: "Did Albert Snyder ever have a serious attack of hiccoughs?"

A: "Yes, it lasted almost five days."

Q: "While he had hiccoughs, Mrs. Snyder, did you put a mercury tablet in his medicine?"

A: "I certainly did not."

Q: "Did you ever file off the label or stamp of 'Poison' on a mercury tablet?"

A: "No, I had no mercury in my house except what Judd Gray sent to me at one time."

Q: "And you never filed a label of 'Poison' off the tablet and gave it to your husband for bismuth?"

A: "I did not; I gave my husband bismuth."

Q: "You never told him that a mercury tablet was bismuth?"

A: "No. What reason would I have for that?"

Q: "You do not want me to answer that question."

A: "Answer it if you will."

Q: "For the same reason that you wanted to pull off the gas tube."

Hazelton objected and the exchange was deleted from the record.

Millard wished to suggest that Mrs. Snyder had planned to poison Gray after he had done her dirty work for her.

Q: "Did you have any poisons in the house, Ruth Snyder?"

A: "I did not, no."

Q: "Didn't you give some poisons to Judd Gray on the night of the murder to take away with him?"

A: "I did not, no."

Q: "Did you have a little bottle up in your mother's room besides the quart bottle of whiskey, with some poison in it?" [2]

A: "I certainly did not."

---

2. Gray claimed that Mrs. Snyder had left a small bottle under the pillow—one whose contents made him ill when he drank it—and a quart bottle in open view in the room. Mrs. Snyder said that she left only a quart bottle under the pillow.

Q: "Did you not express to Judd Gray on a number of occasions a desire to get rid of your husband?"

A: "No, I did not."

Q: "In fact, did you not invariably raise the subject whenever Gray was drunk?"

A: "No, never."

Millard asked Mrs. Snyder to repeat what had happened from the time she, Albert Snyder, and Lorraine arrived home until the time that she was discovered by Mrs. Mulhauser. She recited precisely the same story that she had told under direct examination, even breaking down and crying at the same place, the point at which she regained consciousness and pulled the covers off her husband.[3] After composing herself, Mrs. Snyder was momentarily flustered when Millard stood mute in front of her. Justice Scudder intervened, telling Millard that he could proceed. "Why, your Honor," Millard replied, "I'm waiting for the rest of the answer." Mrs. Snyder glared at Millard and finished her set piece.

Asked if she had ever participated in a divorce setup, Mrs. Snyder admitted that she had. She then listened as a letter was read and introduced into evidence:

In my rotunda, February 28, 7:00 P.M.

Sweetheart mine:

This might come to a short stop; but I'll do the best I can while here.

Well, darling the 'whole works' went over beautifully. Of course it was all pre-arranged and all took place at 101 E. 1st Street the worst neighborhood in N.Y. I was scared most to death, and if you ever saw the woman, you'd die of fright too. Such a cold-blooded way of doing things but it went over as intended and we were fine in all, just witnesses—that was plenty too.

Had another battle with the "G" darn fool—Gee I'm mad.

---

3. Mrs. Snyder even repeated the mistake of referring to the towel that bound her husband's hands as "bandaging." All listeners were of the opinion that Mrs. Snyder's story sounded as if she was reciting from rote.

Went down to see Vincent Lopez at the Jam[aica Theatre, a vaudeville house]; then stopped off to see Catherine[?], then home at 5:30.
Had dinner at 6:15 and now Damit ain't got a thing to do, am going out
for a walk after we get baby to bed.

My troubles are all over dear, stopped yesterday afternoon. Oh, so
good. Tried to get M[other] to go to H[igh]B[ridge] for a day or two, so
that my chances for Friday will be better for staying over. Do you really
want me dear to stay? Wouldn't you rather go right on home so that
you'll be nearer the bank on Saturday? Yes you do—huh?

Please don't put yourself out for me dear. I love you just as much as if
you saved that $8 for yourself. Maybe we shouldn't be quite so extravagant.

Sweetheart dear, I love you with all my heart and soul because you're
the dearest and bestest kid I have or ever had. Much love,

All yours,

Momie

The implication was that, had Mrs. Snyder wished to obtain a divorce,
she was capable of arranging a similar frame-up on her own behalf.[4]

Millard handed the witness People's Exhibit 62, her statement. "Will
you kindly take that alleged confession, Mrs. Snyder, and point out to the
jury, or tell me, what parts, if any, are true? Just read aloud the parts that
are true." Mrs. Snyder read the preliminary portions describing her early
years, then lapsed into silence. Occasionally she started reading aloud
again and trailed off. At one point, she exclaimed, "Oh, this is not true—
I can't read this!"

In the end, all that Mrs. Snyder would confirm was Gray's visit to the
house on the night of Monday, 7 March; the receipt a few days before
the murder of a thick packet containing a letter from Gray that arranged
the meeting on the night of Saturday, 19 March; her actions at and after

---

4. After vacillating, Mrs. Snyder had agreed to help in the framing of Patrolman Edward Pierson, but would only act as the bait. The starring role was played by the woman
referred to in the letter, perhaps a prostitute. Mrs. Snyder lured her friend Pierson to the
hotel room, where the leading lady serendipitously materialized out of the bathroom
just as Ethel Anderson and two witnesses came in the door.

the Fidgeon party up to the point of talking to Gray in Granny Brown's bedroom; and her behavior after Gray had left the house. She refused to confirm the account for practically the entire block of time from the moment she entered her mother's bedroom to the moment Gray left the house—more than three hours.

Cross-examination for the prosecution was conducted by Assistant District Attorney Charles Froessel, a great bear of a man and a vitriolic questioner when aggravated. He could not have been better disposed toward the witness by the fact that his watch had been stolen during the melee outside the courtroom Friday morning.[5] Hazelton, as though unwilling to leave his client at Froessel's mercy, remained standing, arms folded, chewing gum furiously.

Brandishing a long yellow pencil like a conductor's baton, Froessel began.

Q: "You could have kept Gray out by locking the doors, yes or no?"

A: "I could have—"

Q: "Yes or no, madam."

A: "Yes."

Q: "You had enough fur coats and dresses, did you not?"

A: "My mother bought me my fur coat."

Q: "I asked you, 'You had enough fur coats and dresses, did you not?' Yes or no, madam?"

A: "Yes."

Q: "Your home in Queens Village was almost free of its mortgage?"

A: "Yes."

Q: "Your husband maintained a Buick sedan?"

A: "Yes."

Q: "And he also had a bungalow out on the beach, is that correct?"

A: "Yes."

Q: "And you say you were unhappy?"

A: "Yes."

---

5. "I hope Charlie *never* gets that watch back!" Mrs. Snyder joked just before being transferred to Sing Sing.

Q: "Your husband didn't spend a great deal of money on his own clothes, did he?"

A: "Not a lot, no."

Q: "Of course you did nothing in your married life to make your husband unhappy, did you?"

A: "No."

Q: "In other words, you want the jury to believe that you were a perfect lady?"

Hazelton objected and the question was withdrawn.

Q: "Madam, your answer is that you did nothing whatsoever to make your husband unhappy?"

A: "Not that he knew about."

The courtroom audience tittered, and Scudder issued another warning.

Q: "Oh, you knew that he didn't know about the life you were leading?"

A: "He didn't know."

Q: "He never talked to you about his suspicions concerning your staying away at night?"

A: "He never did, no."

Q: "So that you thought that while you were carrying on with the defendant Gray, you were putting it all over on your husband, didn't you?"

A: "No."

Q: "You thought that you were doing him a favor?"

A: "No, I did not."

Froessel established that, prior to Leroy Ashfield's visit to the Snyder residence, Albert Snyder carried only one thousand dollars of life insurance. Mrs. Snyder admitted that she had spoken to Ashfield before he came to speak to Albert Snyder.

Q: "You wanted your husband heavily insured?"

A: "I did not."

Q: "You wanted him to take out more insurance?"

A: "I did."

Q: "What did you think was more insurance in amount?"

A: "Well, the way Mr. Ashfield—"

Q:"Just answer that by figures."

A:"Whatever my husband should consent to taking out."

Q:"I asked you what did you think."

A:"I didn't think."

Q:"In other words, it might have been any amount from one to fifty thousand dollars as far as you were concerned?"

A:"Yes."

Q:"One-fourth of your weekly allowance you paid to the insurance company?"

A:"Yes."

Q:"On the $50,000 policy?"

A:"Yes."

Q:"And in addition to that, you were to pay the premiums on the old $1,000 dollar policy, on the $1,000 policy taken out in 1925, [on] your own life and on your daughter's life?"

A:"Yes."

Q:"By the time you got through, didn't you have to give half of your weekly allowance to the insurance company under that arrangement?"

A:"No, I did not."

Q:"When Ashfield left the house that night, the only thing that was definitely agreed upon was that Albert Snyder would take the $1,000 policy, is that not correct?"

A:"No."

Q:"Do you mean to tell us that your husband in the presence of Ashfield and yourself agreed to take out fifty thousand dollars' worth of insurance?"

A:"No, he did not."

In a rearguard action, Mrs. Snyder argued that her husband had access to her private safe-deposit box.

Q:"You mean to tell us that he had access to the safe deposit box kept in the name of 'Ruth Brown'?"

A:"Yes, he did."

Q:"Did he give his signature to the bank on that particular box at any time?"

A:"No, he did not."

Q: "And yet you want to tell us that he had access to that safe deposit box?"

A: "Yes, he did."

Q: "You mean he had access through Ruth Brown?"

A: "Yes, through me."

This was utterly unconvincing. And the safe deposit box was not Mrs. Snyder's only little secret from her husband.

Q: "Why did you instruct that the Prudential policies be delivered to you personally during the day, when your husband was at work?"

A: "For no particular reason."

Q: "Why did you tell the postman to give only into your hands any correspondence from the Prudential Life Insurance Company?"

A: "For no particular reason."

Q: "Why did you ask that the telephone bills be placed into your hands only?"

A: "Because I did not want my husband to see them."

Q: "Why did you ask that mail addressed to 'Jane Gray' be given only to you?"

A: "Because I did not want my husband to see my correspondence with Gray."

The prosecution had an ace up its sleeve in the form of some jottings in Mrs. Snyder's handwriting found between the pages of a book in the Snyders' living room. Just before the noon recess, Froessel led her into the trap.

Q: "Were you interested in the particular character of the insurance?"

A: "Yes, to a certain extent."

Q: "And did you try to become familiar with the provisions incident to the various kinds of insurance that you had in mind?"

A: "Yes."

Q: "It was last summer [1926] that you became familiar with what would be paid under the provisions of that policy in case of an accident?"

A: "Yes."

Q: "And it was then for the first time you learned that you would get, in the case of Albert Snyder's death, on all these policies the sum of ninety-seven thousand dollars if the death was by accident?"

A: "Yes."

Q: "Now did you sit down and figure out how it would be paid or anything in connection with it?"

A: "No, I did not."

Mrs. Snyder had played into Froessel's hands. He introduced People's Exhibit 90, a scrap of paper on which Mrs. Snyder had scrawled some figures.

Q: "I show you a paper and ask you if this is in your handwriting?"

A: "That was figured—"

Q: "May I read these figures, your Honor? First five years, $10,000, $199.70. After five years, $374.50. $50,000, 5, a line, $998.50. $100,000 multiplied by 0.04, a line, $4,000, equals $78 per week."

In other words, under the "modified life" plan chosen by Albert Snyder, each $10,000 of insurance was to cost $199.70 per year, a total of $998.50 for the $50,000 of insurance taken out. After five years, the premiums would nearly double to $374.50 per $10,000. One-hundred-thousand dollars invested at four percent (roughly the yield on a savings account at the time) would yield $78 per week in income. Mrs. Snyder had erred twice on the side of optimism: only forty-five of the fifty-thousand dollars of insurance taken out by Albert Snyder carried the double-indemnity clause, and $4,000 divided by 52 is equal to $76.92, not $78.[6]

Q: "These are your figures, you said?"

A: "Yes."

Q: "And you figured on the basis of one hundred thousand dollars didn't you?"

A: "I do not recall figuring that."

Q: "Your husband was a good, big, strong man, was he not?"

A: "Yes."

Q: "And you were figuring, when you made the figures, on the basis of one hundred thousand dollars?"

A: "I wasn't figuring on any basis."

---

6. She had divided 4,000 by 50 in her head to get 80, then knocked it down a bit to adjust for the two extra weeks.

Asked about the "modified life" payment scheme, Mrs. Snyder answered that it was not intended that the policy should last five years.

Q: "Oh, it was to run until March 19th last?"

A: "No. It was to run for three years."

Q: "Why three years?"

A: "Because that was the time span necessary to obtain the cash surrender value of the policy."

Lunch recess was a welcome break for Mrs. Snyder and her lawyers, but there was no relief in sight when court reconvened. Canceled checks made out to the Prudential Life Insurance Company, checks that Hazelton claimed Albert Snyder knew all about, were introduced into evidence. Although drawn on the joint checking account, not one check was signed by Albert Snyder.

Q: "When you made out these checks in payment of the premiums, did you keep a record of them in your check stub book?"

A: "Yes."

Mrs. Snyder was asked to go through her checkbook for any stubs recording the checks. There were no records.

Q: "You forgot to put them in, did you?"

A: "Well, I suppose I must have."

Q: "Did you start to keep a household ledger shortly after you were married?

A: "I believe I started, but I never kept it up."

"Perhaps this will refresh your memory," said Froessel, placing into evidence a set of notebooks and handing the witness an impeccably kept ledger in her handwriting running from 1916 up to the day she was taken into custody. In it were records of income tax payments, payments on burglary, fire, theft, and automobile insurance, premiums on the $1,000 policy taken out by Albert Snyder on the occasion of Leroy Ashfield's house call, premiums on his old $1,000 policy, and premiums on insurance policies on Mrs. Snyder, Lorraine, and Granny Brown. But there was not a single entry related to the fifty-thousand-dollars' worth of insurance, allegedly obtained by irregular means, which was by far the largest item in her household budget.

Froessel badgered the witness for half an hour on the exact amount that would have to be paid in premiums over three years.

Q:"So, in order to get at the end of three years a cash surrender value from those two policies of $650, you had to pay the insurance company $2,612?"

A:"But that was not the way it was explained to me."

In late afternoon Froessel, having done enough damage on the insurance front, turned to moral turpitude.

Q:"How did you meet Harry Folsom, who subsequently introduced you to Gray?"

A:"Through a girlfriend of mine, Mrs. Kaufman."

Q:"You two women were alone, weren't you?"

A:"Yes."

Q:"You had no escorts then."

A:"No."

Q:"Isn't it a fact that you became acquainted with Harry Folsom in the presence of Mrs. Kaufman by a flirtation in Henry's Restaurant?"

A:"I could not say that, no."

Q:"It might have been, though, eh?"

A:"It might have been, but it was not that way."

Q:"It might have been that you met Harry Folsom through a flirtation in Henry's Restaurant?"

A:"Yes, but not through my flirtation."

Q:"No buts. Mrs. Kaufman never knew him before that day?"

A:"No."

Q:"And you did not know him before that day?"

A:"No."

Q:"As a matter of fact, in the language of the vernacular, he picked you up in the restaurant, did he not?"

A:"Not me."

Q:"Oh, he picked her up?"

A:"Yes, he spoke to her first."

Q:"But you were there at the time? . . . So that, as a matter of fact, you know that you became acquainted with Harry Folsom purely on a flirtation?"

A:"Not on my part, no."

Q:"But on the part of someone in your presence?"

A:"Yes."

Q:"And with whom you were eating that day?"

A:"Yes."

If Froessel could not prove that Mrs. Snyder was herself a loose woman, then at least he had the satisfaction of establishing that she had eaten lunch with one.

Subsequent to meeting Harry Folsom, Mrs. Snyder had gone to his office and bought hosiery at wholesale prices. Sometime in the early part of July, Folsom introduced her to Judd Gray at Henry's. The first time she met him, she arranged to buy a corset from him when she returned from Shelter Island in July.

Q:"Oh, you were talking about corsets at that very first meeting?"

A:"Yes."

Q:"You had never met this man before?"

A:"No."

Q:"You said that you had been faithful to your husband up to that time?"

A:"Yes."

Q:"And on that very first meeting of the defendant Gray, you talked about getting corsets from him? Yes or no."

A:"No."

Q:"You did not say anything at all?"

A:"I mentioned corsets then, but I did not talk about corsets then."

Q:"Well, you did mention corsets, didn't you?"

A:"Yes. He mentioned it to me."

Q:"Well, is it your custom to engage in conversation with men you meet the first time and talk about corsets?"

A:"Being his line, I did not see any objection to it."

For once, Mrs. Snyder had deflated Froessel, and the courtroom laughter was on her side.

Mrs. Snyder contended that she did not have intercourse with Gray until their third meeting, at the Hotel Imperial.

Q:"You stayed there overnight?"

A:"I do not know whether I stayed there overnight or not."

Q:"Madam, you say that you were faithful to your marriage vows up to that?"

A:"Yes."

Q:"And you do not remember the first time in fourteen years, or whatever it is, that you violated your husband's—"

A:"I said it was sometime in July or August or September."

Q:"You do not understand my question. You say that you were faithful to your husband during all the years of your married life until this day in September?"

A:"Yes."

Q:"When you were out with the defendant Gray?"

A:"Yes."

Q:"And though this was the first time that you violated your marriage vows, you cannot even tell us now whether it was by day or by night?"

A:"No, I do not remember."

Having established that Mrs. Snyder and Gray had patronized a variety of nightclubs, cabarets, speakeasies, and roadhouses, Froessel attacked Mrs. Snyder's claim to be a moderate drinker.

Q:"You take a drink now and then, don't you?"

A:"Very seldom."

Q:"You do once in a while?"

A:"Yes, once in a while."

Q:"Do you know what is meant by the expression 'plastered up'?"

A:"Yes."

Q:"Have you ever used that expression?"

A:"I have."

Q:"Have you ever said, 'Let's get plastered up'?"

A:"I've said that lots of times."

Q:"And do you know what is meant by 'plastered up'?"

A:"I do."

Q:"What do you mean by 'plastered up'?"

A:"I didn't mean it in the sense that it is intended."

Q:"What do you mean?"

A: "Just to go out and have a good time."

Q: "That is what you mean by 'plastered up'?"

A: "Yes."

Q: "Have you ever heard other people use that expression?"

A: "Yes."

Q: "Don't you know that the common acceptance of that term is to get good and drunk?"

A: "No, I wouldn't say that."

Q: "You wouldn't say that?"

A: "No."

Q: "Has it anything at all to do with drunk, in the common acceptance of the term?"

A: "I suppose it has."

Q: "You know that it does, don't you?"

A: "If you want to take it that way."

Froessel was by now roaring with frustration. "I just want the truth, madam, that is all."

A: "Yes, if you say so."

Q: "What is that?"

A: "I say yes, if you say it that way."

Q: "It isn't what I say, madam, it is what you say. Don't you know that it is the commonly accepted version of that term?"

A: "Well, if it's intended that way, yes."

Q: "In other words, you mean that you can use words to mean anything you want to on earth, whether they are generally accepted that way or not?"

A: "It all depends on how they are used."

Froessel confronted Mrs. Snyder with her "Let's get good and plastered" letter to Gray, written on 24 February 1927.

Q: "Do you remember using this language in that letter: 'Hon, let's get good and plastered; ain't that a nice word?' Do you remember that?"

A: "I do."

Q: "And you meant by that just a good time?"

A: "Yes."

Q: "Nothing with regard to intoxication?"

A: "Not to any great extent, no."

Q: "Oh! Now you admit something in the way of intoxication, do you?"

A: "I was never intoxicated."

Q: "I didn't ask you whether you were ever intoxicated or not. Let me ask you this question. After what I have just read from the letter did not these words follow: 'Beginning to think I am already that way on nothing'? Do you remember that now?"

A: "Yes."

Q: "And you mean to say that you did not mean, 'Let us get good and intoxicated,' when you wrote that?"

A: "No, I did not."

Froessel then asked for and received permission to read the entire letter into the record. Mrs. Snyder dropped her head and chuckled silently at the passage where she described her uncut hair as "beginning to looka like da wop."

Q: "Then you did mean by 'plastered up' intoxicated?"

A: "I didn't mean to get intoxicated, no."

Q: "I did not ask you what you meant to do, I asked you what you meant by that letter."

It was late, she was tired and for once, Mrs. Snyder was at a loss. The witness was silent. When Justice Scudder adjourned court and she stepped wearily down a few minutes later, Froessel had not even gotten to the night of 19 March yet.

17

Day 7, Tuesday, 3 May

THE CROSS-EXAMINATION OF MRS. SNYDER by Assistant District Attorney Froessel continued in the morning with a battle over whether, given the evidence so far—Gray's references to "doing away with the governor" in conversations, telephone calls, and letters since the early part of 1927; finding the sash weight, sleeping powders, and instructions in the package given to her in Henry's Restaurant on Saturday, 5 March; Gray's visit on the night of Monday, 7 March, when Mrs. Snyder claimed to have let him in no further than the pantry and forced him to take back the sash weight; the packet received in the middle of the week preceding the murder; and the telephone call on Thursday night, 10 March, in which Gray said he was coming out to finish "the governor" on Saturday night—Mrs. Snyder had known that Gray intended to murder her husband.

Q: "You testified here, I think, that you knew that he was going to kill your husband the moment you saw the sash weight in the package?"

A: "Yes, but—"

Q: "No buts, madam! So, knowing that he was going to kill your husband and basing your knowledge not only on the correspondence and telephone calls and talks, but upon the giving to you of the sash weight, you returned it to him on Monday night, did you not?"

A: "Yes."

Q: "And it was that night, Monday night, when you returned to him the sash weight, that he said he was coming back Thursday night?"

A: "Yes."

Q: "And you have told us that you did not notify your brother or your husband or the police or anyone?"

A: "No, I didn't notify anyone."

Q: "Knowing that Gray was going to take your husband's life?"

A: "I didn't know he was going to take it until . . ."

Q: "Just a minute, now, madam. Did you not testify that you believed he was going to take your husband's life?"

A: "No, I cannot—"

Justice Scudder intervened, instructing Mrs. Snyder, "Just answer the question." She responded, "Well, yes or no covers so much, Judge, I can't answer."

But the judge insisted: "Just answer questions and do not attempt to explain matters."

Froessel took up questioning again.

Q: "Did you not testify that you knew he would kill your husband?"

A: "That he—"

Q: "Yes or no!"

A: "I can't answer that directly."

Q: "You do not know whether you testified or not?"

A: "I do know I testified, yes."

Q: "Did you not say, according to page 969 of the record, Question: 'Yet from your previous conversation with him you had learned, had you, that he wanted to kill your husband?' Answer: 'He had spoken of it several times, yes'?"

A: "Yes."

Q: "Was not also the following question asked and the following answer given by you? Question: 'You were afraid that he would?' Answer: 'I knew that he would'?"

A: "Yes."

Froessel cited the telephone conversations and letters that were exchanged by the lovers.

Q: "You knowing that he would kill your husband? Yes or no."

A: "Yes."

Gray had threatened to come out on Thursday, 17 March, but only telephoned instead.

Q: "It was on that Thursday night that he told you again that he was coming down on Saturday?"

A: "Yes."

Q: "He also told you that he was coming down to finish the governor, or words to that effect?"

A: "Yes."

Q: "He also wrote you of that large letter that you went after?"

A: "Yes."

Q: "And in that large letter he also told you he was going to kill or finish the governor?"

A: "Yes."

Q: "And all this time you knew that he was going to kill the governor?"

A: "I did not know."

Q: "Didn't you testify that you did know?"

A: "Yes, but . . ."

Q: "No buts, madam. All the time knowing he was coming to kill your husband? Yes or no."

A: "I cannot answer it yes or no."

His client adrift, Hazelton rose to his feet: "I submit if the question cannot be answered by yes or no, then the witness has the right to tell the court so."

Justice Scudder saw little point in further savaging of the witness. He took over questioning himself.

Q: "Just one moment, Mr. Froessel. Madam, do you say you cannot answer the question in that way? Is that is a fact?"

A: "It is a fact."

Q: "Then you may state you cannot answer it yes or no."

A: "I can't answer it yes or no."

Q: "And when you testified to the effect that you knew Gray would kill your husband, what did you mean? Now you may tell the jury."

A: "I knew of the intention he had, but I didn't know directly whether he intended killing him or not. I thought I could persuade him not to, inasmuch as I had done it on two previous occasions."

Q: "That covers your meaning as fully as you are at the present time able to cover it?"

A:"Yes."

"Mr. Froessel, now you may proceed."

Like Millard and Hazelton before him, Froessel took Mrs. Snyder through the events of the fatal evening. She repeated her story up to the point of coaxing Gray downstairs to the living room so she could convince him to leave.

Q:"He still had the revolver in his hand?"

A:"Yes."

Q:"The revolver was loaded, was it?"

A:"Yes."

Q:"You took the revolver from him?"

A:"Yes."

Q:"And laid it on the piano?"

A:"Yes."

Q:"Still knowing, or being afraid that he would kill your husband?"

A:"Yes."

Q:"You didn't take the revolver and put it away somewhere where he couldn't get it?"

A:"No."

Q:"As you did with your jewelry."

Mrs. Snyder was silent.

Q:"You were more interested in your jewelry than you were in your husband's life, were you not?"

Hazelton was on his feet, but Mrs. Snyder was too fast for him.

A:"No!" she screamed at Froessel.

It was her finest moment on the stand. For once, she seemed emotionally involved; interested in more than scoring debating points.

Q:"Bearing in mind the visit of the 7th of March; the telephone conversation on the Thursday of the week preceding; the telephone conversation the Thursday immediately before the murder; the correspondence of at least one letter, the big fat letter . . ."

At this point, Hazelton commented loudly that Froessel seemed to be confusing the letter with himself. The portly Froessel had time to whirl and snarl, "A very bright remark!" before Justice Scudder intervened and rebuked Hazelton. Tempers were allowed to cool for a moment and Froessel returned to his question.

Q: "Knowing or believing that he was coming to your house to kill your husband; bearing in mind all these things, could you not have kept him out of the house by keeping those doors locked?"

A: "Yes."

Q: "As a matter of fact, you did not have one door open, you had two doors left open?"

A: "Yes."

Q: "So that he would surely get in?"

A: "Yes."

Mrs. Snyder claimed that while she was in the bathroom she had heard "a terrific thud" when Gray struck her husband with what Neail had testified was a weak, glancing blow.

Q: "You went into the bathroom?"

A: "Yes."

Q: "And how long were you there?"

A: "Possibly five or seven, eight minutes."

Q: "And at or about the end of that period you heard what you described as a terrific thud?"

A: "Yes."

Froessel elicited that the bathroom and the master bedroom were on opposite ends of the hallway.

Q: "And at the time you heard this terrific thud Gray was in your husband's room?"

A: "Yes."

Q: "And you were in the bathroom?"

A: "Yes."

Q: "With the door to the bathroom closed?"

A: "I do not know whether it was closed or partly closed."

Q: "Are you sure you do not know?"

A: "It might have been closed."

Q: "You were attending to a personal necessity, weren't you?"

A: "Yes."

Q: "The one you told us about the other day?"

A: "Yes."

Q: "You mean to tell us the doorway of that room was open at the time?"

A: "I do not say it was open."

Q: "Then the door of the bathroom was closed?"

A: "I don't know whether it was shut tight or whether I had just pushed it closed."

Q: "Did you not testify yesterday that the door of the bathroom was closed?"

A: "Yes, but it might not have been closed tightly."

Q: "Wait a minute, no buts."

Mrs. Snyder testified once more to rushing into the bedroom and grappling with Gray, fainting, and realizing, when she revived, that she was inextricably tangled up in a murder.

Q: "You fainted, and you say you came to, then you left the room of your husband and yourself?"

A: "Yes, I went to my mother's room."

Q: "And you did not know from any examination that you made of your husband whether or not he was then dead or alive?"

A: "No, I did not."

Q: "And you remained in the room adjoining the body of your husband with Gray for how long?"

A: "For a couple of hours."

According to Mrs. Snyder, she let Gray into the house, she did nothing to help her husband as he lay dying and then, even more incredible, she stuck to Gray's robbery story even when it was clear that it was collapsing.

Q: "Did you tell Police Commissioner McLaughlin that you tried to prevent Gray from committing the murder?"

A: "I don't know whether I did or not."

Q: "Well, think a moment, and let us know; give us your best recollection."

A: "I don't recall what I told him."

Q: "You don't recall some of the things that you told him?"

A: "Some of the things, but I don't recall that."

Q:"Well, madam, wasn't it important to tell the Police Commissioner of the City of New York whether you tried to prevent Gray from committing the murder of your husband or not?"

A:"No, I do not remember that."

Q:"Did you think the police investigation was a joke?"

A:"No."

Q: "And you mean to tell us that after having been taken from your house to the police station on that night, you do not remember whether you told Police Commissioner McLaughlin that you tried to prevent Gray from murdering your husband?"

A:"I don't remember having spoken of it, no."

Q:"Isn't it a fact that you made up that story since you have heard the case of the People here?"

A:"No, it is not."

The "honeymoon bag" was brought out again, prompting Hazelton to object that the State was "parading, for the forty-ninth time, adultery before the jury." Froessel held up various articles and asked Mrs. Snyder whether they belonged to her or to Gray. He finished by brandishing aloft a sanitary napkin.

Q:"And this article—does it belong to you or him?"

A:"To me."

Hazelton demanded, "I submit that the article be named if the District Attorney is going that far with the filth!"

"It isn't my filth."

"Well, you're making it yours!"

Scudder rapped for order.[1]

Like Millard before him, Froessel took Mrs. Snyder through her confession line by line, asking at every point not if the statement was true or false, but simply whether she had made the statement. Her invariable answer was that she wasn't sure; she couldn't remember.

Froessel probed the conditions under which Mrs. Snyder had been

---

1. A package of condoms was also found in the bag. Why did Froessel not hold it up? Delicacy, perhaps. In direct examination, Miller took care to elicit from Gray that all "medicinal items" in the honeymoon bag had been purchased by Mrs. Snyder.

held. She admitted that, contrary to her testimony under direct examination, she had been able to rest from nine o'clock Monday morning until noon and from late afternoon until eight o'clock that evening. Also contrary to her testimony, she admitted that when she signed her edited statement Monday evening, she was reclining comfortably on a couch. She admitted that she had asked if a hairdresser from the neighborhood could be called and had borrowed a curling iron when one was not forthcoming. She did not remember whether she had asked Assistant District Attorney Daly to replace the word "kill" in her statement with "do away with." But she vehemently denied that she had asked matrons about the worst punishment she could get, joked that she would never marry again, or inquired about what would happen to her husband's insurance.

Having claimed to be unable to remember making almost any of the statements in her confession, Mrs. Snyder was now asked to state what was truthful and what was not. "Is this the truth?" Froessel repeatedly asked and then read a sentence from the confession. The description of her marital problems; that she was too young and giddy for Albert Snyder; that he never took her out; that Gray attracted her because she could speak to him about her unhappiness—Mrs. Snyder denied all of it. There had been no fight with Albert Snyder on Saturday, 12 March, in which he threatened to blow her brains out—she never wrote that to Gray. It was also untrue that she was in love with Gray and Gray with her and that none of this would have happened had her husband not threatened her life.

Q: "Is this the truth: 'I saw the weight in Mr. Gray's hand start to travel'?"

A: "No, that is not the truth."

Q: "Is this the truth: 'And immediately heard a thud'?"

A: "Well, I couldn't answer that."

Q: "You did hear a terrific thud?"

A: "Yes. I heard a thud."

Q: "Is this the truth: 'And my husband groaned twice after the thud'?"

A: "No."

Q: "You didn't hear your husband groan at all?"

A: "No, I did not."

Q: "Is this the truth: 'And he then turned my husband's face down on the pillow'?"

A: "I don't know anything about that."

Q: "Is this the truth: 'So that the rag and the blue handkerchief with the chloroform on it would be over his nose and mouth'?"

A: "No, I didn't know anything about that."

Q: "Is this the truth: 'He then covered his head with the blanket to make sure of suffocation'?"

A: "I didn't say that."

Mrs. Snyder began to reel like an exhausted boxer.

Q: "After it was over, you saw Gray downstairs?"

A: "Yes."

Q: "Were you not bound upstairs in your bed?"

A: "Yes."

Q: "Well, then you did not see him out of the house? And you lied just now?"

A: "I didn't lie."

Hazelton jumped to his feet and pointed at Froessel: "Bullying! Bullying! Bulldozing tactics!"

Justice Scudder, his own calm wearing thin, uncharacteristically pounded the bench with his open palm and shouted for silence. Mrs. Snyder dabbed at her eyes with a handkerchief.

The cross-examination ended more with a whimper than a bang.

Q: "Did you make this statement: 'I make this statement with my own free will, without any fear or threat or promise and knowing that anything I say may be used against me'?"

A: "No, I did not."

Q: "You signed your name, did you, under the last statement?"

A: "Yes, I did."

There was little Hazelton could do on redirect to repair the damage. He paid the ultimate tribute to Froessel's devastating cross-examination in his final question.

Q: "During all the time you were at the District Attorney's office and the police station, were you being questioned the same as Mr. Froessel questioned you here?"

A: "Pretty much."

Mrs. Snyder made her way slowly down from the witness stand, sat down in her chair at the defense table, dropped her head into her arms, and wept. It was as if the defendants had changed places. From that point on it was Mrs. Snyder who slouched listlessly with her chin cupped in her hands, while an animated Gray looked about the courtroom and followed every nuance of the proceedings.

Controversy had raged over whether Mrs. Snyder's defense would sink so low as to call Lorraine in a bid for sympathy. Before the trial began, Newcombe promised that the State would fight any such move. In the end, there was a compromise: the child would be called, but not required to take an oath.

As her name was intoned, Lorraine made her way from the judge's chambers wearing a small mushroom cap and a black cape coat that fell down over her shoulders. Scudder motioned for her to come perch next to him on the bench and took her by the hand.

Q: "You understand, don't you, that you have to tell the truth?"

A: "Yes."

Q: "And you are going to try to tell the truth?"

A: "Yes."

Q: "You know that in court you have to tell the truth, don't you?"

A: "Yes, sir."

Q: "You sit down there and listen very carefully to the questions which are put to you. If you do not understand the question, just say, 'I do not understand.' "

A: "Yes, sir."

Q: "And if you do understand the question, then you just answer it, knowing that you must tell the truth."

A: "Yes, sir."

Having established her name and address, he handed her to the court attendant, who led her to the witness chair. "Just lean back in your chair and be comfortable," said Scudder "and look at that gentleman at the end of the table [indicating Hazelton] and do not look at anybody else. Just look right at him."

Hazelton was as smiling and unthreatening as possible—the last thing he needed now was for Lorraine to burst into tears; her mother was already sobbing quietly in her chair. He asked all of three questions.

Q: "Lorraine, do you remember the morning your mother called you?"

A: "Yes, sir."

Q: "Was it daylight or dark?"

A: "Light."

Q: "And how long after she called did you call the Mulhausers?"

A: "Right away."

That was all. There was no cross-examination. Lorraine stepped lightly back through the door three minutes after she had entered the room. Mrs. Snyder gave up her attempts at restraint and cried hysterically. As Lorraine was led from the courthouse, a crowd estimated at five hundred rushed madly to catch a glimpse of the little girl and she, too, burst into tears.

18

A LITTLE AFTER THREE O'CLOCK, Henry Judd Gray walked steadily to the witness stand, dressed in a double-breasted suit with a bit of handkerchief peeking out. Underneath, he wore the brand-new underwear his mother had bought him.

Direct examination was by Samuel Miller, who started with where Gray had grown up, what schools he had attended, what church he worshipped at, and what his domestic situation was at the time of the murder. He established that Gray's average weekly earnings for the past few years had been one hundred dollars.[1]

As Gray began to answer the first question, he almost broke down, but he brushed away a tear and continued. A few seconds later, when asked about his marriage, he choked a bit, but took a long drink of water and was able to control himself. From then on, it was smooth sailing.

He had met Mrs. Snyder in June or July 1925 in Henry's Restaurant through his friend Harry Folsom. The two ended up sitting around swapping stories and having drinks for two or three hours. Mrs. Snyder drank either one or two cocktails.

Q:"And how many drinks did you have at that time?"
A:"That I couldn't tell you, sir, I don't remember."
Q:"Would you say it was more than one?"

1. This refuted a favorite public prejudice—that, while Albert Snyder was a hardworking middle-class striver, Gray was a wealthy playboy. He was not; his expense account just gave him the ability to live more lavishly than his income would otherwise have permitted.

A:"I imagine so, yes, sir, I generally always did."

Q:"Would you say it was more than two?"

A:"I wouldn't be surprised, sir."

A few weeks later, the two men met Mrs. Snyder again in the same restaurant. Harry Folsom left to catch a train and, on his way out, suggested that Gray take Mrs. Snyder back to his office and give her a corset. The office was closed, but Gray had a key. "Mrs. Snyder and I went into the back showroom," Gray testified, "and she removed her dress, and I tried on a garment to see if it was the right size, and I believe that at the time she was badly sunburned, and I offered to get some lotion to fix her shoulders, and it was that first night that we were intimate."

Q:"Did she submit willingly or unwillingly?"

A:"Willingly, I should say."

Gray was exasperatingly eager to leave the impression that he was being truthful. Almost every answer ended in "sir" or the questioner's name; sometimes his questioner got the full treatment:"Yes, Mr. Miller, sir." Believing it more formal, he favored the passive voice:"the restaurant was reached" instead of the more natural "we reached the restaurant"; he was also inclined to legalistic inventions such as "thereinbefore" and "hereinsofar."[2] Wishing to get every detail correct, Gray often turned his head to one side, compressed his lips and reflected before answering. If he was not one-hundred-percent sure of himself even after he had considered the question for some time, he would answer shortly, "I don't know," and force exasperated counsel to rephrase the question. Answers were often prefaced, "To the best of my recollection." But when

2. Gray was what sociolinguists call a "hypercorrector." The most common manifestation of this is when a speaker uses the nominative case of a personal pronoun in the mistaken belief that using the objective case is "common." Thus:"She gave it to him and I" in place of the correct "She gave it to him and me." Hypercorrection is a trait of those who perceive themselves to be social inferiors. Milton MacKaye, in *Dramatic Crimes of 1927*, described Gray as a high-toned drummer whose "either" was always *"eyether."* One journalist wrote that Gray appeared to have committed to memory all the formal language of business correspondence.

Gray *did* recollect, he was a lawyer's dream: the precision of his salesman's memory—dates, names, times—was astounding. And the story line was straight. Whereas Mrs. Snyder's point-by-point insistence that she had done nothing wrong sounded jerky and unnatural, even under direct examination, Gray's testimony flowed effortlessly, needing only occasional nudges from Miller in one direction or another.

In the early part of August 1925, Gray testified, Mrs. Snyder telephoned him at his office and the two met at Henry's.

Q: "Will you please tell us what conversation you had with her that day?"

A: "To my best recollection, she told me about an argument that she had with her husband while she was away on vacation. She said that he had gotten into some difficulty, I believe with one of the guests at their hotel, and that she intended to leave him." [3]

Q: "And what did you say to her?"

A: "I believe that I asked what the difficulty was, and she enumerated it. I asked her if it could not be ironed out satisfactory. . . . I said to her that it seemed pitiful that a home should be broken up where there was a child concerned. She said that she had been very unhappy, that their marital life had been one continuous row, that they did not get along amicably, that she felt this was the best conclusion of the conditions at home."

During February and August, the buying seasons in the corset business, Gray booked a room at the Waldorf for the entire month so he could entertain customers privately and stay in the city overnight when required. In mid-August, the couple enjoyed the first of their many trysts at the Waldorf. Gray had invited Mrs. Snyder to accompany him to a party with some friends and, if possible, to stay overnight with him. Mrs. Snyder arrived in the midafternoon with a suitcase. The pair had drinks in the room, remaining until six thirty. Then they went out to dinner and the theater. They returned shortly before midnight, and Gray procured some more liquor. Gray's friends dropped by to pick them up, and the

3. Mrs. Snyder testified that she did not speak to Gray about her unhappy home life until January 1926.

foursome went to a roof-garden dance. After the dance, the group went back to Gray's friends' home. At about four o'clock, Gray and Mrs. Snyder returned to the Waldorf and had sexual intercourse. "I don't remember very much about it," testified Gray, "I was very intoxicated."

In September 1925, Mrs. Snyder mentioned that she intended to try to earn some money on the side so she could send Lorraine away to school. Then, in one of their meetings around the beginning of September, Mrs. Snyder brought up the subject of insurance. She asked how much Gray carried. He told her twenty thousand dollars' worth and asked how much her husband carried. "Very little," replied Mrs. Snyder. She then went on to ask about the best kinds of insurance.

It was during the third week of February 1926, when the couple was staying at the Hotel Imperial, that Mrs. Snyder first divulged her terrible secret. The conversation started innocently enough, with Mrs. Snyder complaining as usual about her home life.

Q: "Can you recollect some of the conversation, especially as to what she said to you about her home difficulties?"

A: "Well, if I recall correctly, it was at that particular time that she had had another serious argument at home, and that conditions there were . . . relationships were very strained at that particular moment."

Q: "Did you have any particular conversation with her in the early morning?"

A: "Well, an argument ensued that particular night. I was quite intoxicated when I came in and, as I remember it, she asked me would I think it was terrible if she confided a secret in me of doing away with her husband."

As she had since Gray began recounting the lovers' meetings, Mrs. Snyder sat staring at the table before her. Then she buried her head in her arms and wept.

"I told her that I thought she was terrible," Gray continued. "I don't remember exactly what ensued after that. I remember we had a terrible argument over the thing at that time. . . . She said she did not believe in God. I told her there certainly must be a God, which led to further argument. As I say, I was in a semi-intoxicated condition."

Hazelton interrupted. "You hear, Your Honor, the witness says he was very drunk." "I said I was semi-intoxicated, sir," replied Gray, as if offended.[4]

In March 1926, Gray went on, he visited the Snyder residence for the first time. Granny Brown was there when he arrived at noon and said that she had heard all about him and trusted him to take good care of her daughter. She left at one thirty, but Gray and Mrs. Snyder stayed until the midafternoon.

Q: "What did Mrs. Snyder say to you and what did you say to Mrs. Snyder?"

A: "The question came up at that particular time of her showing me the contents of a bottle."

Q: "Do you recall what she said about the bottle?"

A: "She showed me the bottle, and said it contained a certain poison. I told her it was dangerous to keep poison around that way and asked her to throw it out, and she did."

Q: "What did she say?"

A: "She said it contained arsenic."

Day 8, Wednesday, 4 May

This was to be the day that Gray described the slaying, and by the time Scudder had entered and given his habitual caution against public displays, more than two thousand spectators had crammed themselves into the courtroom. More than one reporter looked queasy—the press corps had been guests of Maurine Watkins at a performance of *Chicago* the night before, with a reception following the show. Members of a troupe of gypsies who, finding themselves camped nearby, decided to take in the trial, added an exotic touch to the scene.

---

4. Gray was squeamish on the stand about his drinking, taking exception, for example, to counsel's characterization of his alcohol consumption as "excessive" and forever insisting that he was "semi-intoxicated," not drunk. When Gray testified for the hundredth time to having had "a couple of drinks," the vaudeville comedienne Nora Bayes put trial goers in stitches by braying, "Why, there ain't that many drinks in the whole wide world!"

Under Miller's questioning, Gray testified that at a meeting in Henry's Restaurant in mid-July 1926, Mrs. Snyder showed him a five-thousand-dollar policy on Albert Snyder's life and asked if he knew anything about insurance.

"I said I knew very little. She asked me to look the policy over, and see if there was anything in it concerning drowning. I asked her why. She said that she thought that her husband might drown that summer while he was down at the bungalow." Gray glanced through the policy and replied that he did not know and returned it to her.

Gray and Mrs. Snyder saw each other some ten to fifteen times during the late spring and summer months of 1926. Gray dated Mrs. Snyder's attainment of complete mastery over him to a rendezvous at the Waldorf in July. On that occasion, Mrs. Snyder brought two bottles of rye whiskey and two vials containing sleeping powders.

"I had quite a few drinks from the rye whiskey. She asked me if I would try out these vials of sleeping powders to see what effect they would have on me. I asked her if they were poison. She said no, they would just put me to sleep, and she wanted to see what effect they would have on me. I had three or four more drinks and tried first one vial. She gave me three or four more drinks of whiskey and then I tried the other vial."

This was at five o'clock in the afternoon. Gray knew nothing more until the next morning at eight o'clock when Mrs. Snyder telephoned and woke him up. She said that he had taken her home in a taxi, but he remembered nothing of this. He felt terrible, so shaky that he had difficulty packing his bags and checking out of the hotel.

In September 1926, Gray and Mrs. Snyder spent a full week together at the Waldorf. Mrs. Snyder complained of her health—she was having trouble with her heart; once she fainted dead away in the street. Things had reached the breaking point at home, she said.

"She stated to me that she was going to do away with the governor. I told her I thought she was crazy, asked her if she had been to see a doctor; she said no. I had told her on previous occasions that I thought she ought to go and have a bump that is on her forehead examined. She said that wasn't necessary. I asked her how she planned to do this thing, and she said by the sleeping powders she had given me. She said that she had tried them out once before upon him by putting them in a prune whip, and they apparently had no effect."

According to Gray, this was the first of repeated murder attempts related to him by Mrs. Snyder. Gray told her that such a scheme was insane and broached the idea of a trip upstate to help Mrs. Snyder cheer up. She jumped at the invitation—she would say that she was going to Canada with a friend; her mother would be more than happy to keep house. Gray explained to her that the trip could not be right away; he had business to attend to first.

Gray went on the road. He received daily letters at his hotels from Mrs. Snyder, who complained of the unbearable conditions at home. When he returned in late September, the pair met at the Waldorf. Mrs. Snyder told him that she had tried to poison her husband with gas while he took a nap in the living room. The attempt failed, and she commented, "It was too damned bad the pipe was not long enough to go up his nose"—the very thing that Mrs. Snyder accused Gray of saying.

"I said that I thought she was crazy to entertain any such thought as this, that there was an easy way out by getting a divorce. She said she had watched him to see if he was going out with other women, but she did not think that he was."

Mrs. Snyder reported that she was going to meet Ethel Anderson to finalize arrangements to frame Edward Pierson.

"I suggested that if he was not going out with other women he might be framed the same way. She said no; that wouldn't do. I asked her why. She said, 'Just because.' "

Mrs. Snyder related that she and her husband had been in another fight and had not spoken to each other in two days. According to Mrs. Snyder, this did not prevent Albert Snyder from forcing himself on her in bed, and she related her disgust.

The upstate trip, Gray continued, had been arranged for the second week of October. On Monday, he and Mrs. Snyder met at the train station in Newark. The pair set off in Gray's car through the glorious autumn colors of the Hudson River Valley, making their first overnight stop at Kingston. This was, Mrs. Snyder declared gaily, her first real honeymoon.

The first night of the trip, conversation centered on sex, Gray testified. "She said that she had never really known what sexual pleasures were with her husband. I sympathized with her, as I recall, that it was too bad, as I felt that was probably one of the greatest reasons for her unhappiness. She told me that when he came over into bed with her it was so disgusting and degrading that she felt like killing him. I told her that I could not understand such a thing as that because I was not unhappy at home with my relations in that extent with my wife. We had considerable talk on sex that night."

From the moment the couple awoke in Kingston, there was a sore point between them: Gray's business duties.

"The following morning I woke her up and told her it was time for me to get up, that I had to attend to my business. I was in very much of a daze and told her that I did not feel like going out to work. She asked me if I could not stay in bed. I said no, that I could not, that this was a business trip as well as pleasure; that I did not feel that it was fair to my firm when I was out on business to lay down on the job. She said 'Well, you go ahead and do your work and I will get up when I am ready.' "

Mrs. Snyder, left to fend for herself during the day while Gray called on customers, began to grow restive.

After Kingston came Albany, Troy, Schenectady, Amsterdam, Glover, Boonville, Watertown, and Syracuse. In Troy, Mrs. Snyder laughed and called it an "old man's honeymoon" because for two nights running, they had stayed in rooms with twin beds. Never mind, she said, and pushed the beds together.

As the trip entered its second week, Gray continued, the couple crossed over into Pennsylvania and spent the night in Scranton. Mrs. Snyder suggested that they "get good and plastered"—that word again— as it would be one of their last evenings together. Gray demurred, pointing out that he had a hard day's work ahead. In the end, a bit of persuasion from Mrs. Snyder had the desired effect, with predictable consequences for Gray.

"I told her the following morning that this thing could not keep up, my physical condition was such, when I woke up I would be in a daze; when I would call upon my trade I could not sufficiently collect my thoughts to know what I was talking about. She said she realized that we had been excessive in our intercourse and the following night, if we stayed over, we would not have any."

Mrs. Snyder was true to her word, and Gray woke up the next day declaring that he felt better than he had ever since they left. But the end of the trip was at hand, and on the tenth day of Mrs. Snyder's "first real honeymoon," she and Gray drove all morning to Newark, arriving at lunchtime. After lunch, Mrs. Snyder took a trolley car to the subway line and returned to her hateful existence in Queens Village.

When they met a few days later at Henry's Restaurant, Gray testified, the first subject on Mrs. Snyder's lips was how desperate the situation was at home. She and her husband had done nothing but quarrel since she returned, she said, and she could stand it no longer. She absolutely had to do something to get rid of him.

"I told her I thought she was foolish to entertain such thoughts as this. I had taken her away on this trip with me to rid her mind of all such ideas, it had not been spoken of at any point during the trip, and I thought she had forgotten it."

Mrs. Snyder had progressed from sleeping powders and gas to chloral hydrate.

"She asked me if I knew anything about knockout drops. I said I didn't. She said, 'Well, you ought to know what they administer in liquor to put people out.' I said I knew nothing about such things. . . . She said that she had been out on a party one night with some friends and this man had given her one drink and she had passed out for hours."

When she asked whether Gray could put his hands on any such substance, he said no.

The next day, Gray went to Queens Village for lunch. Over drinks, Mrs. Snyder showed him how she had kicked off the gas tube in the living room while Albert Snyder slept. She was insane to try such a thing in her own house, Gray said.

"She said she absolutely could not stand him longer, she had to get rid of him. I said, 'Did you try it before?' She said, 'Yes, I did.' I said, 'When?' She said, 'Out in the garage.' I said to her 'How did you do that?' She told me she had brought liquor to him and given him two drinks while he was working on the car one Sunday the previous winter in the garage; that he had had the motor running, but he had come out before anything had happened. I said, 'I cannot understand how anybody can do a thing like this.' She said, 'Well, that is because you don't know him and do not feel towards him the way I do.' "

October gave way to November. Mrs. Snyder asked again about knockout drops; she had obtained sleeping powders but did not think they were strong enough. Could Gray find out what might be used? In the second half of November, again at the Waldorf, Mrs. Snyder began talking about using a combination of sleeping powders and gas. Then came the real point.

"She said she was going to make one more attempt, and that if that failed, that I would have to help her with some plan. I said, 'This I cannot do.' She said she was at her wits' end to know how to get out of her difficulties. I said, 'I cannot help you because I don't know anything about these things.' . . . She brought up the subject again while we were in bed, after I had a number of drinks, and asked me if I would promise that I would find out what she should use. . . . I told her I would try."

In December, Gray testified, Mrs. Snyder wrote that she had again tried sleeping powders twice, in different doses, but without success. She had also once more kicked off the gas tube, but her husband woke up and smelled the gas.[5] Mrs. Snyder told Gray that her husband had threatened her with his pistol. When Gray asked whether Snyder was serious, Mrs. Snyder replied that he was liable to do anything. He had slapped Lorraine, almost knocking her down.

A few days after Christmas, Mrs. Snyder asked Gray if he would be willing to shoot her husband with a revolver. Gray sounded almost indignant as he described his response: "I said, 'Absolutely not!' I never shot a man in my life!' "

Around this time, Mrs. Snyder complained that she was having a hard time paying the premiums on her husband's life insurance.

"I asked her why she did not drop the insurance if she was finding it

5. Gray is a bit confused about the date: the second attempt at gassing Snyder took place, not in December 1926, but in January 1927.

too great a task to keep up. She said she would lose some money. I told her I thought it was better for her to drop it than to try to keep it up if she could not afford to. As I recall it, she didn't say if she would drop it, but said she would think it over."

Miller wished to establish that Gray had never even met Snyder. Accordingly, Gray testified how he and Mrs. Snyder celebrated New Year's Eve together, one day early, over lunch at Henry's Restaurant with a few friends. Afterward, Mrs. Snyder called her husband, who was in another part of the city, to arrange for him to drive her home. Gray walked with Mrs. Snyder until they got close to Stern Brothers, where she was to meet her husband, then he went into a store while she continued alone. When he emerged from the store a few minutes later, Gray saw Mrs. Snyder walking toward him with two men, but didn't know which was her husband. Mrs. Snyder smiled at him and Gray nodded his head politely. It was the first and only time he saw Albert Snyder before the fatal night of 19 March.

The afternoon session opened with Gray's version of Albert Snyder's bout with the hiccoughs. According to his account, the drops Mrs. Snyder gave her husband in heroic quantities only put Albert Snyder to sleep. She then took bichloride of mercury tablets, filed off the "Poison" label stamped on them, and gave him several, telling him it was bismuth. Albert Snyder vomited violently during the night, but awoke to find his hiccoughs had been cured.

"I told her it was a hell of a way to cure hiccoughs," testified Gray, to the loud laughter of the courtroom audience.

Miller questioned Gray about his borrowing from Mrs. Snyder. He had borrowed money from time to time, Gray answered, but never in large sums and he always promptly repaid her. In February 1926, he borrowed two hundred dollars—he repaid one hundred dollars in March when he cashed a check at the Waldorf, gave her fifty dollars later at Henry's Restaurant, and paid the final fifty dollars in late March or early April. Not so long ago, he borrowed seventy-five dollars. He figured that, at the moment, he owed Mrs. Snyder twenty-five dollars on that loan.

Gray testified that in early February 1927, Albert Snyder experienced yet another brush with death. Before going out to a family gathering at his sister's, Snyder took a drink of whiskey that Mrs. Snyder had poisoned with bichloride of mercury, but it only caused him to vomit once and feel sick all evening. A cousin advised that whiskey should be drunk after, not before, dinner. Mrs. Snyder then asked Gray about the proper dosage, complaining that she had tried one tablet, one and a half tablets, and four tablets, all with no success.

When he returned from a selling trip in Pennsylvania on Friday of the third week of February 1927, Gray was met at the station by Mrs. Snyder. They went to the Waldorf, where she had already registered and procured a bottle of gin. After an uptown dinner, accompanied by much drinking, they returned to the hotel about midnight. Mrs. Snyder announced that she felt like getting drunk and, true to her word, had three or four drinks and passed out on the floor. Gray revived her with difficulty and put her to bed.

After they had talked for an hour and a half in bed, their conversation turned, as it invariably did when they were alone, to the same subject. Mrs. Snyder said that she had exhausted all means at her disposal to kill her husband and that it was a matter of absolute necessity that Gray help her. Her latest idea was to wait until he was sleeping, then knock him unconscious and chloroform him. Did Gray think it would work?

"I said that it was possible. She asked me if I would help her do this. I said I would not. She then asked me if I would get the chloroform for her. I said that I would. I asked her if she was going to do this herself. She said she would try it."

In late February or early March—Gray could not remember which—after several drinks before lunch in Queens Village, there was further discussion of the chloroform strategy and Mrs. Snyder asked if a burglary attempt could be faked after the murder.

"I told her I thought it could. She said, 'You are going to help me, are you not?' and I said, 'No, I am not going to help you, only inasmuch as getting the chloroform for you.' She spoke about an instrument to be used, a hammer, if I recall correctly. I think it was my suggestion about a window weight."

The drinking continued after lunch. Gray became very drunk while Mrs. Snyder elaborated on the arrangements to be made.

"She asked me if I would get some colored handkerchiefs and the chloroform and the window weight and a pair of gloves, I believe, if I remember correctly. I was about to leave on a trip and I said I would."

Mrs. Snyder pressed upon him again the vital importance of assisting her in the actual slaying.

"I said I did not think I could do such a thing, that I had never killed anybody in my life."

Mrs. Snyder rode with him on a bus to Grand Central Terminal and, in seeing him off, said, "Do not forget to get the things, and you are going to help me."

Gray repeated that he would get her the requested items but did not think that he would be able to help her in the actual killing.

"I took the train and went to Albany. I got in rather late and I went across the street and had several more drinks. I got to thinking this thing over, and thinking how terrible it was that I should become embroiled in this matter, and I swore to myself that I would have nothing to do with it."

On the evening of Thursday, 3 March, Gray telephoned Mrs. Snyder from Albany and asked if she was really serious about this. When she assured him that she was, he went out and got drunk. Nevertheless, he also bought one red and one blue handkerchief as he had been instructed. The next day in Kingston, he bought the window weight and the chloroform.

He returned to New York carrying these in his sample case. From the station, he went straight to his office, where he consumed several drinks and received a telephone call from Mrs. Snyder. She was bringing Lorraine into the city for a doctor's appointment the next day, Saturday, 5 March, and suggested that the trio have lunch at Henry's Restaurant.

Gray stayed overnight in the city and Mrs. Snyder telephoned again in the morning, saying that she would be at Henry's around noon. Gray told her that he had obtained the pinchbottle she wanted and that he would put the sash weight together with the bottle in a package and bring it along to Henry's. It must have been a rather bulky affair in all—the whiskey bottle, the sash weight wrapped in four or five layers of paper, the "flesh reducer," and a corset. There was, Gray said in contradiction to Mrs. Snyder's testimony, no note.

Gray arrived at the restaurant after fortifying himself with alcohol. He found Mrs. Snyder and Lorraine already seated and being served.

"I kissed her hello. She said, 'My God, what is the matter with you?' I said, 'I am so frightfully nervous; I do not know what I am doing.' "

Gray ordered lunch but barely ate. He placed the package on the fourth chair at the table and Mrs. Snyder asked if the weight was there. He said that it was. It was difficult to communicate because of Lorraine, so Mrs. Snyder also scribbled a note listing the contents of the package and passed it to Gray for confirmation. Gray picked at his food, had another drink, and left after only half an hour.

Mrs. Snyder's plan was gaining momentum. Two days later, on Monday, 7 March, she telephoned Gray shortly after noon and asked him to come to the house. When he said that he did not think he could, she suggested meeting at Jamaica Station. He protested that he had not eaten, but Mrs. Snyder insisted. Gray prepared himself, as usual, with a few drinks and took along a small bottle of whiskey. When he arrived at about three o'clock, he was met by Mrs. Snyder on the platform and he asked if they could get something to eat near the station. Mrs. Snyder suggested a Chinese restaurant.

In the restaurant, Mrs. Snyder laid her cards on the table.

"I asked her what she wanted to see me about and she said relative to doing away with her husband. She said that she had practiced with the window weight and she lost all her strength when she tried to swing it, and that I would have to help her. I told her I did not think I could help her in any way in this respect. . . . I then said, 'You will have to do this yourself.' I told her that I could not do it alone; if I must do it that she would have to help me. I went back to the toilet, finished the bottle that I had brought with me, and I came back, I recall, and spilled a cruet of juice they had on the table and she said, 'My God, you are nervous, aren't you?' I said, 'I certainly am. I hardly know what I am doing.' "

Mrs. Snyder asked Gray whether he would come that night. He agreed, even though he was leaving on the midnight sleeper for Buffalo and his baggage was already checked through. She reminded him to bring the chloroform and handkerchiefs and some rope as well. She would try to get her husband to go to bed early. If it was all right for Gray to come in, she told him, she would leave a light in her mother's window as a sign. If there was no light, he should wait at the kitchen door.

By the time Gray got back to his office, it was five thirty. He had been drinking steadily since early afternoon. During the early evening hours, he drank nearly a quart of whiskey. Since he could not find any rope, he took some picture wire from the office. After stopping off for a sandwich on the way to the station, Gray boarded the Long Island Railroad train and arrived in Queens Village at nine o'clock.

Far gone from drinking, he wandered around the streets until eleven o'clock, passing the Snyder residence several times. There was a light in the cellar, but none in the upstairs bedroom. Gray knew that he had to leave soon to catch his train. At eleven fifteen, he heard a tap at the kitchen window and saw Mrs. Snyder gesturing to him to come in. There was a hurried conference at the back door, her standing in the kitchen and him in the pantry.

"She was in her nightgown. She kissed me and had a bottle of whiskey in her hand with about half a pint in it. She asked me if I would have a drink. I said that I would. I think I drained the bottle, if I am not mistaken. She asked me if I would do the job that night. I said, no, I could not go through with it. She said, 'Won't you stay and we'll go up together?' I said, 'No, I do not think I can go through with it, Mommy.' I asked her if she wanted to keep the things I had brought over there. She said that she did not think she had better, and I agreed with her."

Still carrying the chloroform, the handkerchiefs, and the picture wire, a very relieved Gray hurried to the train station, picked up his sleeper in Hoboken, and went to Buffalo.

Mrs. Snyder sent Gray eight or nine letters during this, his last trip. As usual, he had destroyed them all. In one letter, received in Buffalo, she pressed him again to obtain chloral hydrate. The night of Saturday, 19 March, looked good, she wrote—she and her husband would be going to a party. From Buffalo, Gray traveled to Hornell, where a waiting letter said that she could not be certain about Saturday because her husband's habits were so unpredictable. On Tuesday, 15 March, he traveled to Jamestown, where two more letters were waiting. Mrs. Snyder had written to confirm the arrangement for Saturday night and promised to send further details in a letter, to await him in Rochester. She added that she hoped Gray would be less nervous than he was on the previous occasion.

From Dunkirk, Gray posted a large letter containing her birthday presents, a red and a blue handkerchief—not to be confused with those purchased for the purpose of chloroforming Albert Snyder—as well as some sleeping powders that Mrs. Snyder had requested. This was the "big, fat letter" that had elicited Hazelton's tasteless reference to Froessel's girth.

Gray arrived in Rochester Wednesday, 16 March, and found the promised two letters waiting for him at the Hotel Seneca. The murder was definitely on for Saturday night, Mrs. Snyder wrote. She and her husband and Lorraine would be at the party and her mother would be away on a nursing job. Mrs. Snyder would leave both the cellar and kitchen doors unlocked. Gray was to enter by the latter. If there was a package of cigarettes on the kitchen table, it meant the coast was clear; he was to go up to Granny Brown's bedroom and wait there. If there were no cigarettes, it meant they had come home and he should wait in the kitchen for her to come down. Under the pillow in Granny Brown's room, he would find a bottle of whiskey, a pair of pliers, and the sash weight. Gray was to bring with him the articles he had brought out last time, as well as a five-foot length of rope.

On Thursday night, 17 March, Albert Snyder enjoyed his last bowling night. Gray had intended not to call Mrs. Snyder as he usually did on Thursdays, but he got drunk and could not resist. He asked her if she had received his letter from Dunkirk. She confirmed that she had. She asked him if he was coming out Saturday night. He said he thought he could. This was the last communication between the pair before the night of the murder. On Friday evening, Gray arrived back in Syracuse, checked into the Hotel Onondaga, drank heavily, and went to bed around two or three o'clock in the morning.

On Saturday, Gray ran errands and worked around town in the morning. Over lunch with Haddon Gray, he arranged for the latter to make it look like his room was occupied that night. After lunch, Gray returned to his room, wrote the letters that his friend was to mail, and had a few more drinks. On his way to the station, he stopped off to buy more whiskey and packed it away in his briefcase along with the chloroform bottle, rubber gloves, the cotton rags, blue handkerchief, picture wire, and gauze.

After a short wait on the station platform, Gray climbed aboard the Empire State Limited bound for New York. He ate an early dinner and settled back with his whiskey as the miles clicked away between him and his deadly rendezvous with Albert Snyder.

19

GRAY HAD REACHED the high point of his performance, the moment for which he had been preparing. Miller asked no more questions now. Gray was speaking entirely in his own words. His eyes were closed most of the time, as if he was watching his story unfold before him.

He arrived at Grand Central at ten twenty and, as an experienced traveler, purchased his return ticket to Syracuse on the 8:45 morning train. He walked across town to Penn Station and waited some time for the next Long Island Railroad train. It was after midnight when he arrived at the Snyder residence, having walked a circuitous route from the Queens Village station. He had finished off what remained of a half-pint bottle of whiskey on the way.

He found the side door unlocked as promised and, when he entered, observed a package of cigarettes on the kitchen table. He was unable to remember if the cigarettes meant he was supposed to go upstairs or to wait in the kitchen. Confused, he stood for ten or fifteen minutes listening for signs of life and, hearing none, pocketed the cigarettes and went up to Granny Brown's room.

"I went over to the pillow and found the sash weight, the pliers, which were long-nosed and nickel-plated, and a bottle, I would say probably a four-ounce bottle." He drained the bottle and immediately felt ill. His head spinning, he sat on the floor to collect himself. Gray wasn't sure how long he sat there, but he found a quart bottle of whiskey beside the chest of drawers and took three or four slugs. That helped to pull him together, but he still felt too sick to get up. Sitting on the floor, he opened his briefcase and assembled the items he had brought down from Syracuse. When he felt better, he raised himself into an armchair.

At this point, Gray testified, his nerves got the better of him and he started to leave.

"I got as far as almost the ground floor on the stairs when I heard an automobile coming along and saw the lights pulling up outside the front door. I ran back upstairs."

It had been a false alarm; the car drove by the house. Gray stayed in the bedroom long enough to have five or six more pulls at the whiskey bottle to steady himself, then decided to make another break for it. As he descended the stairs, a car drove up and he heard people coming up the porch steps. This time, there was no question of a mistake. Gray ran back upstairs as fast as his legs could carry him and barely had time to hide on the floor of Granny Brown's room before Mrs. Snyder and Lorraine entered through the front door.

Mother and daughter came upstairs and went into Lorraine's bedroom. A few moments later, Mrs. Snyder came to the door of Granny Brown's room, which was slightly ajar. "Are you there, dear?" she whispered. Gray answered in the affirmative, and she said, "Wait quietly and I will be back shortly." She went into the master bedroom, then walked back down the hallway into Lorraine's room. By this time, she had taken off her dress and was wearing only her slip.

A minute later, Mrs. Snyder appeared in Granny Brown's room and kissed him; then she returned to the master bedroom. Albert Snyder come up the stairs, went into the master bedroom for a few moments, then emerged and went to the bathroom. While he was there, Mrs. Snyder appeared again and asked if Gray had found the items under the pillow.

"She said, 'You've been drinking quite a bit, haven't you?' I said, 'Plenty.' "

Mrs. Snyder went to the bathroom, which had been vacated by her husband, then passed by the door to Granny Brown's room again as she went into the master bedroom.

It seemed to be only a very short time before Mrs. Snyder returned. She said, "You are going through with it tonight, are you not?" to which Gray replied, "I don't know whether I can or not, but I will try."

It was two thirty, Gray estimated. Mrs. Snyder asked how long they should wait. Gray replied that he did not know. She sneaked into the master bedroom a few times to check that her husband was sleeping. Shortly after three o'clock, she returned and said that the time seemed right.

Gray put on the rubber gloves he had brought and Mrs. Snyder put on his buckskin gloves. Picking up the sash weight, he gave Mrs. Snyder a length of picture wire, the handkerchief, the cotton rags, and the bottle of chloroform. The bottle was wrapped in an Italian newspaper that Gray had picked up on the train.

Gray spoke in a low drone that magnified the horror of the story he told. Not a spectator stirred; Gray held them breathless. More than one reporter's pencil fell motionless as its holder, hung over and spellbound, forgot to take notes.

"I had my glasses off. She took me by the hand; we went out into the hall; the door of the bedroom was closed except for a crack. She opened the door; she entered the room, and I followed her. I don't know how many seconds I stood there trying to get my bearings, and I struck him on the head, as nearly as I could see, one blow. I think I hit him another blow because with the first blow he raised up in bed and started to holler. I went over on the bed on top of him and tried to get the bedclothes over his mouth, so as to suppress his cries."

Gray started to break down and Miller rose to ask for a recess. Gray interrupted him. "No, I'm fine. I want to go on."

"He was apparently full of fight. He got me by the necktie, and a struggle ensued, in which I was getting the worse, because I was being choked. I hollered, 'Mommy, Mommy, for God's sake help me!' I had dropped the weight. She came over, threw the bottle of chloroform, wire, and everything onto the pillow, took the weight, and hit him on the head. I finally got him between my knees in some manner and had him by the throat with my left hand, I believe. My right hand was over his mouth with the covers."

"The next thing I knew," Gray recalled, "his hands were tied with a towel, which she had gotten from the bathroom. I called to her to close the window on account of the outcry. The covers were pulled up over his head. If there were rags packed in his nose and mouth I do not because nobody pushed them in there, as far as I know."

Gray said that, in his alcoholic haze, he lost track of events for a minute or two and found himself sitting on the floor. He asked Mrs. Snyder to give him the wire and, learning from her that it was somewhere jumbled up in the bedclothes, asked instead for one of Albert Snyder's neckties. This he tied around Snyder's feet. Gray had found the second piece of wire in his pocket, and he tied this around Snyder's hands.

At this point, Gray sobbed and, leaning forward with his hand to his throat, drank unsteadily from the glass of water next to the witness chair. His mother and sister wept quietly. Mrs. Snyder sat in what had been her characteristic pose ever since her battering at Froessel's hands: drooped forward, chin resting in her hands. Hazelton and Wallace had drawn their chairs close to the witness stand and stared at Gray with the expressions of beaten men. Miller had promised in his opening statement that Gray would repudiate his confession; maybe throw all the blame on Mrs. Snyder; give them something to fight back at. Instead, he was confirming it practically word by word.

"The next thing I remember, we walked back to the bathroom. I washed the blood off my hands. . . . She took off the buckskin gloves she had on and handed them to me. It was there that she discovered blood on my shirt and on my vest. There was blood all over the front of her night-gown, and all over the front of her bathrobe. She said, 'My God, look at me.' We walked back into her mother's room. She said, 'What will we do?' I said, 'I don't know.' She said, 'Well, blood on me will be all right, because I am sick.' I said, 'My God, not that kind of blood!' She said, 'Take off your shirt,' and I guess I did; I don't remember. . . . I waited in her mother's room, and she went out. She came back in the room with a blue shirt, which was new, and told me to put it on."

She must have gone downstairs and burned her bloodstained clothes, Gray testified, because she was wearing a fresh nightgown. A brief domestic interlude ensued when Gray discovered that Albert Snyder's shirt was much too large for him. He suggested that Mrs. Snyder cut a new buttonhole so that at least the collar would fit properly. She brought a pair of scissors and performed the improvised alteration on the spot.

"I asked her what she had done with my shirt and she told me she had taken it down to the cellar and burned it, together with her bathrobe and nightgown; and we went down into the cellar, and I could smell the burning cloth.[1] I reached over into the coal bin and picked up a lump of coal at a time and threw it into the furnace [in order to keep the noise down]. I took a broom and swept around where I had stepped in the coal dust. I asked her what she had done with the window weight, and she told me she had hidden it in a box. She took me over and showed me where the box was, and the window weight had been stripped of its paper and was bare.[2] I went back to the ashes and took some ashes and sprinkled them on the weight. She asked me what I did that for. I said, if I recollect, to make it look as though it had laid there a long time."

Gray and Mrs. Snyder climbed the stairs and sat talking in the living room. They were still there when the milkman went by about four thirty, so they had sat there for over an hour. Then they went upstairs and began disturbing things to fake a robbery. Gray profited from the occasion to return to Granny Brown's room and take a few more drinks from the steadily diminishing quart bottle. The pair then returned to the master bedroom.

"She asked me if he was dead. I said I did not think so. She said, 'He has got to be dead. This has got to go through or I am ruined.' I said, 'I am through with you and everything,' and I started to muss up the room. She asked me to tie some wire around his neck. I tried to and I could not. I took the wire off his hands. I tried to put it around his neck, but I could not. I went out of the room and went back into the mother's room and finished the bottle of whiskey, and I came back into the room again, and whether there was wire around his neck or not, I do not know. I went over to the chiffonnier, started to throw things about. . . . I asked her where his pistol was, and she got it for me out of his clothes press, and she handed it to me.[3] I took the pistol and broke it and I think I touched his

---

1. Mrs. Snyder also told him that she had changed her pillowcase, throwing the bloodstained one in the dirty clothes hamper in the basement.

2. Gray claimed to have kept the paper wrapping on the sash weight because he thought this would lessen the pain of the blow.

3. Mrs. Snyder testified that Albert Snyder's pistol was under the pillow. Gray's ignorance of the pistol finds some corroboration in McDermott's notebook record of the

hand with the pistol and threw it on the bed. I told her to muss up the room downstairs. I know I threw everything about in her room and her mother's room. She told me not to touch her little girl's room. So I didn't."

"The next thing I knew she came back upstairs and I asked her if she had mussed up things downstairs and she said that she had. She asked me if her husband was dead and I told her I thought so; that he was cold. She went over to her bureau and where she got them from I do not know— out of a bag or someplace—she gave me a lot of powders, a box of what she said was bichloride of mercury tablets in a Midol box. She told me at the time that she had a capsule that had enough poison in it to kill twelve people that she was going to keep."

They continued to rip the house apart, with Gray doing "a lot of sense-less things"—like throwing cushions about—because he was drunk. He worked his way through the living room and kitchen to the dining room, where he extracted a fresh bottle from the sideboard and took a few drinks.

"I do not recall whether she took the wallet out of her husband's overcoat or whether I took it. . . . She told me to take the money. I asked her if she knew how much there was there. She said that she had not counted it. I asked her if she had not better keep it. She said no, for me to take it. She thought there was around seventy-odd dollars. She asked me if I would take her jewelry. I said no. She asked me how she could explain it. I said, 'Hide it somewhere, and they will not probably know anything about it.'"[4]

Daylight was breaking over Queens Village; Mrs. Snyder reminded Gray that he needed to get moving. "I went upstairs with her. She asked me if I would hit her on the head to make it look as though she had been

statement that Gray made on the train from Syracuse to New York: "To tell you the truth, if I'd known there was a gun, I never would have gone in there."

4. This contradicts reports, widely circulated at the time of his arrest, that Gray railed in his cell against the greed that had led Mrs. Snyder to safeguard her jewelry and spoil the burglary story. According to Detective Lieutenant McDermott's notes of Gray's statement on the train, Gray said, "I could not take a woman's jewelry."

struck too. I told her I could not.[5] She asked me to tie her up. She laid on her mother's bed and I tied up her feet with rope that she had brought up from the cellar on her first visitation when she burned the clothes. . . . I told her it may be two months, it may be a year, and it may be never before she would see me again, and I left her laying on her mother's bed and I went out."

Gray slumped back in the witness chair and wept. Mrs. Snyder fell onto the arm of her chair and sobbed uncontrollably. There was no question of proceeding further, given the late hour and the dramatic peak that had been reached. Justice Scudder adjourned court, and the prisoners were escorted back to their cells. Mrs. Snyder was stooped and shuffling. Gray was crying but walked upright and defiant until the courtroom door closed behind him, whereupon his knees buckled and he wilted into the arms of his guard. The crowd sat transfixed for a few moments before anyone stirred. A few wags, whistling past the graveyard, began to make wisecracks and small talk. Most did not.

Day 9, Thursday, 5 May

Because several spectators had fainted during Gray's testimony, two emergency room attendants from Saint John's Hospital were posted in the courtroom. Dressed in hospital whites, each carried a small first-aid kit.

On further direct examination by Miller, Gray quickly finished his story of events that fatal night in Queens Village.

Leaving the house by the kitchen door soon after daybreak, he took a taxi from Jamaica to 59th Street and Broadway in order to avoid a long wait for a train. After eating breakfast at Grand Central, Gray boarded the 8:45 train for Syracuse. "I tried to read, but I could not. I tried to sleep, but I could not." Near Poughkeepsie, when the train passed close to the Hudson, he threw in the briefcase containing the empty chloroform

5. Gray's squeamishness in this matter went a long way toward undoing the plot. If Mrs. Snyder had been really found suffering from, as she put it, "an awful whack on the head," the police investigation might have taken a different direction.

bottle and his rubber gloves, then flushed down the toilet the powders that Mrs. Snyder had given him.

It was four o'clock in the afternoon and snowing when he arrived in Syracuse. Gray went straight to the Hotel Onondaga and found his friend Haddon Gray's note on the dresser. He took two or three belts of whiskey. Then he shaved, took a bath, and changed his clothes. He telephoned Haddon Gray and learned that his friend was having a nap and would return the call when he awoke. During the interval, Gray drank some more.

Haddon Gray telephoned and asked if Gray was coming around to dinner as planned. Gray replied that he was and requested a lift. His friend said that his car was being repaired and asked if he could send someone else around to pick him up, but Gray insisted that Haddon Gray come in person. When Haddon Gray and Harry Platt arrived, Gray told them the story he had fabricated about the break-in at Momsie's house in Queens Village.

"Haddon and I had two or three drinks," Gray testified. "I told him a story—I didn't recall what it was until he testified here—about a burglary and about getting blood on my vest in Mr. Snyder's house. I think I showed him my vest. I'm not just perfectly clear about the conversation, but I gave him a black case with a hat in it, my suit, a pair of gloves, a picture, and a briefcase. We went in this other gentleman's car to his office building, where the case was put on top of a cupboard. Then we went to Haddon Gray's house, where we drank quite a little liquor."

At ten thirty or eleven o'clock, as the evening at his friend's house began to wind down, Gray telephoned a salesman acquaintance who was in town. He took a taxi and met him at the Syracuse Hotel, where the two sat around until one o'clock drinking a pint of whiskey. By this time, Gray had been drinking continuously for thirty-six hours; not surprisingly, the alcohol was starting to affect him. He was unable to find his way back to the Onondaga and needed to ask directions from a policeman. Once in his room, Gray had just started to finish off the whiskey he had left when detectives knocked at the door at two thirty.

Miller led Gray through his treatment at the hands of the Syracuse and New York City Police Departments. Apart from claiming that he had asked to see a lawyer and been refused, he expressed no complaints. Gray said he only recalled telling his story to Police Commissioner McLaughlin several days later, when he read it in the newspaper.

Asked by Miller to read aloud the true portions of his statement, Gray read practically the entire document without hesitating. Nothing could have been in greater contrast to Mrs. Snyder's performance when Froessel had asked her to do the same.

It was noon when Dana Wallace rose to cross-examine Gray on Mrs. Snyder's behalf. He had a nearly impossible job ahead of him. The essence of effective cross-examination is to catch the witness in lies and half-truths. Gray, however, was a witness who freely admitted his guilt. Wallace could not even attack Gray's testimony on the grounds that he had made a deal with the prosecution because Gray had made none.

Wallace began by recalling that Gray had testified he took off his glasses and placed them on the dresser before leaving Granny Brown's bedroom.

Q: "Did you take your glasses off because you had in mind that you were about to strike with the sash weight?"

A: "No, sir."

Q: "Can you tell me the reason for taking them off, if you remember?"

A: "Well, the reason was I took them off, I think, in case that anything should happen in the way of a fight or anything of that kind, as far as I can recall. I don't recall just exactly why I took them off, but I did."

Wallace asked Gray to take off his glasses, rise, take the sash weight, and demonstrate just how he had struck Snyder. Gray stood up; at Wallace's request, the court clerk handed him the sash weight, which still bore Mrs. Snyder's signed evidence tag. Gray gripped it with both hands, raised his arms slightly, and gave it a halfhearted downward chop.

"I used both hands like this."

Q: "How hard did you strike, if you recall?"

A: "Well, I know I could not strike him very hard."

Q: "Because you had been drinking so much?"

A: "No, sir, I did not say that."

Q: "Do you remember that yesterday on the stand, when describing the blows you struck, you broke down and cried?"

A:"I don't recall whether I did or not."

Q:"Do you recall showing emotion yesterday afternoon at the time when your counsel asked for a recess?"

A:"I do, yes, sir."

Q:"You had not the same emotions now that you had then, as I was questioning you, did you?"

A:"No, sir, I don't think so."

Q:"Was that because you were preparing yesterday under direct examination to be emotional just at that time?"

A:"It was not, sir, no."

Wallace forced Gray to admit that, of the many deadly plans he claimed Mrs. Snyder had proposed, the only one that culminated in murder was the one in which he played a role.

Q:"Now do you maintain that you went into this plan because she hounded you and that she gained dominance over you?"

A:"I do, sir."

Q: "And you maintain that, irrespective of the fact that you were fighting against it, her power over you was so great that you could not resist it and went through with this. Is that right?"

A:"That is true, sir."

Q:"Now, then, when did that [dominance] begin?"

A:"Well, I couldn't specify the date. It was a gradual thing."

Q:"From the very beginning?"

A:"Yes, sir."

Q:"The very first day?"

A:"I wouldn't say the first day, no."

Q: "Well, how long would you say before you began to realize that you were apt to do things that she wanted you to do against your will?"

A:"From about last May or June."

Gray was forced to admit that, when he and Mrs. Snyder took their upstate trip, he attended to his business each day despite Mrs. Snyder's complaints. Wallace suggested that this was not consistent with the behavior of a helpless slave, but Gray countered that Mrs. Snyder had been fully aware that his professional responsibilities came first.

Wallace then drew attention to the fact that Gray had stated in his confession that Mrs. Snyder was a woman of great charm, but he had skipped that passage when he had been asked under direct examination to read aloud those portions of his statement that were true. Wasn't it true? Gray was flustered, and his attorneys objected to the question, eliciting from Scudder the observation that the passage in question expressed a sentiment, not a fact, and that Gray might have had occasion to change his mind. A roar of laughter, in which both Gray and Mrs. Snyder joined, swept the courtroom.[6]

Wallace next sought to suggest that it was Gray who had tried to convince Mrs. Snyder to insure her husband's life. Some of the questions that followed were fishing expeditions that did Mrs. Snyder no good at all. In fact, Gray's self-assured replies damaged her case. Did Gray not discuss life insurance with Haddon Gray, and did Haddon Gray not write Gray's own life insurance policy? No to both questions. Besides, Haddon Gray's line was fire insurance.[7] Gray reiterated that the subject of insurance first came up in September 1925, when Mrs. Snyder asked how much he carried. It had next been discussed just after Christmas 1926, when Mrs. Snyder complained that she was having trouble keeping up with the premiums, and Gray suggested that she let the policies lapse.

Wallace confronted Gray with Mrs. Snyder's testimony that he was in possession of Albert Snyder's pistol when she came to him in her mother's bedroom.

"I did not have it," Gray answered. "How should I know where it was?"

Q: "You told us that you pressed the revolver in the hands of the deceased, is that right?"

A: "That is correct, sir."

Q: "For any purpose?"

A: "For no purpose, no, sir."

Q: "Was it to show some fingerprints of Snyder upon it?"

6. Gray also omitted that he had always been a gentleman and on the level with everyone. He included, however, that he had a "fine little wife and daughter."

7. True. Haddon Gray was listed in the Syracuse City Directory as a secretary of Hills and Company, a real estate and insurance concern.

A: "I don't know at the time, sir, why I did it."

Q: "You cannot tell us anything better than that, can you, why you did that?"

A: "No, I cannot."

Q: "It was not to show there was a struggle and his hands had been upon the revolver, was that the reason?"

A: "No, I don't know as that was the reason. Possibly it was. I just did it, that's all."

Q: "When did you start to sober up after all the alcohol you had consumed?"

A: "Somewhere between Albany and Syracuse."

Q: "Well, now, were you over it when you went downstairs and swept up the place where your footprints would show? Were you over it then?"

A: "No, sir, I was not."

Q: "You recall that very distinctly?"

A: "I do, sir."

Q: "You recall very distinctly arranging to have the sash weight covered with ashes so that it would look like it laid there a long while?"

A: "I do."

Q: "You were not over it then, were you?"

A: "I was doing things automatically."

Q: "You mean your mind was working now all the time to protect yourself, is that it?"

A: "Not to protect myself necessarily, no."

Q: "Well, then, what did you do it for?"

A: "I couldn't tell you."

Q: "What did you hide this murderous weapon for?"

A: "I didn't hide it."

Q: "Well, you sprinkled it with ashes?"

A: "That I did."

Q: "So that it might look as though it had been there a long while?"

A: "Yes, sir."

Q: "And you were doing things automatically in this state of intoxication?"

A: "In a semi-state of intoxication, sir."

According to Gray's statement to the police, when he went to Queens Village on 7 March, he walked around for two and a half hours. There was no mention of having spoken with Mrs. Snyder.

Q: "Was there any reason that in your confession you did not mention that after walking Queens Village that night you saw her?"

A: "No reason in the world."

Q: "When you had seen the woman you came out to call on concerning this nefarious enterprise, you say it never occurred to you to put in that statement that you had seen her?"

A: "Not any more, Mr. Wallace, than to mention the fact that I met her in the restaurant that day."

Gray insisted that, until the moment he walked into the master bedroom where Albert Snyder slept, he had not really believed that there would be a murder.

Q: "Did you think when meeting her in the Chinese restaurant of doing the same sort of work as you did the night you went out to go through with it?"

A: "I did not go out to go through with it that night."

Q: "What did you go out there for on that Monday night?"

A: "Because she asked me to come out, sir."

Q: "For what purpose did she say she wanted you there?"

A: "To do away with Mr. Snyder."

Q: "Have you not just said to me you didn't go out for that purpose?"

A: "I didn't go out for that purpose, no, sir."

Gray admitted that he had carried a small package containing the picture wire, the bottle of chloroform, the handkerchief, and the cotton rags.

Q: "Now, you were not going to do anything, is that it?"

A: "I didn't think that I would, not in my own mind, no, sir."

Q: "What did you carry those articles for if you thought you were not going out there for any such reason?"

A: "She asked me to bring them out."

Q: "You brought them out for her?"

A: "I did."

Q: "Had you any idea what they were going to be used for?"

A: "She had told me in the afternoon."

Q: "It was her influence over you?"

A: "That and liquor I think, yes."

Wallace then proposed that the visit referred to in Gray's confession, when he had walked around, was not the 7 March visit, but a later one that he made without the knowledge of Mrs. Snyder. Was it not Gray, come to murder Albert Snyder on his own, whom the Muhlhausers saw prowling around the Snyder residence a week before the murder? No, Gray insisted, he had not returned to New York City until the night of 19 March.

Q: "Are you sure that in Buffalo at that hotel on Friday [11 March] you did not make some arrangement similar to those that you made in Syracuse with Haddon Gray in case of your not being seen on Saturday night?"

A: "No, sir, I did not."

Q: "Is it not a fact that you went over there [Queens Village] on 12 March and walked around the home of Mrs. Snyder intending to do this job alone?"

A: "No, sir."

It was late afternoon when Justice Scudder adjourned court. This time, Gray showed no signs of distress or weakness as he was returned to his cell. In fact, he was grinning.

20

WHEN CROSS-EXAMINATION RESUMED, Wallace tried to show that, far from being a helpless pawn, Gray had taken the lead in plotting the murder. He reminded Gray that, when the burglary frame-up was discussed in the Chinese restaurant on the afternoon of 7 March, Mrs. Snyder only went as far as saying she would claim two colored men broke into the house.

Q: "And did she go any further and tell anything about ransacking the house and having herself tied up?"

A: "Not that I recall. I believe I said that she would have to be tied up."

Q: "And then she did not go any further on describing how the plan was to be carried out or what was to be said to the police?"

A: "No, I do not think so."

Q: "From that time on, you took up the plan, didn't you?"

A: "No."

Q: "Now, what else did you suggest?"

A: "I do not think that there was any other suggestion."

Q: "Was anything said about tying the victim up in the way he was afterward tied?"

A: "Not that I recall."

Q: "Was that your suggestion?"

A: "I believe it was not, sir. I do not know."

Q: "Well, now, wasn't it either your suggestion or hers?"

A: "I do not know whether it was my suggestion or her suggestion."

Q: "Now, when you got to your office, you had the rope she asked you to bring on your mind, did you not?"

A: "No, sir. I had my work on my mind."

Q: "Well, what did you do with regard to the wire?"

A: "I picked up the wire about seven o'clock."

Q: "Was your mind on your work then or on the strangulation of Snyder?"

A: "It was not on the strangulation of anybody, sir."

Q: "What was your mind on when you picked up that wire?"

A: "The wire was to tie his hands and feet."

Q: "Well, then, was it on the proposed murder of Albert Snyder?"

A: "It was."

Q: "Was Mrs. Snyder standing over you then, dominating you?"

A: "She was not, no."

Q: "Was her spirit or presence around you in the atmosphere?"

A: "It might have been."

Q: "You believe in that?"

A: "I might."

Q: "Have you told anybody that you thought you were insane?"

A: "No."

Q: "Have you asked for a sanity test?"

A: "No, sir."

Q: "Did you undergo such a test?"

A: "I did."

When Gray mentioned that he had taken six or seven drinks before setting out for Queens Village on the night of 7 March, Wallace's patience broke.

Q: "You will pardon me, Mr. Gray. I ask you this. Is there any day that you know of in connection with this case that you did not drink?"

A: "No, sir, nor any other day since I have known Mrs. Snyder."

Q: "You had never drunk before that?"

A: "I drank very little, sir."

Q: "So the minute you met Mrs. Snyder you began to drink to excess, is that it?"

A: "I wouldn't say that."

Gray claimed that, in going out to Queens Village on the night of 7 March, he was merely following the instructions Mrs. Snyder had given him at the Chinese restaurant.

Q: "Had Mrs. Snyder ever threatened you so that she had you in fear of her?"

A: "I would not say that it was fear, no. It was more magnetism than fear."

Q: "And this magnetic force drew you on even without her presence, is that it?"

A: "In many instances it did, yes."

Q: "And that magnetic force was so great it overcame all your thoughts of your family and child, is that right?"

A: "Yes, sir."

Q: "When did you think of obtaining the cotton rags?"

A: "I happened to see the rags on the street in Rochester and picked them up."

Q: "What did you pick them up for?"

A: "I don't know, I picked them up just to put with the handkerchief, that was all."

Q: "You don't know why—a man of your intelligence walked along the street and picked up some rags and carried them with you down to New York and back to the Snyder home?"

A: "I didn't carry them around with me, sir. I put them in with a lot of stuff that I was carrying, with my trunk."

Wallace managed to make Gray's version of waiting for two hours in the Snyder residence sound foolish. There was ample opportunity to abandon the task that he supposedly found so repugnant and leave. Mrs. Snyder had not been there to exert her magnetism, yet Gray remained. Gray protested weakly that he had made two attempts to leave.

Q: "And the influence overcame you?"

A: "No."

Q: "What did, then?"

A: "Automobiles driving up."

Q: "So every time that your power became paramount and you got ready to go, an automobile came up and destroyed the thought?"

A: "Yes."

Gray insisted that he went to Queens Village on the night of 19 March, just as he had on the night of 7 March, with no intention to commit murder, only because Mrs. Snyder had summoned him. When he left Syracuse, he was still undetermined about what course of action to take.

Q: "You were going, then, to see if you could have nerve enough to do it?"

A: "That is true, sir."

Q: "But you felt so sure that it might happen that you prepared your alibi, did you not?"

A: "I prepared my alibi to cover myself being away from there, Mr. Wallace."

Q: "Do you wish this jury to understand that all of this alibi was done without any thought that it was to be an alibi for the proposed murder?"

A: "Mr. Wallace, I didn't think myself when I went down there that this thing would ever be consummated."

Q: "Well, what did you prepare the alibi for?"

A: "Simply to cover myself up in Syracuse due to my absence, that was all."

Q: "Cover you for what?"

A: "That is what I would like to know, Mr. Wallace, sir."

Wallace was getting nowhere, even with his demands that the witness drop the "sir" and "Mr. Wallace."

Q: "Do you have any idea what you expected to gain by aiding and bringing about the death of Albert Snyder?"

A: "No, sir."

Q: "And without any reason for it that you know of, a man of your intelligence struck a man over the head with a sash weight?"

A: "I did."

Q: "And you want to tell this jury that you do not know why you did it?"

A: "I'm telling you that, sir."

Q: "What did you intend to do after it was all over?"

A: "I didn't intend to do anything. I was through."

Q: "You thought well enough of your future affairs to shoot right up to Syracuse and protect your alibi, did you not?"

A: "I did that automatically, sir."

Q: "Now it never occurred to you to telephone down and find out how Mrs. Snyder was getting along, did it?"

A: "I didn't have the opportunity because I was taken into custody that night."

Q: "You had no means of finding out how it had all come out? You had used the long distance telephone before, had you not?"

A: "Never on a Sunday."

The cross-examination degenerated as Wallace failed to make any headway. He switched subjects rapidly and managed to trip up Gray on a few minor details. The questions came so fast that Gray, who insisted on taking his time, became confused, and even the court stenographer asked Justice Scudder to intervene. Gray admitted that he could not remember whether Mrs. Snyder led him into the bedroom by the right or the left hand. However, he could remember clearly that she was in the room.

Q: "You can see her standing there?"

A: "Yes."

Q: "Standing at the threshold or inside with you?"

A: "Inside."

Q: "Is that because you insist that she be placed inside the room?"

A: "No, sir."

Wallace contrasted Gray's clear memory regarding Mrs. Snyder's position with his hazy recollection of which hand she had held.

Q: "Is it because the first involves you and the second involves her?"

A: "No, sir. I am already involved."

A reporter for the *Daily News* calculated that, in the last hour of Wallace's cross-examination, forty points of evidence, major and minor, were touched on in rapid-fire and randomly ordered questions without causing Gray to alter his direct testimony. In twelve hours of cross-examination, Wallace had failed to shake the witness.

There was no need for the prosecution to make a major assault. After a short recess, District Attorney Newcombe rose to begin the State's cross-examination. His manner was that of a sorrowful parent rebuking a wayward son. Entirely ignoring questions of what was planned and where, and avoiding details, Newcombe took Gray through the minimum of facts necessary to establish that he and Mrs. Snyder had committed murder on the night of 19 March: that they entered the room together, that Gray struck Snyder once or twice with the sash weight, that there was a struggle during which he called to Mrs. Snyder for help, that she then also struck her husband.

Newcombe picked up Gray's confession.

Q:"And you personally dictated this statement?"

A:"I believe I did, yes."

Q: "Don't you recall that in substance, after I had asked you if you were prepared to make a statement and you said, 'Yes,' and I called in the stenographer, you said, 'Where should I begin?' and I said, 'From the day you met this woman.' Does that refresh your recollection?"

A:"No, sir. It does not."

Q:"You do not say that was not said, Gray?"

A:"Oh, no. Oh, no, I don't say that. If you say so, Mr. Newcombe, it must be true."

Q:"Your statement is in your dictation, is it not, Gray?"

A:"It must be, because it is practically true all the way through."

Q: "There was no compulsion or duress or threats were there, Mr. Gray?"

A:"Not that I recall."

Q:"Well, if there had been, you would recall it, would you not?"

A:"I presume I would."

Q: "It was your voluntary statement, made frankly and freely in my office, was it not?"

A:"Yes, sir."

Q:"Now you very minutely and very definitely described the events of 19 March and the events of 20 March, Mr. Gray. You realized the statements you made and the effect of those statements?"

A:"I have only tried to tell the truth."

Q:"And what you have told is the truth?"

A:"It is, sir."

That was enough for the People of the State of New York.

After the midday recess, Gray's defense team presented a short parade of character witnesses, none of whom was on the stand for more than five minutes. In every case, they testified to the defendant's unimpeachable reputation for telling the truth.

It was barely three o'clock, but lawyers for both defense teams requested an adjournment until Monday morning to allow them to review testimony and prepare their closing arguments. Justice Scudder suggested proceeding after a brief recess, but the defense lawyers insisted on more time for preparation. The State made no objection. Commenting that justice would not suffer if they took their time, and apologizing to jurors for their continuing incarceration, Scudder granted the request for an adjournment.

The jurors, who had become restive during Wallace's minute cross-examination of Gray, had looked forward to the weekend. They delegated juror number 7, Lewis Ruckdaschel, to request a two-day furlough. Justice Scudder observed, however, that their lives were very precious to the State of New York at the moment, dashing any hope of escape from the Kew Gardens Inn.

21

AFTER THE CLOSE OF TESTIMONY, Mrs. Snyder issued a statement: "I don't see how anyone can possibly believe Judd's story. I feel sure the jury will see through his lies and his unspeakable charges against me." These were brave words for a woman who, if she was reading the newspapers, knew that Gray's testimony was being hailed as the absolute truth told by a man who had abandoned earthly concerns.

Gray released one of his rare statements: "I am not afraid of the chair. I suppose I am going to get it, but I feel better since I told the truth. Considering everything, I still haven't given up hope."

The comments made by Gray's mother on Friday afternoon were widely quoted: "Judd is not interested. He is indifferent about the jury's decision. He told the truth. He couldn't tell anything else because of the hereafter."

Sunday, 8 May, was Mother's Day, and a predictable amount of attention was lavished on the mothers in the case. Lorraine was photographed signing a Mother's Day card and handing it over for delivery to the Queens County Jail. The card itself, with its painstaking signature, was reproduced in Sunday's *Daily News*. Mrs. Snyder sent a telegram to Granny Brown: "I have many blessings and I wish to be thankful for all that you have done for me. Love to you and kiss Lorraine for me." She requested a permanent wave and an employee at a nearby beauty shop willingly arrived with the tools of her trade, but Warden Fox refused her admittance.

Granny Brown, who received reporters while she cooked a chicken dinner, was less sanguine than her daughter as the usual crowd of curiosity seekers cruised past the house. "I don't know what the jury will do," she said. "Men are so strange."

She could not take her mind off the day of the murder. "Ruth phoned me that day and told me that she hadn't bought any groceries and meat for the Sunday dinner. She said she and Albert were going to the party and that they would probably sleep late and we'd go out for a ride afterward and eat out."

She denounced Gray as she mashed potatoes. "Judd Gray made Ruth what she is today. She wouldn't think of doing murder. She never drank before she met him. I told her he was no gentleman when I first met him. I didn't like him; he seemed like a slick fellow to me. Few salesmen are gentlemen anyway; they run around too much. If only I had been home that night, Judd Gray would have had to face me. He couldn't have bluffed me. I'd have gotten him out of this house. And to think that I was just sitting around in Kew Gardens, doing nothing!"

Mrs. Gray also received a Mother's Day telegram from her son, but did not divulge its contents. "It was just a Mother's Day telegram," said Gray's sister Margaret. "You know, telling her she's the most wonderful mother in the world. He's always sent her a wire on Mother's Day. Always a thoughtful boy, Judd was." What Mrs. Isabel Gray received, if anything, went unrecorded.

Sash weight stickpins for the gentlemen and scarfpins for the ladies, selling for ten cents apiece, became the novelty items of the season. There were also large brass buttons with the inscription "This husband protected by W. J. Burns Detective Agency." In the city's diners, lunch counters, and coffee shops, the current slang for coffee and a Danish pastry was "sash weight and arsenic." A Long Island Railroad conductor was disciplined for announcing: "Sash Weight Junction!" at the Queens Village stop.

The defendants' mailbags were brimming. A Texas rancher said that, when Mrs. Snyder was released, he would be in front of the Queens County Jail, wearing a yellow chrysanthemum in his lapel so she could recognize him. A horse breeder in Kentucky named one of his fillies "Mrs. Snyder." A new practical joke emerged on Wall Street. The idea was to leave a message on someone's desk directing him or her to return a call from Mr. Gray at Stillwell 6017—the number of the Queens County Jail.

The task before the jury was not altogether simple. There were four possible verdicts. The extremes, acquittal and guilty of first-degree murder, were straightforward. Court attendants were giving five-to-one odds in favor of first-degree murder for Mrs. Snyder. She might benefit, though, from the sympathy factor if Gray managed to win a reduced verdict—the jury would be reluctant to condemn one defendant while sparing the other.

The question was whether Gray could squeak by with second-degree murder, taking a life without premeditation, or, even better, with manslaughter, taking a life without the intent to kill but with reckless disregard. His claim to have been constantly intoxicated was not a defense in and of itself because voluntary drunkenness does not excuse one's actions in the eyes of the law. If, however, the jury believed that his drunkenness was not voluntary, that he really was under some sort of undue influence, then he stood a chance of winning a reduced verdict. Second-degree murder carried a penalty of twenty years to life, with a likely reduction to fourteen years for good behavior.

Gray and Mrs. Snyder attended church services on Sunday, avoiding each other scrupulously as usual. After church, each was given the opportunity for a brief private session with Reverend Johnson, who encouraged them to pray and to keep their spirits up. Both slept well and did justice to the Sunday pot roast dinner.

Day 11, Monday, 9 May

Because Mrs. Snyder's team had led off the opening statements, Gray's team was first to present its closing argument. This arrangement was advantageous to Mrs. Snyder because it gave her the last word, at least before the State spoke. At ten o'clock Monday morning, Millard rose to speak for Gray.

"May it please the Court and gentlemen of the jury, in the dark shadow of this frightful crime, this frightful tragedy, I come to you to speak for my friend, Judd Gray."

Putting his arm around Gray at the defense table, Millard continued, "I am going to plead with you before God to render justice in this case. I am going to plead as I never pleaded before, just as though Judd Gray were my own boy, for I believe in him."

His tone darkened.

From a wholesome, homelike atmosphere, where the fires of the home hearth were burning continually with love and devotion, suddenly in June 1925, a sinister, fascinating woman came across his path. Oh, gentlemen, what a catastrophe! . . . This woman [gesturing], this peculiar creature, like a poisonous serpent, drew Judd Gray into her glistening coils and there was no escape. . . . This woman [gesturing] was abnormal. Just as a piece of steel jumps and clings to the powerful magnet, so Judd Gray came within the powerful compelling force of that woman and she held him fast. This woman [gesturing], this peculiar venomous species of humanity, was abnormal, possessed of an all-consuming, all-absorbing sexual passion, animal lust, which seemingly was never satisfied.

"Through excessive indulgence, . . . she sapped his strength; sapped his vitality," Millard continued. He was again at Gray's side and once more draped his arm over Gray's shoulder.

"You know the inevitable result. . . . Under those circumstances there is always, in the exhausted vitality, a craving for a stimulant, always. Sometimes the weakened individual seeks a narcotic drug, that dreadful menace, one of the greatest menaces confronting civilization today. At other times it is whiskey, eagerly striving to bring back for the moment that vital spirit, that fire, that vitality which is ebbing low."

Mrs. Snyder took advantage of Gray's increasing thirst for whiskey to badger him every time he was drunk about the murder of her husband, Millard argued. After a year and a half of patient effort, Gray was like a trained mannequin: a human dummy, ready to do anything Mrs. Snyder told him to do.

Mixing metaphors with abandon, Millard thundered, "The match had been placed to the powder, the poison had been sipped, and it began to do its deadly work, just as though a typhoid-ridden patient, acting under the spell of another, were doing the act, exactly the same, just as though a child of five years were acting under the powerful, dominating influence of a master mind."

Gray blindly went to Queens Village on 7 March as ordered, bringing with him chloroform, wire, and cotton rags. What was the first thing Mrs. Snyder did when Gray arrived? Why, it was to give him a big drink of whiskey, naturally. But, whiskey or no whiskey, Gray had not been able to go through with it. "She saw that he could not do it, that he was too weak, shaky, and drunk to do it, that she could not exercise that control." So Mrs. Snyder was forced to wait for another occasion.

That brought Millard to the night of the crime. He played down Gray's preparation of a complicated alibi for the night of Saturday, 19 March, comparing it to the instinctively feigned innocence of a schoolboy caught misbehaving in class. He fixed in the jury's mind the image of Mrs. Snyder socializing with her husband at the Fidgeons' party to leave the impression that she was on good terms with him.

"Isn't that the diabolical mind of a fiend?" he asked. "That is hardly a human mind."

With no real evidence to back it up, Millard advanced the claim that Mrs. Snyder had planned to poison Gray after he had served his purpose.

[Gray went up to the mother's bedroom] and there, under the pillow, was the sash weight and what? A four-ounce bottle of liquid. I want you to remember that little bottle, a four-ounce bottle of liquid under the pillow, with the instruments of death. Outside, not underneath the pillow but nearby on the dresser, was a quart bottle of whiskey. . . . What on earth was the reason for the little bottle of four ounces when there was a quart bottle of whiskey on the dresser?[1]

I am going to tell you why it was there. Ruth Snyder thought that when Judd Gray went into her mother's room he would take that quart bottle of whiskey, as was his custom, and he would drink and drink and drink, and by the time she returned with Albert Snyder and Lorraine, he

1. Millard stated that the quart bottle was on the dresser; Gray had testified that it was on the floor next to it.

would be pretty well drunk. She left it handy for him. He could not miss it. But not the little bottle.

She thought that when she came home and was ready for this deed, this tragedy, that then they would go to the pillow and that he would be in such a drunken condition that he would take that little bottle without any trouble. But instead of that, gentlemen, he reached under the pillow and, intuitively, a natural thing, he finds the little bottle. [He drank the contents of that little four-ounce bottle and it made him immediately so dizzy that he sat on the floor.]

Ruth Snyder had a very much more clever plan, a sure-fire plan, no such stupid plan as was actually perpetrated on the night in question. . . . Gentlemen, Ruth Snyder had planned it only too well. Do you suppose that she was going to take the chance of leaving a surviving witness of her crime to travel around the country? Her mind did not work that way. Not a chance in the world. Not a chance.

She thought that Judd Gray, the poor fool, after he drank the quart bottle of whiskey, just before the time for the perpetration of this crime, would drink from that little bottle, and that by the time the blows were delivered the contents of that bottle would begin to do its deadly work, and she had planned to put that pencil in the wire around the neck of Albert Snyder to point to Judd Gray. And she thought that after her husband had been killed that the poison would do its work, and that Judd Gray would also die. . . . He would be there, his pencil used in tightening, the sash weight there, Judd Gray there with a bottle, an empty bottle of poison near his side. . . . But he drank the whiskey, an immense amount of whiskey, and he didn't die.[2] He may have been dizzy for a short time, but he didn't die.

If what Ruth Snyder planned had gone through that night, she would have had nothing to fear, and she would have cashed in on the ninety-seven thousand dollars' insurance and been on Easy Street, with

---

2. In other words, the Tom Dawson whiskey from the quart bottle served as an antidote to the poison in the small bottle. See "Lingering Questions" at the end for my commentary on Millard's theory.

nobody living that could point to her crime. There lies the only motive in the case.

This brought Millard to one of the strongest points of Gray's defense, that he had had no motive for murdering Albert Snyder. Snyder's wife was already available to him whenever he wanted, and he would not profit directly from an insurance claim on Albert Snyder's death.

> You cannot—as honest, conscientious men, find a motive for Judd Gray. That is the all-important fact which you are going to consider when you get by yourselves tonight. Where is the motive for Judd Gray? I defy the mortal mind to find one. Even Ruth Snyder could not find one. "What reason on earth had Judd Gray to desire the death of your husband?" I asked her. She could not find a motive. . . . He had never even met Albert Snyder. He had absolutely nothing to gain by Albert Snyder's death. Simply the blind following of a controlled, operated, human mannequin. Simply because Ruth Snyder wished it, wanted it, blindly, groping, following her. Absolutely no motive on earth. That in itself would be enough, gentlemen, in the year 1927 of our Lord, to set Judd Gray free.

Millard made much of the fact that Gray had not made any attempt to flee or to avoid discovery.

> This poor, groping, blundering fool left the Snyder home. . . . Just then what does he do? . . . He goes within a couple of blocks and talks to a stranger, right near the scene of the crime, with a policeman in uniform within four feet. Think of it. . . . Think of it, gentlemen, right near the scene of the crime, standing and talking and waiting for a bus, without the faintest effort of disguise, his face clearly in view, with a policeman in uniform standing right by him. . . . A shrewd, calculating criminal with criminal intention? It is not in his makeup. He has not got a criminal hair in his head or in his whole makeup up, and you know it. There is not a blot on his whole character, not a stain throughout his life from the cradle to the present moment.

Having presented the substance of Gray's case, Millard wound up for his closing peroration.

Gentlemen, let those who cannot comprehend, who cannot understand the pitfalls and snares of human life, from their self-erected pedestals of pious intolerance and scorn, cast the stones of contempt and hatred of the poor victim of tragic misfortune. Let them cast the stones, but you and I, my brothers, will go down into the mire and morass to rescue a human soul who has fallen the prey of a cruel, calculating, cunning serpent of a human being who by her flame, passion has become a demon in disguise. We will rescue that human being. . . .

There is a law higher than any human law. A law that transcends any man-made law, and that is the law of conscience. That still small voice must dictate our every action, else we may never rest. We must be able to go home to our loved ones and look them in the face with the smile of a contented conscience.

Gentlemen, I have been a public prosecutor, I know what it is to prosecute offenders against the law of the land, and, fully conscious of my responsibility, I solemnly and sincerely say to you that the ends of justice would be fully met, the laws of the State would be fully vindicated, and you would never have the pangs of regret or the reproach of conscience, if you found this poor human victim guilty of manslaughter. That is the extreme culpability of that defendant in this case. Absolutely as a man I tell you that I would to God that you could find it in your conscience, knowing all the facts, to set him free and tell him to go home to his mother because he fell a victim and a prey to this atrocious woman. But I do really appreciate and readily understand how some of you may feel, that a certain measure of culpability and blame may rest on the shoulders of that poor man because he allowed himself to become the prey of this woman. Yet I actually feel that God's will would be done if he were freed.

Mrs. Snyder's attorneys had been muttering to each other as Millard declaimed and, when he rose to speak for Mrs. Snyder, Wallace was in a fine, perhaps drunken, fury.

I am going to remark at the outset in no uncertain terms, that this is a case of Henry Judd Gray and the State of New York versus Ruth Snyder. She is sandwiched in between two prosecutors and the District Attorney need only sit idly by and watch the condemnation of this woman [gesturing] by this codefendant [gesturing].

And also at the outset I take a few of the remarks that Mr. Millard said in conclusion, that he, too, has been a public prosecutor. So have I, for many years, in this county. And for twenty-six years of a somewhat active life in the criminal legal field, I have endeavored to do for the commonwealth and the individual my duty as I saw it. And I thank God that that experience is a matter known to perhaps a great many of you here, or some of you, just because of hearsay, if nothing else, because then you know I will have a right to call upon that experience and say . . . that there [gesturing] is the most despicable man who has ever walked on God's footstool as far as I have known men and as far as the pages of history recall. . . .

Nothing can convince me that this woman [gesturing] has not been put in one of the most unfair positions possible before an American court of justice. This miserable filth of the earth [gesturing] is allowed to sit here, and . . . he makes his squealing appeal for mercy to you. Not a defense, an appeal of mercy, and it has rung from the minute he took and defamed that woman to the last note of his counsel's voice died away, not once a defense, but a plea for mercy.

Wallace lost his train of reasoning and sputtered to a halt. He took a long drink of water and arranged his thoughts.

Gray's defense, he continued, if it could be called that, amounted to a string of broken promises. Citing Miller's opening address, Wallace reminded the jury that Gray's counsel had promised to show that his confession had been obtained under duress. Clearly, that plan fell through. "When he opened this thing he was going to fight, he was going to perjure himself, but . . . he dropped that and said, 'I will plead for mercy.' "

Then there was Miller's promise to present a tear-jerking, heart-wrenching drama about a man sapped by lust and abnormal relations. Wallace was dismissive. "I believe that in the pages of history . . . we have heard of men almost as amorous as Mr. Gray and I have not heard of any of them talking about their minds being sapped. In fact, some of them stand up pretty well in the business world, if we can believe the daily newspaper reports."[3]

Finally, Miller had promised to prove that Gray was not of rational mind when the crime was committed, that he was hopelessly drunk. "Well, gentlemen," continued Wallace, "I have seen men under the influence of liquor, and I believe that you have, but when they tell about this human anaconda, as far as the moist goods of the earth are concerned, a quart of whiskey will not have any more effect on him on a night like that than storming Gibraltar with a popgun!"

The only point of Gray's defense for which a scintilla of evidence had been brought forward was his contention that Mrs. Snyder dominated him.

Very well, let us see how much of that went on. . . . He was the superior in education. He was better equipped by forebearage. He had a home of luxury as compared with hers. . . . They meet in this restaurant so equipped. She with strained relations, which she admits, and he with a lovely home and family. Now then, do they meet to combat equally or not? They do not. Here is a man of the world whose business was influence. That was his business—to talk women into things. . . . He gets her over to his office and they drink, and he discovers he ought to put a corset on her and he knows where to get the cold cream to fix up the sunburn on her bare shoulders. Oh, she dominated him, did she, from that time on?

3. Probably a reference to real estate tycoon Edward "Daddy" Browning. The Kew Gardens Inn, where jurors were sequestered, was notorious at the time of the Snyder-Gray case because it was the residence of portly fifty-two-year-old "Daddy," his sixteen-year-old bride, "Peaches" (née Heenan), and her formidable protector, "Ma" Heenan. Shortly after the wedding, "Peaches" decamped with her mother, accusing "Daddy" of unspeakable acts (including the introduction of an "African honking goose" to the bedroom) and demanding a prodigious divorce settlement. She lost the case, but had the last laugh: when Browning died in 1934, she inherited his estate.

Ironically, Wallace was repeating Gray's account of the seduction, not his own client's.

> So, the next thing we hear, he became the guinea pig of experimentation. He decided to try a sleeping powder on himself. Well, let me inform you, and I am quoting the trial record right and I know it, that when he took that sleeping powder he said she brought over two bottles of rye and two vials. He says, "I drank the rye.". . . Well, I wouldn't wonder if a fellow dallied with a sleeping powder and swallowed two quarts of rye whiskey that he would not know much until eight-thirty in the morning. That is the evidence, and yet this man who voluntarily chose to make a swine out of himself as far as liquor is concerned lays it to what? To this woman's domination.

Wallace appealed to the jury's experience as men of the world. Surely if Gray had been under the domination of Mrs. Snyder, he would have started to neglect his family or his business. There was no evidence that he had. The letters in evidence were more consistent with Mrs. Snyder being under Gray's spell than the reverse.

> Their defense has been the domination of this woman over him, the magnetism of this woman over him, the hypnotic influence of that woman over him; . . . but his answer to me when I asked, "What caused you to do this?" was "I don't know." He didn't say, "Her domination." He didn't say, "Her magnetism." He said, "I don't know." Well, hereafter when one should desire to slay in this county, let it be mixed up with some female, and then say, "It was her domination over me; so I killed him; I had no material object, and why I killed him, I don't know."

Turning to the insurance issue, Wallace argued that Snyder had been an outdoorsman and a motorist; he had needed insurance. In fact, not to speak ill of the dead, it was an outrage that he only carried insurance worth one thousand dollars before Mrs. Snyder encouraged him to take out more. If Mrs. Snyder was confused about whether she would recoup her investment if she continued to carry the policy, well, who could really claim to understand their own insurance policy? "I can easily understand how a man or woman could be misled by a life insurance agent . . .

because I have seen a life insurance agent when he got through with me make me believe that, at the end of three years, I was going to have the City Hall and a certificate of election for mayor for eight years, and you have all had the same experience."

Maybe Mrs. Snyder had tried to hide the premium payments from her husband. But, then, what wife did not sometimes try to conceal expenses from her husband to avoid a domestic dispute?

Wallace reminded the jurors that no direct evidence had been introduced to show that Mrs. Snyder had tried to kill her husband. There was only the testimony of Gray, who referred to letters that, conveniently for him, had been destroyed: "Not a letter about poison, not a witness brought concerning poison, not a neighbor who saw him [Albert Snyder] sick after the asphyxiation with gas or the bichloride tablets, not a human being brought here to substantiate his [Gray's] testimony, and the only evidence is in letters which he has destroyed, but of which he has such a splendid memory, every word and line."

Like Millard before him, Wallace tried to fix in the jurors' minds a mental image of the preparations for murder—but with the roles reversed. Where Millard had referred to Mrs. Snyder crouching like a tiger beside her husband until he was asleep, Wallace described Gray unpacking the murderous implements (including, naturally, the sash weight) from his brief case and arranging them on the floor in Granny Brown's bedroom.

Mrs. Snyder, oblivious to the deadly scene that was being prepared, was in the bathroom all this time. "They have made a great hullabaloo in several questions here as to whether or not, if she went to the bathroom, the door would necessarily have been closed. It might be just a little ajar because, with the relations which existed for two or three years between them, I do not think modesty had run to such a pinnacle that she much cared whether he looked in the bathroom or not, in my opinion. Why make so much out of that?"

When she heard the thud, Mrs. Snyder rushed into the bedroom and seized Gray by the necktie—it was not Albert Snyder Gray had struggled with, it was Mrs. Snyder, trying to drag him away from her husband. Gray claimed that he lost his senses for a few minutes during which Mrs.

Snyder finished the job; Mrs. Snyder claimed that that she fainted away and Gray finished the job.

> Who would be the most likely to swoon—the man charged, as he said, steeled with liquor, prepared for the assassination, or a woman in the state when, as every physician within the sound of my voice and every woman knows, the female of our species can be brought into an aggravated condition by the slightest form of excitement, much less the viewing of a murder? Who was the most likely to swoon—this man who was steeled with rum, who took two quarts of rye and some sleeping powders to sleep six or seven hours, or a woman who admits she fell hopelessly in a faint after drinking three glasses of intoxicating liquor? . . .
>
> Now then, put yourself in this woman's place. . . . He said, "It's over," and he said, "You are in it just as much as I am; I can arrange the perfect defense; I have already arranged the perfect alibi; it must look like a robbery.". . . From that time, I believe that most all the human race would rush to self-preservation except some of those stolid and strong hearts that have, thank God, made history. But how would the average woman view it, with some feeling in her heart because of the adulterous relations? It would be "It is safety first; it is self-preservation. It is me. It is Lorraine. I didn't want to get into the mess, but I am in it; and now . . . I better follow his advice."

Wallace was especially outraged by the fact that, despite having arranged an alibi, Gray thought it would be a good idea to put Albert Snyder's fingerprints on his revolver to corroborate the burglary story: "This semi-intoxicated man does that which would damn him with every one of your fathers, . . . the most brutal thing I have ever heard in the annals of criminal history, back to the Middle Ages. By God, he goes there to the cold hand of Snyder and . . . tries to shove into his hand the handle of that revolver so that fingerprints might be there . . . to show that this valiant man fought back. Think of it, making yourself a hero, almost, after death."

Wallace concluded with Dr. Neail's testimony, devastating to Gray's version of events, that there was no evidence of a struggle. "Dr. Neail says that not only the third or the second, but that any one blow would have rendered Snyder unconscious. Gray says he was there and Dr. Neail was not. And again in his flippant manner he says, 'I am a murderer, but please let me inform you that Dr. Neail, the most astute medical examiner on Long Island, doesn't know what he is talking about, but I do.'. . . If Neail tells the truth, . . . Ruth Brown Snyder is innocent."[4]

Where Millard had pleaded the jury to consider the remote possibility that his client was innocent, Wallace had dared the jury to find his client guilty. Even Gray admitted that it had been quite a show. He turned smiling to a court attendant and whispered, "What do you think of those fireworks? He must think it's the Fourth of July!"

4. Mrs. Snyder was even innocent, claimed Wallace, if the jury chose to believe her confession. Both of these points were fantastical. As Wallace must have known, Justice Scudder would instruct the jury that Mrs. Snyder's confession, if accepted, was sufficient to convict her of first-degree murder. And while it was true that Dr. Neail's testimony contradicted Gray's claim of a struggle, the jury was free to return a guilty verdict against Mrs. Snyder even if they believed that she had not struck her husband.

22

AS WALLACE HAD PUT IT SO WELL, District Attorney Newcombe had no real work to do. Taking the floor after a short midday recess, he described the friendship between the defendants and reminded jurors that Snyder had been an encumbrance to them—a nuisance with a $97,000 price on his head.

> Relations had not progressed very long before the killing of Albert Snyder was discussed, before plans for the killing of Albert Snyder were made. He says that she suggested it and planned it, and she says that he suggested it and planned it, but it does not make much difference in this case, gentlemen of the jury, who first suggested it and planned it. . . .
>
> They talk about motive. . . . Can't you see what it was? They had their plans to divide that insurance in some way. Whether it would have been a case of cheating cheaters or not, I don't know, but that was their plan.

Newcombe was dismissive of Mrs. Snyder's counsel's claim that Gray was in Queens Village on 12 March: "I do not know whether he was or not. It does not make a particle of difference to the case whether he was or not."

Then he demolished the two weakest points of Mrs. Snyder's defense—the sash weight and the open doors. As to the sash weight: "Imagine the temerity of the woman to sit there on the witness stand and tell you twelve men that because she did not want Gray to murder her husband— she knew that he wanted to and was fixed and determined upon it—she gave him back the weapon with which he was going to kill him. You talk about romancing. Is there a more complete romance than that yarn? She kept that sash weight and she kept it until Saturday night, 19 March."

232

As to having left the doors open: "Gentlemen of the jury, if she hadn't been as bent on that plan as Gray, if they both had not been determinedly and definitely bent on the murder of Albert Snyder, wouldn't she have locked the doors of the house and kept Gray out? She is sane; she is a bright, intelligent woman. That is what she would have done. But no, she leaves those doors open and she goes on to the party with Albert and the little girl."

Gray claimed that he was an automaton, a walking zombie blindly following Mrs. Snyder's instructions with no idea that he was actually going to commit a murder. But why would he have arranged an elaborate alibi if he had not known that he was going down to Queens Village to kill Albert Snyder?

As to Gray's defense of drunkenness, Newcombe said,

> He tells you about this drinking, but as Mr. Wallace brought out, he was drinking to steel his nerves, to get his courage up to the sticking point of carrying out that murder. Was he drunk after the commission of that murder? Gentlemen of the jury, no. He remembered every single detail as if it happened yesterday, as if he had not had a drink. He remembers [all the details about] changing his shirt. [He remembers] going down to the cellar and picking up the coal piece by piece so it would not make a noise and brushing up his footsteps where he would step into the coal bin to get that coal. Was that man drunk? Was that man under any domination or hypnotism? That man, gentlemen of the jury, was just as clear-headed and clear-thinking as you are this very minute.

Like Millard, Newcombe fixed the jury's imagination on the image of Mrs. Snyder lying awake in bed next to the husband she was going to murder. "When he was fast asleep, she went and got Henry Judd Gray and together they came in and committed the cold-blooded, atrocious murder, the most vicious murder that has ever happened in the annals of Queens County or the State of New York. And, gentlemen, they talk to you of sympathy. After Albert Snyder had been struck, he rose up and there he saw in the act of killing him his own wife and her lover, Gray. My God, gentlemen, think of that man's thoughts with a realization that he was being murdered by his own wife and her lover."

Until then, Newcombe had spoken quietly and dispassionately, but his voice rose as he turned to Mrs. Snyder's behavior on the morning after the murder.

> Did she tell Police Commissioner McLaughlin, gentlemen, one single word as to the defense she has now? Did she tell Mr. McLaughlin that Gray took the revolver and threatened to shoot her unless she permitted him to kill her husband? Did she tell Mr. McLaughlin that she got him downstairs and got the revolver away from him and then had to go up to the bathroom to attend to personal needs, and that Gray came upstairs while she was in the bathroom, that she heard this terrific thud and went into her room and there was Gray on the back of her husband, and she pulled Gray off and Gray struck her and she fainted? Did she tell that to Mr. McLaughlin? No, gentlemen, not a single word of that story.
>
> Gentlemen of the jury, that story she told on the witness stand was a fabric of lies, never conceived and thought out until the eve of this trial. If that had been the truth . . . why would not she have told that story to Assistant District Attorney Daly? . . . Because it was a cock-and-bull story that had not been conceived at the time.

Newcombe defended the fairness of the treatment Gray and Mrs. Snyder had received while in custody and thus the admissibility of their confessions. He demolished Mrs. Snyder's contention that her statement had been altered, using material taken from Gray's, by reminding the jury that, according to testimony, her statement had been signed before Gray arrived in New York.

Ultimately, it was the confessions that would matter, and Newcombe made sure he referred to them in closing.

> In these statements, she says that they killed Snyder together, and he says that they killed Snyder together. . . . Gentlemen, our whole great nation, all of our American institutions are built and founded upon the sanctity of the American home, and if in this case there should be a failure of adequate punishment, that foundation, that cornerstone of those American institutions, will totter and fall. . . . On behalf of the people of Queens County, on behalf of the people of the State of New York,

whom I represent here and now, the State of New York asks you to bring in the verdict that is warranted by the evidence and that is murder in the first degree as against both defendants.

After Newcombe had finished, there was a short recess, and then Justice Scudder issued his instructions to the jury. He began with the standard caution that both defendants were innocent until found guilty and advised the jury of the meaning of reasonable doubt.

"The joint trial is only a matter of convenience," he said. "Each defendant must be considered as being separately tried. A verdict against one does not necessarily apply to the other."

He instructed them on the various degrees of homicide, pointing out that intent, deliberation, and premeditation were the essential elements of murder in the first degree.

Justice Scudder defined the meaning of "principal to the crime" and warned that if the jurors found either one of the defendants to be a principal, they could not consider the uncorroborated testimony of that defendant as evidence against the other. As a corollary, he stipulated that if the jury found that the defendants had acted in concert to slay Albert Snyder, neither defendant could be convicted on the testimony of the other alone.

As anticipated, he directed that each confession, if the jury found that it had been obtained without duress and deception, was sufficient in combination with the corpus delicti to convict the defendant who made it of first-degree murder.

Scudder gave restrictive instructions on compulsion. "The defendant Snyder contends that whatever part she may have taken in the crime . . . was due to compulsion. In order to prove compulsion, there must be proof of immediate bodily harm and danger of loss of life. Future danger or threat against life is no excuse that compulsion was exerted." If she participated in the killing under compulsion and then continued to play a role after the fear of immediate bodily harm had passed, she was as guilty of the homicide as if there had never been compulsion in the first case.

By contrast, Scudder was more sympathetic to Gray's claim that he had been hopelessly intoxicated. He instructed the jurors that if they found Gray to have been so drunk that he was unable to form intent, they should bring in a verdict lesser than murder in the first degree against him.

Scudder then asked if counsel for the defense had any special requests regarding instructions to the jury. Counsel for Gray was satisfied. Mrs. Snyder's counsel was not.

Hazelton handled the legal points. Some of these involved merely points of evidence. For instance, he asked the judge to remind the jury that in her confession, Mrs. Snyder never specified that she placed the murder instruments under the pillow (she only said she put the implements in her mother's room) and never stated that she struck her husband. Scudder was amenable: so instructed.

Hazelton next asked Justice Scudder to instruct the jurors that, should they find that Gray and Snyder were accomplices, then evidence given by Gray against Mrs. Snyder must be corroborated, not merely by evidence linking her to him, but by evidence linking her to the crime itself. So instructed.

Finally, there was the judge's inevitable but deadly instruction that the fact of the murder and the defendants' respective signed statements, if accepted, would support a verdict of first-degree murder against each. Hazelton asked Scudder to charge the jury that, if they rejected Mrs. Snyder's confession in favor of the story she told on the stand, she must be acquitted despite Gray's testimony regarding the fatal night, because the latter was uncorroborated. So instructed.

Hazelton's last request concerned Mrs. Snyder's crucial claim that she had sought to dissuade Gray from committing the crime. "I ask Your Honor to charge that, if the jury have a reasonable doubt as to whether or not the defendant Snyder advised and requested the defendant Gray not to commit the crime on the morning of March 20th, 1927, before the defendant Gray left the bedroom of the mother to commit the crime, as testified to by the defendant Gray, then the jury must give the benefit of the doubt to the defendant Snyder and acquit her."

In other words, if the jury believed Gray's version right up to the commission of the crime, but believed that, at that point, Mrs. Snyder had tried to dissuade Gray, they must acquit her. Justice Scudder agreed, but cautioned that it was entirely up to the jury to decide whether such abandonment took place and, if so, when.

At five thirty, the jury members filed out of the courtroom to consider their verdict. Mrs. Gray rushed to her son's side to encourage him. The spectators surged forward and bailiffs struggled to disperse the crowd. Then, as if there had been a signal, the tide shifted and the crowd began to move back toward the exits. One elderly man who lost consciousness was pushed upright and swept along by the mob. Eventually, the courtroom crowd thinned, and the defendants were led to the holding pens to await the verdict.

Mrs. Gray decided not to wait and left for New Jersey. "I will never like crowds again after this," she remarked. Granny Brown had chosen to stay home, but Mrs. Snyder's brother, Andrew, was there to give encouragement. Photographers asked the pair to pose together, but Mrs. Snyder vetoed the idea: "Leave him out of it. I'm the one being hung here."

The Queens County records for the shortest and longest jury deliberations in a first-degree murder case were three minutes and fifty-one hours, respectively. At seven o'clock, after a bit less than ninety minutes, the jury sent word that it had reached a verdict, and the defendants were brought back into the courtroom. As the documents necessary to record a verdict were ready, the jury sat uncomfortably for several minutes while attendants dashed to collect the required materials. "Absolute silence! Absolute silence here!" shouted court attendants.

Once the paperwork was in order, Justice Scudder directed the defendants to rise. They stood, separated by their counsel, as foreman William Young brought in the jury's verdict—guilty of first-degree murder as charged against both defendants in the indictment.

There had been three ballots. The first vote was unanimous for murder in the first degree against Mrs. Snyder. The second vote was nine to three in favor of murder in the first degree against Gray with one abstention and two in favor of manslaughter in the first degree, that is, killing without design, but in a cruel and unusual manner. A half hour of discussion followed, in which Gray's "love slave" defense received a moderately sympathetic hearing, but the third ballot was unanimous for murder in the first degree against Gray.[1]

Gray took the verdict well. His head dropped for a moment, but he quickly regained composure. Mrs. Snyder crumpled, sobbing, into her chair, and buried her face in her hands. However, a few seconds later she looked up, dried her eyes, and calmed down. The prisoners were led in front of the court clerk, who took their "pedigrees."[2] Mrs. Snyder squared her shoulders like a soldier and thrust her hand in the air, palm upright as if to take an oath. She stood, ramrod straight, for ten seconds before realizing that she was not to be placed under oath. The taking of pedigrees was an informal affair. When asked whether she was married, Mrs. Snyder answered, "Yes," provoking an outburst of laughter. Further merriment ensued when Gray answered, "Yes," upon being asked whether he was temperate.

While the pedigrees were being taken, Justice Scudder and attorneys for all sides met in a huddled conference at the bench. Scudder was in favor of imposing sentences immediately, but Mrs. Snyder's counsel argued that they needed time to prepare motions for setting aside the ver-

---

1. Most jurors had little or nothing to say when contacted by reporters; the exception was Charles Meissner: "The Bible tells us 'An eye for an eye and a tooth for a tooth' and it is this book on which we base our belief. It was not a question of mercy for a woman. That was settled when we were accepted as jurors. Why should she get off with ten or fifteen years when she was just as guilty as anyone? Perhaps we believed some of that part of her story of her home life with Snyder. But there he was, a fine, good fellow, gave her most of his pay. See what he got! It only goes to show that a man should marry a woman of his own age."

Foreman William Young received a rude shock after the verdict. The $45 due to him for jury duty, at a rate of $2.50 a day, were attached by an attorney who claimed that Young owed him $47.50 for services rendered two years previously. He forgave the remaining $2.50 of the debt, commenting that Young was entitled to at least that much for his public service.

2. Even today, following a guilty verdict in New York State, the prisoner is led to the court clerk's desk, where a "pedigree"—name, date of birth, religion, trade, and so on— is taken. The practice was instituted in the second half of the nineteenth century by criminologists who hoped to establish statistical regularities in the profiles of convicted criminals.

dict. Scudder consented to a one-week delay, until the following Monday, 9 May, and the prisoners were escorted back to their cells.

The speed of the verdict allowed all the newspapers to get their "bootjacks"—so called after the hooks they used to pick up bundles of newspapers—on the streets with extra editions in time to catch the pretheater Broadway crowd. Front-page mock-ups with the headline "GUILTY!" had been already prepared by all the papers. The *Telegram* had three presses up and running with a boilerplate guilty story even before the verdict came in. The flash arrived at one minute to seven, and the first copies of the extra edition were on the street at one minute after. By seven thirty, the new edition containing the "makeover" story, that is, the boilerplate with a few details thrown in to describe what actually happened, was rolling off the presses. In a stroke of genius, the circulation director sent three thousand copies to the courthouse itself where, as the first newspaper on the scene, it sold out instantly.

Back in his cell, Gray said to his guard, "I told the truth and my conscience is clear. My mother is glad I told the truth and God Almighty knows I told the truth."

Mrs. Snyder managed to strike a defiant pose for reporters as she was escorted from the courtroom: "I haven't lost my nerve. My attorneys know that I have not had a fair trial, and we will fight this verdict with every ounce of strength." To the attendant who assisted her from the courtroom, she said, "I am no more likely to go to the chair today than I was before the start of this trial." Greeted by the Queens County Jail Catholic chaplain George Murphy, to whom she had grown close despite continuing to attend Protestant services, she moaned, "Oh, Father, I thought they'd believe me . . . I thought they'd believe me."

As the defense attorneys left, they were mobbed on the steps of the courthouse. Reporters were so intent on their catch that District Attorney Newcombe almost managed to slip away unseen. An alert photographer spotted him, however, as he reached street level and, diving down the steps, grabbed him by the arm and dragged him back up. Jovial handshakes were exchanged all around for the benefit of cameramen. "As always, friendly enemies," commented Newcombe.

Gray asked that food be brought to him and ate Hungarian goulash with gusto. He then stayed up late writing letters. Mrs. Snyder, less stoic, fell on her cot gasping for breath. Three physicians were called to attend her and, based on the rigidity in her jaws and the fact that her fingers appeared to be drawn up into claws, suggested that she might be suffering from epilepsy. This was music to Hazelton's ears, and he immediately began to consider basing Mrs. Snyder's appeal on medical grounds. The attacks continued, off and on, through Monday night, leading physicians finally to give her an injection of morphine. If her condition deteriorated, they warned, Mrs. Snyder would have to be moved across the square to Saint John's Hospital.

Granny Brown heard the bad news from detectives assigned to guard the Snyder residence and took to her bed in hysterics. Lorraine had already been sent away to stay with her uncle Andrew and his wife.

One intrepid reporter braved the dangers of Norwalk to record Mrs. Isabel Gray's reaction to the verdict. The only person home when he rang the bell of the Brundage residence was Isabel's mother, Mrs. Kallenbach, who burst into tears when she heard the news, but quickly recovered. "I'm glad that woman got it, anyway!" she said with spirit. Brundage arrived a moment later with a policeman in tow to deal with reporters, but even he was unable to suppress a comment: "I can't believe it even now. Why, Judd and I were very close. And I don't understand about all this drinking. He never drank when he came out to our house—never more than one drink at the most."

A report was leaked that Gray had asked for a chance to talk with Mrs. Snyder. Gray himself, however, triple-denied this through Miller, Queens County Under-Sheriff William Desmond, and Warden Fox. "Why should I love her?" he said according to one of these. "If it were not for her, I wouldn't be in this jam. I don't want any more to do with her."

It was at this time that Mrs. Snyder initiated a momentous friendship with the notorious Jack Lait—journalist, editor, playwright, vaudeville-act writer, film writer, novelist, critic, radio commentator, muckraker, and man about town. Editor of Hearst's King Features Syndicate, Lait wore bow ties and favored a fedora hat with a rakish upturned brim. He smoked Home Run cigarettes and drank from a hip flask as he composed copy.

Perhaps it was a given that Lait and Mrs. Snyder would hit it off, and so they did. Mrs. Snyder sent word through Warden Fox that she wished to give a series of exclusive interviews to Lait, and the request was permitted.

According to Lait, Mrs. Snyder began their conversation by commenting, "Oh, baby, won't those other reporters rave when they see you got an inside story. Say—they'll *burn!*" Supplementing the interviews with material gleaned from Granny Brown, Lait wrote "The Price We Pay: Ruth Snyder's Own Life Story," a feature series that ran in Hearst's *American* and was syndicated through King Features.

Lait played up the undying love angle for all it was worth: "I love him. I can't help it. He could have done anything to me and with me—I guess he did, almost everything. I try to hate him. But I can't. I forgive him. Oh, I don't admire him any more, and I yield nothing of what I said on the stand. But he has a power over me that fights through all of it. I'm helpless against it."

This may have sold newspapers, but could not have been farther from the truth.[3] When Mrs. Snyder first heard the bogus reports that Gray wanted to see her, she was amenable, but quickly changed her mind. She wrote to her mother, "Have you ever heard such a liar as that beast of a man? Would you ever think he even cared five cents worth for me? No— I should say not. He's just a filthy, dirty skunk."

The epilepsy theory lost ground fast. On Tuesday, Mrs. Snyder again suffered two of her mysterious attacks. After reexamining her, the physicians announced that she was suffering not from epilepsy, but from nervous strain. Her cell door was kept open so that other female prisoners

---

3. In "Ruth Snyder's Own True Story," ghosted by Lait some months later based on the same interview material, Mrs. Snyder just as enthusiastically expresses her hatred for Gray. Another theme that Lait played for all it was worth was that of Mrs. Snyder as a tough, salty dame: "No, when they put that little steel plate on Ruthie's marble brow, they won't hear a whine, a squawk or a sob—take it from me, brother, I've gone through worse and nobody ever heard me whimper."

could drop in to chat, and a matron remained with her at all times. The usual jail crockery was replaced with aluminum pans to thwart a suicide attempt, and Mrs. Snyder was given specially dulled forks and knives. That night, the jail physician gave her chloral hydrate to help her sleep.

When Scudder discovered he was scheduled to be sitting elsewhere on Monday, he moved the sentencing to Friday, 13 May, with no objection from the defense counsel. Whether the defendants had any reaction be being sentenced on Friday the 13th is unrecorded.

Mrs. Snyder spent her remaining days in Queens County Jail pleasantly, stringing beads for a handbag and perusing the ten or twenty letters she received each day.[4] She usually answered the ones that enclosed stamps. "If I had a life sentence to do," she remarked to one of the jail attendants, "I'd like to do it in Queens." On Thursday, four college girls dropped by to pay her a visit. They went away disappointed because they were not permitted to see her, but, as Mrs. Snyder remarked, "It's the thought that counts." She was cheered that many of the celebrities who had attended the trial expressed their opposition to capital punishment. This must, she thought, have an effect on public opinion. She was also buoyed by the fact that Scudder himself was an opponent of the death penalty.

Although jammed, as usual, with spectators, the courtroom had a different feel on Friday. The celebrities of stage, screen, and pen had vanished after the verdict—exceptions being the determined Marquess and Marchioness of Queensberry. The tables that had been set up for the press had been disassembled, so the roughly one hundred reporters present milled around the courtroom.

As the defendants and lawyers waited in the holding pens, Mrs. Sny-

4. According to Warden Fox, who estimated that Gray received about twelve letters a day. Both these figures are net of the crank letters that were screened out and discarded. Fox added a few more details about the prisoners' lives in Queens County Jail. During the hours when their cell doors were open, both exercised by walking a mile up and down their tiers, a matter of fifty laps. Mrs. Snyder had a table outside her cell door; it was here that she read and answered letters. Gray chatted with Warden Fox for half an hour to an hour each day.

der was in high spirits, giggling like a schoolgirl. Hazelton lost his temper and spoke sharply to her. "Stop that laughing! You are about to be sentenced to death." Ever attentive to appearance, however, when he entered the courtroom at nine forty, he took care to smile and joke as though he had not a care in the world. Miller entered five minutes later, less ostentatiously cheerful. Millard followed him and looked downright grim. Finally, District Attorney Newcombe, making no effort to hide his good mood, walked into the court. Wallace was otherwise occupied and did not attend, nor did any of Newcombe's assistants.

Justice Scudder took the bench at ten o'clock and the defendants were led before him. Mrs. Snyder came first and stood to the left of the bench. Gray came second and stood some five feet away from her. For once, the pair was not separated by a bevy of attorneys, only by an officer of the court. Mrs. Snyder wore the black dress that had done service throughout the trial. No longer constrained by having to appear before a jury, she had also applied makeup, with good effect. Matron Irene Wolfe stood a bit behind and to the left of Mrs. Snyder. Her right hand rested lightly on the prisoner's back, but she was sure that her charge would not collapse. Mrs. Snyder gazed sweetly at Scudder. Gray stood ramrod straight, clutching his daughter Jane's copy of *A Child's Book of Prayer*.

To the frustration of those in the back, the proceedings were conducted without benefit of loudspeakers. Eager spectators stood on the radiators and bailiffs circled the courtroom pulling them down from their perches. The protests and curses made it even harder to hear. Justice Scudder asked counsel if there were any legal reasons why the death sentence should not be pronounced. Hazelton mechanically read a lengthy statement on behalf of Mrs. Snyder. It amounted to a summary of all the exceptions that counsel had taken during the trial.

"The Court," said Scudder, "is of the opinion that these exceptions should be overruled, and they are overruled." Hazelton took exception to the overruling of his exceptions, and with that, the legal barriers to the sentencing of Mrs. Snyder were exhausted. The court clerk then repeated the question whether there were any further reasons why sentence of death should not be pronounced. This was Mrs. Snyder's opportunity to declare she was pregnant. Apparently thinking it was an opportunity for a speech, she opened her mouth to say something, but Hazelton quickly moved to her side and responded to the clerk that there was none.

Justice Scudder, the opponent of capital punishment who had done his best to avoid trying the Snyder-Gray case, had no desire to inflict a lecture upon the defendants. The only words he spoke were those required by law:

> The judgment of the court is that you, Ruth Snyder, for the murder in the first degree of Albert Snyder, whereof you are convicted, be, and you hereby are, sentenced to the punishment of death; and it is ordered that, within ten days after this day's session of court, the Sheriff of the County of Queens deliver you, together with the warrant of this court, to the agent and warden of the state prison of New York at Sing Sing, where you shall be kept in solitary confinement until the week beginning Monday, the 20th day of June 1927, and, on some day within the week so appointed, the said agent and warden of the state prison of the State of New York at Sing Sing, is commanded to execute and do execution on you, Ruth Snyder, in the mode and manner prescribed by the laws of the State of New York.

Mrs. Snyder shifted from foot to foot and flashed an odd smile at the judge, but he merely stared at her. The same ritual was repeated for Gray, but the exceptions offered by Millard were less lengthy. As the prisoners were taken out of the courtroom, Mrs. Snyder gave way to an impish desire to tickle Matron Nan Hart.

After sentencing, Gray released a handwritten statement:"I am one of the best examples of what whiskey, lust and sin will ultimately lead one into. I have seen so many pitiful cases here as an inmate of this jail, as to what liquor and improper relations will exact in retaliation that it makes me more than anxious to urge my fellow men to see the light of God as our only true salvation."

Mrs. Snyder conferred with Father Murphy and announced her desire to convert to the Catholic faith. Murphy had a comment for reporters:"I think she has a deep and profound sense of repentance. That, I believe, is the fundamental of real religion." To minimize publicity, Murphy told reporters that the conversion would take place at a later date. In fact, he performed it practically on the spot.

Mrs. Snyder received a visit from her mother and discussed practical affairs. She also asked attendants if stops were permitted on the way to Sing Sing. "There is a good roadhouse I know up there," she was reported to have commented. "I'd like to stop for a lobster dinner."

PART THREE

Last Days

*Mrs. Snyder leaves Queens County Jail for Sing Sing Prison,
in Ossining, New York, 16 May 1927*

23

SIX MOTORCYCLES, two of them equipped with armored sidecars carrying police riflemen, were waiting outside the courthouse after sentencing. The artillery was to accompany the prisoners' convoy as far as the New York City limits. After that, speed alone would be sufficient to deliver the prisoners safely.

Ten thousand spectators thronged the streets around the courthouse hoping to observe the famous pair as they left Queens County, but they waited in vain. At the request of their attorneys, the prisoners were allowed one last weekend in Queens County Jail to settle personal matters. "Well, it looks like we won't be leaving your boardinghouse just yet," remarked Gray when Warden Fox told him that he and Mrs. Snyder would not go to Sing Sing until Monday.

Over the weekend, Gray signed a document transferring his liquid assets to his wife. Mrs. Snyder signed documents giving temporary custody of Lorraine to her mother and requesting that Granny Brown be made Lorraine's legal parent.

On Sunday, crowds gathered on Jackson Avenue across from the jail to catch a glimpse of Mrs. Snyder. She did appear briefly at her cell window in the late afternoon and waved at the crowd. Some reporters jokingly beckoned her to join them down below. Mrs. Snyder laughed, shook her head, and elaborately shrugged her shoulders, palms upright, in a gesture that said it just couldn't be done.

The crowd that assembled on Monday morning was about half the size of the one that had been disappointed on Friday. Hopefuls began to arrive at six o'clock; by nine, the sidewalks were choked. Many people perched on parked cars, sometimes to the curses of owners, who arrived to find their vehicles crawling with humanity. Red Cross volunteers took advantage of the crowd to solicit donations for victims of the great Mississippi River flood.[1] Patrolmen did their best to restrain the sidewalk crowds, and mounted policemen pranced their horses menacingly back and forth on the avenue itself. All regular traffic had been diverted.

At ten twenty-five, Gray, handcuffed to two deputy sheriffs, descended the back stairs of the Queens County Jail. Another deputy and Sheriff Joseph Quinn himself waited at the foot of the stairs. All five men entered one of two curtained black Cadillac seven-passenger sedans that were parked with their motors idling. These cars were the automotive monsters of their day, capable of maintaining a steady 120 miles per hour on the open highway. A few moments later, Mrs. Snyder left the jail handcuffed to Matron Irene Wolfe, closely followed by Warden Fox. Under-Sheriff William Desmond and a deputy were waiting for them in the second Cadillac. Fox returned to the jail and reemerged carrying several bags of Mrs. Snyder's belongings, which he deposited in her vehicle. He looked sad as he went back up the stairs and disappeared from view into his somehow diminished jail.

Rumbling mightily, the procession of six motorcycles and two automobiles approached the gates of the rear yard of the jail-courthouse complex. Sirens screamed as the gates slowly swung open. The motorcycles came out first and, when they did, all attempts to control the crowd collapsed. Spectators surged past patrolmen into the street. Mounted policemen cursed as they wielded their batons to force passage for the lead motorcycles. As the convoy started to break away, a woman darted forward to peek into Mrs. Snyder's vehicle and was rewarded by a nasty blow from the butt of a sidecar-mounted policeman's rifle.

Once free from its pedestrian pursuers, many of them women who ran after the convoy shaking their fists in the air and screaming imprecations at Mrs. Snyder, the procession headed toward the Queensboro Bridge. Press vehicles were able to get away from the jam only in fits and

---

1. Comedian Will Rogers, who helped raise funds for flood victims, joked that the timing of the disaster was unfortunate because it had to compete with the Snyder-Gray case for headlines.

starts. As a result, fourteen cars in clumps of two and three straggled behind and the convoy proceeded through mid-morning traffic like a drunken accordion playing catch-up with itself. Among the vehicles in this Keystone Kops parade was that of Queens Alderman James Murtha, who, exercising a hitherto-unknown privilege of office, took advantage of the event to give his family an outing.

The convoy drove across the bridge, where throngs were waiting on the Manhattan side, and then crossed Central Park at 72nd Street. Traffic police had been warned about the motorcade, but they were so eager to watch that they confused their hand signals and made traffic even worse. Once on the West Side, the vehicles drove up Riverside Drive and entered the Henry Hudson Parkway, picking up speed. At that point, the armored sidecar motorcycles dropped off and the high-performance Cadillacs geared up to cruising speed.

Alderman Murtha's car was unable to sustain the pace and limped to a halt, billowing smoke. Then a press car caught fire, and its occupants emerged cursing. Just like in the movies, they hailed a passing driver, waved a twenty-dollar bill in his face, and piled in, shouting, "Follow that car!"

Between Dobbs Ferry and Irvington, there was a near disaster. The commander of the motorcycle escort skidded on a patch of oil and was thrown. When Mrs. Snyder saw the policeman hurtle through the air, she buried her head in her hands and screamed. Fortunately, he was thrown clear of traffic and was not seriously injured. After picking himself up out of a ditch, he climbed back on his motorcycle and caught up with the convoy just as it reached Sing Sing, where a trusty at the prison hospital treated his scrapes and bruises. Gray expressed his gratitude that the officer was unhurt, remarking that there had already been enough tragedy connected to the case.

Mrs. Snyder ignored the taunts shouted at her by the crowds that continued to turn out as she passed through the small towns of Westchester County. Asked how she felt, she said, "As well as might be expected, under the circumstances." Yet she perked up sufficiently to remark that she was unafraid and hoped to pass back over the same route someday under happier circumstances. When Matron Wolfe asked if the handcuffs should be readjusted, Mrs. Snyder said, "No, I don't think so. They'd get me there just the same." Gray said little and smoked four cigarettes during the hour and twenty-minute ride. He expressed concern that his cigarettes would be taken from him when he entered the Death House and was relieved to learn he could buy more from the prison store. As they approached Sing Sing, Gray got a view of the prison complex. One of his escorts lamely pointed out the ball field to Gray and remarked that he might make the team if his sentence were commuted. "I used to be pretty good when I was a youngster in school," remarked the prisoner.

The south gate of the prison, choked as expected with newspaper reporters and curiosity seekers, swung open and the vehicles pulled into the outer yard. Inmates and guards competed on equal terms for a chance to glimpse the celebrity prisoners buried in their curtain-shrouded vehicles.[2] A guard, jumping onto the running board of Gray's vehicle before it had come to a halt, shouted, "The woman goes in first!" A green gate in the original prison wall slid open—whenever Sing Sing grew, new walls were simply built around old—and the Cadillac carrying Mrs. Snyder passed into the inner compound, where the Death House was located. She descended from the car with Matron Wolfe and walked the few steps into the building.

With perfect timing, a *Daily News* airplane that had been tailing the convoy made a low pass over the prison, the photographer aboard madly snapping pictures. The plane repeated the maneuver a few minutes later when Gray's vehicle entered the compound and its occupants descended. Gray strove even then to keep up appearances by draping a green sweater over his handcuffs.

Sing Sing's warden, Lewis Lawes, its principal keeper (P.K.), John

---

2. Old hands said that only once in thirty years had there been so much interest in a new arrival, and that was when New York City Police Lieutenant Charles Becker was delivered to the Death House in 1914. As head of the Vice Squad, Becker was leader of a protection racket that collected a quarter of all organized gambling and prostitution revenue in New York. His downfall came when he was convicted of ordering the murder of a recalcitrant casino owner. In his white shirt and tie, Gray was said to be the best-dressed man to enter the Death House since the ill-fated Becker.

Sheehy, a trusty clerk, and an assistant keeper met Mrs. Snyder in the combined office and visiting hall of the Death House.

Lawes had been born in 1883 into a prison family—his father was an employee of the state reformatory at Elmira—and after running away from home as a teenager and spending three years in the Army, he joined the prison service as a guard. He rose through the ranks and in 1919 was appointed warden of Sing Sing, a job in which his predecessors had lasted an average of eleven months. Lawes instituted a series of reforms that catapulted Sing Sing into the forefront of American penal practice and made its warden an influential spokesman on issues of all kinds. Author, speaker, social scientist, and tireless advocate of prison and legal reform, Lawes was, at the time of the Snyder-Gray case, known from coast to coast.

Mrs. Snyder's personal details—name, date of birth, and so on—were taken by the trusty, and she signed a form giving prison officials permission to read her mail. Sheehy and his assistant escorted her into the "Women's Wing." There she was required to disrobe and was weighed, showered, examined by Sing Sing Chief Physician Charles Sweet, who certified that she had no contagious diseases, and given prison clothes. These consisted of prison-manufactured underwear and cotton stockings, a blue-and-white spotted cotton housedress that Lawes had purchased from a shop in Ossining, and a pair of felt slippers. She was photographed and, although the Bertillon system had long since been abandoned in favor of fingerprints, went through the ritual of having a lengthy set of physical measurements recorded.

The moment Mrs. Snyder passed out of the reception area, Gray was shown in and the procedure was repeated.[3] He received blue jeans and a plaid work shirt to wear.

---

3. The *Evening Journal* reported that the following exchange took place between Warden Lawes and Gray:

"What are you here for?"

"I don't know."

"Well, what were you convicted of?"

"First-degree murder."

Having perhaps read of the laughter in Long Island City when Gray described him-

Having learned that her wedding ring would be taken from her, Mrs. Snyder had given Granny Brown the platinum band she had worn so prominently during the trial. She arrived at Sing Sing with $15.28 in her pocket. In addition to the bags she had brought from Queens County Jail, Mrs. Snyder carried a small rosary given to her by Father Murphy. When her personal details were taken, Mrs. Snyder gave her religion as Catholic, and her first Death House visitor was Father John McCaffery, the Catholic chaplain of Sing Sing. This was the first open acknowledgment that she had converted.

Gray had traveled light; his only possession, apart from $8.58, was the prayer book he had held while being sentenced to death.

The Death House complex (the "Slaughter House," in prison slang) was a prison within a prison. It had its own kitchen, its own exercise yards, and a small hospital, complete with an operating room, which had occasionally been used to perform surgery necessary to keep prisoners alive until their execution date. The building was lozenge-shaped, almost square, with the office and visiting room at the northern end and the death chamber at the southern end. The northeast and northwest sides of the lozenge housed the so-called East and West Wings, each containing six cells apiece. The "Women's Wing," of which Mrs. Snyder was the only resident, was really just a hallway off the office and contained three cells.

Prisoner Number 79,891 (Gray) and Prisoner Number 79,892 (Mrs. Snyder) were lodged in identical cells, each ten feet wide by twelve feet long and containing a washbasin, a toilet, and a bolted-down cot. The side and back walls were unpainted concrete; the front consisted of a barred sliding door. Prisoners were allowed to pull a dark curtain when they desired privacy.

A corridor led straight down the principal axis of the lozenge from the office to the death chamber. Ten yards from the latter was a room (the "Dance Hall") containing six holding cells arranged in a lazy semicircle

---

self as "temperate," Lawes was having none of that: the Death House registration book reads "Intemperate."

so one guard could view all six cells at once. Here, there were no curtains and no privacy: these were the holding cells to which prisoners were removed a few hours before their execution. The execution chamber ("Out Back") had its own outside entrance and a tiny coatroom for witnesses. Off the execution chamber was a rudimentary morgue (the "Ice Box") where autopsies were performed.

The first application for the position of Death House matron for Mrs. Snyder had arrived at Sing Sing the day after the indictment. In the end, three women, Mrs. Lillian Hickey, Mrs. Lucy Many, and Miss Mary Kopp, were chosen for the job; they alternated eight-hour shifts so that Mrs. Snyder was never left alone. Her cell, the middle cell of the three on her hallway, was considered lucky. Its last occupant, Mrs. Fanny Soper, who killed her husband and feigned insanity, had her death sentence commuted to a twenty-year term of imprisonment; her predecessor, Mrs. Anna Buzzi, was acquitted of murder after obtaining a new trial on appeal.

Lucky or not, Mrs. Snyder's cell was totally isolated from everyone except the matrons. Gray at least had neighbors on his hallway in the East Wing, and although prisoners could not see each other, they could talk.

Monday was a busy day for new arrivals to the Death House. Half an hour before Mrs. Snyder and Gray arrived, Charles Doran, a twenty-three-year-old taxi driver convicted of murdering a gas station attendant in Albany, had been admitted. A quarter of an hour later, it was the turn of Peter Seiler, a twenty-one-year-old office clerk who had killed a policeman while holding up a Manhattan speakeasy. Doran, Seiler, and Gray occupied neighboring cells on the East Wing; the West Wing was full with six prisoners.

Warden Lawes gave a press conference in his office at which he emphasized that no communication between the two prisoners would be allowed. "They will live separately and, if they do not obtain commutations, they will die separately." To prevent meetings between relatives of the condemned prisoners, Lawes had staggered visiting days—Gray's would be Tuesday, Thursday, and Saturday, as they were for all the other male inmates; Mrs. Snyder's would be Monday, Wednesday, and Friday.

Lawes squelched rumors of a final lovers' reunion and told the reporters that it was even a distinct possibility that the murderers would not be executed on the same day.

Sing Sing inmates regarded capital punishment with horror and the carnival atmosphere surrounding the new arrivals, not to mention the fact that a woman was involved, had upset them. As Lawes was speaking to reporters, an aide rushed in and took him by the elbow. There was trouble; the inmates had refused to eat their lunch of pork and beans. And they were threatening a strike. Lawes fought his way out of his office and rushed to the mattress shop. Men stood silently beside their machines. Would they go back to work, or did they want to be locked up in their cells? Lawes demanded. No one moved, and Lawes gestured to the keepers to escort the prisoners back to their cells. Then he went to the license plate shop, where it was the same story.

By mid-afternoon, all of Sing Sing was under lockdown. Lawes, who had a great gift of knowing when to play his cards and when to fold them, conferred with a few trusted old cons. How had the pork and beans been, anyway? Like marbles with rancid fat, the prisoners replied without hesitation: inedible. Lawes immediately summoned representatives from the Prisoners Welfare League and promised them that the head cook would be called on the carpet. Thus ended what went down in Sing Sing history as the "Bean Rebellion."

With the famous prisoners consigned to the Death House, journalists were deprived of real news about the case. In desperation, they turned to Mrs. Snyder's hair, discovering that it had been dyed with peroxide, which she could not obtain in Sing Sing. The source for the story was P. K. Sheehy, a garrulous Irish egotist who was unable to keep his mouth shut once a reporter got him going.[4] On Saturday, 21 May 1927, with Lindbergh midway across the Atlantic, the *Daily Mirror*'s front-page

---

4. Once Gray was in a bad mood and Sheehy asked him what the problem was. "Lay off of me!" snapped Gray. "Everything I say in here I read in the papers the next day." Naturally, Sheehy relayed the story to reporters. Sheehy ran Sing Sing with an iron hand, for which Lawes tolerated his big mouth as well as his petty brutality and corruption. One of Sheehy's favorite tricks was to allow a poker game to progress until the stakes

headline read: "Over Open Sea, Going Strong." Mrs. Snyder's tresses, however, were important enough to make the back-page headline: "Mrs. Snyder's Hair Is Black."

Not only was Mrs. Snyder's hair black, Sheehy told the rapt press corps, but she was gaining weight. She had weighed 152 pounds when she arrived at Sing Sing; within a week, she estimated that she was approaching 155. There were no more mile-long walks up and down the corridor; she received only two twenty-minute exercise periods per day in the tiny concrete-paved exercise yard reserved for female prisoners.[5] She requested and was given a rubber ball that she could bounce back and forth.

Because Warden Lawes's taste in dresses did not correspond to her own, she was also allowed to have several plain housedresses sent from New York. After Mrs. Snyder had settled into the Death House routine and was found to be an easygoing prisoner, Granny Brown was allowed to bring some of her more fashionable dresses from home. Although the prisoner was not permitted to wear these, as a treat, she was allowed to sit with them in the cell next door during the day. Just being in the same cell with them made her feel better.

Prison rules were bent to allow Mrs. Snyder to use face powder and cold cream. To her frustration, however, she was not allowed to keep the box of face powder out of fear that she would throw it in a keeper's face. Instead, each morning a dose was passed to her on a piece of paper. Mrs. Snyder was also upset to learn that chewing gum was forbidden. Not only could it be used to jam the lock on the cell door during a suicide attempt, but an ingenious inmate had, two years previously, succeeded in constructing a club out of a rolled-up magazine fortified with wads of hardened chewing gum stuck between the pages.

Gray's only complaint was that it was too hard to get cigarettes. He started smoking a pipe but found that the tobacco mixture dispensed by

---

were high, then break it up and confiscate the pot, paying a small commission to the snitch who had passed him the information.

5. Gray was luckier. He could play basketball or handball one-on-one with the guard who supervised him in the East Wing exercise yard.

the State was not to his liking. After discussions with Reverend Anthony Peterson, the Protestant chaplain of the jail and a pipe smoker, Gray settled on a brand that he could order through the prison commissary. Matches were not allowed in cells; Gray had to ask a keeper each time he needed a light. Reading material was freely available, but all staples were removed from magazines.

At this point, Gray began what would develop into a rich correspondence with attorney Samuel Miller. The two had formed a deep friendship during the trial; as Gray was to say later, Miller became almost more of a brother than a lawyer. On his second day in Sing Sing, Gray wrote that he had arrived safely, that the cell was large and immaculate, the food excellent (since the Death House had its own kitchen, he had not been subjected to the offending pork and beans), and everyone splendid. The same cheerful triviality pervaded all of Gray's letters, which invariably contained a sentence—sometimes a paragraph—about the weather and concluded with the hope that Miller's family was well.

During Mrs. Snyder and Gray's first week in the Death House, the three members of the State Lunacy Commission—psychiatrists George Smith, head of the commission, Joseph Moore, and Paul Taddiken—happened to be at Sing Sing on other business and took the opportunity to observe the pair. They reported to Lawes that the prisoners appeared to be sane and normal in every respect. The commission would submit a formal finding in due course.[6]

Gray's glasses, which were taken from him until it could be ascertained whether he showed suicidal tendencies, were returned in light of his calm behavior and his inability to read without them. Gray's neighbor Doran let it be known through his attorney that Gray was "a hell of a nice fellow." They played checkers during the day, each calling out moves to his neighbor.

Both prisoners continued to receive an abundant volume of mail. Incoming correspondence was screened to weed out letters that were of-

6. Mandatory sanity hearings for condemned prisoners were instituted in New York State in 1924 after an autopsy on the body of Alberigo Mastrota, executed for beating his uncle to death, revealed what were interpreted as organic signs of insanity.

fensive or inappropriate, such as marriage proposals. The bulk of Mrs. Snyder's mail was from religious correspondents who either praised or condemned her turn to Catholicism. Both prisoners spent much of their time sleeping. Gray slept ten hours every night; Mrs. Snyder slept eight, but took a two-hour nap each afternoon.

Granny Brown took advantage of Friday visiting hours to make the trip to Ossining. Visiting conditions in the Death House were atrocious, especially after the easygoing atmosphere of the Queens County Jail. The prisoner would be brought into the reception area and seated in a tiny wire-mesh cage; the visitors would sit in another, five feet away. Between them, one and sometimes two guards were stationed. The prisoner and visitors were forced to speak in raised voices just to make themselves heard across the void. Worn out by the journey from Queens, Granny Brown burst into tears when she saw her daughter under such circumstances. Mrs. Snyder, by contrast, was composed and spoke of her determination to make sure that Granny Brown was appointed Lorraine's guardian.

Mrs. Snyder proved that she had not lost all of her charms. Some Death House inmates had looked forward to her arrival under the delusion that they would be able to converse with her. This was, needless to say, impossible: she was isolated in her own wing and her postage-stamp-sized exercise yard was not visible from either of the men's corridors. Death House cook James "Dummy" Dugan managed, however, to strike up a correspondence with her by smuggling notes in with the food. Mrs. Snyder replied with notes smuggled out underneath the dirty dishes. Dugan soon fell madly in love with Mrs. Snyder and was immune to reason, even when Death House barber Vincent de Stefano[7] reminded him that the woman had killed her husband.

---

7. Vincent de Stefano occupied an unusual position at Sing Sing. He had been in and out of prison for more than ten years, and his path crossed so frequently with Lawes's that a friendship developed. He acted not only as Death House barber, but as Lawes's chauffeur and secretary of the Prisoner's Mutual Welfare League. He lived in Lawes's home and had the run of the prison and town. De Stefano was an intimate of, among other major figures in New York crime, Albert Anastasia, Lucky Luciano, Frank Costello, and Joseph Valachi.

Dugan hid himself every day at a barred window through which he could elaborately blow kisses to Mrs. Snyder when she was in the exercise yard. She good-humoredly, but discreetly, returned his kisses when matrons were not watching. It was all settled, Dugan told de Stefano: "She's sure to get off and, whatever happened with her and her husband, it'll be different between her and me."

The hearing for guardianship of Lorraine was scheduled for 31 May before Queens County Surrogate Daniel Noble, with Hazelton appearing for Granny Brown. Because one of the points being raised by Warren Schneider was the negative effect Death House visits would have on Lorraine, she had not accompanied Granny Brown to Ossining. Pending court action on the matter, Mrs. Snyder signed a document waiving all parental rights, including visitation rights, over Lorraine.

One thing was clear: whoever won custody of Lorraine would immediately sue for payment of the ninety-seven thousand dollars in life insurance. Not surprisingly, the Prudential Life Insurance Company issued a statement declaring that it would fight all claims on the life on Albert Snyder.

Legal precedents were mixed. In 1923, a Seattle man named Plumlee took out five thousand dollars of life insurance, naming his wife as beneficiary. Five hours later, Mrs. Plumlee poisoned her husband with strychnine. She eventually confessed to the crime and was imprisoned. The Equitable Life Insurance Company resisted paying the resulting claim, and the first trial judge directed the jury to return a verdict in its favor. The U.S. District Court of Appeals, however, reversed the lower court, citing that there was insufficient evidence that insurance money was the motive for the slaying.

A New York State case, also in 1923, had reached a different conclusion, however. Kay Pendleton Smith of Brooklyn, who had a $1,000 life insurance policy payable to his wife, murdered her and was duly executed. The trustees of his wife's estate sued the Metropolitan Life Insurance Company for payment of the policy. The court decided that Mrs. Smith's estate could gain ownership of the policy only from the estate of Mr. Smith, which would amount to Mr. Smith's having been permitted to enrich his estate by killing his wife.[8] The case was therefore decided in favor of the insurance company.

On Friday, 27 May, Hazelton and Wallace filed Mrs. Snyder's appeal with the clerk of the Queens County Court. This automatically stayed the scheduled 20 June execution. It was a pro forma appeal; the making of legal arguments would wait until the full trial record, preparation of which was paid for by the State, was available. District Attorney Newcombe informed Warden Lawes of the stay immediately upon receiving notice of appeal. Mrs. Snyder, when she heard the news, remarked, "Well, that settles things for a while." She also learned that, at the request of Warren Schneider, the hearing for custody of Lorraine had been delayed until 7 June.

Over the long Armistice Day weekend, Gray received his first visitors: his sister, Margaret, his brother-in-law, Harold Logan, and Samuel Miller. Because he was neither blood relative nor counsel, a court order was required in order to admit Logan. Mrs. Snyder received a holiday surprise in the form of a large chocolate cake from Cox Bakeries, of which Hazelton was vice president.

Sunday was a beautiful day, and hundreds of cars filled with families descended on Sing Sing to gaze upon the stone walls that confined Gray and Mrs. Snyder. As usual on the Sabbath, motorists hoping to glimpse Lorraine or Granny Brown besieged the Snyder residence in Queens Village. Passing cars were left in peace, but policemen chased away families who parked in front of the house and unpacked box lunches.

On Monday, Mrs. Snyder's brother, Andrew, journeyed to Ossining to see her, only to be informed that visitors were not permitted on holidays. When he protested that he could only get away from work on bank holidays, prison officials relented.

On Thursday, 2 June, Mrs. Isabel Gray made an appearance for the first time since her visit to the Queens County Jail immediately after her

8. Prisoners under sentence of death were considered legally dead, as a result of which only Smith's estate, not Smith himself, could receive the insurance benefit.

husband's arrest. One lone reporter had doggedly remained in Ossining, refusing to leave until Mrs. Gray visited the Death House. She arrived, accompanied by her protective brother-in-law, Frank Brundage. Brundage was at first refused admittance, but went to White Plains and obtained a court order that permitted him to see the prisoner. As he sped off in search of the order, Mrs. Gray entered the Death House on the arm of Elise Chisolm, Warden Lawes's personal secretary.[9]

According to keepers who were present, the meeting between husband and wife was a purely formal encounter during which no signs of affection were discernible. After one and one-half hours together, Mrs. Gray left her husband and went to Lawes's office for a discussion. Would it be possible, she asked, for this and any future visits to be kept secret? "Just try it!" retorted Chisolm.

Gray detested the very mention of Mrs. Snyder's name, and his keepers and corridor mates respected his feelings. He had his lighter moments, however, even where Mrs. Snyder was involved. When Death House barber de Stefano was giving Gray his weekly shave, he remarked that he would next see Mrs. Snyder, who wanted her hair trimmed. Gray sent a message through de Stefano to Mrs. Snyder that he was sorry he could not shave the back of her neck the way he used to. Mrs. Snyder received the message with a laugh and asked de Stefano to do as good a job on her neck as her former lover had.

State Lunacy Commission members, who continued to drop by and chat with the prisoners, reported that they appeared normal. Gray, tongue in cheek, expressed satisfaction that his mind had not deteriorated to any marked extent since his arrival. Mrs. Snyder spent long periods sitting silently on the edge of her cot, hardly unusual for a prisoner under sentence of death. In Chicago, attorney Clarence Darrow expressed his opinion that Gray had not been properly analyzed before his

---

9. It was rumored that Chisolm wrote the better part of Lawes's books, that the pair had a long-standing love affair, and that Mrs. Lawes's 1937 death in a suspicious fall from Bear Mountain Bridge was suicide committed in despair over her husband's philandering. Lawes and Chisolm were married in 1938.

trial. This elicited a blast from Samuel Miller: "Darrow is a mile away from the facts."

Gray told Reverend Peterson he was ashamed that he was blessed with time to prepare for his fate while Albert Snyder had been murdered with his sins full upon him. He pored over the religious tracts Peterson left him, happily reading them aloud to his neighbors when they asked. According to Peterson, Gray emerged as the unofficial leader of his wing, settling minor disputes, giving personal advice and the like. In a letter to Samuel Miller, Gray spoke of his earnest desire to be of service to his neighbors, and his frustration at not being able to do more to help them.

Mrs. Snyder, who also consulted Peterson despite her new religious preference, was more easygoing with him. When Peterson and his wife toured the West Coast, they sent her a postcard from California, which she forwarded to Lorraine. When the minister returned, she listened avidly to his stories and expressed a wish to travel. Mrs. Snyder was enormously cheered on 8 June when her old friend Father Murphy from Queens County Jail dropped by for a visit. Also helping to sustain her were the almost daily visits from Mrs. Lawes. These remained the best-kept secret of Sing Sing: Lawes drew a firm line when it came to his family, and any newspaper that had dared to print the story would have found its reporters barred from the prison.

The legal hearing to determine Lorraine's fate was held in Jamaica on 7 June, but resulted only in the filing of briefs and the scheduling of a second hearing on 18 June. On 11 June, Samuel Miller filed a pro forma appeal for Gray, who was informed by the District Attorney's Office of the automatic stay of execution.

Meanwhile, trouble broke out with the members of the State Prison Commission. Although they were permitted access to prisoners as part of their official, largely philanthropic, duties, Warden Lawes barred the commissioners from the Death House on the grounds they were merely curiosity seekers; his stand was supported by New York State Commissioner of Corrections Raymond Kieb. There was also trouble with the general public: a previously little-known and less-invoked privilege allowed residents of New York State access to Sing Sing for a brief official tour of the facilities. When the daily volume swelled from twenty visitors to three thousand, the open-prison policy was suspended.

The Prudential Life Insurance Company petitioned Justice Scudder for a court order to permit it to return the premiums that Mrs. Snyder had paid—the first step toward voiding Albert Snyder's insurance policies. When Scudder granted the order, the Prudential mailed off a check, but, on advice of counsel, Mrs. Snyder returned it uncashed. On 17 June, attorneys James H. McIntosh and Solomon Weit of Beiber and Weit, which had been retained by the Prudential, visited Sing Sing to tender, as the court order permitting them access stated, "certain monies and papers." After listening politely, Mrs. Snyder persisted in her refusal, and the disappointed lawyers returned to New York.

To add insult to injury, Mrs. Snyder applied to Warden Lawes for permission to continue paying the premiums on her husband's and her own insurance policies. Permission to pay premiums on Albert Snyder's policies was denied pending court action, but granted for her own policy, there being no compelling argument against it; in due course, the Prudential received the prisoner's signed check. Mrs. Snyder also formally requested that the principal beneficiary on Albert Snyder's policies be changed to Lorraine. The Prudential denied the request and, escalating the war of nerves, announced that, because Mrs. Snyder and Gray would be probably not be alive to give evidence by the time the lawsuit came to trial, it would seek permission to take depositions from the prisoners in the Death House.

On the Fourth of July, Gray and Mrs. Snyder enjoyed one of the three special dinners served in the Death House—the others being served on Christmas and Thanksgiving. The menu was roast chicken with all the trimmings. As a treat, a loudspeaker was placed in the Death House so that condemned prisoners might listen to the radio broadcasts freely available to other inmates.[10]

10. One of Warden Lawes's principal humane reforms in the early 1920s had been wiring Sing Sing for radio and providing each cell with earphones. The Death House was not hooked up to the system. A portable radio was sometimes brought in, in addition to which, some relief from the monotony was provided by a phonograph that was

The day was marred by tragedy when a canoe capsized in the Hudson, drowning three vacationers in plain view of the prison. Clinging to their overturned craft until the current swept it away, the canoers struggled in vain to reach shore. Hundreds of inmates, watching in horror, clamored to be allowed to dive into the river to save them, but they were restrained by rifle-brandishing guards. A sullen mood spoiled the rest of the holiday at Sing Sing.

The electric chair had been idle an unusually long time, since early April. Activity picked up again on Thursday, 14 July. Although death warrants specified only the week during which sentence was to be carried out, Warden Lawes invariably chose Thursday nights at eleven o'clock. The condemned prisoner was William Wagner, a twenty-three-year-old German waiter who steadfastly refused to give his real name in order to protect his family in Europe. Wagner had left his boarding house on Hicks Street in Brooklyn with a suitcase that the landlady's daughter believed (mistakenly, as it turned out) to be filled with stolen valuables. She struggled with him in the doorway. Another boarder ran up and assisted her, whereupon Wagner pulled out a pistol and killed him. As Wagner was taken to the Dance Hall, he went through the melancholy ritual of saying farewell to his corridor mates. Gray patted him on the back and told him to bear up. Mrs. Snyder, isolated on her own corridor, had asked to be allowed to say good-bye to the condemned man as he was taken to his fate, but was denied permission. "It's a pity he's lost," she said, and Gray wrote Samuel Miller of the emotional difficulty of losing neighbors.

Seven days later, it was the turn of Peter Heslin, twenty-eight, of Manhattan, who was convicted of shooting a police patrolman who interrupted him during a holdup.[11] "I was planted on circumstantial evi-

---

carried between the two men's corridors and, when it was occupied, the Women's Wing.

11. A poignant touch was added by the fact that Heslin (true name: Robert O'Neil) had rescued barber de Stefano's older sister from a brutal stepfather years before. De Stefano was almost incapacitated by grief when he cut Heslin's hair before the electrocution.

dence," Heslin said as he settled into the electric chair. "You are now watching an innocent man die." The following Thursday saw a happier turn of events when Thomas "Red" Moran won a reversal of his conviction from the New York State Appeals Court.[12]

Around this time, a report circulated that Mrs. Snyder had offered Gray a deal. According to the story, Mrs. Snyder asked Gray to take upon himself all the blame for the murder. Once she was free, she would devote her energies and resources, including the insurance money, to saving his life. Between her efforts and the popular disinclination to execute one killer while the other went free, Gray was practically guaranteed to escape the chair. Lawes had no comment on the report.

In the meantime, Mrs. Snyder's defense team was thrown into disarray when the long-simmering tension between Hazelton and Wallace boiled over. The joint practice was dissolved and Wallace set up his own office. The two attorneys continued to work together on Mrs. Snyder's appeal, but Wallace was less and less involved as time went on. Hazelton took a long vacation in Montana, leaving preparation of the appeal in the hands of Joseph Lonardo, who was heavily assisted by private investigator Frank Bambera.

Lonardo, who entered the country in 1904 as a stowaway, got his start in law by shaving Wallace in his uncle's barbershop. When he complained that his uncle refused to send him to school, Wallace took Lonardo, who was so young that he had to work standing on a box, under his wing. After graduating from Brooklyn Law School, Lonardo went into criminal practice. Since his heavy Italian accent doomed him as a courtroom advocate, Lonardo became one of the first lawyers in the country to specialize in handling appeals. When Wallace became district attorney in 1923, he hired Lonardo to establish the Appeals Branch of the Queens District Attorney's Office. Since he was Wallace's protégé,

---

12. As it turned out, Moran was reconvicted and executed on 14 December 1928. Leader of a gang that had perpetrated a series of ugly armed robberies, the 18-year-old Moran shot and killed two policemen when they pulled him over for a minor traffic violation.

Lonardo found it necessary to go into private practice when Wallace lost his bid for reelection.

On 11 July, attorney Richard Beiber of Beiber and Weit went to Sing Sing and served Mrs. Snyder with a citation issued by the Queens County Surrogate's Court to show cause why an administrator should not be appointed for the estate of Albert Snyder. The Prudential's application for an administrative decision voiding Albert Snyder's policies was made before New York State Supreme Court Justice Thomas Crain on 25 July. Company attorneys enumerated twenty-six points of fraud and deception practiced upon it and Albert Snyder by the defendant Ruth Snyder. Hazelton argued for Mrs. Snyder that the Prudential had failed to establish a cause for action and, more important, that the proper venue for such an application was a court of law, in a civil suit decided by a jury trial. Crain ruled against Hazelton, arguing that the company could not sue because it had not sustained any actual damages yet.

The full trial transcript was still not finished; in the second week of August, both defense teams successfully filed for extension of the appeal deadline until 3 October, when the New York State Appeals Court began its autumn session. Public interest in the case reached rock bottom, not only because of the traditional summer holiday, but also because local and national attention was riveted on the execution of the anarchists Sacco and Vanzetti in Massachusetts. Lorraine and Granny Brown slipped away for a well-deserved month in the country.

Desperate for copy, reporters returned to familiar themes, the color of Mrs. Snyder's hair and the prisoners' reading habits (the Bible for Gray; detective and true-romance magazines for Mrs. Snyder); one newspaper ran an entirely fictitious story that Gray had taken up knitting, a charge he indignantly denied through Samuel Miller. It was a hard time for Gray. He was depressed because his wife had not returned to see him and Haddon Gray had not visited.[13] To make matters worse, he came down with a nasty cold that persisted for weeks.

13. Although the newspapers reported that Haddon Gray received a court order permitting him to visit the Death House, the log of activities related to prisoners awaiting

On 7 September, Queens County Surrogate Daniel Noble awarded Granny Brown custody of Lorraine. Noble issued no comment on his decision; in a letter written some weeks later, Warren Schneider claimed he had withdrawn his custody application. Whatever the reason, the Snyder home in Queens Village was the scene of unrestrained joy. Lorraine danced around and insisted on being photographed even though she had just had three teeth pulled. "I am just about as happy as anybody could be," said Granny Brown. "With conditions as they are I can't celebrate, but that doesn't mean I am not the happiest I have been in months." She immediately made plans to sell or rent the ill-fated house and to move in with her son, Andrew, and his family on Woodycrest Avenue in the Bronx. It remained for Surrogate Noble to appoint a trustee for Lorraine's financial interests, a role that Granny Brown had pointedly not sought to win for herself. "At my age, money doesn't mean much," she observed. Noble accordingly declared Lorraine a ward of the New York State Supreme Court in financial matters and *ad litem,* that is, so far as litigation went.

The trial record was made available to attorneys on 13 September.[14] To the dismay of both defense teams, the New York State Court of Appeals set 24 October as the date for hearing both appeals. Due to the delay in obtaining the printed trial record, attorneys had not expected the case to reach the Appeals Court before late December.

Death House inmates got a treat on 23 September when they were allowed to listen to the direct radio broadcast of the Dempsey-Tunney fight from Chicago. Gray rooted for Dempsey; Mrs. Snyder favored the winner, Tunney. On 29 September, the electric chair claimed another of its Thursday-night victims. This was Charles Albrecht of Manhattan, a 33-year-old Manhattan train motorman who had raped and murdered

---

execution notes no such order on behalf of Haddon Gray. Gray died without ever again seeing his friend.

14. On 12 September, Gray wrote to Samuel Miller: "I read in the paper today that you are still awaiting the rest of the two-thirds of the minutes to be printed and am sorry that you are being held up so." It is typical of Gray that he was more concerned about Miller being inconvenienced than about delaying the date of his execution.

the 7-year-old daughter of a family who took him in during the 1926 subway strike, a period when he was without income. He was "crazy drunk" at the time and only meant to scare the girl's mother, he explained before dying.

In September, the Snyder-Gray case claimed another victim, albeit one who played a minor role. Ethel Anderson, Mrs. Synder's fun-loving cousin and bosom companion, succumbed to tuberculosis aggravated by the strain of publicity surrounding the case. A number of figures familiar from the case—Granny Brown, Andrew Brown, Patrolman Edward Pierson, and others—gathered at Woodlawn Cemetery on a dreary morning and saw her laid to rest. She was 28 years old when she died.

THERE WERE NO SURPRISES in the appeals, which were argued before the New York State Court of Appeals by Hazelton and Miller and rebutted by Assistant District Attorney Froessel. Hazelton contended that Justice Scudder had denied Mrs. Snyder a fair and impartial trial when he refused her motion for a separate trial. "In effect," ran the brief, "Gray became a prosecution witness, with the benefit in aid of the People's cause that Gray's credibility was beyond question, because his testimony relating to his own participation in the crime was tantamount to a plea of guilty."

Miller, for Gray, focused on a point that Justice Scudder had given to the jury in his instructions—that the prisoner might have been intoxicated because he was under the influence of Mrs. Snyder and, as a result, had been incapable of premeditation.

Froessel's reply was that the guilt of Mrs. Snyder, and premeditation and intent on the part of Gray, were so evident on the face of the matter that it offended common sense to argue otherwise. This argument carried the day, and when the opinion of the court was announced on Monday, 21 November, it was devastating to both appellants. Writing for a unanimous court, Justice Irving Lehman stated the bare facts of the case in a few paragraphs. "Extended analysis of the testimony produced at the trial," he wrote, "would serve no serious purpose. Both defendants testified in their own behalf. Each attempted personal exculpation by throwing as much of the blame as possible upon the other. A mass of circumstances belied the claim of exculpation of either. The jury might well find that each defendant by testimony in open court had established the guilt of both." As to the statements made to the police, although each one ascribed greater blame to the other party, "Each confession, if accepted as true, would be sufficient to establish the guilt of the person making it for the crime of murder on Albert Snyder."

Lehman expressed the court's view that Justice Scudder had conducted an exemplary trial and had exercised "scrupulous care" in protecting the rights of the accused. He had allowed the jury to consider every claim of innocence presented by each defendant, even though for some of these contentions there was little, if any, evidence. He had ruled, wrote Lehman, in favor of the defendants whenever there was the slightest room for doubt.

This left only Mrs. Snyder's objection to the joint trial. Not only had Justice Scudder ruled fairly based on the knowledge at his disposal, the court asserted, but the possible damage to Mrs. Snyder arising from presentation to the jury of Gray's case was not substantial when her own confession showed her guilt.

The Clerk of the Court of Appeals drew up death warrants bearing the signatures of all seven justices and delivered them to Sing Sing. The warrants scheduled the execution for the week of 9 January. Gray and Mrs. Snyder were now in desperate straits. Not only had the Court of Appeals ruled against them, but it had done so unanimously. Governor Smith, like his predecessors, was especially reluctant to extend clemency when the appellate court spoke with one voice.

The Court of Appeals orders reaffirming judgment did not arrive at Sing Sing until Thanksgiving Day, 24 November, but Lawes ordered that the prisoners be informed of the adverse judgment as soon as court rose. Gray heard the news from P. K. Sheehy during a holiday visit from his mother. Gray thanked him in a firm voice, saying that he was not surprised, and continued speaking to his mother. Sheehy proceeded to the Women's Wing and told Mrs. Snyder that her appeal had been rejected.

"What does that mean?" she asked.

"It means that, unless the Governor intervenes, then in six weeks, or maybe a little bit more, you go out back."

The prisoner began to sob hysterically. For close to five hours, she was incapacitated. When she recovered, she sent a telegram to Hazelton: "Come immediately—Ruth Snyder." In a macabre touch, affixed to the corner of the telegram was a Thanksgiving sticker of a fat, grinning turkey under a full moon.

Hazelton arrived as bidden and the two went into conference. Mrs. Snyder was furious. She and her mother had spent over thirteen thousand dollars on her defense. She had reason to believe that this was double the amount Gray and his family had paid, and she seemed to be receiving only half the service. She wanted Hazelton off the case; from now on, she would be represented by Lonardo and was writing him to that effect.

Hazelton put on a good face as he left the prison, telling reporters that Mrs. Snyder had given him a new angle to work on. He could not divulge his plans, but he was confident of obtaining a new trial, even an acquittal. Back in New York, there was an angry meeting between Lonardo and Hazelton. The upshot was that Lonardo went to Sing Sing, soothed Mrs. Snyder, and argued that it would be suicidal to change horses in the middle of the stream. She backed down and Hazelton remained the attorney of record.

Reporters who went to Queens Village for Granny Brown's reaction to the Court of Appeals decision received a rude shock; they were greeted at the Snyder residence only by a "For Sale" sign. With Lorraine safely placed in an Ursuline boarding school in Westchester County, Granny Brown had made good on her plan to move back in with her son, Andrew. The house grounds and garden, already under siege when Granny Brown and Lorraine were in residence, had been picked clean by souvenir hunters. Gone were the rose bushes that Albert Snyder planted beside the front steps, gone was the birdhouse he had made in his basement workshop.

In Connecticut, reporters again enjoyed the inimitable hospitality of Frank Brundage and departed knowing as little of Mrs. Isabel Gray's feelings as they had known when they arrived. Albert Snyder's relatives reacted with glee. Warren Schneider was "tickled to death," and one sister proclaimed that she had prayed every night on her knees for the execution of her brother's murderers and would continue to do so until the switch was thrown. Justice Scudder was presiding in Staten Island when the decision was handed down. A note was passed up to the bench; he glanced at it, nodded slightly, and continued hearing testimony. He had no comment for reporters afterward. District Attorney Newcombe commented only that the interests of justice had been served.

All the tabloids started polls. "What would *you* do if *you* were Governor?" asked the *Daily News,* soliciting readers to send in comments of less than 100 words. The *Daily Mirror* went a step further. From Thanksgiving on, it paid twenty-five dollars per day for the best letter against Ruth Snyder and twenty-five dollars for the best letter in her favor. These letters were published together with the writers' photographs and short biographies. The response was enormous; one sea captain even polled his crew and dispatched a cable (in favor of mercy) from the mid-Atlantic. Public opinion in the polls started three to one against Mrs. Snyder, four to one among female respondents.[1]

Frustrated in the courts and hoping to take advantage of the principle that a person who is mad may not be executed even if he or she was sane at the time of the crime, Hazelton launched a psychiatric offensive at the end of November. He discovered that the bump on Mrs. Snyder's forehead that Gray had referred to on the witness stand had recently started growing. Working on the assumption that the bump could have led to insanity, he requested that Mrs. Snyder be examined by the illustrious Dr. Clarence Neymann of Northwestern University in Chicago. Hazelton harbored hopes of proving that his client was, as he put it, an "erotomaniac"; this would, of course, be an answer to Gray's prayers. Samuel Miller, seeing nothing to lose and everything to gain, announced that he would cooperate fully with the Snyder defense team to have the prisoners examined. Dr. Thomas Cusack, the defense psychiatrist who had previously examined Gray, would collaborate with the Chicago physician.

Hazelton was acting as much out of personal conviction as legal expe-

---

1. Unfortunately, Mrs. Snyder had to compete for sympathy with Francesco Caruso, an illiterate Sicilian who, moments after his son died of diphtheria, murdered the attending physician. The doctor had made an appallingly callous remark after the boy expired, and this was a case of diminished responsibility if ever there was one. Caruso's first-degree murder conviction was reduced to first-degree manslaughter on 29 November.

dience. He had long felt that Mrs. Snyder was a borderline psychiatric case, the more so since she had resisted even the slightest suggestion of an insanity defense. He was struck also by the fact that Mrs. Snyder repeatedly exhibited iron self-control in public, only to collapse after returning to her cell. Such repression of feelings, felt Hazelton, was the very stuff of lunacy. There was no question, he emphasized, of seeking a new trial at which an insanity defense could be introduced. He was merely looking for evidence of diminished responsibility that should properly be considered by the governor.[2]

On Monday, 28 November, Neymann, an enormously corpulent little man, arrived, accompanied by his wife, aboard the Twentieth Century Limited. He closeted himself at the Biltmore Hotel with attorneys, the trial record, and the psychiatrists' report on Gray.

But then a problem developed. Prison physician Charles Sweet denied the existence of the mysterious bump. Members of the State Lunacy Commission who had examined her said they, too, knew nothing about it.[3] Commissioner of Corrections Kieb, himself a psychiatrist, asserted that no psychiatrist other than properly appointed commission members would be admitted to Sing Sing. After an hour-long conference with Governor Smith, Kieb emerged with an even stronger point—Dr. Neymann was not licensed to practice in the State of New York. The Chicago physician, said Kieb, was "an interloper."

Outraged, Hazelton promised that he would go all the way to the

2. In retrospect, Hazelton's comments seem disingenuous: at this very moment, Joseph Lonardo was meeting with the Clerk of the New York State Court of Appeals to discuss scheduling a possible petition to reopen the case on the grounds of newly discovered evidence.

3. Gray advised Samuel Miller to stay away from the controversy:"I would steer clear of this new turn of events if I were you. That is merely a suggestion as I leave it all to you. But it seems a bit late in my estimation. That specific growth I am positive in my history given you at Long Island and my suggestion of its examination was made two and a half years ago as stated therein the copy you hold. To me seems—well, I can tell you better on seeing you. But just as soon not have my name linked with it. Keep up the stand you have taken for it is honorable."

U.S. Supreme Court if necessary to see that Mrs. Snyder was examined by the physician of her choice. "Oppression and tyranny of the high-handed type that have led to the downfall of empires is badly apparent in the attitude of Commissioner of Corrections Kieb," Hazelton fumed. "The man is clearly affected by a childish case of professional jealousy," he said, and proceeded to rattle off a list of Dr. Neymann's impeccable academic and clinical qualifications.

Neymann was being retained by Hazelton out of his own pocket, and the doctor's fees rose daily as he and his wife languished at the Biltmore. After a week, Hazelton gave up, and Neymann returned to Chicago a disappointed man. He promised to send a report based on the review he had made at the Biltmore, but this was a poor substitute for a physical examination.

Just as Neymann was settling back into his Chicago routine, the prisoners underwent the required official sanity examination at the hands of the New York State Lunacy Commission. On the same day, Granny Brown, dressed in black mourning and escorted by a *Daily Mirror* reporter, managed to go to the State House, penetrate the governor's chambers, and burst in on him unannounced while he was in conference with his legal adviser, Edward Griffin.[4] The distraught woman, practically incoherent, was assuaged by Governor Smith's promise that her daughter would receive every consideration during the regularly conducted clemency hearing.

Dana Wallace, meanwhile, had not been entirely idle. He managed to dig up a crank named David Chambers, who swore he had seen Gray conspiring with various malefactors in Syracuse in January. When the story hit the newspapers and Wallace demanded a conference with District Attorney Newcombe to consider this new evidence, Gray was livid. "That man Wallace is as crazy as [Chambers] is . . . it looks like any old port in a storm and Wallace at the helm," he wrote Miller. Gray furnished

---

4. Such staged confrontations with the governor were common in this less security-conscious age. One J. C. Bashford offered to set up an encounter for Samuel Miller, speculating that attorneys for Mrs. Snyder might wish to join in the spectacle.

incontrovertible proof that he had been elsewhere on his salesman's rounds at the time and Wallace's effort collapsed as quickly as it had sprung to life.[5]

On 16 December, George Ricci, a thirty-one-year-old Brooklyn building superintendent, and Peter Seiler, who had entered the Death House on the same day as Gray and Mrs. Snyder, went out back. They were executed two and a half hours later than the usual eleven o'clock so that their electrocution would not interfere with the staging of the Christmas show, "That Sweet Little Devil," in the prison auditorium. Ricci had murdered a wealthy contractor who had employed and then fired him. Governor Smith used the occasion of Seiler's execution to make a rare comment on a denied clemency appeal—usually, he maintained his silence and allowed the law to take its course. "Practically every case which comes to me," he said, "is of that of a good boy who never had a chance, who will never stray from the fold again, etc., etc. This is of no consequence so long as he has been justly convicted according to the laws of the legislature of the State of New York and there has emerged no compelling evidence which was unavailable to the judge and jury."

The holiday spirit was swinging newspaper polls in favor of clemency, a trend that encouraged Mrs. Snyder. She and Gray received a number of anonymous Christmas gifts, including several small checks. Gray said that he had enough money already and refused to cash his. "What's the big deal?" said Mrs. Snyder when she was told of his reluctance, and went ahead and pocketed the money. She also received a three-foot-tall doll for Lorraine; this was forwarded to Granny Brown. She had precious little to occupy her these days. Since the Court of Appeals decision, her knitting needles and sewing materials had been taken from her.

---

5. In his 29 December letter to Samuel Miller, Gray wrote:"Thank you, old man, for taking care of that matter for me, for I was greatly concerned over developments. I simply could not stand by and see any poor innocents embroiled by such fanatical minds, without a shred of truth. I simply wanted to thwart any plans they might be laying to persecute somebody innocent. She should have known better than that, Sam, to allow them to do such a thing. Right is right and that was *all* wrong." This is the only mention of Mrs. Snyder in Gray's letters to Miller.

On 22 December, the New York State Lunacy Commission met and unanimously found that Mrs. Snyder and Gray were sane. They delivered their report to Governor Smith, who would neither divulge its contents nor comment on them. The prisoners' fates were now in his hands, and his alone.

The *Daily News* exploded a bombshell on Saturday, 31 December: District Attorney Newcombe, the paper reported, had suppressed a recommendation by the psychiatrists who had examined Gray before the trial that he be allowed to plead guilty to a lesser charge. The story was leaked to the *News* by Hazelton, who had learned of it from Miller, Millard, and Drs. Cusack and Block in the course of a meeting with Dr. Neymann on 7 December. At that meeting, Neymann remarked that he was surprised that his New York colleagues had not been called as witnesses to give evidence of Gray's "almost self-evident psychoses." "So were we!" chimed in the psychiatrists. They claimed to have fully briefed Gray's counsel, indicating that their examination would support a reduction of the charge to second-degree murder. The attorneys had promised to pass along this news to Justice Scudder. When the psychiatrists never heard anything more, they simply assumed that Scudder had refused the offer.

Not quite, said Miller and Millard. They had not been able to see Scudder personally; the best they could do was to pass the psychiatrists' recommendation along to Newcombe, who then went alone to Scudder's chambers. A few minutes later, he had come out and announced, "No deal!" Their theory was that he had relayed to Scudder only that Gray was willing to plead guilty to second-degree murder, omitting any reference to the results of the psychiatric examination.

For three weeks, Hazelton had sat on the story. He wanted Miller and Millard to be the ones to bring it out. After all, it was their client who had been wronged. They, in turn, hoped that the panel of psychiatrists would spontaneously come forward; that way, the tale would have the aura of disinterested scientific truth. But the psychiatrists, particularly Cusack, did not want to compromise themselves and their profession by appearing to inject themselves into the legal process after they had served their appointed role. It was a stalemate.

Finally, Hazelton decided that he could wait no longer. If Gray was insane, then what did this say about the sanity of his own client? Who could guess what sort of perverted relationship existed between the murderers?

Hazelton wrote an impassioned ten-page letter to Governor Smith. In it, he trusted that the governor would join him in wishing that the avenue down which the State propelled his client should be overcast by no lesser shadow than the Great Inscrutable One who waited at its end. He trusted that the governor was not intent on thrusting Mrs. Snyder into the electric chair as though it were a pagan god demanding sacrifice. He trusted that the governor was not a follower of Nietzsche.

The upshot of all the expressions of trust was a request for a thirty-day stay of execution. During this period, the panel of psychiatrists could be called before the governor to give their opinion, Scudder could be asked whether he had been informed before the trial of Gray's diminished responsibility, and Mrs. Snyder could be examined by "a reputable practitioner of the newer school of psychiatric technique." The members of the State Lunacy Commission, added Hazelton, were "openly intolerant" of modern psychiatry.

The *News* did not bother to check with Newcombe before running its story, and he was furious when he learned of it. "Anyone who says I agreed to recommend taking a plea of second degree murder from Gray is a liar!" he exploded to a reporter who tracked him down at a New Year's Eve party in Atlantic City.

Psychiatrist Sylvester Leahy was cagey when asked whether the panel had, in fact, recommended a lesser charge: "I'd rather not commit myself. Mr. Newcombe is a very good friend of mine. Besides, our function was only to decide on the question of legal sanity and we found him to be legally sane."

Dr. Thomas Cusack took refuge in the same nice distinction. The panel's finding of "not insane" meant that Gray was legally sane, he told reporters. The idea of pleading guilty to second-degree murder originated not with the psychiatrists, but with Miller and Millard during the course of discussions. Reporters pressed him and asked, regardless of who came up with the idea, had the panel in fact unanimously agreed that it would speak in favor of a lesser charge? No comment.

Dr. Stephen Jewett remembered some suggestion about a reduced charge being made to Newcombe, but wasn't sure if it had originated with psychiatrists or attorneys, or even whether he had joined in it. With regard to the psychiatrists giving testimony at the clemency hearing in Albany, Jewett was all for it. The legal definition of insanity was hopelessly behind the modern psychiatric definition, he said.

Dr. Siegfried Block was in Florida and could not be reached for comment right away; a few days later, he wrote a letter to Governor Smith stating that the psychiatrists had made no recommendation of leniency and that their finding that Gray was legally sane rested in part on their observation that, as evidenced by his preparation of an alibi, he had calculated the odds of being caught and figured he could beat them.

Both prisoners continued to be in good spirits. Samuel Miller visited Gray on Tuesday, 3 January, to update him on preparations for the clemency hearing and found him resigned to his fate and drowning his sorrows, as usual, in religion.

Joseph Lonardo and Frank Bambera visited Mrs. Snyder and described her as confident and cheerful. She was buoyed when she learned that Justice Scudder had been asked by Governor Smith to write a private letter spelling out his views on the justness of her death sentence. She apparently did not realize that it was normal in all executive clemency reviews for the trial judge and district attorney to be asked to state their positions in writing. She had already selected the dress she would wear when she was transferred to Auburn Prison to serve out her life sentence. "I feel sure there will be a delay," she told day Matron Kopp. "At any rate, I've told my mother to be sure to visit me on Friday the 13th."

The next day, however, she was depressed. First thing in the morning, the Lunacy Commission, accompanied by the prison physician, Dr. Sweet, visited her and Gray again to make sure that there were no previously overlooked signs of insanity. It was a purely routine visit, they told reporters, but in view of its length and the storm raging in the newspapers about the prisoners' sanity, no one believed them. Then Granny Brown, whom Warden Lawes was now allowing to visit daily, paid a call. After her visit, a few members of the ever eager-to-serve New York State Prison Commission managed to get in; they reported that Mrs. Snyder was "hard-boiled and unrepentant." By the time Lonardo and Bambera showed up in the late afternoon, Mrs. Snyder was exhausted from her steady stream of visitors. She had given up hope, she announced, and wished to make her will. Lonardo whipped out a yellow legal pad, drew up the brief document, and called in P. K. Sheehy to serve as witness along with Bambera.

There was nothing sensational about the will. It disposed of Mrs. Snyder's property equally and in general terms between Granny Brown and Lorraine, appointing the former sole executrix. The most significant item was, of course, Albert Snyder's $97,000 in life insurance, currently in litigation. Mrs. Snyder expressed particular concern that jewelry still in the custody of District Attorney Newcombe be given to Lorraine. The equity in the house, the value of the automobile, Mrs. Snyder's insurance policy, and her stocks and bonds together amounted to fifteen thousand dollars. Mrs. Snyder asked that Father McCaffery be the one to give a copy of the will to her mother. Lonardo did his best to cheer her up, but it was no use. She wept continuously through the evening after he left, then tossed and turned until, at the suggestion of Matron Hickey, she was provided with a sedative to help her sleep.

25

ALBANY HOTELS BEGAN TO FILL UP on the night of Wednesday, 4 January, for the clemency hearing. Reporters lounged around hotel lobbies with their hip flasks and passed the time concocting various absurdities: Mrs. Snyder had requested to be executed in a silk evening gown; she wished to be buried by her husband's side in the Schneider family plot; she was being allowed the use of an electric curling iron in her cell, and so on. There was little real news; all were forced to admit that the outcome of the clemency hearing was a foregone conclusion. There had been no reply to Hazelton's thunderous letter. Governor Smith's office refused to acknowledge even its receipt.

At least three points of political logic argued against clemency for Mrs. Snyder; Gray did not even count because he was ready to die. First, there was Mrs. Snyder's highly publicized conversion to Catholicism, which, sincere or not, had been widely interpreted as a bid to win Smith's sympathy. In his quest for the Democratic presidential nomination, Smith was battling against the twin handicaps of being a Catholic and a Wet. He had already been forced to issue a point-by-point rebuttal of the argument that his loyalty to Rome would interfere with his oath of office.[1] The Vatican did nothing to ease his position by harshly criticizing

---

1. In April 1927, New York lawyer Charles Marshall, a devout Episcopalian, published a nine-page open letter in the *Atlantic Monthly* challenging Smith's ability to steer a course independent of Rome. Governor Smith was at first reluctant to respond, but was told by his advisers that not to do so would be political suicide. Smith's reply, drafted by his staff and minutely reviewed by Church authorities, was published in the May issue of the *Atlantic Monthly*. Most commentators gave the exchange to Smith hands down.

Prohibition. At the time of the Snyder-Gray hearing, the Women's Christian Temperance Union was vowing to fight Smith tooth and nail, and John Roach Stratton was touring the country fulminating against him.[2] The last thing Smith needed was to extend clemency to a bleach-blonde adulteress who murdered her husband while he was drunk on bootleg whiskey.

Second, Smith did not want to cast any doubts on the performance of Justice Scudder. The rumors that Scudder was likely to run for governor on the Democratic ticket should Smith move on to run for President appeared confirmed when Smith picked him to head up the judicial probe into the exploding Queens County sewer scandal.[3] This investigation provided a custom-made opportunity for the judge to cloak himself in the robes of civic virtue.

Third, Smith needed to take into account the precedent laid down by Governor Theodore Roosevelt, the last New York governor to move on to the White House, in the case of Mrs. Martha Place. During the nineteenth century, New York, like other states, rarely executed women.[4] In 1899, Mrs. Martha Place, a Brooklyn housekeeper who had married her former employer and become jealous of her beautiful stepdaughter, cruelly mutilated the girl's features with acid and smothered her. Mrs. Place

2. The Snyder-Gray murder epitomized the case for Prohibition, said Mrs. Clem Shaver, wife of the Chairman of the Democratic National Committee, in a Washington luncheon speech. "Nothing but whiskey caused that man and woman to lose all moral restraint."

3. Since 1917, not one foot of sewer pipe had been laid in Queens County that was not of the miracle "Lock-Joint" brand available only from contractor John "Fifty-Fifty" Phillips. As a result of this happy arrangement between Phillips and Borough President Maurice Connolly, the taxpayers were fleeced out of sixteen million dollars.

4. When it did, the crime was usually the murder of a husband. Mrs. Elisabeth van Valkenberg in 1846, Mrs. Mary Alice Runkle in 1849, and Mrs. Anna Hoag in 1852 were all hanged for murdering their husbands. Mrs. Roxelana Druse shot her husband in 1887 and, despite a strong plea of self-defense, was hanged in the yard of the Herkimer County Jail. She had dismembered her husband's body and burned it in the stove, an act the public imagination transformed into feeding it to the pigs. Mrs. Druse's daughter received a life sentence merely for assisting in disposal of the body.

then buried an ax in the head of her husband, who nevertheless survived to testify against her. The case received nationwide attention and public opinion ran strongly against the execution of a woman. Governor Roosevelt was besieged from across the country with petitions for mercy. He dismissed most of the appeals as "mawkish sentimentalism" and decisively rejected the appeal for clemency:"The law makes no distinction of sex in such a crime. This murder was one of peculiar deliberation and atrocity. To interfere with the course of the law in this case could be justified only on the ground that never hereafter, under any circumstances, should capital punishment be inflicted on a murderess, even though the victim herself was a woman, and even though the victim's torture preceded her death."

In the 1909 case of Mrs. Mary Farmer, who had murdered her neighbor over tea in order to possess her house, Governor Charles Evans Hughes had followed Roosevelt's precedent that, in cases involving "peculiar deliberation and atrocity," the sex of the murderer was no ground for clemency.

The clemency hearing was scheduled for noon in the formal Executive Chamber on Capitol Hill. The lines began forming at eleven o'clock, and the doors opened at noon. This crowd, unlike the one at the Queens County Courthouse, was subdued. People walked softly and spoke in hushed tones under the gaze of the former governors whose portraits hung from the mahogany-faced walls. Reporters were already in the room when the general public was admitted. A dozen state troopers in plain clothes stood guard as about three hundred people filed into the room. There were few chairs left after counsel and relatives had been made comfortable; the public stood ten deep against the walls.

Hazelton and Wallace were the first of the principals to arrive, accompanied by Granny Brown; then District Attorney Newcombe and Assistant District Attorneys Froessel and Conroy took their places, and finally Miller and Millard, together with Mrs. Gray and Gray's sister, Margaret. Counsel sat in armchairs a few feet in front of the governor's massive ceremonial desk, which dominated the front of the room. Chairs behind counsel had been reserved for families of the condemned, but as the crowd surged forward, the families were left sitting in pathetic isolation, crying intermittently.

Governor Smith had been entertaining friends in his private office just off the chamber. At twelve fifteen, a side door swung open and in marched, not the governor, but Mrs. Smith, accompanied by a half-dozen elegantly gowned New York society matrons, who settled into chairs that had been reserved for them around the governor's desk. Finally, Governor Smith himself came in at the rear of the procession and took his place. At one elbow were the six bound volumes of the trial transcript; at the other was the Criminal Code of the State of New York.

"This is a public hearing into the question of executive clemency for Ruth Snyder," Smith announced. "Who speaks for her?"

Hazelton rose to his feet and introduced himself and Wallace.

"How much time do you want?" asked Smith.

"Oh, not more than half an hour or so," Hazelton answered.

With the exception of a grandiloquent reference to vines kissed by the setting sun (in Queens Village), Hazelton managed to keep himself under control. He declared that Mrs. Snyder had been an excellent housewife and mother. He reminded Smith that the Court of Appeals had not endorsed, in any way, the state's contention that the motive for Snyder's murder was insurance.

Then he dove into his precious psychiatric material. "I have been told that Ruth Snyder is suffering from a psychosis, or at least there is a strong possibility of it. There is a borderline insanity which does not come within the strict legal definition of insanity, but which renders her only partly accountable for the crime which she committed."

Hazelton repeated his request that Smith delay the execution so that he could hear what the psychiatrists had to say. Only then could he make an informed decision.

"After all, what class can you put Ruth Snyder in? Can you put her in with gunmen and thieves? No? With women of the street? No? Well—I don't know—where *can* you put her?"

Then Hazelton turned to the fiasco of Gray's sanity examination and the findings of the team of psychiatrists. He reminded the governor that one member of the team had said that if Gray had seen a psychiatrist, he would not have found himself in his current situation. And if Gray was insane, Hazelton argued, then who could say what forces had warped the already susceptible Mrs. Snyder?

In closing, Hazelton reminded the governor that there was a chance that the New York State legislature would soon adopt a bill abolishing the death penalty. "You are famous as a humanitarian. I will ask you to give us the benefit of this twilight zone of insanity, and I ask you to have the psychiatrists come before you and tell you just what is the matter with Mrs. Snyder. I commend my client to your heart and to your wisdom and, above all, to your conscience."

Smith, facing a portrait of Theodore Roosevelt hung at the back of the room, had not moved a muscle during Hazelton's appeal. He took off his glasses and nodded at Wallace, who rose and thrust his hands into his pockets. Burning the candle at both ends had started to catch up with him, and Wallace's face was a ghastly yellow. He knew the "twilight zone" insanity argument was a waste of time; all the governor wanted to know was whether anything new had emerged since the trial.

"There is one thing you should know, and that is that we have found evidence since the trial which would set aside the theory that Mrs. Snyder dominated Gray. There was intense feeling against this woman at the time of the trial and it was that feeling which convicted her. We gladly lay this matter in your hands, Governor, confident that this is a case where clemency should be exercised."

"We will now take up the case of Henry Judd Gray," said the governor, and Millard stood up. He gave a recapitulation of his closing address to the jury: Gray was raised in a splendid home (at this Mrs. Gray broke down in tears); his boyhood and youth were unsullied by the slightest stain; what a tragedy that he and Mrs. Snyder had ever met.

Millard and Miller had struck a deal with Hazelton and Wallace—they could vilify Mrs. Snyder as much as they wanted at the clemency hearing as long as the accusations fed the claim of "abnormality" and supported the psychiatric argument. "I knew this woman to be abnormal the first day I looked into her eyes," Millard said. "I do not come here to condemn Ruth Snyder—if we were psychiatrists we would say she should have been put in an institution long ago or placed under the care of a physician."

Since his disastrous meeting with her, Gray had been living in "continuous delirium" caused by "excesses and continually applied drink," all of which were ultimately to be blamed on "the unquenchable fire within Ruth Snyder." Three of the four psychiatrists who examined Gray did not believe, Millard knew for a fact, that Gray should suffer the extreme penalty. Millard asked the governor to listen to them before he made a decision. "I am aware that the mob is calling for vengeance, the same mob that cried 'Crucify him!' I know the yelping of these human coyotes will not affect your decision. I know you will treat this case with Christ-like sympathy and I beg you to commute the sentence of these two sinners to life imprisonment."

Then Miller rose and stressed the lack of motive. There was not a word in the trial transcript that gave a hint as to motive. Gray had never been able to explain to counsel, nor to the psychiatrists, why he had murdered Snyder. In fact, he had not even been able to explain it to his wife and mother.

"Gray has searched his brain and racked his mind night after night and for the life of him cannot tell what drove him into that crime."

At the very least, said Miller, the governor ought to grant a thirty-day stay of execution so Gray could be reexamined by psychiatrists. Smith could then hear their conclusions and speak with the four experts who had found Gray "not insane," as well as with ex-Police Commissioner McLaughlin about the shape Gray was in when he was arrested.

District Attorney Newcombe coasted through the People's rebuttal. "I have conscientiously examined this case in search of extenuating circumstances," he began. "I have found none, and today I have heard none. I don't mean to be harsh, but . . ." He then proceeded to dismantle Hazelton's portrayal of Mrs. Snyder as a good mother with the evidence that Lorraine had been present when Gray transferred the murder weapon to Mrs. Snyder. Only avarice and greed, as indicated by Mrs. Snyder's connivance to see to it that her husband was heavily insured, could explain this "revoltingly brutal crime." Newcombe went on to enumerate the damning details of the slaying as Smith listened, chin in hand.

"Of this matter of the psychiatrists, I can only read you their report. It shows, beyond any doubt, that they were not in any perplexing middle ground of indecision. They were satisfied as to his sanity. So are the eminently capable and thoroughly disinterested members of the State Lunacy Commission."

To drive home his point, Newcombe brandished a letter, dated the day before, from Doctors Leahy, Cusack, and Jewett, in which they reaffirmed that they had found Gray legally sane. He closed on a familiar refrain: "If ever there was a case in the annals of the State of New York where capital punishment would be warranted and justified, it is this case."

Smith probed the psychiatric angle. "Was any defense based on Gray's mental condition put in evidence at the trial?"

"None," answered Newcombe.

This was too much for Miller, who jumped to his feet and pointed accusingly. "We had an agreement with Mr. Newcombe!" he sputtered. "We could not bring up the question of responsibility because we had already accepted the finding that Gray was legally sane."

"Well, why didn't you have the psychiatrists examine this twilight zone stuff when they examined Gray before the trial and put their findings in their report?"

"We didn't have the right to do that. All the psychiatrists were permitted to report on was whether Gray was legally sane or insane."

"Of course you had the right. This twilight zone talk you're making now should have been your defense; it should have been heard during the trial, not brought before me here.

"What's the use of all this? It seems to me that the law is perfectly clear. Now, listen." Smith picked up a volume of the Criminal Code and read aloud the familiar statute: a person is punishable for murder in the first degree if he knew the nature and quality of the act and realized that it was wrong.

In response, Millard explained "I mean that Gray was not a free agent.

I mean that his mentality, his resistance, his will, his physical self were so drained and so sapped by his relations with Mrs. Snyder that he was virtually living in another world."

"If your arguments were followed," Smith replied, "that Gray was insane by reason of excesses, all it would be necessary for any prospective murderer to do would be to go out first and do these same foolish acts in preparation of his defense. It seems to me you're writing a new interpretation of a perfectly understandable law."

Hazelton intervened, "We'll concede that both of them were able to distinguish between right and wrong. But in the light of modern psychiatry, there were conditions which, even if they realized their guilt, made them abnormal and unaccountable for their acts."

Smith raised his right arm and waved it in a weary gesture of dismissal. "[T]here is something abnormal about anyone who commits murder. Stay off this psychiatric stuff; it doesn't enter my mind. Stick to the law. I'm not going to be concerned about psychosis. And while you're talking about the psychological background to this crime, don't forget there's a background to me also. I mean my oath of office. Here [tapping the Criminal Code] is the statute of the law. I swore before God to support these statutes. That's my background. So keep out all this other stuff."

Hazelton refused to give up. "Yes, but Your Excellency will remember that Saint Paul said, 'The letter of the law killeth, but the spirit of the law giveth life.'"

The audience leaned forward and waited for what Smith would have to say about Saint Paul. "I know, but the New York State Legislature says different, and that's a later authority than Saint Paul and the one which I am sworn to uphold."

Hazelton flushed. "What Saint Paul said is a cardinal rule of constructive legal interpretation!" he rejoined, but everyone else knew it was over; Smith's barb had brought the proceedings to a close.

"Well, if there's nothing more . . ." Smith surveyed the principals but no one stirred. "Then this hearing is over."

The governor rose, shook hands with the lawyers, and walked out two hours after he had walked in. A sob-sister rushed to Granny Brown's side, notepad in hand. Had she sensed sympathy in the governor's voice? "No, I couldn't find much sympathy." That was an understatement.

Half an hour later, Governor Smith again broke his usual silence and emerged to explain why he had decided to deny clemency to Charles Doran, scheduled to die that night. Smith felt impelled to give the public a lecture on the legal treatment of homicide committed in the course of a felony. A great deal of pressure had been brought to bear on behalf of Doran, a hard-luck case who had been convicted of a gas station robbery in Albany during which an attendant had been shot to death. He alone, of the quartet that committed the robbery, had drawn the death sentence. Gray's old neighbor and checkers partner, Doran, left to a chorus of "Bye-bye, Charlie!" from his hall mates.

Doran stopped for a moment at Gray's cell and spoke in hushed tones. His younger brother, Henry, had told him during their farewell visit, he said, that the hearing that morning had not gone well. It looked bad for Gray and Mrs. Snyder. "Take it easy, kid," advised Gray, and, indeed, Doran died game, giving witnesses a ghastly ear-to-ear grin as the mask was placed over his head. Henry Doran forlornly hung around the prison gate because he did not have enough money to transport his brother's body back to Albany. Reporters covering the Snyder-Gray case took up a collection to rent a hearse. Also going out back that night, though less lamented, was Louis "Smiley" Mason, who died cursing a confederate whose sentence had been commuted to life imprisonment in return for testifying against him.

Mrs. Snyder did not hear the bad news until Granny Brown visited on Friday, but she sensed what was coming. Hazelton and Lonardo had promised to see her after the hearing, but never showed up. "They won't tell me!" Mrs. Snyder screamed to Matron Kopp. "Cowards! They're afraid to tell me!" Later in the evening, she was calmer as she reflected on the fate of Doran and Mason. "Two more going and no hope. God help them both!" Mrs. Snyder said, and threw herself face down upon her cot.

Governor Smith announced that he would withhold judgment on the clemency application until Monday, but, with not even the tabloids bothering to pretend that there was any mystery about how he would decide, the attorneys began grasping at straws. On Thursday night, Hazelton filed with the New York State Supreme Court a writ seeking a jury trial in *Prudential Life Insurance Company v. Snyder et al.* This would require that Mrs. Snyder be kept alive until she could testify before the jury. The chief issue in the case was not one of law, Hazelton argued, but one of evidence. Did Snyder know or did he not know what he was signing? A judge could be reasonably expected to weigh the evidence based on the record of *State of New York v. Snyder and Gray,* but if there were a jury, then denying Mrs. Snyder the right to appear before it would be highly questionable.

Beiber and Weit, counsel to the Prudential, displayed only feeble opposition to Hazelton's move. They were sitting on a strong case and knew it. Mrs. Snyder alive and testifying, they reasoned, posed little threat. Mrs. Snyder dead, by contrast, was a potential reversible error. Thus, when Hazelton's writ came before Justice Aaron Levy of the New York State Supreme Court on Friday, 6 January, the clerk announced that, because attorneys for both sides had affirmed that they were busy at the moment, arguments for and against the writ would be heard on Friday, 13 January, that is, one day after Mrs. Snyder's probable day of execution. Hazelton prepared to petition Justice Levy for a stay of execution on the grounds that, were the application for a jury trial granted, Mrs. Snyder's testimony would be required.

Did Levy have the power to issue such a stay? According to him, he did, even though the law clearly stated otherwise. According to Section 495 of the Criminal Practices Code, in cases not involving an appeal or writ of error, no judge, court, or officer other than the governor was permitted to delay an execution except the sheriff (and only then in cases of newly discovered insanity or pregnancy).

The closest precedent was the 1917 case of Patrius von der Corput. On the night before his scheduled execution, lawyers for a group called the "Humanitarian Cult" succeeded in obtaining from a New York State Supreme Court justice a stay of execution on the grounds of new evidence. The stay having been granted, lawyers sought a writ of habeas corpus from the New York State Court of Appeals, which was refused on the grounds that the entire affair was in clear contravention of Section

495. Von der Corput was executed one day behind schedule. "The Supreme Court has no power to stay the execution of a death sentence in order that the defendant may be brought before the court on a writ of habeas corpus," wrote the Court of Appeals. Legal language is seldom plainer than that.

Lawes and New York State Attorney General Albert Ottinger had already experienced one run-in with Justice Levy. Just after Thanksgiving, Levy had signed a court order allowing one Courtney Terrett to visit Mrs. Snyder. When Warden Lawes discovered that Mr. Terrett was a reporter for the *Telegram,* he ignored the court order and referred the matter to Ottinger, who supported the warden's decision without hesitation. Asked by reporters what he would do if presented by Justice Levy with an order staying Mrs. Snyder's execution, Lawes replied that he would again be guided by the advice of the attorney general.

As if Mrs. Snyder did not already have enough troubles, pandemonium broke out over the weekend, thanks to Jack Lait. Lait had succumbed to temptation to churn the material from his feature series in the *American* into something more ambitious. The hook was that it would be Ruth Snyder's actual Death House autobiography, smuggled out of Sing Sing. Lait had spoken to Victor Watson, editor of Hearst's *Daily Mirror,* who agreed to run the feature under Mrs. Snyder's byline as a *Mirror* exclusive, "My Last Story." A syndicate was formed to sell it to over a dozen newspapers across the country. Having struck a financial bargain with Granny Brown, Lait sat down and started to bang away on his typewriter.[5]

But if "My Last Story" really was Ruth Snyder's last story, how could the *Mirror* prove it? Here, Lait hit upon a scheme. A few pages of his masterpiece would be smuggled to Mrs. Snyder, who would then copy them over in longhand. Her handwritten text, smuggled out, could be reproduced in the *Mirror* as proof of the story's authenticity. Lait proposed the

5. Lait first admitted to having ghosted "My Last Story" in his "Broadway and Elsewhere" column in the *Daily Mirror* of 29 August 1950; he described the proceeds, which went to Granny Brown and Lorraine, as "handsome." Editor Watson of the *Mirror* described them as "enough to send Lorraine through a girl's college." Perhaps this was the Ursuline convent school in Westchester County.

deal to Granny Brown, promising that he would incorporate any other material her daughter sent out with her longhand copies, so Mrs. Snyder would be his partner in writing.

Speaking to each other in Swedish across the visitor's room, the two women agreed to Lait's proposal and hit on an easy method to exchange material. When Mrs. Snyder went to and from the exercise yard, she would ask for permission to use a small washroom normally reserved for the matrons. Granny Brown would ask to use the same washroom when she came to visit. Material would be left hidden behind the toilet.

And so it was. Granny Brown brought in selected pages of Lait's text, and brought out flawless copies—not a stray mark—in Mrs. Snyder's hand. Also smuggled out were a few pages of Mrs. Snyder's own composition in which she described her childhood. The matrons never suspected anything.

On Thursday, 5 January, the *Mirror* kicked off its one-week-to-live countdown by running "My Last Story" on the front page under the byline "Ruth Snyder," complete with one facsimile of the original manuscript on page one.

Lawes was apoplectic. Not only had security been breached, but an "exclusive" story emerging from Sing Sing was an egregious violation of the rules of engagement between him and the press. The publishers of other New York papers were howling in protest. At first, Lawes suspected Mrs. Snyder's legal advisers and issued an order barring Lonardo and Bambera from visiting the Death House. But the accused culprits were also perplexed by the turn of events and protested their complete innocence.

Mrs. Snyder was upset: "I feel bad," she said on Saturday. "I understand that Warden Lawes is angry at me. They accuse me of sending out stuff for the newspapers," she said. "I wrote some things, but I didn't know what it was for. I know I didn't get any money. If my mother got any, I don't know. I feel terrible."

The fact that Mrs. Snyder had been able to get a manuscript out implied that someone could have brought something in. Mrs. Snyder was summarily moved to another cell and she and all of her possessions were subjected to a minute search. For a moment, she panicked, thinking that she was being taken to the electric chair. The privilege of sitting amid her fine dresses was taken away.

On Saturday night, Lawes got a tip that it hadn't been Lonardo and Bambera; it had been Granny Brown. When the old woman arrived on Monday morning to pay her usual visit, she was escorted not to the Death House, but into the warden's office, where Lawes grilled her. Having administered a stern lecture, Lawes signed Granny Brown's admittance slip anyway. Granny Brown spoke with her daughter for about an hour and then permitted two reporters to take her to lunch. "I feel terrible," she confessed. "She knows she must die. I told her it was useless to keep up faith any longer. Ruth is very blue, but she's taking it better than me. She has been a brave girl."

Grief did not prevent Granny Brown from doing her sums. It was reported that she made two thousand dollars on "My Last Story," without telling her daughter about it, if Mrs. Snyder's reaction is to be believed. And now she admitted to reporters that was trying to talk her daughter into accepting a cash settlement in *Prudential v. Snyder.*

As it turned out, "My Last Story" and "Ruth Snyder's Own True Story," the King Features Syndicate pamphlet based on it, amount to a denial of any guilt whatsoever; a hysterical reaffirmation of the story that Mrs. Snyder had told on the witness stand and a heaping of blame and abuse on Gray. The circulation of the *Daily Mirror* was boosted by more than one hundred thousand copies nonetheless, with orders for extra copies being received from as far away as Pittsburgh.

Warden Lawes formally announced on Saturday that the executions would take place Thursday, 12 January. Twenty-four witnesses—twenty journalists and four medical doctors—were selected from among the thousands who had besieged him with requests.[6] Invitations were sent on Monday, 9 January, as was a letter to the New York State executioner,

---

6. A disproportionate number of requests came from doctors who asked to be present for scientific purposes. Many applicants included checks in varying amounts that were returned uncashed.

Robert Elliott, requesting him to be at Sing Sing Thursday night and to confirm his availability by return telegram. A formal notification of the day and hour of the execution was sent to Governor Smith.

Smith was otherwise engaged: on Saturday night his wife had developed acute appendicitis in the couple's suite at the Biltmore. She had been taken to Saint Vincent's Hospital for emergency surgery. Even as he rushed to her bedside, Smith was assaulted by reporters wishing to know if he had reached a decision on executive clemency. "I will have absolutely nothing to say on the Snyder matter!" he snapped. "I will talk about it when I am good and ready. I do not wish to be asked about that case again. I am concerned with my wife at the moment."

The press had already started warming up the public before the weekend. Thus the *Evening Journal* of Friday, 6 January:

> The Grim Specter of Death waved his wand over the hysterical form of Ruth Snyder in her melancholy death cell today to the rhythmic beat of a macabre dirge: *"I'm next! I'm next!"* Like a giant trip hammer this expression beat on her brain. Next! Next to enter the "little brown door"! Next to feel the grip of the shackles on the death chair! Next to experience that quick, relentless thunderbolt of science that would hurl her headlong into eternity! *"I'm next! I'm next!"*

And a precious surviving relic from the *Evening Graphic*:

> Don't fail to read tomorrow's *Graphic*. An installment that thrills and stuns! A story that fairly pierces the heart, and reveals Ruth Snyder's last thoughts on earth; that pulses the blood as it discloses her final letters. Think of it! A woman's final thoughts just before she is clutched in the deadly snare that sears and burns and *fries—and kills!* Exclusively in tomorrow's *Graphic*.

As if they were covering a coronation or a royal wedding, the papers flooded their pages with details of the execution protocol. Would Mrs. Snyder be escorted to the chair by a female matron? Well, there would certainly be at least one matron present, said Lawes. Or better yet, would she be accompanied by Alfred Coynes, the longest-serving Sing Sing temper and the only one who had been present at the execution of Mrs.

Place? Coynes was constantly sought out for his opinion on how Mrs. Snyder would behave. One day, her sanity was slipping from her and she would have to be carried hysterical to the chair; the next day, she was bearing up well and would die defiant. One day, Lorraine would be admitted to the Death House for a farewell visit; the next day, Lorraine would not be allowed anywhere near it. Finally, a delirious reporter had it both ways: Lorraine would not be admitted to the Death House while her mother was alive, but would be admitted after she was dead so she could accompany the body back to New York.

The silk evening gown story that had started making the rounds before the clemency hearing was unstoppable. On Friday, the *Mirror* reported: " 'Bring me my silken things—my prettiest dresses and softest lingeries,' [Mrs. Snyder] begged today. 'I want to be buried in something pretty and soft and clinging. The prison cottons are so hard and rough and uncomfortable. My skin has been scratched until it's rough and raw. Now that I must die, I want my prettiest things on when I am buried.' "

When the *Daily News* ran its story on Monday, it was a black silk party dress and black silk underwear. On Tuesday, it was "the black silk dress she wore so often at the house parties she attended." By Wednesday, it was "the black silk carefully packed away in a cedar chest." Such a handsome payoff in speculation, as Mark Twain once wrote, from a trifling investment of fact.

26

ALMOST LOST IN THE UPROAR, apart from his role in contradictory stories about which prisoner would be executed first, was Gray. Yet he, too, had the urge to put his thoughts down on paper. Famous Features Syndicate offered him five thousand dollars for his life story; Gray went to work and wrote thirty thousand words. Then there was a hitch. Model prisoner that he was, Gray asked Warden Lawes for permission to send out the manuscript, and Lawes refused. The best that could be done would be for Gray to read the manuscript to his sister every time she came to visit, then she could relay the story to a ghost writer, and the feature would run under the byline "Henry Judd Gray as told to his sister, Margaret."

That knocked down the price to three thousand dollars, but it was better than nothing, and the feature ran in about forty dailies around the country. Aside from minor details, it adhered to the testimony given by Gray on the witness stand and, by extension, to his original statement. It consisted in large part of remorse and religion, but Gray also wrote candidly about the lackluster marriage in which he had found himself.

On Sunday, Gray was visited by his mother and Miller. He made out a will leaving to Jane all property not already transferred to his wife, with his mother as executrix. The Gray family continued to sing his praises to any reporter who made the trip to West Orange. "Judd's courage in the face of what seems inevitable has given us strength to bear our sorrow," said his sister.

"He is paying for something his normal mind would never have permitted him to do," added Mrs. Gray. "His mind is normal now, however, and his awful deed is a nightmare to him. Hours and hours of thinking

have failed to furnish him with a reason for his act. He says that the act itself is a dream." She had forgiven Judd, the boy she knew could never
have done such a thing. "He is now the same sweet little boy he always
was." [1] She lifted a handful of letters: "So many letters we get, and not one
of them condemns Judd. Judd is pleased that we are not looked upon
with shame for what he has done."

Security remained tight in Norwalk. Six policemen guarded the
Brundage residence, and taxi drivers were told that their licenses would
be revoked if they took reporters to the house. Yet, when the *Daily News*
managed to get a reporter through to Frank Brundage, surprisingly, he
consented to say a few words.

"Mrs. [Isabel] Gray has nothing to say. Her nerves are shattered, she is
prostrate on a bed upstairs and she has no desire to make any comment.
She has nothing to explain or announce. All she can do is to suffer until
it is over and, by the end of the week, this seven-day wonder of a crime
will be forgotten."

He took a philosophical view of affairs. "We all liked Judd. It's one of
those things you can't understand, but there it is. I've managed to protect
his wife from the time of the trial up to the present and I guess I can stick
it out for the rest of the week."

Brundage made no attempt to conceal the rift separating Mrs. Isabel
Gray from Gray's mother and sister. "I can't understand those people.
Why they should peddle such garbage [perhaps alluding to the Famous
Features Syndicate piece then running] and permit themselves to wallow
in the publicity of the whole affair is more than I can understand."

On Monday, Mrs. Isabel Gray made the trip to Sing Sing, her second
and last, to say good-bye to her husband. The time was arranged so she
would not cross paths with Gray's mother. She arrived early in the morning, accompanied by Frank Brundage, in a curtained car. Reporters were
able to observe that even with the curtains drawn to protect her from
cameramen, she had her hat pulled down and kept her hands clenched
tightly over her face.

She and Gray talked about practical affairs, how to dispose of Gray's

1. Gray was thirty-five years old.

insurance money, Jane's upbringing, and the like. At noon, Mrs. Gray left, bidding her husband a businesslike farewell.

An hour later, Gray's mother showed up and, as usual, had a few words for the reporters. Did she have anything to say about her daughter-in-law's visit? Nothing at all.

· Over the weekend, Mrs. Snyder's defense suffered another crisis. Lonardo, his visiting privileges restored by Lawes,[2] showed up at Sing Sing at six o'clock Sunday afternoon to discuss applying in federal court for a writ of habeas corpus based on the argument that the joint trial was unconstitutional. Having exhausted the New York State appellate courts and with the New York State Supreme Court off limits thanks to Section 495, Federal court was their only chance. In order to make the application more dramatic, Lonardo proposed to draft it in the first person and have Mrs. Snyder sign it personally.

On his arrival at Sing Sing, Lonardo was shocked to discover that Hazelton, chief attorney of record, had ordered Warden Lawes to remove his name from the list of counsel permitted to confer with Mrs. Snyder.

The reason was a simple dispute: Lonardo was in favor of going to the federal court in Manhattan right away; Wallace figured there was nothing to lose and was amenable; Hazelton wanted to wait for Governor Smith's clemency decision. Fuming, Lonardo got word of what was happening to Mrs. Snyder. "I think I know the best way to adjust this situation," Mrs. Snyder remarked to a matron as she passed her an express-mail letter to Granny Brown in which she renewed her decision to fire Hazelton and appoint Lonardo chief counsel. She sighed that she had no more hope and would prefer death to spending her life in prison. On Monday night, she liquidated her Death House bank account and ate $4.50 worth of chocolate.

A peace conference between Lonardo, Hazelton, and Wallace was scheduled for Tuesday afternoon at Wallace's new office in Jamaica. Shortly before the meeting, Lonardo spoke to reporters in his Long Island City office. "Mr. Hazelton says he is through. Whether for financial

---

2. The warden did not restore those of Frank Bambera, who was, he discovered to his horror, not an attorney but merely a private investigator.

or other reasons, I do not know."[3] The telephone then rang. It was Hazelton and the conversation degenerated quickly. "How dare-a you-a say you get-a me disbarred if I-a try to be-a chief-a counsel?" Lonardo shouted in his heavy Italian accent, as reporters scribbled furiously. The upshot of what followed was that Lonardo no longer recognized Hazelton as chief counsel.

Despite the animosity, the afternoon parley went well enough for the three lawyers to draft a joint telegram to Mrs. Snyder: "Owing to constructive work on your behalf we are unable to see you today. Our combined efforts needed here."

For reporters there was a typewritten statement: "We are anxiously awaiting the Governor's answer to our plea for clemency. Further actions contemplated by us must necessarily depend upon this."

According to Hazelton, there was no fundamental disagreement between counsel; the important thing was to make sure that no one lawyer could do anything without all three being in agreement. He launched into an oration on the frail health of Granny Brown and how she would never withstand the shock if her daughter were executed.

Lonardo stuck to the subject: he was making no attempt to supplant Hazelton and would hold in abeyance his plans for a Federal appeal until Governor Smith had spoken. In return for holding back, Lonardo was now an attorney of record, an associate of Hazelton and Wallace, rather than just the hired help. The dispute had nothing to do with money, he emphasized; he had been paid for drafting Mrs. Snyder's appeal but was now working pro bono. Privately, Lonardo said he feared that Hazelton was planning some spectacular publicity stunt that might throw his precious appeal off track.

Shortly before six o'clock on Tuesday evening, 10 January, a desk clerk told the dozen reporters killing time in the Biltmore lobby that the

---

3. Hazelton had plenty of reasons to drop the case. He was acting as head counsel for the Queens County sewer contractors at the time. There was far more political potential in that case than in Mrs. Snyder's forlorn hopes. The *Sun* wrote that Hazelton simply felt that further heroics on Mrs. Snyder's behalf were a waste of counsel's time and Granny Brown's money.

governor wished to see them on the fourteenth floor. They arrived and were admitted to the outer room of the executive suite. The bedroom door opened, and Governor Smith entered the room. With him were his legal counsel, Griffin, and his personal secretary, the latter carrying a sheaf of mimeographed papers, which he distributed. Smith looked fatigued and sighed. "Well, this is my decision," he said as he sat down and started to read:

> In the matter of the application for executive clemency for Ruth Brown Snyder and Henry Judd Gray.
>
> This case has received my anxious consideration, not merely since the hearing before me upon the application for executive clemency, but ever since the Court of Appeals unanimously affirmed the conviction of the defendants.
>
> The execution of this judgment on a woman is so distressing that I had hoped that the appeal to me for executive clemency would disclose some fact which would justify my interference with the procedure of the law. But this did not happen. I have searched in vain for any basis upon which my conscience, in the light of my oath of office will approve on which I might temper the law with mercy.
>
> Up to this writing there is no extenuation shown for what the seven judges of the Court of Appeals, in agreement with the twelve jurors and the trial justice, have found to be a deliberate and premeditated murder committed by these defendants.
>
> The application for executive clemency is therefore denied.

Smith held up his right hand to dismiss any questions and announced that he was going to visit his wife in the hospital.

Warden Lawes had no reaction to the news other to say that no formal notice of the governor's decision would be given to the prisoners. If Mrs. Snyder or Gray learned of Smith's statement at all, it would be through a relative or the prison grapevine.

Asked yet again about what Mrs. Snyder would wear, Lawes erupted. "She will wear one of her ordinary dresses. She will wear just what she happens to have on at the time. We have no uniform for women prisoners and when Mrs. Snyder came here we bought her three cheap, washable calico dresses. She will wear one of them—probably whichever is cleanest." On that distinctly unromantic note, he dismissed reporters from his office and went home to dinner. "DISAPPOINTED NOT TO DIE IN SILK DRESS," punted the *Post*. The best the *Daily News* could manage was that, if she had a favorite among her three prison dresses, she would be permitted to wear that one.

Hazelton, his strategy in tatters following Governor Smith's decision, suddenly discovered the virtues of silence. Now that the governor had spoken, he would meet with his colleagues to determine strategy and have no comment until then. "I was never so close-mouthed as I will be from now on," he said, as if he had ever been able to keep his mouth shut.

Miller went to Sing Sing late Tuesday night and discussed with Gray plans to apply, like Lonardo, for a federal writ of habeas corpus on the grounds that the joint trial was unconstitutional. Gray agreed, but warned that he himself would have nothing to do with the process. Let his mother sign the application if she wished, he said.

Gray wrote a letter to Lawes disposing of the twenty-one dollars remaining his Death House account, dedicating fifteen dollars to buying a first-class meal for the ten men left after he was gone, and earmarking the remaining six dollars for Frank "Dixie" Baldwin, murderer of a Steuben County farmer, to buy cigarettes. Baldwin, who was destitute and had no relatives to visit him, was so deeply touched that he wept.

Mrs. Snyder confirmed to matrons that she would be attended by Catholic chaplain McCaffery when she died. She was depressed; she ate little breakfast Tuesday morning and spent long hours on her cot staring at the ceiling. "She has clung to some faint hope, but she appears to sense the situation," Warden Lawes said.

When Granny Brown and Andrew came to visit on Wednesday, they brought along an old friend—Father Murphy from Queens County Jail. Mrs. Snyder's family was admitted immediately, but Murphy was refused entry even though he had in hand a New York State Supreme Court order granting him admittance. Lawes argued that, unless Mrs. Snyder declared a preference for Murphy over her present adviser, Father Mc-Caffery, Murphy had no business with the prisoner. Father Murphy insisted that Commissioner of Corrections Kieb be contacted and waited for two hours outside Lawes's office until the Commissioner responded. Kieb agreed with Lawes. Murphy insisted on speaking to Kieb himself and argued that this rebuff was "arbitrary, illegal, inhuman, and irreligious." On each of these four points, he gave a brief disquisition.[4] Lawes and Kieb had not heard the last of him, he sputtered—and he was right. Murphy telephoned the Biltmore, made his case to Edward Griffin of Governor Smith's staff, and immediately received an order permitting him admittance on Thursday.

While Murphy was fuming, Granny Brown and Andrew spent the afternoon with Mrs. Snyder and broke the bad news of Governor Smith's statement the night before. "There is still time for something good to happen," Mrs. Snyder observed. She was sufficiently composed to write a brief note to Warden Lawes, thanking him for his many kindnesses while she was in his custody. There was a flurry of excitement when a packet of white powder was found in her cell; however, it turned out to be bicarbonate of soda issued from the prison pharmacy when she had an upset stomach.

Gray was, if anything, even calmer and more resigned since his farewell visit with Isabel. He was certainly fit: he played handball with Father McCaffery and won every game.

Dr. Joseph Moore of the New York State Lunacy Commission examined the prisoners and determined that they were not showing signs of insanity. The opinion of only one member of the commission was sufficient for the execution to proceed, so no further examinations were called for.

Mrs. Snyder's mail continued to arrive at a steady rate, but little of it was brought to her now. Letters were received from twenty-five women offering to die in Mrs. Snyder's place; there were also a handful of black-hand letters threatening retribution if she was executed, one of them

---

4. Kieb, who wanted nothing more than to wash his hands of Mrs. Snyder, blamed Father Murphy for publicity that had arisen from Mrs. Snyder's conversion in Queens County Jail; Murphy protested that he had not sought publicity. Reporters hypothesized that Father McCaffery himself sought to have Murphy excluded because he wanted no competition in his moment of glory.

bearing the signature "The Jolly Roger" over a skull and crossbones. The "Soul Mates' Union" of Washington, D.C., wrote asking Warden Lawes to permit the murderers to spend their last night together. Someone sent a matched pair of rabbit's feet to the two prisoners for luck; Gray was amused and wore his until the end.

Ossining was beginning to fill up with reporters. There was no real hotel left in town since the one-hundred-year-old Weskora Hotel had burned down the week before with a loss of three lives. Prices at the single boarding house rose by the hour, as the proprietor set the room rate at whatever the market would bear. Reporters who had arrived early and locked in cheap rates found lodging in private homes and sublet their rooms at a profit to latecomers.

In Sing Sing, reporters were permitted to install themselves in the clerk's office just outside Lawes's, where they took up all the bench space normally used by visitors. Tension arose between photographers and prison officials, who were concerned about having their security arrangements, not to mention themselves, photographed. Matron Hickey was so upset that her picture had been published in the *Evening Journal* that, when she saw the guilty cameraman at the prison gate the next day, she assaulted him with a pair of boots she was carrying.

Warden Lawes barred reporters from using prison telephones, even the single pay phone, nor would he allow extra telegraph wires to be run into the prison. At first, reporters coped by taking taxis a mile up the hill to the town in order to wire their copy. This would be out of the question on the night of the execution, so they arranged for a dozen telegraph wires to be run up Dunstan Avenue, the road winding along the ice-sheeted Hudson from the prison to the town. The wires terminated in the back room of the Hudson View Inn, known to locals as "Duck Inn," a broken-down yellow clapboard roadhouse a few hundred yards from the main prison gate. Tables were set up in the back room and squads of operators from the Postal Telegraph Company and Western Union installed themselves, along with the telegraph and teletype machines. Duck Inn also happened to have the nearest pay telephone, and the proprietor's ten percent cut on outgoing calls was soon amounting to over ten dollars per day.

Daily News reporter George Kivel had a brainstorm when he saw an abandoned hot dog stand next to the prison gate. He contacted its owner and, having duly rented it for fifty dollars a day, set about arranging for his own exclusive wire hookup. This gave the *News* a ten-minute advantage in wiring its copy, and Kivel received a $100 bonus for his ingenuity.

On Wednesday night, against the odds, Mrs. Snyder hit the legal jackpot. All afternoon, Hazelton, Wallace, and Lonardo had discussed strategy at Wallace's office. Wallace had been in one of his alcoholic smashups a few days before and was nursing a broken collarbone. At three o'clock, Lonardo emerged. Hazelton had finally consented to his plan to seek a Federal writ of habeas corpus, Lonardo declared to reporters, although he refused to join in it.

No sooner had Lonardo set off to Sing Sing to obtain Mrs. Snyder's signature than Hazelton and Wallace snuck out the back door and headed to the chambers of New York State Supreme Court Justice Levy at Manhattan County Courthouse in lower Manhattan, where Hazelton argued that Mrs. Snyder's execution should be stayed at least until her evidence in the insurance case could be heard. According to the ruling of Queens County Surrogate Noble, Lorraine was a ward of the Supreme Court so far as the insurance litigation was concerned. Mrs. Snyder was one of only two people alive, the other being Leroy Ashfield, who could testify as to how the insurance had been taken out and, if she were not heard, Lorraine might be placed at a disadvantage in the lawsuit. A deposition from Mrs. Snyder might not be good enough because she was presently in a disturbed state of mind.

Having heard two hours' worth of arguments, Justice Levy was convinced and issued a writ ordering Warden Lawes to appear before him at ten o'clock Friday morning to show cause why the execution of Mrs. Snyder should not be delayed until her testimony could be heard or her deposition taken. In theory, the latter could be accomplished in time for the execution to take place before Sunday, the deadline set by the Court of Appeals in the death warrant. In practice, such a rush job would be difficult. If the execution did not take place by midnight Saturday, the matter would revert to Justice Scudder, who would have to sentence her again. It was considered highly unlikely that he would set an execution date less than one month away.

Alexander Orban, veteran court reporter from the *New York Daily News,* heard through the grapevine that Mrs. Snyder's lawyers were in conference with Levy. Smelling a story, he was nonetheless fearful to wait at the courthouse, where he would be seen by other reporters. Instead, he waited for Levy outside a drugstore that he knew the judge always passed on his way home. Waylaid, Levy explained that he was considering a stay and would announce his decision following dinner at his club, the Grand Street Boys Club on West 55th Street. It was a reporter's dream. Orban wrote up his story on the assumption that the stay would be issued and waited outside the club. When Levy emerged at ten o'clock, Orban got his confirmation, the story ran in a final midnight extra edition under the headline "RUTH SAVED!" and the other papers were left writhing in confusion.

Meanwhile, at Sing Sing, Lonardo steered Mrs. Snyder through the habeas corpus legal papers, which required her to fill in certain details. She made random noises and asked how to spell the simplest words. She signed her name six times on the legal forms; each signature laboriously written and none bearing any resemblance to the other. "I'm a young woman," she said as she signed. "I'm young and I'm in the prime of life. I'm young and they're going to kill me. It don't seem right, Lonardo. Oh, I'll go all right. I'll have to go. But I seem so young and full of life."

When Lonardo, returning with Mrs. Snyder's signatures on the petition, descended from the midnight train at Grand Central, he was assaulted by reporters brandishing the *Daily News* extra. As mystified as the pressmen, he said he would hold his plans in abeyance until after the hearing in Justice Levy's court.

How was Mrs. Snyder bearing up? "Mrs. Snyder looked like a dead woman. She touched my hand and she was cold as ice. I took her other hand; it was another piece of ice. I touched her forehead. It was frozen. Her face was red from crying. She had been lying down all day before I arrived."

Her wit had not entirely deserted her, however. She joked forlornly that she had been sentenced to death on Friday the thirteenth and was now to die on Thursday the twelfth.

Levy's writ had to be served on Warden Lawes before noon Thursday. Frank Bambera got sweet revenge for his exclusion from the Death House by taking a few reporters in tow and rousing the warden at two thirty in the morning. Lawes made the best of it, saying that, as a humane man, he would welcome any legal directive sparing the condemned prisoner, but would, as an agent of the State, have to defer to legal counsel. He referred the matter to Commissioner of Corrections Kieb, who immediately forwarded it to Attorney General Ottinger for an opinion. Lawes also telephoned Governor Smith at the Biltmore and was told to await further instructions. "Sometimes the law is tough for a layman to understand," the warden told reporters with good humor. "So I've got a lawyer working for me. My lawyer is the Attorney General."

Governor Smith held a breakfast conference with Edward Griffin, who advised him that Levy's writ was assuredly illegal. A telegram from Miller and Millard arrived, praying that, "in simple justice," Smith grant Gray any reprieve he extended to Mrs. Snyder. Not to do so, they argued, would be "frightfully unfair." This was unnecessary. Lawes had already declared that he would execute both or none that night.

Attorney General Ottinger convened a meeting with his assistants and the solicitor general. The consensus was that the writ was in clear contravention of Section 495, which meant they would advise Warden Lawes that he was free to execute Mrs. Snyder tonight. The problem was that Lawes was also within his rights, writ or no writ, to delay the execution until midnight Saturday. In view of the confused situation and his opposition to capital punishment, he might do just that.

Governor Smith, who was outraged at Justice Levy's arrogance, telephoned Ottinger mid-morning and ordered that the pair be executed that evening without fail. At the time, his suite at the Biltmore was being guarded by extra detectives. His desk was piled high with telegrams and special delivery letters pleading for Mrs. Snyder's life, among them a letter containing a map of Sing Sing Prison with a large cross marking the spot where the writer promised that two 300-pound bombs would be dropped from a plane during the execution. The letter further stipulated that the plane would be using "an improved bombsight that we have rea-son to believe is an innovation."

Ottinger had an idea on how to break the impasse. He drafted, in the form of a letter responding to Lawes's request for advice, an opinion in which he differed respectfully from the learned Supreme Court judge and ordered Lawes to disregard the stay of execution. The attorney gen-eral simultaneously telephoned Lawes with his finding, transmitted the letter, released copies to reporters, and dispatched New York State Deputy Attorney General Robert Beyer of the New York City office to hand-deliver a copy to Justice Levy along with an ultimatum: hold an im-mediate hearing on the writ and vacate it, or suffer the humiliation of seeing it ignored.

Levy was sitting on the bench at noon when a reporter managed to get a note passed up to him stating that Ottinger had instructed Lawes to ignore the writ. "I don't care what Ottinger holds," Levy scrawled on the note and handed it to the clerk to pass back. When court adjourned for its midday recess, Levy was in an only slightly less belligerent mood. "Ot-tinger's opinion is just as good as any other lawyer's," he remarked on his way back to chambers.

Beyer was waiting for him with his message, and Levy agreed reluc-tantly to move up the hearing. "If the Attorney General feels so deeply that an immediate hearing is essential to the execution of justice in this state, I will accommodate him." Levy agreed to hear arguments at two o'clock. Hazelton, whom by sheer luck they were able to contact in Brooklyn, rushed to Manhattan and begged for more time to prepare. The hearing was put off until three fifteen.

As word spread, every downtown lawyer with time on his hands crowded into the courtroom to hear the arguments. A considerable cast of characters was there—Hazelton, Wallace, Lonardo, Miller, and, of course, Beyer. Everyone gathered around Justice Levy's bench for a pho-tograph. Then the hearing was called to order and Levy, looking ill at ease, invited Beyer to present his argument. The deputy attorney general rose and was immediately interrupted by Hazelton, who frantically de-manded to know if arguments would be on technicalities, namely, the power of the New York State Supreme Court to delay the execution, or on the merits of the case, namely, whether Mrs. Snyder's testimony really was necessary to protect Lorraine's interests. If the latter, Hazelton said he would object because those arguments had been scheduled for ten o'clock the following day. Levy announced that arguments on both sets of issues would be heard, regardless of Hazelton's objection.

Deputy Attorney General Beyer led off on a technicality: the application for the writ was wrongfully made to Justice Levy since his jurisdiction did not include Sing Sing Prison. He warmed to his argument with an attack on the merit of the appeal: Mrs. Snyder's counsel had been blessed with all the time in the world to see that her deposition was taken and to ensure that Lorraine's interests were defended. If Mrs. Snyder's execution were stayed so she could testify in the civil case, it would open the way for Hazleton and Wallace to fight tooth and nail to delay its trial. Beyer closed on his strongest point: Section 495 explicitly stipulated that the New York State Supreme Court had no right to delay an execution. He bowed to Hazleton and sat down as the latter rose.

Where Beyer's manner had been subdued and his voice modulated, Hazelton's manner was wild and his voice cracked with strain.

"Before you is a little girl whose father is dead and whose mother's life is about to be taken by the State. The child, so far as property rights are concerned, is poverty stricken—a pauper. All the child has are certain property rights vested in her by her mother—they may be worth nine dollars or they may be worth ninety thousand dollars, but whatever they are worth, they are hers."

Having no law to fall back upon, Hazelton conceded as much by brushing contemptuously aside a stack of law books at his elbow. "I would as soon throw these out the door. We are not concerned with what was done before but with what should be done now. I am not here to prevent an execution but to protect the rights of a fatherless, and almost motherless, child."

Beyer, in rebuttal, merely noted that sympathy should not play a role in this decision. "Consider the source," he said acidly of the testimony that Hazelton claimed was so vital to Lorraine's interests and yet had not bothered to secure by deposition during these many long months.

Justice Levy had sat with his eyes closed during the arguments. He opened them when the lawyers were finished and noted with regret that the gravity of the situation required him to make his decision in haste and that his comments were to be understood as impromptu. He turned first to the legal technicalities, particularly Section 495, and disagreed with Beyer. He then candidly admitted that he had changed his mind on the merits.

"This discussion discloses that the child could in no way be served by these proceedings [that is, a jury trial] even if the moving party were to be successful upon this application. I am persuaded of the claim of the Attorney General that this move has no definite or fixed purpose except to accomplish indirectly what could not be gained otherwise—that is, that the day for effectuation of the solemn judgment of this Court [the New York State Supreme Court] in another judicial department is sought to be delayed. It is a sad day for the child, but as the Court can conceive of no machinery in law available to relieve this child's misery in respect to her rights in this impending litigation, this motion is denied and the stay vacated."

When reporters swarmed counsel for all sides, Miller suggested they retreat to his offices on nearby Lafayette Street until the crowd thinned. Friend and foe alike recognized the wisdom of his offer and followed him, but to no avail. Reporters had already laid siege to the office building. As the news spread, reporters upstate even tracked through a field of mud to inform Commissioner of Corrections Kieb, who was inspecting the site for a proposed new state prison at Attica.

At four thirty, Miller and Lonardo, who had struck up a friendship, went to the chambers of federal judge Henry Goddard in the Woolworth Building to present their clients' applications for writs of habeas corpus.

Gray's chances for a stay were already almost nonexistent. At noon, Miller had tendered Gray's application, signed by his mother. Judge Goddard sent Miller, as was customary, to give the application to the senior law clerk, who looked it over and shook his head—nothing Federal in it. Miller insisted on seeing Goddard again and was told that he could have a few minutes with the judge before Lonardo's appointment later in the afternoon. Miller went in and harangued Judge Goddard for half an hour, to no effect; he emerged looking haggard. Lonardo went in to plead for Mrs. Snyder, with the same result.

The attorneys returned to Miller's office and issued a joint statement: "We are going to say good-bye to our clients. Tomorrow the public will have its cup of blood."

27

THE PRISONERS HAD AWOKEN ON THURSDAY MORNING, 12 January, each in a good mood for different reasons. Gray rose at eight forty five, relieved that his ordeal was drawing to a close. He ate breakfast and read his Bible until eleven when Dr. Sweet dropped by to look him over. After eating lunch at noon, Gray sat down to write thank-you notes to people who had done him favors. Mrs. Gray, whom prison officials described as "dignified and pleasant," arrived with Margaret and brother-in-law Harold Logan at two o'clock for their last visit. Before leaving home, Mrs. Gray had told reporters that all she wished for was to kiss her sweet boy's forehead once more on this earth in the ebbing hours of his life. She had no hope left and final plans had yet to be made for the burial. The sad trio left Sing Sing at four thirty, and Logan practically ran down a flock of reporters as he tore away from the prison.

Mrs. Snyder rose at nine thirty. She had heard through the grapevine of Justice Levy's stay and heartily ate a breakfast of toast, oatmeal, orange juice, and coffee. She even walked back and forth and sang a bit in her cell. This was nothing like her lethargy the day before, when she had drunk a bit of orange juice, groaned, and crawled back into bed with the covers over her head until one o'clock. Dr. Sweet examined her at ten fifteen, and Lawes dropped by at eleven to officially inform her of the stay.

When Warden Lawes received instructions from Attorney General Ottinger at noon to ignore Justice Levy's stay, he went straight to the Death House to break the bad news to Mrs. Snyder, but, once there, he could not find the heart. She was more cheerful than she had been in months; she chatted freely and strode firmly up and down the tiny corridor just as she had in the Queens County Jail. They spoke for a few minutes and Lawes left her secure in her delusion.

Granny Brown and Andrew arrived at one o'clock and, as an exception, were allowed to visit Mrs. Snyder in her cell. The two women traded memories and giggled like schoolgirls until three thirty. In more serious moments, the conversation centered on Lorraine, Mrs. Snyder's innocence, and her desire to see Father Murphy. Mrs. Snyder's parting words to her mother and brother were "Take care of Lorraine. God knows I'm innocent!" As far as the visitors knew when they left, Mrs. Snyder was safe at least until Friday. Perhaps, though, Granny Brown had a premonition, for on the way back to the Bronx she asked the driver to pull over in Tarrytown and instructed her son to telephone the prison and reiterate the vital importance of Father Murphy's visit.

At five o'clock, with Granny Brown and Andrew safely out of the prison, Warden Lawes went again to the Death House to inform Mrs. Snyder that her last chance was gone. "Any news from New York? What are they doing?" Mrs. Snyder pleaded. Again, Lawes's courage failed him. "I have heard nothing definite. They're still fighting in Levy's court." Fifteen minutes later, in desperation, Lawes turned to the golden-tongued P. K. Sheehy and asked him to be the messenger of death. When told that her last hope was gone, Mrs. Snyder cried out once and then burst into tears. Lawes ordered that, in view of her mental state, nothing special be brought to her for her last dinner. She got the ordinary Death House fare—Spanish omelet—at five forty-five and ate little of it.

At five o'clock, Gray was moved to the far cell on the West Wing of the Death House—it was out of the question that both he and Mrs. Snyder would occupy cells in the Dance Hall—where he dined at six. He ate chicken soup, roast chicken, mashed potatoes, celery, stuffed olives, and ice cream, followed by coffee and cigars.[1] Gray had said good-bye to his

---

1. No detail was more lovingly reported than the menu chosen by a condemned prisoner. Strange to say, it always consisted of precisely the same fare. Obviously, there was no choice about it—condemned prisoners simply received the Death House "special" on their last night. The whole idea of "ordering" a last meal was an invention that newspapers cynically persisted in publishing week after week.

tier mates in the East Wing with the easy savoir faire of an ambassador paying his respects before leaving a country to take up a new post.

After dinner, Death House barber de Stefano came, shaved Gray, and clipped a three-inch patch of hair from the back of his head to allow for better contact of the electrode. De Stefano was more nervous than Gray, whom he nicked several times. Gray spoke again of his hope that Mrs. Snyder's soul would be saved and asked de Stefano if he drank. Fearing another of Gray's temperance lectures, de Stefano answered cautiously: "Well, not in here."

"Then, when you get out," said Gray to the barber's amazement, "have a drink for me. Save me a toast."

Shaken, de Stefano packed up his implements in a hurry, shook Gray's hand, and left with his escorts for the Women's Wing. There he supervised while Matron Hickey clipped the back of Mrs. Snyder's head. Both women cried the whole time. At seven twenty, Mrs. Snyder was moved to the Dance Hall, less than twenty-five feet from the door to the death chamber.

The crowd of reporters, off-duty prison guards, and townspeople had been steadily growing at Duck Inn. Down the road, outside the main prison gate, Ossining residents and curiosity seekers who had driven from as far as Massachusetts and Rhode Island swelled the crowd to five hundred. One hundred private motorcars were parked in two rows, many with their lights on, illuminating the strange scene. Four guards stood outside the gate to keep order. Babies cried, children wailed, young couples on dates necked and sipped from hip flasks. Parents fretted that their high-school-age children were paying no attention at all to the Regents Examinations coming up on Monday. Old-time Ossining residents were reminded of years before the war, when half the town would turn out on execution nights and cheer when a black flag was hoisted on the prison turret to indicate that the execution had taken place.

Hazelton, Wallace, and Bambera (his visiting privileges restored *in extremis*) arrived at eight; they were able to get in to see Mrs. Snyder for only fifteen minutes. When they emerged from the prison, Wallace and Bambera wanted to get away, but Hazelton, as usual, was willing to talk to reporters. "She is too far gone to know what she is doing. I never saw anything more terrible. I cannot describe her terror, her misery, her agony. I died a thousand times while we were with her. It was awful."

They went to Duck Inn, where more reporters awaited them. Hazelton again rose to the occasion. "We went down with our colors flying. Death has won a transient victory, but the stains of this carnival of blood will not have faded until capital punishment itself is dead."

Wallace was practically in tears. "She is bearing up and has made her peace with God. She is reconciled to the inevitable and said, 'I bear no malice against the world or anybody in it.'" Pronouncing themselves emotionally incapable of remaining until the executions were finished, Hazelton, Wallace, and Bambera went up to the railroad station, where yet more reporters lay in wait. Hazelton, more composed than he had been back at Duck Inn, described what had transpired at the meeting.

"Mrs. Snyder sat with her head in her hands. All of us felt so bad that we did not say anything. Finally I said, 'Have you asked God to forgive you?' She said, 'Yes, I have and he has forgiven me. I hope that the world will.' Then she put her head back into her hands. We sat there. She said, 'Is Mother coming back?' I said no. 'Baby?' she asked. I said no again. Finally, embarrassed, she lifted her head and said, 'Well, good-bye.' What could we do? We got up and left."

Lonardo and Father Murphy arrived together just after Mrs. Snyder's previous visitors left. Murphy had no trouble getting in and Mrs. Snyder greeted him with joy. Lonardo left the two alone in the visitor's area and Murphy heard her confession and granted her absolution.[2] "She's bearing up in the faith of God," said Murphy as he stepped out and Lonardo reentered the room. Lonardo asked Mrs. Snyder if she had any messages she wanted to leave. She looked at the clock.

> I have an hour and fifty-five minutes to live. I am terribly sorry I have sinned, but I am paying dearly for it. I only hope that my life that I am giving up now will serve as a lesson to the rest of the world. If the world

---

2. Father Murphy belonged to the Brooklyn Diocese, which at that time covered Queens. Patrick Cardinal Hayes gave him special dispensation to administer the sacrament outside his diocese.

will only benefit by it, I am satisfied. Judd and I sinned together, and now it looks as though we'll go together—God knows where. If I were to live over again, I would be what I want my child to be—a good girl, really making the fear of God a guide to a straight life.

She rose and prepared to go. "If there is any penitent in the world, it's me." Then she turned and walked back to the Dance Hall and the waiting Father McCaffery. There was a sink in her holding cell; she decided to wash her hair and asked McCaffery to go back to her old cell to get her shampoo.

Mrs. Snyder had been writing letters off and on all evening. There was one to each of the three matrons thanking them for their kindness. More importantly, and unknown until the *Evening Journal* sprung it as a scoop on Friday, she had asked for and received permission to send a brief note of farewell to Gray. It contained only a few lines, but it cheered Gray up and he immediately requested a pencil and reciprocated in kind.[3] "I am very glad," he said. "I had hoped she would forgive me. I hope God will forgive both of us."

Mrs. Snyder wrote to Father Murphy just after he and Lonardo left. The letter duly appeared in the Friday's *Daily Mirror,* along with the usual facsimile to establish its authenticity:

My dear Father,

Little did I think some months ago that I'd be asking you to deliver prayers for the dead.

This time, Father, I am going to ask you—do this big favor and say a few prayers over me before my clay is laid to rest? Perhaps I am asking too much, am I? Please don't refuse me.

My poor dear mother is so heartbroken, she has been a wonderful mother through it all. I am so proud of her and my baby. How I hate to leave them with so much sorrow. What disgrace have I brought to my

3. According to Lawes in *Meet the Murderer!:* "These brief letters [read by officials] contained nothing more than a few formal words and by no stretch of the imagination could honestly be described as frenzied declarations of love."

loved ones, and I have prayed to be forgiven. It all seems too selfish to leave so much on them.

I don't fear death—for all will be over in a minute, but the hours, days and months of sorrow for my poor loved ones appalls me—oh for what and why did I stray away? If I could but suffer the agonies alone— my sufferings are nothing to those of my mother's and others. I know he [Gray] would want to carry more as myself, if it were only possible. I offered up my communion for him last Sunday—I have no hate in my heart, and I don't think he does either.

When I go, I am going clean in heart, body and soul. Goodbye, Father, dear, and many thanks for all you have done for me.

Sincerely,

Ruth

Appearing in the same paper was Mrs. Snyder's last letter to her brother, Andrew, and his wife:

My dearest brother, Margaret,

Time is fast passing by and I have the inclination to write; I thought I'd tell you what is on my mind.

I don't want anything but the simplest of everything—I only ask that Father Murphy say a prayer for me before I am laid away.

Mother will probably buy a plot—and have papa moved—if you intend not to rest with us, then only two double graves will be necessary— I would like to have my baby with me when the time comes.[4]

Could I ask you again, before I am called, to either adopt Lorraine for me or else have mother adopt her? We cannot have her leave us after I am gone. Won't you do this? Ask Hattie [?] to love her for me; Margaret too.

---

4. The letter is a little jumbled here. Harry Brown was buried in a crowded area; if the family was going to be interred together, it would be necessary to buy a plot and move his remains. If Andrew and Margaret intended to make their own arrangements, then two double graves would be required—one for Harry and Josephine and the other for Ruth and Lorraine.

Be kind to poor dear mother, try to take my place and help her if you can—and watch her too!

This is my last letter, Andrew—Bear up and help Mother bear her heavy burden.

Goodbye, Andrew dear. I am sorry for all the pain and trouble I have caused to you all—forgive me, please.

Love,

Your sister,

Ruth

Remember—only the most simple burial, no mass, no inscriptions, very plain.

I want to go out of this world as I came into it—just a poor soul.

As for Gray, between the strength he derived from religion and the note from Mrs. Snyder, he was in excellent spirits when Miller visited him in his cell just before ten o'clock. He was proud of having bared his soul and cleared his conscience. "I'm not a real criminal," he said. "Circumstances just got the better of me."

After ten o'clock, the last of the visitors departed and Sing Sing had the prisoners all to herself. Armed guards patrolled the surrounding roads and checked identity papers. A direct line, as customary, had been established between Lawes's office and Governor Smith, who was still installed at the Biltmore while his wife convalesced.[5] Attorney General Ottinger was taking no chances. He ordered his deputy, Beyer, to camp out in the warden's office to serve as babysitter until the executions were carried out.

Lawes went to Gray's cell at ten thirty to say good-bye. Gray gave him the manuscript he had prepared for Famous Features Syndicate with instructions to pass it along to his sister, Margaret. This manuscript, generously supplemented by the editors, formed the basis for Gray's autobi-

---

5. As if to underscore his indifference to the case, Governor Smith spent the evening with a family friend. Gray's family, expecting to be besieged in West Orange, spent the night at a hotel in the city. Granny Brown spent the evening at home in the Bronx, either unaware or choosing not to know that the last act of the drama was being played out.

ography, *Doomed Ship*. Gray requested that Warden Lawes give his Bible to his mother and expressed hope that his example would help other men steer clear of the rocks. Then he went back to praying with Reverend Peterson. Mrs. Snyder was also praying, with Father McCaffery, when Lawes dropped by her cell, and the farewell lasted only a few seconds. She gave him some letters to give to her mother. "It's better to go now than live the life I lived before," she said. Lawes shook her hand, bowed quickly, and left.

Among those who had been most confused by the last-minute flurry of legal actions was executioner Robert Elliott. A Richmond Hill electrical contractor who had long worked as a chief engineer and electrician in the New York State Prison system, Elliott had served as a junior assistant to "Professor" Edwin Davis, who inaugurated death by electrocution in the State of New York in 1889. Upon his forced retirement in 1914, Davis sold his patented electrodes to the State for ten thousand dollars and was replaced by his senior assistant, John Hulbert. After ten years, the strain of the job began to get to Hulbert. One night, he collapsed before an execution and the prison doctor had to ply him with brandy to revive him sufficiently to throw the switch. Only moments before another execution, he lost his temper over a trifle and flung a set of electrodes across the execution chamber. He finished by abruptly resigning and, in January 1926, was replaced by Elliott.[6] Although short in tenure, Elliott was long in experience and had already officiated at two spectacular multiple executions: Sacco and Vanzetti in Massachusetts and the four Reid Ice Cream bandits in New Jersey.[7]

Elliott's first task was to close the electrical circuit by throwing a large switch on his control board; this was accomplished by pulling the switch up, not down, to ensure that gravity or a casual slip did not result in a horrible accident. The control board was located in a closet-sized alcove

6. Hulbert became despondent in retirement and shot himself in 1929, two bullets being required to do the job.

7. Elliott was frequently "imported" by neighboring states. Christopher Barone, Louis Capozzi, Joseph Juliano, and Nicholas Juliano were four young Newark gangsters who in 1926 robbed the payroll of the Reid Ice Cream Corp. The heist was masterminded, and the getaway car driven, by Robert Boudreau.

room behind and to the right of the electric chair. Elliott could observe the chair from the open door, but the prisoner was unable to see the executioner.[8] Elliott's second responsibility was to regulate the voltage using a transformer; keeping all the while an eye on the prisoner, a voltmeter, and an amperage meter.

The application of electricity to muscular tissue induces contraction; electrocution causes instantaneous paralysis of the heart muscles. If this was all there was to it, there would be an excellent chance that the heart would start up again when the current was shut off, as happens to the many people who survive being hit by lightning. By maintaining the current, however, the body temperature is raised to a level—some 140° Fahrenheit as measured on the surface of the skin—sufficient to destroy the nervous system.

But herein lies the executioner's nightmare: applying so much current that the body is incinerated.[9] Elliott had perfected a system of repeated shocks. First he hit the condemned with a full two thousand volts for a few seconds, then he lowered the voltage for a minute while the body heated up. Then he applied a second full surge of current and, if necessary, repeated a third and fourth time. The heart could not withstand the repeated shocks, but the body never became hot enough to undergo severe burning. As to minor burning of the hair and the flesh where the electrodes were attached, Elliott had finally concluded that it was unavoidable.

8. Some photographs purport to show the control panel at Sing Sing, complete with a sign displaying instructions for bell signals: one bell, turn on generator; two bells, turn on current; three bells, more current; four bells, reduce current, and so on. In fact, this control panel was at the power plant at Clinton Prison in Dannemora, where executions were carried out until 1914. The practice at the time (roughly the turn of the century) was for executioner Davis, who donned evening dress when he worked, to observe the condemned and send bell signals to the power plant, where the current was actually controlled.

9. As in the case of the first execution by electricity in 1889, which was such a nightmare that it nearly brought back the gallows. Having failed to kill William Kemmler with the first shock, which lasted only twenty seconds, Davis then proceeded to pour on four minutes of uninterrupted current. Kemmler's body was the color of overcooked meat and his brain a lump of charcoal by the time he was finally declared dead.

He tried to portray himself as a technician, a disinterested servant of the state, and a humanitarian. Elliott was in fact a tormented man, obsessively torn between the money he made and the revulsion he felt for his task. He earned far more as executioner than he did as an electrician; a small fortune of nearly sixty thousand dollars for the close to four hundred criminals he executed before he died in 1939.

In the days running up to the execution, Elliott began to misbehave. First, he started talking to the press. While eating breakfast at Sing Sing after executing Doran and Mason, he became downright chatty over coffee. "They never suffer in my chair," he said philosophically. "They used to hit 'em with the electricity all at once. It wasn't scientific. I work the current in and out." On Monday in Pennsylvania, where he went to execute two men, he spoke to reporters about how much hair it would be necessary to clip from Mrs. Snyder's head to assure good contact with the electrode. Then, the day before the execution, he discovered that Davis had received a bonus—$250 instead of $150—for executing Mrs. Place and Mrs. Farmer. He petitioned Lawes for the same sum, but was turned down flat. He continued to talk to any reporter who approached him, but the message had changed. Now it was "I hate like hell to do this job. I hope it ends capital punishment in New York State."

By the day of the execution, Elliott had worked himself into such a state that a chronic stomach ulcer became aggravated and he was in severe discomfort. He telephoned Warden Lawes in the early afternoon asking what to do and was told to report to the prison as planned. Fighting pain, Elliott packed a workbag with his electrodes, put on a jaunty double-breasted plaid overcoat, and caught a ride up to Sing Sing with one of the medical doctors invited to witness the execution. The idea was to confuse the crowd waiting outside the prison, who had no idea who the doctor's passenger was when the car pulled up at the gate.

After checking in at the warden's office, Elliott tested the eight straps on the chair—one chest, one waist, two upper arm, two wrist, two ankle—to make sure that they were solid and that the buckles were in good order. He checked the control panel and performed his routine test—hooking up the electrodes to the two lead-in wires, immersing them in a pail of water with a double pinch of salt, and bringing it to a boil—to satisfy himself that the apparatus was working well.[10] The lead-in wires, one for the head electrode and one for the leg electrode, were run through a metal pipe under the floor and emerged next to the chair.

The electrodes, Elliott's own invention, each consisted of fist-sized piece of sea sponge in which a piece of fine copper wire screen the size of a silver dollar had been embedded. This was attached to a short length of wire which was hooked up to the lead-in wire with a thumbscrew. Before being plastered to the condemned's skin the sponges would be soaked in saltwater to conduct the current. Elliott, a sort of Edison of limited domain, had also had a brainstorm regarding the head electrode, which tended to come loose, resulting in sparks, burning, and flames mounting from the head. He took a regulation leather football helmet, lined it with rubber, and drilled a hole in the back at roughly the point corresponding to the occiput. The head electrode was placed inside the helmet with the wire sticking out the back; the helmet was then placed on the condemned's head and the chin strap was pulled tight.

The electrodes hooked up, the football helmet resting next to a bucket of salt water just in back of the chair, Elliott retired to the warden's office, where he lounged around the waiting room smoking his pipe, making small talk with the guards, and nursing his inflamed stomach.

New York State law required the presence of twelve members of the public, usually consisting of reporters and medical doctors, in addition to prison personnel. Two doctors had been selected by District Attorney Newcombe: Assistant Medical Examiner Howard Neail and psychiatrist Sylvester Leahy, who were already involved in the case and were personal friends of Newcombe. Two others, Doctors Neil Lundell and Thomas Price, had been nominated by the Sheriff of Queens County, who had delivered the prisoners to Warden Lawes and therefore required a legal accounting of their fate. Dr. Sweet and his chief assistant, Dr. Harold Goslin, as Sing Sing staff physicians, were present as a matter of course. Dr. Robert Bloom, an Ossining surgeon, managed to procure an invita-

---

10. Gruesome as the test may sound, it could have been worse—executioner Davis used to insert his electrodes into a piece of raw beef and roast it.

tion on the excuse that his wife, Winifred, a registered nurse, worked for Dr. Sweet. Bloom was missing his left leg just above the knee and walked on crutches.

Lawes had selected twenty reporters from among the fifteen hundred who had asked to attend. Doctors Neail, Leahy, Lundell, and Price and eight of the reporters would act as the twelve required official witnesses; the additional reporters were, so to speak, an extra service to the public. Only one female reporter, Zoe Beckley of Famous Features Syndicate, asked to witness Mrs. Snyder's execution, but she did not wish to see Gray's. Lawes ruled this out.

Thus did Ruth Snyder, "man crazy," as her sister-in-law had called her, die in front of an audience that, except for Matrons Many and Hickey, was exclusively male.

The twenty reporters came from Duck Inn at ten thirty. They had their passes checked at the main prison gate and were directed to the administration building. There they were parked for fifteen minutes in the reception room, where prisoners were processed and visitors checked in. The medical doctors were already in Lawes's office. At ten forty-five, a clerk emerged and escorted the reporters to the warden's office, where Lawes, seated at his desk while reporters stood in a semicircle around him, gave a briefing on recent developments.

He described the prisoners' last meals and summarized their final words to him. He put the reporters out of their agony by answering the single most asked question in recent days: who would go first? It was the practice in the case of multiple executions to execute the most distressed prisoner first and, between Mrs. Snyder and Gray, it was no contest: Mrs. Snyder would lead the way. Just then, the telephone rang. It was Edward Griffin at the Biltmore. There was no change. Lawes hung up, explained what the call had been about, and continued the briefing.

Absolute silence and decorum were to be observed in the execution chamber; neither smoking nor drinking from hip flasks was allowed. On no account would anyone be permitted to leave the room until the proceedings were finished. Journalists should report exactly what they saw and nothing more; too much trash had already been written about this case.[11] Lawes had heard a rumor that one of the reporters would try to take a picture of the execution using a "watch-camera." Rather than ordering them searched for cameras before entering the death chamber, Lawes trusted it would be sufficient to place them on their honor.

"The hour has come," he said and rose. The eight reporters who happened to be nearest Lawes's desk were asked to sign in advance the register that attested they had witnessed the execution; the doctors had already signed. Lawes led the way, and each man was handed a yellow slip of paper as he filed out the door. The procession passed out of the administration building and, turning to the right, quickly came to the gateway to old inner compound through which Gray and Mrs. Snyder had passed seven months before. A guard at the gate collected the slips of paper. "Single file, gentlemen, please," he murmured as they passed through. It was bitterly cold, and the gravel crunched under their feet as they covered the few yards to the back entrance to the Death House. Dr. Bloom swung himself along on his crutches. On the right was the old Death House, which had been converted into a greenhouse and in season was surrounded by a beautifully landscaped garden.[12] Now, in the dead of winter, it was a bitter remnant of its summer self. On the left stood the outer wall of the prison and, above it, a line of leafless treetops was silhouetted against the illuminated sky.

A door stood open, beaming yellow light, at the end of the walk.

---

11. Warden Lawes had pointedly refused to invite a representative from the *Graphic* to witness the execution.

12. The domain of Charles Chapin, ex-city editor of the *New York World,* who was sentenced in 1918 to twelve years to life for shooting his wife. Among the many privileges that Chapin enjoyed in the supposedly classless Sing Sing was the opportunity to indulge his passion for gardening. Lawes also placed Chapin in charge of his voluminous scrapbooks of newspaper clippings related to all aspects of crime and punishment. In these scrapbooks, which now reside with Lawes's papers at John Jay College in New York, is a newspaper photograph of executioner Elliott. Across his brooding face is drawn in crayon a skull-and-crossbones. "WRETCH! the love of money" runs the clumsily written text below. According to Gauvreau in the embellishment was added by Lawes's nine-year-old daughter, encouraged and counseled on spelling by Chapin.

When they entered it, the men found themselves in a tiny anteroom, where they hung their coats; then they passed with no ceremony into the death chamber itself. This was a roomy place, 30 feet square with a 12-foot ceiling, painted white and brilliantly illuminated by six wall lights. At one end, some 10 feet out from the wall, stood the electric chair on a rubber mat. Against the wall in back of it and looking, if possible, even more menacing, was a high-wheeled gurney cart with a white porcelain top. Elliott stood in his closet in the left corner of the room fiddling with the controls; he peeked out and nodded to one or two acquaintances from previous executions. Just next to the control booth, in the middle of the left-hand wall, was a door leading to the white-tiled autopsy room. The door through which the condemned would enter—not little and green, as legend had it, but wide and of light stained oak—was to the right of the electric chair and just a bit behind it; thus the first sight the condemned had was a slightly oblique view of the chair and, beyond it, of Elliott in his control room. Over this door was an imposing placard bearing one stark word—"Silence."

The witnesses settled into four rows of oak church pews, each accommodating five persons. Anticipating that he might have trouble taking his seat, Dr. Bloom leaned up against the wall. Warden Lawes stood at the back of the room, and blue-coated, brass-buttoned keepers ringed the walls. Prison doctors Sweeney and Goslin stood by the door to the autopsy room, stethoscopes looped around their necks. Goslin sported a dashing white rose in his lapel. The room was crowded: by one count, there were forty-three spectators in all.

Five minutes dragged by after the men settled into their seats, minutes made longer by the infernal hissing and clanging of a steam radiator at the back of the room. P. K. Sheehy glanced at Lawes and slipped out the door. Ten seconds later, he returned, followed by Mrs. Snyder, who was flanked by Matrons Many and Hickey. Father McCaffery, dressed for the occasion in a black cassock and purple stole, followed close behind reciting the Catholic service for the dead.

Mrs. Snyder swayed and leaned heavily on the matrons, but she moved under her own power. Her face was swollen and red from weeping and her hair, still wet from its last-minute shampoo, hung in limp strands around her face. She carried a large crucifix in her left hand. In the event, she wore a black cotton skirt hanging to the knees and over it a voluminous heavy brown smock with white imitation pearl buttons. It was the sort of outfit an artist might wear, or a housewife about to do dirty work.[13] She wore black stockings, one of which had been rolled down to the ankle in order to attach the leg electrode, and felt prison slippers.

"Jesus have mercy upon me, Jesus have mercy upon me," she said shrilly—a child's voice, one reporter wrote—as she was propelled toward the chair. As she sat down, she instinctively pulled her skirt down, but the chair was large and roomy and maneuver was clumsily done: reporters noted that her underwear was blue.

In less than thirty seconds, Sheehy and three guards had attached the straps, and Elliott had dropped to his knee and affixed the leg electrode. Father McCaffery read the prayer of consolation in a muffled voice. The matrons and P. K. Sheehy huddled in front of Mrs. Snyder to shield her as much as possible from the gaze of the witnesses. Elliott placed the football helmet with its electrode over her head and tightened the chin strap. Then he slipped a black leather mask—really just a strip of leather some eight inches wide and twelve inches long with a slit for the nose and mouth so that the prisoner would not be suffocated—over Mrs. Snyder's face and cinched it tight to the head post in back. As he did so, she distinctly said, "Father, forgive them for they know not what they do!" McCaffery administered last rites in a rush and took the crucifix from her. Mrs. Snyder could be heard still repeating, "Jesus have mercy," from under the mask.

13. The smock did more than preserve modesty, just as the woolen suit worn by condemned male prisoners was not just for formality. In hoisting dead prisoners off the electric chair, guards were occasionally burned when they came into contact with bare hot flesh. One guard was rather seriously burned when handling the body of just-executed Frances Creighton, who, having collapsed in her cell, was electrocuted wearing only a thin nightgown in 1936.

There was a loud click as Elliott closed the switch in mid-sentence, and Mrs. Snyder's body surged against the restraints.[14] Five seconds later, Elliott cut down the voltage and her body settled back. McCaffery stopped reading and retired to the right side of the room, where he stared intently at the crucifix Mrs. Snyder had held. Lawes stood, looking at the floor with his arms folded across his chest as if to throw a barrier between himself and the chair. The transformer buzzed steadily and crackled twice, but the sound was almost drowned out by the clanking radiator. Mrs. Snyder's exposed flesh turned brick red and, as her hands reflexively turned inward and clenched, her left forefinger seemed to rise and point accusingly at her own face.

One minute later, Elliott hit her again with the full two thousand volts, and Mrs. Snyder again strained against the straps. White smoke rose from her head as her hair caught fire. Another minute passed and Elliott gave her a third surge. Because he had never executed a woman, he wanted to err on the side of caution.[15] Matron Many, who had turned to the wall, was wracked with sobs. Warden Lawes hurried to her side and, fearing that she was about to collapse, contravened his own order by sending her from the room.

Three minutes after he had turned it on, Elliott switched off the current. P. K. Sheehy stepped forward with Dr. Sweet and removed the helmet and mask. Mrs. Snyder's mouth lolled open in a stupid grin and there was considerable foaming, but mercifully her eyes were shut. Sheehy opened her shirt a few inches and wiped away the sweat from her chest with a towel. Dr. Sweet applied a stethoscope and, as a courtesy, allowed his assistant, Dr. Goslin, to listen as well before he pronounced the woman dead. Two keepers slipped white surgical tunics over their blue coats and began to detach the leg electrode and to unfasten the straps. A

14. Elliott also cut off Gray in mid-sentence. It was better to close the switch when the condemned's lungs were empty, or at least not full, of air. Otherwise, there was a sickening gurgle as the lungs were forcefully emptied.

15. One of the more flagrant and predictable canards about the execution was that Elliott miscalculated the voltage, causing Mrs. Snyder's breasts to explode.

burn mark roughly the size and color of a small eggplant could be seen where the leg electrode had been attached.

Another keeper wheeled up the gurney cart and draped a towel over Mrs. Snyder's legs to prevent any immodest display when she was hoisted from the chair. One of the white-tunicked keepers took Mrs. Snyder under the armpits, the other took her around the knees, and they lifted her onto the cart. As she was wheeled away into the autopsy room, a keeper snatched the towel from Mrs. Snyder's legs and wiped the chair.

While keepers were disposing of Mrs. Snyder, Elliott fished a second set of electrodes out of the bucket of brine and readjusted the dials on his machine. Father McCaffery and Matron Hickey, having discharged their duties, departed and went to comfort Matron Many. The gurney cart reappeared and guards removed their white tunics. Elliott nodded his readiness to P. K. Sheehy, who slipped out the door. It seemed only a few seconds later that the door reopened and Gray was led in.

Between the massive P. K. Sheehy in front and the bulky Reverend Peterson behind, he looked tiny. He was attired in a well-pressed gray pinstriped suit with a generous tug of mauve handkerchief protruding from the pocket. He wore no tie in order to facilitate application of the stethoscope. The right trouser leg, slit up to the knee to accommodate the leg electrode, flapped crazily as he walked. Like Mrs. Snyder, Gray wore felt slippers.

He walked firmly, without support. When Gray sat down in the chair, he creased his trousers at the knees and settled back as if he were about to be served tea. He did not have his glasses on and blinked myopically at reporters. Reverend Peterson, decked out in the magnificent robes that were allowed him as a doctor of divinity, hovered around reciting the Beatitudes as the mask and helmet were put in place. Gray began to intone the Twenty-third Psalm in a guttural voice and no sooner had he started than Elliott hit him with the current.

Gray's death was as uneventful as Mrs. Snyder's, except that Elliott gave him only the usual two shocks. His right sock caught fire in a blaze of blue sparks, and three large curls of white smoke rose from his head. As Gray strained against the straps, he seemed to be trying to look at the ceiling overhead, where stars were visible through a barred skylight. The slit in the mask revealed his mouth to be wide open, and his exposed flesh, like Mrs. Snyder's, was a fiery crimson. When the mask was removed, Gray's eyes were half shut and appeared to have flowed with tears while the current was applied. The guard had some trouble unbuttoning Gray's shirt and finally snapped the button loose with a jerk—it sounded like a pistol shot in the silent room. Gray had gone to his death wearing long johns, and it took another moment to unbutton his undershirt and to wipe away the sweat. Dr. Sweet again stepped forward, listened through his stethoscope, and declared Gray dead.

Lawes raised his head and inclined it silently toward the door through which the witnesses had been admitted. They rose and started out. Mrs. Snyder had entered the room at one minute after eleven and was declared dead five minutes later. Gray had entered at eight minutes after and was declared dead at eleven thirteen. Keepers were just heaving Gray's body onto the gurney cart as the last of the witnesses filed out into the cold night air.

Back in Lawes's office, reporters were told that they were free to go. As they were escorted out the south gate, their names were checked off to make sure that none had stayed behind. Then chaos erupted as they dashed to their cars and careened toward Duck Inn, where open teletype wires waited.

Doctors Sweet and Goslin, meanwhile, set to work in the autopsy room.[16] The papers had been crowing for days about the lovers "sharing

---

16. In a bizarre aspect of the case, Lonardo had earlier that day presented Warden Lawes with a motion signed by Granny Brown and Mrs. Snyder's brother, Andrew, requesting that no autopsy be performed on Mrs. Snyder. Lonardo then contacted a friendly doctor in the vicinity and requested him to wait just up the road from the prison with an ambulance and a massive dose of adrenaline with which to revive his client. Lawes telephoned Ottinger for advice and was instructed to ignore the motion out of hand in light of Section 507 of the Criminal Code, which expressly required that an autopsy be performed on every prisoner who died while in the custody of the State of New York. Lonardo recalled later that he had told Mrs. Snyder of his intentions during their last meeting. She had smiled wanly and shaken her head, saying, "No, that chair kills you." The story received a charming but completely bogus embellishment from Gauvreau in "Thou Shalt Not Kill." According to this, a rumor that Mrs. Snyder was to

their last intimacy on a mortuary slab." Starting with Gray, the bodies were stripped, washed, weighed, and found to be well nourished. The skulls were opened and the brains removed; they were found to be normal. The torsos were opened from throat to abdomen and the organs were found to be normal, with one notable exception: Mrs. Snyder had an enlarged thyroid gland. The autopsies were leisurely and thorough; each took more than an hour.

At four in the morning, after most of the crowd had deserted the prison gates, a black hearse was escorted into Sing Sing by a police car. When the two vehicles emerged five minutes later, the hearse bore Gray's body in a cheap plywood box. It drove down the New York side of the Hudson River, followed by twelve cars filled with bleary-eyed reporters and close to fifty cars belonging to citizens intrepid enough to have waited through the cold night. At the Holland Tunnel, where the procession would cross into New Jersey, the police escort infuriated reporters by suspending traffic through the tunnel, including press vehicles, until the hearse was on the Jersey side. The pressmen drove desperately and managed to catch up just as the hearse reached the Colonial Home Funeral Parlor, ironically housed in the mansion of Edgar Ward, founder of the Prudential Life Insurance Company.

Mrs. Snyder's body left Sing Sing in a gray hearse an hour after Gray's. The only difference was that she received no police escort—to the very end, Gray seems to have gotten the better treatment—and, Gray having already drawn off most of the curiosity seekers, Mrs. Snyder's last journey was a calmer affair. In Yonkers, the driver of the hearse got lost and the entire procession circled the main square three times. Having found his

---

be revived started to make the rounds a few days before the execution. Editors busily calculated how much it would cost to purchase Mrs. Snyder's impressions from the great beyond, and vaudeville producers dreamed of how much they could earn from sending her on a coast-to-coast tour. According to this story, the *Daily Mirror* was so worried about being scooped that it assigned one of its reporters, Ray Doyle, to stay behind after the execution and view Mrs. Snyder's corpse in the autopsy room. "If she's going on stage, then I'm [vaudevillian] Eva Tanguay," Doyle growled as he joined his colleagues outside the Death House.

bearings, the driver went to Grand Concourse Funeral Home in the Bronx, where Mrs. Snyder's body was embalmed and changed into a fancy white dress. Then it was transported in the same hearse to Wood-lawn Cemetery, where it was received by her brother Andrew and placed in a receiving vault pending finalization of burial arrangements. Mrs. Snyder's brother was shaken by the sight of his sister's body and com-plained about the ear-to-ear cut left by the autopsy.[17]

With Mrs. Snyder's burial on hold, it was Gray, for once, who got most of the publicity. At nine o'clock, crowds began to gather on the sidewalks outside the funeral parlor and, by noon, the surrounding streets were mobbed. A detail of a dozen patrolmen was assigned to keep order. At two thirty, a squadron of six police motorcycles drove up to the gate with sirens screaming and escorted in a car containing Mrs. Gray, Mar-garet, her husband, Harold, and Mrs. Isabel Gray. For good measure, there was a second car packed with East Orange plainclothes policemen. The detectives waited outside while the women, their fur collars pulled high up to hide their faces, were shown to the chapel where Gray's em-balmed body lay in a half-open casket.

His hair had been arranged to hide the bald spot as well as possible, and he was dressed in a black suit. The mortician had applied heavy makeup to conceal marks left by the autopsy, and the head had been turned to conceal extensive burns on the right cheek. Between the thick makeup and strange angle of the head, Gray looked like a store man-nequin with a twisted neck. At Mrs. Gray's request, the body was half-smothered with red roses, Gray's favorite flower. The arms were folded across the chest and the right hand grasped a single stem.

The women prayed for several minutes, and Reverend Victor Likens of Trinity Presbyterian Church in South Orange read a short service.

---

17. To examine the brain, a bone saw is used to cut across the forehead just above the eyebrows down to the ears. The scalp is then rolled back to reveal the skull and a second cut is made down from the crown of the head to join the first incision. The front half of the skull can then be removed. When the autopsy is complete, the skull is replaced and the scalp is rolled back down, leaving only an ugly cut across the forehead from ear to ear to indicate what has been done.

When the funeral procession emerged to take the body to Rosedale Cemetery for burial next to Gray's father, there was a serious disturbance. Police motorcycles and the detectives' car slowly forced passage through the crowds surging around the hearse and the two heavily curtained cars that followed it. When finally free, the procession careened wildly through the placid suburban streets, sometimes hitting fifty miles an hour, pursued, of course, by press cars. It was a miracle no pedestrian was hit.

Police had shown up at Rosedale Cemetery at noon to bar spectators, but, by then, it was too late: over three hundred people had entered the grounds during the morning. Since chasing everyone out was beyond question, police contented themselves with setting up rope barriers to keep spectators back from the canvas tent that had been erected to hide the newly dug grave. Less than five minutes from the time the casket was carried into the tent, it was lowered into the grave. As the first spades of earth were strewn over the coffin, Mrs. Isabel Gray collapsed into the arms of her mother-in-law.

It had been raining off and on all day, and when the mourners emerged, it began to pour. Entering the car that had brought them, Gray's widow leaned heavily on her mother-in-law. As the cars passed through the cemetery gates, something striking happened: the skies suddenly cleared and a brilliant rainbow appeared in the east.

THE CASE WAS GOOD for one more convulsion of publicity. As reporters were shown out of Sing Sing, one of them whom the regulars did not know was observed to be limping badly. The defect was even more noticeable because of the ridiculous "collegiate," or bell-bottomed, trousers he was wearing. They were all the rage on campus, but it was unusual to see a pair on anyone much over twenty. The man inside the trousers, Thomas Howard, accredited to the Chicago Tribune News Service, climbed into a powerful Cadillac touring sedan that screeched away from the prison at top speed.

In fact, Howard had not gotten into the Cadillac, which was a decoy car in case state troopers were sent in pursuit of him. He had slipped into the back seat of a modest Ford sedan parked next to it and crouched low as it left the prison. Moaning in pain, he loosened the tight metal strap that attached to his ankle the custom-made one-shot camera that he had used to take a photograph of Mrs. Snyder as Elliott's second blast of electricity passed through her.

The photo plot was long in planning. It had originated with *New York Daily News* publisher Joseph Patterson, who had already attained a circulation of one million, the highest in the world, and was setting his sights even higher. He and his managing editor hit on the death-photo idea. They needed to get a photographer, not a reporter, into the execution chamber, but they knew that if they used a local man, other reporters would know what was up and blow the whistle. Therefore, they imported Howard from Chicago and managed to get him an invitation to the event.

Howard lay low for days in a hotel room, where he spent time prac-

332

ticing with the camera. A long cable ran up his trousers leg into his left pocket, where the shutter could be activated by squeezing a bulb. After discussions with *Daily News* reporters who had attended executions, Howard decided to set the focus for a distance of fifteen to twenty feet and the shutter for an exposure of six seconds. By dint of scrambling, Howard was able to get a seat in the front row of the death chamber and everything went just as planned.

By one o'clock Friday morning a print, enlarged, cropped, and retouched, had been etched onto a zinc plate and the *Daily News* was on the streets with a 40-pica one-word headline over the photo: "DEAD!" For added effect, the exclamation point was set at an audacious oblique slant. The circulation of the *Daily News* shot up to one and a half million on the strength of the picture. It was the largest sale of any single paper on any single day in American history, even more than when Lindbergh landed in Paris.

Howard earned himself a hefty bonus and was sent to Havana on assignment until the heat died down. When some U.S. Marines approached him in a bar, he was sure that the jig was up; that they had come to arrest him. Instead, when they found out who he was, they clapped him on the back and bought him a drink.

Apart from Howard, who was on the run, everyone involved in the execution took a well-deserved rest. Executioner Elliott was shaken and, although he did not collapse, as the tabloids gleefully reported, his physician gave him sedatives. The crisis was of short duration—Saturday morning, reporters found him placidly adjusting the carburetor of his car in Richmond Hill.

Warden Lawes had hardly gotten to bed before he was roused to deal with a crisis. Mrs. Snyder's last admirer, Death House cook "Dummy" Dugan, had taken her death badly, and keepers discovered him roaring drunk on distilled prune juice, methodically destroying the Death House kitchen. It took two keepers and all of Lawes's skills as a negotiator to restrain the rampaging cook, and it was dawn by the time the warden finally made it back to bed. He slept until noon, whereupon he departed with his family for Palm Beach, saying that he had never been under a greater strain in his life.

Both matrons who had witnessed the execution were upset. Mrs. Lillian Hickey broke their long silence to tell reporters that Mrs. Snyder had been a perfect lady, no bother at all, and had been more interested in listening to the matrons' problems than complaining about her own.

Granny Brown was good for two days of headlines; thus, under the subhead "PHYSICIANS WAGING DESPERATE BATTLE FOR HER LIFE," readers of the *Evening Journal* learned: "Physicians vainly sought an antidote for grief, but no medical prescription, they found, could cure a tortured mind. The wax-like body seemed already to have withdrawn from life. Andrew Brown, his wife and other members of the family strove to revive the tired woman, but she looked at them out of sunken orbs of misery. The thing they feared had come—a deadening reaction from an appalling tragedy."

In fact, Granny Brown bore up as well as could be expected. The day after the execution, she remarked, "Well—perhaps it was better that Ruth died."

There were no follow-up stories about Mrs. Margaret Gray's reaction. The press took it on faith that her years of breeding allowed her to keep a stiff upper lip and wrote it up that way. Mrs. Isabel Gray, was, as usual, incommunicado.

Reporters were still game, if tired, but their editors discovered a strange thing: the public no longer cared about the case. After the tear-jerkers about Granny Brown's health and much pompous introspection about the execution photo, there was nothing more to say. None of the Sunday editions even bothered to recap the case; all the papers had done that ad nauseam in the days leading up to the execution. When Mrs. Snyder was laid to rest in Woodlawn on Wednesday, no one even bothered to cover the event. So the readers, too, got a well-deserved rest.

APPENDIXES

SOURCES

ACKNOWLEDGMENTS

INDEX

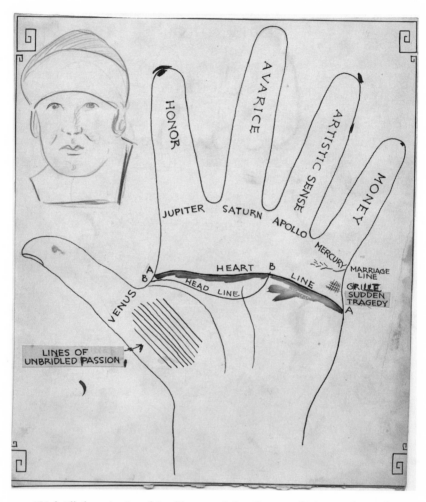

"Unbridled passion" and *"sudden tragedy"*—*diagram of Mrs. Snyder's palm*

APPENDIX A Lingering Questions

DAMON RUNYON REFERRED to the Snyder-Gray homicide as "The Dumbbell Murder—it was that dumb," for which there is abundant evidence. There seems little doubt that substantial justice was rendered according to the standards of the time. Yet several tantalizing aspects of the case bear looking at.

What really happened the night of 19 March 1927?

I think Gray essentially told the truth.

Gray's defense never really recovered from Dr. Howard Neail's forensic testimony that there were no signs of the struggle that Gray had said took place. Gray relied on this story to support his contention that he dropped the sash weight and that Mrs. Snyder picked it up and struck her husband. Miller and Millard's failure to elicit at least that the corpus delicti was consistent with Gray's story of a struggle was a colossal blunder.

Neail made much, in his testimony, of the fact that Albert Snyder's pajamas and the sheets under his body were not rumpled. But a competent cross-examination would have honed in on the scrapes and bruises on Albert Snyder's neck, face and hands. The five abrasions on the right side of the neck and the two on the left side were probably inflicted by the fingers and thumb of Gray's left hand as he held off Snyder while wielding the sash weight with his right hand. The gouge on the left side of Snyder's nose may have been inflicted by Gray's thumb as he groped for a purchase. Minor scrapes of the sort reported on Snyder's hands are common in victims involved in hand-to-hand combat at the time of their deaths. There was more evidence of a struggle on the inside of Snyder's mouth, where there was a contusion on the inner cheek opposite the upper left third, fourth, and fifth teeth. This is precisely the type of injury that would arise if Gray had held Snyder off with his left hand as described above, punching at him with his right after he dropped the sash weight.

But was Albert Snyder too drunk to fight? Alexander Gettler stated in a later interview *(Collier's,* 6 October 1945) that Albert Snyder was "practically comatose" when he was assaulted, concluding from this that Gray's story of a struggle was false. Snyder's blood blood alcohol content (BAC) was 0.3 percent. A BAC of 0.1 percent is sufficient today to establish drunk driving; 0.4 percent is commonly associated with death due to respiratory paralysis. Contrary to his wife's testimony, Snyder was staggering, passing-out drunk when he died.

On the other hand, heavy drinkers like Snyder can develop a physiological, biochemical, and pharmacological tolerance to alcohol and can function at a very high BAC. Snyder had, after all, managed to drive home and get himself to bed. Nevertheless, alcohol was certainly a contributing factor in Snyder's death. Drunk, stunned, bound hand and foot, his mouth and nose jammed into a chloroform-soaked rag with blankets piled over his head, Snyder was a dead man with or without the strangulation that Neail found to be the actual cause of death.

Bolstering Gray's version of events is the fact that under cross-examination, Mrs. Snyder's story of having given the sash weight back to him collapsed about as completely as it is possible for testimony to collapse without the witness issuing an outright retraction.

For reference, the passage in Mrs. Snyder's statement reads: "When I went into my mother's room, Mr. Gray had the window weight which I was shown in the District Attorney's office. I had brought the window weight up from the cellar that afternoon, March 19th, 1927 to have it all ready for Gray. These details were all arranged during the week in the correspondence between myself and Mr. Gray."

Gray's statement reads: "When I got to the house the implements were under the mother's pillow. She had put them there and instructed me to find them there, together with liquor. She wrote that to me. The implements referred to were the sash weight, a pair of pliers and a small bottle. These implements were under her mother's pillow. She had written me all about the plans and what I was to do."

The matter of the sash weight was crucial to Mrs. Snyder's defense. It was bad enough that she had left the doors open for Gray, knowing his murderous intent, but she hoped to squeak by on the strength of her claim that she thought she could dissuade him. Add to this that she had also concealed the murder weapon as previously arranged and Mrs. Snyder's story lost all credibility.

Mrs. Snyder boxed herself even further in by her insistence that she had done absolutely nothing wrong. She would have done herself little harm by admitting that, fearing for her life, she had helped Gray arrange the cover-up. As it was, she insisted that she sat in her mother's room for some two hours doing nothing at all. This beggars the imagination.

Did Mrs. Snyder attempt to murder her husband before the night of 19 March 1927?

By the time he finished testifying, Gray had listed over six attempts on Snyder's life: putting sleeping powders in his prune whip, taking him whiskey in the garage while he was working on the car in hopes that he would pass out and die from carbon monoxide poisoning, giving him bichloride of mercury when he had the hiccoughs, doctoring his whiskey with bichloride of mercury in various doses on several occasions, and twice kicking off or removing the gas tube while Snyder took a nap; first in July 1926 and again in January 1927.

If the question is whether she seriously tried to murder him, I think the answer must be no. Bringing someone a drink while he is working on his car in the garage must surely qualify as one of the lamest homicide attempts in the annals of crime history. Other episodes, particularly the two gas incidents, appear to be more serious attempts, and there is corroborative evidence in the form of the anecdotes related by Snyder's relatives. However, even these episodes have a distinctly unrealistic air. Let us paraphrase Edward G. Robinson's outburst in the film *Double Indemnity*: in the long history of homicides, by shooting, stabbing, slashing, beating with blunt instruments, poisoning, strangulation, pushing from high places, and so on, how many murders have been committed by turning on the gas while someone took a nap?

What about the alleged attempted poisonings? These fell into two groups, those involving "sleeping powders or so-called sleeping powders," as Gray described them in his confession, and those involving bichloride of mercury. Barbiturates were developed in the nineteenth century; if the "sleeping powders" were such compounds, then a dose administered in conjunction with the whiskey that Albert Snyder consumed heavily would have been an effective murder weapon. So effective that the sleeping powders used by Mrs. Snyder, if any were in fact used, must have been over-the-counter compounds, probably bromides. Even in the 1920s, it was rare to dispense prescription drugs, but not over-the-counter drugs, in powder form.

The evidence of the poisoned whiskey, together with Gray's statement and testimony, strongly suggest that Mrs. Snyder did have at least one poison, bichloride of mercury, in the house, but so, probably, did half the housewives on the block. Bichloride of mercury was commonly kept in household medicine cabinets in the form of tablets stamped "POISON," which, when dissolved in water, produced a solution that could be used as an antiseptic or disinfectant ("mercurochrome").

The compound certainly passes clinical muster as a deadly poison: once ingested and broken down, mercury concentrates in the liver and kidneys and death follows in one day to two weeks as a consequence of renal failure. But a single dose large enough to cause death would likely be vomited right back up, and a series of small doses would usually cause an array of symptoms (metallic taste, thirst, vomiting, and bloody diarrhea) sufficiently alarming to send the victim to a doctor. Bichloride of mercury is a highly unlikely poison; I can think of only one notable American homicide in which it was the weapon.[1]

1. In 1925, David Stephenson, the politically ambitious grand dragon of the Indiana Ku Klux Klan, kidnapped, raped, and brutalized a young woman named Madge Ober-

In view of these inconsistencies, I would suggest that those murder attempts which did take place were playacting—that Mrs. Snyder was toying with the idea of murder, rather than seriously attempting it. All the murder attempts, both those Mrs. Snyder halfheartedly carried out and those she did not, were reported to Gray in order to inflame him and to implicate him emotionally in her desire to get rid of Albert Snyder. I draw this interpretation in part from Filson Young's introduction to his *Trial of Frederick Bywaters and Edith Thompson* (Edinburgh: Hodge, 1923), the notorious English case of 1922 that has some parallels with the Snyder-Gray case.

Did Mrs. Snyder intend to poison Gray after he had killed Albert Snyder? Did she intend to frame him?

I think the likely answer to the first question is no. Millard's theory that Mrs. Snyder tried to poison Gray with the whiskey left underneath the pillow is ridiculous. As Gray testified, the arrangement for the evening was that the sash weight, a pair of pliers, and a bottle of whiskey were to be hidden under Granny Brown's pillow. If Mrs. Snyder had wanted to keep a bottle of poisoned whiskey in reserve for Gray, she would never have put it under the pillow. Had she done so, she would have run the risk of arriving home from the party to find a retching Gray desperately ill on her mother's bedroom floor. The most likely explanation is that a quart bottle of whiskey is difficult to hide under a pillow, and Mrs. Snyder would have been hard pressed to explain it away if Albert Snyder noticed something lumpy under his mother-in-law's pillow.

Having promised to leave some whiskey under the pillow, Mrs. Snyder placed the small bottle there. On reflection, she realized that this would not go far toward satisfying Gray's thirst, so she put on the dresser the quart bottle of Tom Dawson that she had purchased for her party. If

---

halzer, who in her despair swallowed bichloride of mercury and kept it down. She died in agony seventeen days later, having accused Stephenson in a deathbed statement. The trial, which resulted in a second-degree murder conviction and a life sentence, effectively marked the end of the Klan as a political force in Indiana.

Albert Snyder had asked what it was doing there, she could easily have made up some excuse.

As to Millard's claim that taking a few swigs of Tom Dawson could counteract the effect of the poisoned whiskey in the small bottle, in all of toxicology, there is no poison for which whiskey is the antidote. Perhaps the small bottle contained bad bootleg whiskey that made Gray sick. Alternatively, Gray's sudden dizziness after draining the small bottle might have just been a panic attack.

If Mrs. Snyder did not poison the whiskey under the pillow, then what about the poisoned whiskey found in Gray's possession? According to Gray in *Doomed Ship,* he himself prepared the deadly potion after returning to Syracuse, presumably using the bichloride of mercury tablets that Mrs. Snyder had given him when he left the house. While relating his troubles to Haddon Gray and Harry Platt, he flourished the bottle and threatened to drink it, but they dissuaded him.

On the train to New York, again according to *Doomed Ship,* Gray complained of a sore throat and asked if he might take some throat medicine. He opened his suitcase, produced the bottle from a sock, and moved toward the washroom. McDermott, sensing something in Gray's demeanor, took the bottle and said, "Hey, you know, I have a cold, too! Let me have some." "My God!" said Gray. "Don't drink that, it's poison!" The problem here is that McDermott makes no reference to this episode in his otherwise comprehensive detective's notebook.

Another version reports that while Gray, McDermott, and Brown were sitting in the diner across from Jamaica Precinct House, one of the detectives joked, "Hey, Judd! We found that whiskey in your bag! Looks like good stuff, too!" whereupon Gray warned them not to drink it because it was poisoned.

These stories, although unconfirmed, remind us that there are many possible explanations for the poisoned whiskey. A straightforward one is that Mrs. Snyder gave it to him when he left: "Here, take this. It is poisoned whiskey. Make sure you don't drink it."

Even though Millard may have been wrong about Mrs. Snyder's intention to poison Gray, I think he may have been on to something when he claimed in his closing address that Mrs. Snyder planted Gray's gold pencil in order to implicate him. Recall that police found one length of picture wire wrapped around Snyder's neck and a second length, with the pencil attached, hidden beneath the body. If Gray had used the pencil as a turn stick to garrotte the already unconscious Snyder, as Mrs. Snyder claimed, the pencil would have been found entangled in the wire around Albert Snyder's neck. Gray maintained in his statement that Mrs. Snyder carried the picture wire (as well as the chloroform) with her into the bedroom and threw everything "into" (he means "onto") the bed when Snyder rose up and started to struggle. According to this version, then, the pencil was already clipped to the wire, ready to ready to serve as a turn stick. It seems likely that Gray would have remembered an operation so complicated as preparing a garrotte. All in all, I would not put it above Mrs. Snyder to have extracted Gray's pencil from his jacket pocket while he was otherwise occupied and planted it beneath Albert Snyder's body.

Was there an insurance motive?

"Once it popped into Ruth's bird brain that by insuring Mr. Snyder she could make him support her *in absentia,* his days were numbered," wrote Alexander Woolcott. Yet Gray swore to his dying day (in *Doomed Ship* and elsewhere) that insurance was never a motive. In *Meet the Murderer!* Warden Lewis Lawes reports that Mrs. Snyder paced her cell muttering, "Divorce was impossible," and gives his opinion that what Mrs. Snyder desperately wanted was her freedom.

However, the weight of evidence is crushing: the irregularity with which Snyder's policies were obtained, the burden of the insurance payments (which consumed over one-sixth of Albert Snyder's gross salary and close to one-fourth of Mrs. Snyder's household allowance), the omission of these payments from the otherwise complete household ledger, the peculiar arrangement with the postman regarding delivery of mail from the Prudential, the storage of the insurance policies in Mrs. Snyder's personal safe deposit box rather than the one she jointly held with her husband, the jotted calculations of the income she would receive in the event of Albert Snyder's death by misadventure. Mrs. Snyder may never have told Gray about the insurance, and it may have been a secondary factor in her calculations, but it seems inescapable that when Leroy Ashcroft rang the doorbell in November 1925, Mrs. Snyder was, as Woolcott put it, making plans for life after Albert Snyder.

An obvious source of insight into the insurance angle is *Prudential Life Insurance Company v. Snyder et al.,* tried at the end of October 1928 by New York Supreme Court Justice Jeremiah Mahoney. Unfortunately, the case was a nonevent. Granny Brown swore Snyder knew all about the insurance. Ashfield admitted that he traced Snyder's signature onto the form requesting that the original application for one policy be changed to an application for two policies, but denied that he intended to commit fraud. Asked why he didn't go back and ask Snyder to sign the amendment form himself, Ashfield was hesitant in answering. "I wasn't sure how much he knew about it."

In finding in favor of the Prudential, Justice Mahoney had it both ways. Snyder may have been duped into thinking he was signing for a small policy in duplicate, wrote Mahoney; on the other hand, he may have known exactly what he was doing. In either case, the subsequent irregularity on Ashfield's part—tracing Snyder's signature onto the amendment form—rendered the policy null and void. There had been no meeting of the minds; therefore, there was no and had never been any insurance contract.

Did Gray suffer from diminished responsibility?

Gray's "love slave" defense appears rather fatuous today. To begin with, his assertion that he never drank heavily until he fell under Mrs. Snyder's thrall, a claim that went over well with his psychiatrists and with contemporary authors such as Kobler, rings false. Alcoholic capacity on the scale of Gray's is not developed overnight. Today we are more attuned to the practically limitless ability of alcoholics (particularly those who frequently travel) to hide their drinking from friends and family until some event, such as a fall or car accident, betrays their secret. Mrs. Isabel Gray had objected to Gray coming home from business entertainment with liquor on his breath long before he met Mrs. Snyder. Did he have more than one drink when he met Mrs. Snyder at Henry's Restaurant? asked his counsel Samuel Miller. "I imagine so, I generally always did" was the reply. More than two? "I wouldn't be surprised."

That Mrs. Snyder was in control of the relationship is not to be denied, but this is a far cry from the sort of master-slave relationship that Gray described on the witness stand. Based on Gray's childhood, his crushing Oedipus complex, his line of goods, and the outlines of his relationship with Mrs. Snyder, it seems plausible that he was secretly homosexual. There is no proof of this, however. The psychiatric report on Gray has disappeared and only fragments survive. In one of these, Dr. Thomas Cusack wrote, "Gray is very effeminate because of his unusual dependence on his mother." Asked what attracted him to women, Gray told the psychiatrists, "I am drawn to women not by physical charm so much as by neatness and intelligence."

What comes across most clearly in Gray's statement and testimony is that he was effete, eager to please, and unable to say no; someone who could easily find himself on a slippery slope. In February 1926, Mrs. Snyder told him she was thinking of doing away with her husband. "I told her I thought she was awful." In March, she showed him poison she was keeping around the house. "I told her it was dangerous." In September, Mrs. Snyder told him about putting sleeping powders in her husband's prune whip and turning on the gas while he napped. "I told her she was crazy." By November, she began pestering him to obtain chloral hydrate; by February 1927, she was asking him to shoot her husband. In late February or early March, Gray took a step too far when he promised to obtain chloroform for Mrs. Snyder. From that point on, Mrs. Snyder's demands rapidly escalated, culminating in the brutal events of 19 March.

In addition to comments quoted above, one extended comment from Gray's psychiatric examination remains, this one written by Dr. Siegfried Block:

Henry Judd Gray's lack of experience in love affairs and in dealing with women who may be described as ultra-worldly were contributing elements toward the downfall which has placed him in the shadow of the electric chair. His deterioration from a keen-minded, alert young businessman to the weakling possessed of a cringing inferiority complex was the distinct result of associations with Ruth Snyder—superinduced by the over-indulgence in bootleg liquor which the woman encouraged.

Gray recounts, in *Doomed Ship*, that, while he was explaining how Mrs. Snyder dominated him, one psychiatrist asked, "Gray, don't you consider yourself just a plain damned fool?" An even better story, related by the psychiatrists and referred to by Millard in his closing argument to the jury and by Hazelton in the clemency hearing, has a member of the team placing his hand on Gray's shoulder and intoning: "My boy, if you had consulted a psychiatrist, you would not find yourself in this situation."

What of the psychiatrists' mysteriously aborted offer to support a reduced charge of second-degree murder? The true story will never be known, but I have a theory. The psychiatrists communicated to Miller and Millard their unanimous opinion that, despite being legally sane, Gray suffered from diminished capacity. "Why, then we should offer to plead guilty to murder in the second degree!" exclaimed counsel. Off went Miller and Millard to District Attorney Newcombe, who heard them out. Newcombe then briefed Justice Scudder fully, including the psychiatric angle, presumably expressing hostility to the reduced charge.

Scudder was an old-school patrician who had done everything possible to avoid this sensational trial and the attendant publicity. Newcombe's opinion aside, the last thing Scudder wanted at this time (recall that he was being touted as a favorite to run for Governor on the Democratic ticket) was to be associated with neuroses, psychoses, complexes, "erotomania," "excessive intercourse," and gin-soaked "abnormal desires." The record would read like *Psychopathia Sexualis*; there would be even more controversy than there had been over the Leopold–Loeb case.

Why, then, did Gray's attorneys not call the psychiatrists to testify to Gray's state of mind? When Governor Smith pointedly asked this question at the clemency hearing, Gray's attorneys had no answer. One possibility is incompetence; the other—and I think more likely—is that they discussed this strategy with Gray, who rejected it. Gray, after all, was in the throes of a religious rebirth and deeply convinced that his troubles were due to having left the true path, a version rather different than the one that the psychiatrists would present—not to mention what they might say about his relationship with his mother. If this version of events is true, then in a sense, Gray committed judicial suicide in order to keep up appearances. This would also explain why Miller and Millard were reluctant to take the lead in breaking the story.

Did Mrs. Snyder suffer from diminished responsibility?

Almost all the newspapers arranged for phrenologists, psychics, preachers, palm readers, and the like to examine photographs of the accused and expound on what they saw. Most, not surprisingly, divined that Mrs. Snyder exploded with animal lust and that Gray lacked moral strength. The *American,* happily, had the sense to enlist a medical doctor, and he made an interesting observation: judging from a photograph made some years before the murder, Mrs. Snyder suffered from a goiter, or enlargement of the thyroid gland, at the base of the throat. Another photograph from 1926 clearly reveals the same condition. When Mrs. Snyder's body was dissected following her execution, Sing Sing physician Charles Sweet noted that Mrs. Snyder's thyroid gland was enlarged.

Enlargement of the thyroid gland is usually caused by hyperthyroidism, in which thyroid stimulating hormone (TSH) is overproduced, causing the gland to grow beyond its normal size. It is more properly known as Graves' disease, after the nineteenth-century Irish physician who first described it. Graves' disease , the most common endocrine disorder, is most often found in women aged thirty to fifty. Today, some 2 percent of women in this age group suffer from the condition; the percentage was much higher in 1927 before the introduction of iodized salt.

Among the symptoms of Graves' disease are excitability, nervousness, sweating, diarrhea in varying degrees, weight loss despite strong appetite, changes in menstrual patterns, and rapid pulse (Arthur C. Guyton and John E. Hall, *Textbook of Medical Physiology*, 10th ed., Philadelphia: W. B. Saunders, 865ff.)

More than half, but not all, hyperthyroid patients exhibit the exophthalamia (bulging eyeballs) that is the most dramatic manifestation of the condition. Mrs. Snyder did not.

Among the symptoms of Graves' disease that Mrs. Snyder *did* exhibit are

1. missed menstrual periods, to such an extent that she wondered aloud to Gray whether she was undergoing menopause;

2. a tendency to break out in sweats; observers noted in court that her skin turned red, that she sweated profusely, and that she mopped her face incessantly; this is, of course, not unknown among defendants on trial for their lives;

3. palpitations of the heart ("pounding heart"), about which she complained to Gray;

4. nervous agitation, depression, and neurosis; and

5. prodigious appetite, a point on which all reports agree; she was known to consume half a roast chicken and spaghetti at one sitting (complaining that the spaghetti did not have enough sauce) and to drink a quart of milk a day.

It is possible that Mrs. Snyder's inability to tolerate moderate amounts of alcohol was related to the metabolic acceleration associated with Graves' disease. The disease could also explain her evident ability, night after night, to engage in sex until two and three in the morning and to then rise and shine after a few hours' sleep.

According to Alfred M. Freedman and Harold I. Kaplan (*Comprehensive Textbook of Psychiatry*, Baltimore: Williams and Wilkins, 1967), although there is no proof, there is "widespread agreement" that "prolonged tensions and chronic emotional stresses" may precipitate Graves' disease. Psychological and emotional "causes," using the term loosely, are observed in about 80 percent of all cases. Based on extensive surveys of patients, the psychoanalytic theory of the etiology of the disease is as follows:

There is in childhood an unusual emotional attachment and dependence on a parent, usually the mother, and any threat to this protection
or approval is found intolerable. Often there is inadequate support
given to the patient as a child because of economic stress, divorce,
death, or multiple siblings. The persistent threat to security in early life
leads to unsuccessful and premature attempts to identify with the object of dependence and cravings. Because of this failure, the patient
continuously strives towards premature self-sufficiency and tends to
dominate others by smothering attention and affection. There is a need
for the patient to build defenses against a repetition of the unbearable
feelings of rejection and isolation that occurred in childhood. Should
these break down, the condition may result.

The information we have on Mrs. Snyder's childhood, at least as she
reported it, her smothering of Gray with maternal affection, and her
"Tommy" persona—the zany bleached blonde who was on a first-name
basis with every man in the neighborhood—are all consistent with the
passage above.

Graves' disease is easily treated; most patients respond to medica-
tion and suffer no relapse. A combination of psychotherapeutic drugs to
treat agitation and anxiety and psychotherapy to address underlying neuroses may be indicated; in serious cases, the thyroid can be surgically
removed.

Although it provides an interesting medical and psychological footnote, Mrs. Snyder's thyroid gland is of no legal relevance. However un-
pleasant the condition, suffering from Graves' disease would not have
been a reasonable legal defense in 1927 (much less today) to bludgeoning,
chloroforming, and strangling an unlikable husband.

Was Mrs. Snyder's confession coerced or "doctored" so it would dovetail with Gray's?

Most people would be amazed at the liberties that police are permitted to
take with suspects prior to their formal arrest—not informing them of
their right to see a lawyer, lying to them ("Once we clear up a few ques-

tions, we can all go home . . ."), and so on. As a criminal lawyer friend once advised me, "If the police ever tell you they just want to clear up a few questions, get a lawyer . . . they have already decided to arrest you."

Mrs. Snyder's treatment in custody seems to have been reasonably proper given the wide discretion that police are allowed. Assistant District Attorney Daly testified that Mrs. Snyder signed her statement at eight o'clock on Monday evening after a long nap. Gray did not arrive in New York until some four hours later. It is just possible that someone who had heard Gray's confession on the train descended and telephoned New York with the particulars, but this seems unlikely. After all, Police Commissioner McLaughlin testified that Mrs. Snyder's signed statement was substantially the same as the oral confession she had made to him.

Yet it is undeniable that Newcombe's staff used wide editorial discretion when, at Mrs. Snyder's request (according to Daly) they reduced the fifty-two page transcript of her oral statement (which has disappeared) to the eight-page document that she later signed. This, in and of itself, is not troublesome. The idea in taking a statement is not to produce a verbatim document, but rather a coherent text by which all parties are willing to stand. Moreover, Mrs. Snyder kept changing her story as she spoke. For example, at the beginning, she said she had gone downstairs after her husband was asleep and let Gray in; later, she stated that Gray had been waiting in the house.

The result of the editorial intervention is that in her statement Mrs. Snyder was held on a shorter leash than Gray, whose statement, however precise Police Commissioner McLaughlin found it to be, shifts backward and forward in time and is filled with excursions, asides, and background information. This contrasts with Mrs. Snyder's statement, which is strictly linear and all business, reading as if it were written by a prosecutor, which it more or less was.

Was the joint trial fair?

The New York State Court of Appeals unanimously found Justice Scudder's decision judicially correct. One defendant had demanded a separate trial, the other had just as vociferously demanded a joint trial, and the judge had not known for certain what their respective defenses would be. Scudder was in possession of the confessions, which did not substantially conflict with each other. He was free to believe the confessions—each of which was sufficient to condemn the person making it—so long as he did not share his opinion with the jury. Legally speaking, then, Justice Scudder was entitled to hold a joint trial. In the broader sense, however, this decision placed Mrs. Snyder at a severe disadvantage, as discussed above. "Much law, little justice," runs the old saying. Be that as it may, the fact remains that Mrs. Snyder effectively condemned herself in her confession and testimony, which failed to withstand cross-examination.

As the "Prisoner's Dilemma" from game theory reminds us, the best strategy for Mrs. Snyder and Gray in the joint trial would have been for *both* defendants to stay off the witness stand and to repudiate their respective confessions. The lawyer for defendant A could then stand before the jury and say simply, "If you believe A's confession, then A is guilty. A claims that this confession was obtained under duress and is not true. It is up to you to decide whether to believe this. Do not trouble yourself, as regards my client, with whether you accept the confession of defendant B. As the judge will instruct you, that confession may not be considered as evidence against A."

The lawyer for B would do the same, leaving the jury with a strong temptation to wash its hands of the matter by letting the pair off on a reduced charge. At the very worst, Governor Smith might have been able to point to confusion that justified commuting the sentences of both defendants—for if one defendant was entitled to mercy, then assuredly they both were.

Perhaps this is the logic that led to a comment made by a member of District Attorney Newcombe's office under condition of anonymity after the verdicts came in: "The biggest mistake the defendants made was taking the stand. The best the State could have hoped for if they'd stayed off the stand would have been guilty of murder in the second degree. The state's case was made puncture-proof when they became witnesses."

Mrs. Snyder's problem was that Gray was determined to do public penance on the witness stand. This appears evident even in his choice of counsel. Why on earth fire James Hallinan, a first-rate criminal lawyer (as witnessed by his later election as Queens County district attorney and eventual accession to the New York Supreme Court), in favor of general practitioner Samuel Miller? Perhaps because Hallinan would take the case only if he was allowed to fight aggressively, something Gray was unwilling to let him do.

Should Mrs. Snyder have stayed off the stand anyway, daring the jury to believe the calumnies her codefendant heaped upon her? In hindsight, the answer is yes. Nothing could have been worse than her disastrous testimony.

The burial of Judd Gray, Rosedale Cemetery,
East Orange, New Jersey, 13 January 1928

Dispositions

People

Granny Brown did, as her daughter had hoped, buy a plot in Woodlawn Cemetery, where **Ruth Snyder** is buried under a stone engraved "May R. Brown." After the execution, Granny Brown lived in the Bronx, first with her son, Andrew, and daughter-in-law on Woodycrest Avenue, then later by herself on Mahon Street. She died at home of heart disease at six A.M. on 11 October 1939 (surviving executioner Robert Elliott by less than twenty-four hours) and took her place in the family plot. Last to arrive were **Andrew Brown** and his wife, Margaret, who died in 1970 and 1975, respectively.

When, in 1951, Mrs. Mamie Thake, Albert Snyder's sister, ordered a stone to mark her recently deceased husband's grave in the Schneider family plot in Mount Olivet Cemetery, she also ordered a second stone, engraved simply "Brother," for the unmarked grave of **Albert Snyder**. The stone is almost buried by shrubs, which look as if they were planted for that purpose. Perhaps she was still concerned about curiosity seekers. Mrs. Thake and Miss Mabel Schneider, who died in the 1970s, are buried in the same plot; the other Schneider siblings found their final resting places elsewhere.

Judd Gray is buried in a neat, modestly marked grave in the family plot in Rosedale Cemetery. His family, exhausted emotionally by grief and financially by the combination of legal fees and the Depression, kept a low profile. His sister, **Margaret,** swore that she would devote the rest of her life to fighting capital punishment, but she had little of it left: she died prematurely, in 1936, and joined her brother in the Gray family plot. The indomitable **Mrs. Margaret Gray** moved away from the Oranges, eventually dying in Metuchen, New Jersey, in 1947, at the age of eighty-one. She is buried, naturally, next to the boy she loved. Brother-in-law **Harold Logan** is not in the Gray family plot: having been widowed in his forties, he presumably made a new life for himself.

"Life insurance," Gray reported he once told Mrs. Snyder, "is a good investment for a family man." So it proved in his case, for, on the day following his death, **Mrs. Isabel Gray** received a check for twenty-five thousand dollars from the Union Life Insurance Company of Cincinnati. What with the life insurance, about seven thousand dollars in stocks and bonds, and equity in the house in East Orange, which proved easy to sell, she was left in comfortable circumstances. She stayed in Norwalk, where she lived quietly and raised her daughter, Jane. She took an active part in the Grace Episcopal Church, leading its Women's Guild from 1948 to 1956. There was a rumor in 1930 that she was to be remarried, and an even stronger one in 1934, but both proved to be false. She died after a short illness in 1957, aged sixty-five. Her protector, **Frank T. Brundage,** died suddenly at his Florida home in 1955.

Lorraine Snyder and **Jane Gray** grew up, married, and lived uneventful lives. I refrain from saying more to protect their privacy.

A few months after the trial, **Townsend Scudder** was remarried, to a woman twenty years his junior. The couple moved to Round Hill Road in Greenwich, Connecticut. He remained a force to reckon with on Long Island and was associated with Robert Moses in the development of Jones Beach, where a memorial to him stands. In the 1930s, Scudder became embroiled in a three-year legal dispute, which he won, with the Town of Greenwich over his right to keep dogs. In 1955, on the occasion of his ninetieth birthday, Scudder reminisced in a *New York Times* interview that Gray "had the appearance of a divinity-school student," whereas Mrs. Snyder was "loud, frivolous, and coarse." Scudder died in 1960, at the age of ninety-five, having only the year before sold his last twenty dogs when he could no longer take care of them.

Richard Newcombe was elected Surrogate of Queens County in 1929, an office he held for only thirty days before dying prematurely of a heart attack. His assistant district attorneys—"Newcombe's Boys," they called themselves—continued to meet annually in his honor. There is a small square in Uniondale named "Newcombe Square"; this contains a simple granite monument erected in his memory in 1939. Newcombe's photograph hangs in Queens County Surrogate's Court.

Peter Daly became city magistrate, then a justice of the City Court; in 1936, he was elected to the New York State Supreme Court, where he sat until a year before his death in 1967, at the age of seventy-five.

In 1937, **Charles Froessel** was elected to the New York State Supreme Court; in 1949, he was elected to the New York State Court of Appeals. One year before retiring in 1962, he voted with the majority to clear the way for construction of the World Trade Center in lower Manhattan. In 1968, Governor Nelson Rockefeller asked Froessel, then seventy-five years old, to come out of retirement to head a commission appointed to study New York's restrictive abortion law. After the public hearings, New York adopted the least restrictive abortion law in the nation. His passions were Freemasonry (he became grandmaster mason within New York State), the Boy Scouts, and big-game hunting. He died in 1982, at the age of eighty-nine.

Dana Wallace refused his share of the fund for Mrs. Snyder's defense, giving it to Granny Brown for the support of Lorraine. In 1930, Wallace's wife of twenty-nine years, Estelle, sued him for divorce, citing his excessive drinking. Wallace ran for the office of district attorney on the Republican ticket in the same year, but was beaten by James Hallinan, Gray's first lawyer. After again injuring his shoulder in yet another automobile accident, Wallace sought the Republican nomination in 1932, but failed to collect enough signatures to be put on the ballot. In 1937, Wallace was suspended from the bar for one year as a result of his connection to an ambulance-chasing scandal; he supported himself that year by taking out fishing parties on his boat. In ever poorer health since the 1940s, he died in 1951, at the age of seventy-five, survived by Estelle, with whom he had patched things up some ten years before.

Edgar Hazelton, hungry for political success and finding none in Queens, moved to Suffolk County soon after the trial. He installed himself and his family in the Northport house that had been occupied by Jimmie Walker, the disgraced former mayor of New York City, following his return from exile in Europe. From 1937 to 1950, Hazelton was Suffolk County attorney; from 1951 to 1960, Suffolk County surrogate. He died in the early 1960s.

After their moments of fame during the Snyder-Gray trial, the other defense lawyers faded into relative obscurity. **Samuel Miller** never recovered from the tragedy of losing both the case and his friend Judd Gray. In failing health, he gradually withdrew from practice. He died in 1957, at the age of sixty-four. **William Millard,** apparently bearing no grudge, managed the 1928 Bronx campaign of **Albert Ottinger** against Franklin Roosevelt for the governor's seat. In 1932, he defected to the Democrats and supported Roosevelt for president. Millard died in 1939, at the age of sixty-six. **Joseph Lonardo**'s most notorious client after Mrs. Snyder was German-American Bund leader Fritz Kuhn, whose appeal on charges of sedition Lonardo unsuccessfully argued in 1939. In 1953, toward the end of his career, Lonardo became a member of the Supreme Court Bar. He died in Queens in the early 1960s.

Continuing his stormy tenure, New York State Supreme Court Justice **Aaron Levy** presided over two cases involving the failed Bank of the United States in 1929. Not until five months into the second case did he disqualify himself on the grounds that he owed over one hundred forty thousand dollars to the bank. Shortly after retiring from the bench in

1951, he was called before the New York State Crime Commission to explain, among other things, why he had turned over the administrative operations of his court to his son-in-law. "I didn't trust my own employees," replied the imperturbable jurist. Levy died of a heart attack in 1955.

The policemen in the case did well. **Michael McDermott** became embroiled in a departmental dispute that resulted in his being exiled to Staten Island. As a result, he took early retirement, after which he prospered, ending his career as chief of security for the Manhattan Project in Oak Ridge, Tennessee. **John Gallagher** stayed the course, retiring after World War II and marrying his companion of twenty-five years. **Martin Brown** became chief inspector of the Police Department and died of a heart attack during the great blizzard of 1947. Although the press reported he was stricken while shoveling snow, in fact, he died while watching the Ed Sullivan Show.

Four months after the execution of Ruth Snyder, the Richmond Hill home of **Robert Elliott** was badly damaged by dynamite, presumably planted by sympathizers of Sacco and Vanzetti, although no one was ever arrested. The list of those executed by Elliott reads like a Who's Who of murder in New York in the 1930s—Francis "Two-gun" Crowley in 1932; Albert Fish, Francis Creighton, and Edward Applegate in 1936; and so on. In the late 1930s, Elliott embarked on an ambitious series of ghost-written articles that were published in *Collier's* and other magazines. He died in Richmond Hill in 1939 after a long illness.

Lewis Lawes retired from Sing Sing in 1941 and spent World War II as chief adviser of the prison industries section of the War Production Board. He died in 1947 at the peak of his form, when he was only sixty-three.

In 1941, based on a series of tests performed on Sing Sing inmates, **Dr. Charles Sweet** established a new treatment, consisting of a massive five-day intravenous infusion of antibiotics in place of the standard eighteen-month series of injections, for advanced stages of syphilis. He retired from Sing Sing in 1951, when he reached the compulsory retirement age, but remained an active surgeon in Westchester County. He died in 1963, at the age of eighty-two, still listed as consulting surgeon for Sing Sing Prison.

Death House barber **Vincent de Stefano** was released from prison in 1934 and, after a false start when a vindictive parole officer sent him back for eighteen months on a trumped-up charge, stayed out of jail. He became a contractor in New Jersey and prospered by doing work on the houses of his Mafia friends. He remained friendly with Granny Brown and Lorraine until the former's death and the latter's marriage: "I never want to ever hear about the case again as long as I live," Lorraine once remarked to him. De Stefano died in 1953, survived by his wife and two daughters.

As a result of his rampage, **"Dummy" Dugan** was relieved of his job as Death House cook, which went to a Chinese prisoner. Ninety days were added to his sentence.

Photographer **Thomas Howard** died in his Chicago home of a heart ailment in October 1961, at the age of sixty-eight. At the time of his death, he was chief photographer for the *Chicago Sun-Times*. Apart from its intrinsic value as marking the apogee, or nadir, depending on your point of view, of an era in American journalism, his photograph of Mrs. Snyder in the electric chair is one of the best-known photographs in the world. In 1960, it was one of fifty-seven photographs chosen by the National Press Photographers Association for their book *Great Moments in News Photography*.

Jack Lait continued his rake's progress through American journalism. He stayed at King Features Syndicate until 1936, then edited the *New York Daily Mirror* until forced by illness to take a leave of absence in 1952. Lait became a rabid Roosevelt hater and Red-baiter during the Depression, a tendency that culminated in the early 1950s with his trashy and vastly successful *Confidential!* series. Toward the end of his career, Lait turned to radio broadcasts and wrote a script dramatizing Mrs. Snyder's final hours in the Death House. Lorraine's husband learned of the script and pleaded with Lait not to air the show. Lait agreed and put the case to the show's producers, who allowed him to pull it. He died, much loved and much hated, in California in 1954, at the age of seventy-one.

Places

The Snyder residence in Queens Village, put on the market for its assessed value of eleven thousand dollars, proved to be a slow seller. It was not until August 1930 that a reasonable offer of eight thousand dollars was received. Pleading the burden of the four-thousand-dollar mortgage and real estate taxes, Granny Brown successfully appealed to the New York State Supreme Court (Lorraine's financial guardian) for permission to sell at the reduced price. Thus did Harry Schlicting, a Jamaica bricklayer, move into a white-collar neighborhood at a blue-collar price. He paid dearly in terms of aggravation, however, for he was harassed by curiosity seekers and pranksters. "Go 'vay! Go 'vay! Der iss no vun!" Schlicting hissed at John Kobler when the author knocked at the door. In the 1939 *WPA Guide to New York,* Queens Village is referred to as "site of the notorious Snyder-Gray murder," and cars from as far away as California slowly cruised past the house right up to the eve of World War II.

In 1944, Schlicting sold the house to Henry and Elizabeth Olkowski, who raised a large family in it, and who reported no ghosts, though they occasionally received crank letters. They sold the house in 1968, at which point I will drop the story to protect the privacy of the current occupants.

The house is unchanged in any significant way. A high wooden fence blocks the back yard from public view, and a low chain-link fence surrounds the modest fringe around the front of the house. A lurid plaster Madonna stands by the front steps where Albert Snyder's roses were ripped up by souvenir hunters. The garage which he built and where he spent so many hours still stands.

Like the city and borough it served, the **Queens County Courthouse** fell on evil days. In the 1970s, an Office of Court Administration report noted that the building was in gross violation of the fire code, the heating was erratic, the electrical system was deficient, and light bulbs went unreplaced because the building custodian did not have a ladder high enough to reach them. Because the building was not air-conditioned, it was shut for five months every year; eventually, it was used as nothing more than a traffic court. During these spells of inactivity, the building earned its keep as a film location for, among other films, *The Wrong Man, Panic in Needle Park,* and *Crazy Joey.* In 1970, the Weatherman faction of Students for a Democratic Society exploded a bomb in the telephone booth just outside the courtroom where the Snyder-Gray trial was held. There was no structural damage to the building, but the oak doors were ripped off the courtroom, marble fittings were shattered, the elevator cage was twisted out of shape, and the glass dome over the stairwell was shattered. No arrests were ever made.

The courthouse's fortunes improved in 1973, when the antidrug Rockefeller Laws came into effect. So great was the crush of cases that the building was fixed up and went back to work as a criminal court. In 1976, the Landmarks Preservation Committee declared the building a landmark. Limited maintenance work was undertaken, including even the replacement of the stained glass skylight. In the late 1980s, the Citicorp building, the first skyscraper in Queens, was built on the other side of Court Square. It altered the New York City skyline forever, but development of the neighborhood added impetus to the effort to save the courthouse. As of this writing, many windows have been replaced, the crumbling stonework has been repointed, the heating and ventilation systems have been fixed and major restoration work has been done in the lobby and third-floor courtroom.

The **Queens County Jail,** which came to be known as the "Long Island City House of Detention," had many illustrious residents before closing its doors in 1974. Willie "The Actor" Sutton was housed there during his 1950 trial for robbing the Sunnyside Branch of Manufacturer's Hanover Trust, a crime that earned him a seventeen-year stint upstate and put an end to his criminal career. It was during this trial that Sutton, asked why he robbed banks, was reported (falsely) to have made the famous reply "Because that's where the money is." Vincent "Mad Dog" Coll, perhaps the most psychopathic gangster New York ever produced, spent time in the jail before Dutch Schultz finally killed him in 1932. So did Joe "Crazy Joe" Gallo before the Colombo family murdered him in 1972. Martha Beck and Raymond Fernandez, "The Lonely Hearts Killers," were housed for a while in the jail, as was Jack "Murf the Surf" Murphy, head of the gang that heisted the Star of India diamond from the Americna Museum of Natural History.

In October 1973, the House of Detention was the scene of one of the most serious prison disturbances in New York history. Over three hundred inmates had been crowded into space designed for half that number, with predictable results. They seized seven hostages and demanded successfully that a panel of New York State Supreme Court justices and reporters tour the prison to view conditions. The visitors were appalled by what they saw; when order had been restored, the prison population was reduced to one hundred fifty inmates. For eighteen months under the administration of Warden Adam McQuillen, the House of Detention was viewed as a model facility, but economic conditions forced its closure at the end of 1974 and the transfer of its prisoners to Riker's Island. Ninety-seven signed a petition asking the city to reconsider. The jail was turned over to the Real Estate Department, which tore it down and put up a parking lot.

Sing Sing continues to flourish as a maximum-security prison for males twenty-one years of age and over and as a detention center for males sixteen and over. The prison's name was changed in 1970 to "Ossining Correctional Facility," but the new name never took hold; in 1985, its name reverted to "Sing Sing Correctional Facility." Along with Tappan, a medium-security annex that opened in the mid-1970s, Sing Sing houses over two thousand inmates.

Things

Exhibits from the trial, including the **sash weight** with which Snyder was bludgeoned, the **handkerchief** and **cotton rags** with which he was chloroformed, and the **ticket stub** that broke Gray's alibi, were put on display in the museum of the New York City police force after the executions. There they remained until as late as 1965, when they were photographed for an article in *Action Detective Magazine*. The exhibits subsequently disappeared, along with their display case. Some say they were sent to the Medical Examiner's Museum; others say to John Jay College. Inquiries at these and other likely institutions have not borne fruit.

On Alexander Gettler's retirement, the **toxicological evidence from the case**—small sealed glass ampoules containing chloroform and ethyl alcohol isolated from the brain of Albert Snyder and whiskey poisoned with bichloride of mercury—was given to Morton Helprin, Chief Medical Examiner of New York. The ampoules were on display in the Medical Examiner's Museum at Bellevue until it was closed down to make room for laboratories. Then they were sent to the National Museum of Health and Medicine of the Armed Forces Institute of Pathology at Walter Reed Hospital in Washington. They are presently in storage, but may be seen upon request.

The handcuffs that were used to transport Judd Gray to Sing Sing Prison were returned to their rightful owner, the sheriff of Queens County. In 1931, Sheriff Samuel Burden made a present of them to Alderman Augustus Shipley, who slipped them on to show them off to a friend. The friend playfully snapped them shut. It took a Jamaica locksmith four and a half hours to free the alderman, who suffered painfully swollen arms during the procedure.

The **electric chair** of New York State was last employed at Sing Sing in 1963 to execute Eddie Lee Mays. In 1969, it was placed in storage at

Green Haven Prison, a maximum-security facility in Duchess County. In 1994, it was exhibited at the New York City Historical Society exhibit entitled "Five Murders That Shocked New York." One of these, not surprisingly, was the murder of Albert Snyder.

*Communications equipment being unloaded at Queens County
Courthouse in preparation for the trial, April 1927*

The Snyder-Gray Case on Stage and Screen

Stage

THE SNYDER-GRAY CASE found immediate dramatic outlet in Sophie Treadwell's play *Machinal: A Tragedy in Ten Episodes.* Considered a minor American classic, *Machinal* (Ma-shee-NAHL; French for "mechanical" or "automatic"—one felicitous translation was "The Life Machine") played on Broadway to considerable critical and some commercial success during the 1928–29 season. The Judd Gray character was played by Hal Dawson, an unknown who capitalized on the exposure to join a touring company on its way to California, where he found success under the new name of "Clark Gable."

As befits a work in the Expressionist tradition of Elmer Rice's *The Adding Machine* and Eugene O'Neill's *The Hairy Ape, Machinal's* dialogue consists largely of staccato, telex-style one-liners delivered by a vast number of bit players and interspersed with brief soliloquies delivered by the principal characters. The play is also obviously influenced by the dramatization of Theodore Dreiser's novel *An American Tragedy,* which played on Broadway during the 1926–27 season and was seen by Ruth Snyder and Judd Gray. Gray reportedly commented, "What a way to go!" after the closing execution scene.

Treadwell the journalist, who covered the trial for the *Herald Tribune,* had no ax to grind; Treadwell the playwright, on the other hand, was a woman with a cause. The heroine of *Machinal*—"the Young Woman," as she is called—is an office stenographer who, encouraged by a greedy mother whom she has been supporting, marries the boss. He is a pig of a man—indeed, far worse than Albert Snyder—who tells his bride dirty jokes to relax her before sex, whose greatest ambition is to buy a Swiss watch, and who insistently crows, "They signed on the dotted line!" after every business success. The Young Woman gives birth to a daughter, but motherhood brings her no joy. She tries to talk to her mother, but all the old woman cares about is the money and security that the husband affords. Bereft of love, finding meaning nowhere, the Young Woman happens to meet a man in a speakeasy who impresses her with a tale of killing two bandits in Mexico. She becomes his lover. The two of them conspire to kill her husband, which she accomplishes by clubbing him over the head. The Young Woman's lover abandons her and she is arrested and convicted. "Say a prayer I can understand!" the Young Woman pleads before she is taken to the electric chair, but the idiotic cleric who attends her is incapable of it.

Machinal is not, to say the least, a cheery vision of American capitalism, the American moral landscape, or the American suburban middle-class household. Not coincidentally, it was translated into Russian and played in Moscow in 1935, making Treadwell the first American playwright to receive royalties on a play produced in the Soviet Union.

Despite favorable reviews over the years, *Machinal* has remained a footnote in American dramatic history. Perhaps the *New Yorker's* drama critic Brooks Atkinson was correct in his review. He thought *Machinal* was a good play, but complained that, whereas Ruth Snyder had an undeniable lust for life, the Young Woman drifted through the play as though she were anesthetized, coming off like a sort of aimless, self-indulgent female version of Georg Büchner's Woyzeck. The one-dimensionality of the lead character, the highly stylized Expressionism, and the heavy-handedness of play's political message dogged the two major revivals of *Machinal*—first in 1959–60, a major event in the emergence of off-Broadway theater, and then in 1990–91, when it was directed by Michael Grief for the New York Shakespeare Company. *Machinal* continues to be a staple on the liberal arts college circuit.

William Styron and John Phillips wrote a play *Dead! A Love Story* about the relationship between Ruth Snyder and Judd Gray and its aftermath. Never published, the play was first staged in 1986 by HB Playwrights Foundation and Theatre in Greenwich Village, and directed by Herbert Berghof (HB), legendary in the theater world for having directed the original production of *Waiting for Godot*. Mrs. Snyder was played by Madeleine Potter (best known for her role in the film production of Henry James's *The Bostonians*) and Gray by Alexander (son of Leonard) Bernstein. Costume design was by Anna Johnston, whose credits include *Ragtime, The Godfather,* and *Serpico.* In place of scenery, the production used blown-up contemporary newspaper photographs as a backdrop to the action.

To judge from the unpublished script, the authors of *Dead!* immersed themselves in the atmosphere and the details of the case. The grind of daily life in the Snyder and Gray residences is well depicted in the script and is contrasted with the boozy geniality of Henry's Restaurant. The authors pick up, with excellent effect, on minutiae such as the silver fox fur Mrs. Snyder was wearing when she first met Gray and the prune whip that was Albert Snyder's favorite dessert. They extracted trial dialogue from the record itself. With less success, the authors lace the play with odd conceits—the most bizarre of which is that Mrs. Snyder and Gray are apprehended by police while vacationing in Miami Beach on Granny Brown's life savings! The insurance angle is left out of *Dead!* with no great damage to the coherence of the story; Mrs. Snyder's hatred of her husband is well-enough established as the motive for the murder.

Dead! accepts Gray's "love slave" version of the slaying in its totality. Gray's character starts off as an ethical idiot—mama's boy, alcoholic, drudge to religion—and is practically a zombie by the time Mrs. Snyder has finished programming him. "My thirsty little man . . . what are we going to do about my thirsty little man?" she coos approvingly as he slugs back whiskey in Granny Brown's bedroom. She giggles: "I've got him [Albert Snyder] sleeping on his good ear."

The characterization of Ruth Snyder starts off well. The stage directions when she first appears read: "This is a woman capable of frivolity, giddiness, the inanity of the flapper generation. Yet, also when she considers herself to be betrayed, she is a woman able to indulge in the wildest extremes of ruthlessness, duplicity and cruelty. While not an extraordinary beauty, Ruth emanates a strong and open sexuality. In the cliché of the time, she possesses that imponderable quality called 'It.' "

All true. But, as the play unfolds, *Dead!* practically out-*Graphics* the *Graphic* in its lurid depiction of Mrs. Snyder. The central theme is that a girl needs a real man to make a big fuss over her. A real man would treat a girl right, make her feel like a princess. Snyder, the dumb Kraut, is not a real man at all. Now that fellow Gray, on the other hand, with a little bit of help, he would know how to make a girl feel important, all he needs is a little backbone. "I'm going to make you help me and be a man. A *man!*" Predictably, after Gray has done her bidding, Mrs. Snyder discovers that he, too, is no real man.

In the end, neither *Machinal* nor *Dead!* tells us much about Ruth Snyder. A woman who clubbed, chloroformed, and strangled a husband whose worst flaw was his sour disposition makes an unconvincing feminist heroine—but, even so, she was more than a spoiled schoolgirl looking for a fellow who knew how to treat a girl right.

Screen

Hard-boiled detective fiction writer James M. Cain adapted the Snyder-Gray case for his novella "Double Indemnity," serialized in the magazine *Liberty* in 1936 and subsequently published with two other stories under the title *Three of a Kind* (New York: Knopf, 1943). The tale attracted the attention of veteran scriptwriter and recently turned director Billy Wilder in 1944. Because Cain was busy working on other films, Wilder turned to Raymond Chandler to write the screenplay. It was an unhappy collaboration. Chandler polished off a script in five weeks, but Wilder insisted on spending six months reworking it with him, and then made Chandler stay around the studio, sober, during filming. Wilder also made the mistake of remarking to Chandler that his work reminded him of Cain's, which Chandler detested.

Cain's novella had already departed far from the facts of the case. Wilder now departed still farther, moving away from Chandler's screenplay. He had a hard time getting anyone to take the Judd Gray role. Fred

MacMurray, whose career had been in comedy, accepted, despite his fears the seamy plot would end his career. In the event, his weak-willed, superficial drummer is in the right direction. The highlight of the movie, however, is Tom Powers's devastating portrayal of the hard-drinking, foul-tempered, penny-pinching husband. Powers's Albert Snyder is far more compelling than Barbara Stanwyck's sultry Ruth Snyder, who was in real life more drab, more neurotic, and much less intelligent. Nonetheless, Stanwyck was nominated for Best Actress, and *Double Indemnity* for Best Picture, Best Director, and Best Cinematography, at the Academy Awards.

There was an altogether forgettable remake of *Double Indemnity* for television in 1973, with Richard Crenna and Samantha Eggar in the leading roles. Crenna resurfaced, not as Judd Gray, but as Albert Snyder, in the 1981 cult favorite *Body Heat,* written and directed by Lawrence Kasdan, with William Hurt and Kathleen Turner starring as the murderous pair. This is probably the only instance of an actor appearing at different points in his career as both murderer and murder victim in the same case. Usually described in the cable television guides as "critically acclaimed," "trashy," "steamy," and "graphic," *Body Heat* is notable in large part for the amount of sex it managed to pack in while hanging on to an R rating.

Both *Double Indemnity* and *Body Heat* play to the hilt the femme fatale duping her gullible lover into a murder conspiracy, intending all the while to get rid of him after he has served his deadly purpose. As we have seen, there is only the slimmest evidence for this in the Snyder-Gray case, in the form of the poisoned whiskey.

Albert Snyder, ca. 1925

Albert Snyder and Jessie Guischard, ca. 1910

Sources

"TO HAVE AND HOLD the premises herein granted unto the parties of
the second part, their heirs and assigns forever . . . SUBJECT TO . . . that
the parties of the second part shall quietly enjoy said premises."

> –Deed conveying Lot 1, Block 10741, in the Borough and County
> of Queens, from Charles K. and Frances Hrostoski, parties of the
> first part, to Albert E. and Ruth M. Snyder, parties of the second
> part, recorded 6 January 1923, *Liber* 2471, Page 1310.

Primary Sources

THE KEY SOURCE DOCUMENT for the Snyder-Gray case is the typewritten trial transcript, which is stored in three medium-sized cardboard
boxes in the Records Room of the Queens County Clerk's Office. As
the case went to appeal, the minutes were edited into a six-volume trial
record for review by the New York State Court of Appeals. Forty-five
sets of the record were printed and bound. One set remains with the
county clerk in Queens, another is on deposit at the New York Public
Library, catalogued under "New York State Court of Appeals," a third is
in the New York State Library in Albany, and a fourth (Assistant District
Attorney Peter M. Daly's copy) is in the Special Collections section of
the Sealy Library of the John Jay School of Criminal Justice in New York
City. I am in possession of Samuel Miller's copy, and this is the source of
all trial extracts. The verbatim text has been edited for continuity and
readability.

Also in the Records Room, rolled up and thrust into one of the boxes containing the trial minutes, is the entire official Queens County Court paper trail of the Snyder-Gray case (recall that when the judge first assigned the case fell ill, Queens County Court was supplanted by the New York State Supreme Court). The documents start with Indictment 9460 and proceed through the brief arguing in favor of a separate trial filed by Mrs. Snyder's lawyers, the briefs in opposition filed by Gray and the People, and the notices of appeal and denial thereof. They end with the statement by Sing Sing Prison doctor Charles Sweet that, on autopsy, all vital organs of the prisoners were found to be normal. All documents except the notice of denial of appeal from the New York State Appeals Court bear the original signatures of lawyers, judges, and prison officials. The prisoners' signed "pedigrees" are also in the Records Room.

The New York State Archives in Albany contain a number of Sing Sing prison records related to the condemned prisoners, starting with the admission register containing personal information and ending with the notice of the time at which sentences were carried out. The personal papers of Warden Lewis Lawes are deposited in the Special Collections Room of the Sealy Library of the John Jay School of Criminal Justice, although they contain disappointingly little information on the Snyder-Gray case.

All original material related to the investigation and prosecution of the murder has been destroyed. This distressing note appeared in the *New York Times* on 7 December 1949:

> Memories of some of Queens County's most notorious crimes, including the Snyder murder, will flare briefly today when several tons of legal papers are pushed into the furnace of the seventy-year old County Courthouse in Long Island City. J. Irwin Shapiro, chief assistant district attorney, announced yesterday that he would burn at 11 a.m. most of the papers accumulated in the prosecutor's office from 1898, when Queens became part of New York City, through 1933. They include copies of indictments in cases that have been closed, exhibits, Grand Jury minutes, memoranda, work sheets and statements of witnesses.

. . . Permission to destroy the papers was given by the State Department of Education, which has jurisdiction over archives.'[1]

Photographic evidence has also disappeared: in 1989, a burn order was issued for all pre-1930 crime scene photographs in the files of the New
York City Police Department (NYPD) Photo Unit. Consequently, files
in the Photo Unit storage room go back only to December 1930. Unfortunately, the NYPD Crime Scene Unit has destroyed all pre-1950 crime
scene reports.

The exception to this dearth of original material is the detective's
log book kept by Detective Lieutenant Michael McDermott and made
available to me by his son. It contains only a modest amount of material
related to Mrs. Snyder, but is more or less comprehensive regarding
the Syracuse end of the investigation and includes McDermott's notes
of Gray's confession aboard the Empire State Limited. It is also the
source for the story of Dana Wallace's attempt to pack the Snyder-Gray
jury.

Death House letters from Gray to Samuel Miller were made available
to me by Miller's daughter, Mrs. Sylvia Coman. Although these add
nothing to our legal understanding of the case, they provide invaluable
insight into the personality of Judd Gray. Also contained in this collec-

---

1.When he left office, Queens District Attorney Richard Newcombe entrusted
personal files related to the prosecution to his associate and eventual law partner Elmer
Ellsworth Wigg. This is not unusual—in New York State, district attorneys, being employees of the State who are elected and work at the county level, fall into a sort of
archival limbo. The tendency over the years has been for them simply to take their papers with them when they resign or are voted out. According to Irving Goodstein, sole
surviving partner of Pressinger, Wigg, and Goodstein (originally, Pressinger, Cunningham, Newcombe, and Wigg), who worked with Wigg from 1946 until his death in
1963, Wigg never mentioned the Snyder-Gray files. Wigg died childless, so the trail died
with him. As to truly valuable material—Mrs. Snyder's fifty-two-page statement, which
was boiled down into the eight-page signed confession read into the trial record, and the
five-hundred-page psychiatric evaluation of Gray—I fear that the report in the *Times*
leaves little room for hope.

tion are several letters to Gray from Mrs. Margaret Gray and Mrs. Isabel Gray, perhaps given to Miller for release to the press.

Telephone calls to descendants of other legal principals in the case and to legal associates and associates of associates—Martin Green, Esq., of Millard, Green, and Udell, and Irving Goodstein, Esq., of Pressinger, Newcombe, Cunningham, and Wigg—yielded a few anecdotes, but nothing in terms of diaries and papers.

For information on the Schneider, Brown, Gray, Kallenbach, and Guischard families, I relied on city directories; birth, death, and marriage certificates in the relevant jurisdictions; and the enumeration sheets of the U.S. Federal Censuses of 1900, 1910, and 1920; the New York State Censuses of 1895, 1905, 1915, and 1925; and the New Jersey State Censuses of 1905 and 1915. Returns from the 1890 U.S. Federal Census were destroyed in a fire, and returns from post-1925 censuses were not yet released at the time of writing. Descriptions of neighborhoods and houses were taken from the Belcher-Hyde and Bromley atlases of New York City and the Franklin atlas of Essex County, New Jersey. Names of New York City employees and officials were checked against the *New York Civil List*; lawyers' ages, office addresses, and law school credentials are from the *Martindale-Hubble Law Directory*.

Books and Book Chapters

John Kobler's *The Trial of Ruth Snyder and Judd Gray* (Garden City, N.Y.: Doubleday, Doran, 1938) is the natural starting place for a student of the case.[2] Kobler's introduction still offers the best overall discussion of the case, even though it suffers from numerous errors of fact, some serious enough to jar the knowledgeable reader.

Kobler's rather old-fashioned analysis of the case is well comple-

---

2. Doubleday launched a series counterpart to the famous Notable British Trials series (Edinburgh: Hodge), adopting the same format of an introductory essay followed by the edited trail record. Sadly, the American series was an utter flop; the only other volumes published were *The Trial of Lizzie Borden,* edited by Edmund Pearson, and *The Trial of Richard Bruno Hauptmann,* edited by Sidney Whipple.

mented by the feminist interpretation given by Ann Jones, who devotes almost a chapter of her book *Women Who Kill* (New York: Holt, Rinehart and Winston, 1980) to the Snyder-Gray case. Jones bases her analysis on tabloid press accounts and has done her homework thoroughly, especially for someone treating the case only as part of a broader study. Her critique of the unfairness with which the public treated Mrs. Snyder, compared to the kid-glove treatment which Gray received, is on target. However, Jones goes too far when she argues that Mrs. Snyder's version of events was as plausible as Gray's, implying that the jury's choice of one version over the other was largely a result of prejudice against the woman in the case. I entirely disagree with this view.

So much for extended critical treatments of the case. Fred J. Cook's *The Girl in the Death Cell* (New York: Fawcett, 1953), originally published in 1936, is a down and dirty paperback in the Gold Medal series. One hundred and fifty of the book's less-than two hundred pages consist of trial extracts, so Cook adds little value. Recently, Leslie Margolin worked from tabloid coverage to produce *Murderess!* (New York: Kensington, 1999), an airport bookstore-style true crime paperback. Although a step above *The Girl in the Death Cell,* with a good appendix about movies based on the Snyder-Gray case, *Murderess!* is essentially a rechurning of already published newspaper material.

Historian Karl W. Schweizer's lengthy print-on-demand account of the case, *Seeds of Evil: The Gray/Snyder Murder Case* (Bloomington, Ind.: 1stBooks, 2002; available online at www.authorhouse.com), focuses on the human drama of these "ill-fated actors on the stage of life, caught in a deadly web of passion, deception, and murder." Despite an impressive wealth of detail, Schweizer offers no new information about the case, historical or otherwise; his fictitious conversations and streams of consciousness are tedious; and his moralistic diatribes are more suited to a sermon from the late 1920s than to a work of serious intent.

The Snyder-Gray case was given chapter-length treatments, all of them in varying degrees inaccurate, with the exception of Nigel Morland's relatively accurate chapter from *Background to Murder* (London: Werner Laurie, 1955), in a number of mostly prewar books: Ione Quinby, *Murder for Love* (New York: Covici-Friede, 1931); C. E. Bechhofer

Roberts, *The New World of Crime* (London: Eyre and Spottiswoode, 1933) and Milton MacKaye, *Famous Crimes of 1927* (Garden City, N.Y.: Crime Club, 1928). Detective Inspector Arthur A. Carey devotes practically a chapter of his biography *Memoirs of a Murder Man* (Garden City, N.Y.: Doubleday, Doran, 1930) to a quite inaccurate account of the case. A cut above all these is the chapter in *The Story of Queens Village* (New York: Centennial Association, 1974) by Vincent F. Seyfried, the foremost historian of Queens. Any number of Snyder-Gray feature articles of the "When Justice Triumphed" variety have been published in New York and Long Island newspapers over the years; notable among these is "That Cosmo Girl" by Joseph McNamara in the *New York Daily News* Sunday magazine of 24 April 1988. All of these shorter treatments contain errors, some of them whoppers; all of the entries on the Snyder-Gray case in the various popular encyclopedias of crime contain errors of fact.

Executioner Robert G. Elliott describes the pair's execution in his autobiography *Agent of Death: The Memoirs of an Executioner* (New York: E. P. Dutton, 1940). This volume was ghosted by Long Island newspaperman Albert R. Beatty. There is also a chapter on the case in Leo W. Sheridan's *I Killed for the Law: The Career of Robert Elliott and Other Executioners* (New York: Stackpole, 1938). Warden Lewis E. Lawes's *Life and Death in Sing Sing* (Garden City, N.Y.: Doubleday, Doran, 1928) is an excellent source of information on the Death House and practices surrounding executions at Sing Sing; for general information on death by electrocution, Frederick Drimmer's *Until You Are Dead: The Book of Executions in America* (New York: Pinnacle Books, 1990) is accurate, but Craig Brandon's *The Electric Chair: An Unnatural American History* (Jefferson, N.C.: McFarland, 1999) is better. Lawes devotes an informative chapter of *Meet the Murderer!* (New York: Harper, 1940) to the Snyder-Gray case and his revulsion at the publicity surrounding the pair's execution; the story of Death House cook "Dummy" Dugan's affection for Mrs. Snyder is told by Lawes in *Invisible Stripes* (New York: Farrar and Rinehart, 1938) and also by Principal Keeper John Sheehy in his essay "Life in Sing Sing," published in Kurt Singer's *Crime Omnibus* (London: W. H. Allen, 1961).

More off the beaten track is "Thou Shalt Not Kill!," an unpublished biography of Lawes by Emile Henry Gauvreau,[3] the manuscript of which is deposited along with Lawes's papers in the Special Collections room at the Sealy Library of the John Jay School of Criminal Justice.

Indispensable for any student of crime in New York State is Daniel Hearn's *Legal Executions in New York State: A Comprehensive Reference, 1639–1963* (Jefferson, N.C.: McFarland, 1997). All New York execution dates, as well as incidental information on the nature of the crime, were taken from this source. The collection of the Ossining Historical Society is rich in all information related to Sing Sing Prison and includes a superb collection of newspaper clippings related to executed inmates and audio tapes of interviews with former keepers.

The Snyder-Gray case was the topic for a number of articles in the trade weekly *Editor and Publisher* from March 1927 through January 1928. General sources for New York journalism in the 1920s are Simon Michael Bessie's *Jazz Journalism: The Story of the Tabloid Press* (New York: Russell and Russell, 1938); and two books by Silas Bent, *Ballyhoo: The Voice of the Press* (New York: Boni and Liveright, 1927); and *Newspaper Crusaders: A Neglected Story* (New York: Whittlesey House, 1939). Gauvreau's "Thou Shalt Not Kill!" is particularly useful for atmospheric information on the journalistic side of the execution.

Newspapers

Tabloid journalists spent much of their time in the no-man's-land between news and entertainment and, engrossing as it may be, their coverage of the case must therefore be read with caution. Arthur Mefford, a reporter formerly of the *Daily Mirror* and, at the time of the case, of the *Daily News,* was bitter and to the point when quoted in *Editor and Publisher* (14 May 1927): "Never, in my opinion, was there another story in which so much bunk got into print; nor another story so badly faked. The reporters themselves were to blame for this. The District Attorney's

3. Bernarr MacFadden's close associate and editor at the *Graphic,* Gauvreau was subsequently editor of the *Daily Mirror.* Gauvreau's standards of truth were elastic, but not infinitely so; his biography of Lawes is a fairly serious piece of work.

Office handed out great quantities of pure bunk; so did the police; so did Gray's attorneys; so did Mrs. Snyder's counsel; so did the sheriff's office and jail attendants. And the reporters, fighting frantically among themselves, swallowed it whole and begged for more."

The nontabloids—*New York Times, American* (Hearst), *Herald Tribune, Evening Journal* (Hearst), *Telegram* (Scripps-Howard), *World, Sun,* and *Post* (not yet a tabloid at that time) are more reliable sources and correspondingly less fun to read.

Six weeks after the appearance of the *Evening Graphic* in 1924, someone at the New York Public Library (NYPL) decided that it was beneath the institution's standards and stopped subscribing. Not until 1928 did a more enlightened librarian renew the subscription. The incomplete microfilm in the NYPL collection is the master copy for all other holdings of the *Graphic* listed in the national newspaper collection catalogue. Thus, incredible as it seems, half the entire run of the New York tabloid with the third-largest circulation has disappeared without a trace. Passages from the *Graphic* quoted in this volume are from two secondary sources: Stanley Walker, *Mrs. Astor's Horse* (New York: Frederick A. Stokes, 1935) and Lester Cohen, *The New York Graphic: The World's Zaniest Newspaper* (New York: Chilton Books, 1964); see also Frank Mallen, *Sauce for the Gander* (White Plains, N.Y.: Baldwin Books, 1954).

While the *Evening Graphic* may have disappeared, a trace remains. Late in this book project, a notice appeared on eBay offering for sale a batch of original photographic prints related to the Snyder-Gray case. The photographs reproduced in this book represent a selection of these. They are stamped "Evening Graphic" on the back, so the source is clear. According to the seller, his grandfather had a friend who worked in the newspaper business; presumably this friend pilfered the prints when they were discarded after use. The cover of this volume reproduces an original *Graphic* cut-and-paste composograph of Mrs. Snyder and Gray. Courtroom sketches of the defendants and Mrs. Snyder's palm diagram are also part of this treasure trove.

It was with great anticipation that I turned to the *Long Island Daily Press* for the local perspective; I am sorry to say that it added surprisingly little to the news service material that provided the bulk of its coverage.

The same apples to the *Orange Daily Courier* for the New Jersey angle. A check of the *Syracuse Herald Journal* morgue revealed no material of importance.

Among the dozens of journalists who covered the trial, the consummate metropolitan Damon Runyon stands out. He pulled no punches, leading off his trial coverage for the *American* as follows: "A chilly looking blonde with frosty eyes and one of those marble, you-bet-you-will chins, and an inert, scare-drunk fellow that you couldn't miss among any hundred men as a dead set-up for a blonde, or the shell game, or maybe a gold brick."

A more rock 'em-sock 'em example of the inverted-pyramid style—big picture first, details later—would be impossible to find. Runyon continued to write his regular sports column while producing thousands of words of trial copy every day. Runyon's coverage of the Snyder-Gray and other trials has been edited and reissued in *Trials and Other Tribulations* (New York: Dorset Press, 1991), originally published in 1947. Jonathan Goodman excerpted some of Runyon's Snyder-Gray work in his edited collection *The Pleasures of Murder* (London: Allison and Busby, 1983).

The work of the "trained seals"—novelists, movie stars, playwrights, producers, preachers, and other social notables hired to write their impressions of the case—was, without exception, execrable.[4] Difficult to classify but eminently readable is H. L. Mencken's essay "Death of a Good Man" published on the subject of Judd Gray in the Baltimore

4. It "represented merely the pre-conceived notion of the writers on current events in general, and could have been written by almost anybody, at home, about almost anything," according to the *New Yorker's* "Talk of the Town" column of 30 April 1927. Ben Hecht devoted the whole of his "Reporter at Large" column in the same issue to the inanity of the "trained seals." He called their work "simple minded and idiotic" and suggested that they might as well sit in a display window of Gimbel's blowing soap bubbles under a sign reading "Notable Authors." This did not stop Hecht from writing a somewhat overheated piece of his own for the *American*. The Snyder-Gray case also provided the *New Yorker* with "Reporter at Large" columns from Morris Markey on 2 April, a piece containing a scandalous number of factual errors, and from Elmer Davis on 7 May, this a rather good piece entitled "Clytemnestra: Long Island Style."

Evening Sun on 2 January 1928. This piece was reproduced in *A Mencken Chrestomathy* (New York: Knopf, 1949).

The Prisoners' Autobiographies

The King Features Syndicate 1928 "one-off" pamphlet "Ruth Snyder's Own True Story," and Gray's memoirs *Doomed Ship* (New York: Horace Liveright, 1928), though both useful for autobiographical material, add few insights to our understanding of the murder. Each author simply re-asserts, with greater vehemence, the story told on the witness stand.

*Judd Gray in custody in Syracuse,
New York, waiting for the train,
21 March 1927*

*Judd Gray, center, in custody in Syracuse,
New York; his friend Haddon Gray, right,
tries to hide his friend's face from
photographers, 21 March 1927*

Acknowledgments

FOR HELP in putting this story together, I am indebted to the following persons and institutions, none of whom, as usual, should be held responsible for my mistakes:

The staff of the Queens County Clerk's Office, for help in finding the original trial material; the staff of the Queens City Register's Office, for help in tracing the history of the Snyder residence.

James Folts, head of research services at the New York State Archives (whose mother as a young girl named her cat "Judd" on account of its gray color), for making available records from the Sing Sing Prison Death House and giving advice on documents related to the appeal and application for executive clemency.

Richard McDermott, for making available the detective's log book kept by his father Michael McDermott; Mrs. Sylvia Coman, for making available correspondence from Gray to her father Samuel Miller; Sadie Scudder, Townsend Scudder III, and Thayer Scudder; Dana Wallace Jr. and Dana Wallace III; Mrs. Richard McCormack (daughter of Dr. Stephen Jewett); Mrs. Jean Knapp (niece of Matron Lucy Many); Robert Peter (son of Assistant District Attorney Peter) Daly, Esq.; John (son of Assistant District Attorney Thomas) Thornton, Esq.; Ed (son of Police Lieutenant Martin) Brown and his cousin Harry Brix. All these individuals responded generously to inquiries about diaries, papers, and reminiscences left by players in the case.

Roberta Arminio of the Ossining Historical Association, who was my principal guide through material related to Sing Sing; also Byron

Saunders of the Queens Historical Society and Judy Haven of the Onondaga Historical Association.

Patterson Smith, bookseller and expert on rare-book aspects of American criminal history, who has been my source of published material, as well as a constant provider of encouragement in all things criminal.

Kenneth Cobb of the New York City Municipal Archives, for genealogical material; the staff of the U.S. National Archives in New York, for the same; the staffs of Woodlawn, Mount Olivet, Cypress Hills, and Rosedale Cemeteries, for grave locations.

William Asadorian, curator of the Long Island Room at the Queensboro Public Library, for use of the collection and much general advice on the project; Luc Sante, for information about the *New York Evening Graphic*; Vincent Seyfried, historian of Queens; Barbara Milstein of the Brooklyn Museum of Art; Jon Peterson and Leo Hirschorn of the History Department at Queens College.

Mark L. Taff, M.D., former president of the New York Society of Forensic Sciences at Lehman College in the Bronx, for comments on Dr. Howard Neail's autopsy report; Professor Lawrence Kobilinsky, Department of Sciences, John Jay School of Criminal Justice, for comments on serology; Donald Hoffman, M.D., toxicologist, New York Medical Examiner's Office, for comments on bichloride of mercury; William Eckert, M.D., International Reference Organization in Forensic Medicine and Sciences (INFORM) in Wichita, Kansas, for information on the career of Dr. Alexander Gettler.

Joseph Baume, Esq., president of the Queens County Bar Association, for putting me in touch with old-timers familiar with the case, among them Samuel Tripp, Esq., former president of the Bar Association; Irving Goodstein, Esq., of Pressinger, Wigg, and Goodstein; and Martin Green, Esq., of Millard, Green, and Udell, all of whom provided information on the lawyers involved in the case.

Michael O'Brian, Esq., formerly of the Appeals Branch of the Queens County District Attorney's office, for legal material and comments.

George Andrews, clerk of the Long Island City Courthouse, for historical information on the courthouse and jail.

Elisabeth Perry, Women's History Department, Sarah Lawrence College, and Robert Wesser, History Department, State University of New York, Albany, for information on Governor Alfred E. Smith.

Glen Paris, artistic director of HB Playwrights' Foundation and Theatre, New York City, for making available the script of William Styron and John Phillips's *Dead! A Love Story,* and Edith Meeks of the original cast, for discussing the production.

John Podracky of the New York Police Museum, Ellen Borakove of the New York Medical Examiner's Office, and New York City Police Sergeant John Cashman (retired), for clues that resulted in finding toxicological evidence from the Snyder–Gray case in the medical museum of the Armed Forces Institute of Pathology in Washington, D.C.; also Alison Wilcox and Alan Hawk of that institution, for running the leads to ground.

New York City Police Officer Kathy Reed of the Commissioner's Office, Sergeant Bob Stewart of the Police Photo Unit, and Detective Jerry Donahue and Sergeant Malloy of the Crime Scene Unit, for help in establishing, once and for all, that crime scene photos and records from the Snyder–Gray case no longer exist.

Jodi Etsell, daughter of Sing Sing Death House barber Vincent de Stefano, for information on Sing Sing in general, and the prisoners' last days in particular.

Dan McGuire and Dick Case of the Syracuse *Herald-Journal,* for checking their morgue for material on the Syracuse end of the case; Emma Smith of the Calvary Baptist Church, for checking on the papers of John Roach Stratton.

Erasmus wrote, of a library, "In no forest is there happier hunting," and I am indebted to more librarians and their assistants than I can remember. Gratitude is due to the staff of the main research branch of the New York Public Library, where I was for many months a daily fixture at the microforms desk and in the genealogy, business, and map rooms; to the staff of the old New York City Public Library Annex on 43rd Street; to Theresa Capone of the Special Collections department of the Sealy Library of the John Jay School of Criminal Justice, for making available the papers of Sing Sing Warden Lewis E. Lawes; to Neil Jordahl of the

Humanities Collection of the Baltimore Public Library, for finding Mencken material; to Bernard McTigue of the University of Oregon Library, for information on the papers of Jack Lait; to the staff of the Billy Rose Library of the Performing Arts at Lincoln Center, New York City, for material related to the Snyder-Gray case on stage and screen; to the staff of the New York Academy of Medicine Library, for material related to Graves' disease; to Frank Ferro and the staff of the Norwalk Public Library, for material from the Norwalk *Hour*; to the staffs of the West Orange and Orange Public Libraries, for material from the Orange *Daily Courier, Weekly Advertiser,* and *Weekly Transcript.*

I am especially grateful to Faiji Rosenthal, Peter Edelman, and the staff of the *New York Daily News,* for giving me free run of their superb clipping and photograph morgue.

Index

Page number in italic denotes illustration.